For Charles,
Who's daughter did the
right thing —————— and yes,
they _are_ charismatic.

[signature]

FORGED IN 25 March 2011
WAR Charleston, SC

2010

Surprise! ☺

Enjoy reading about
these fascinating and
charismatic leaders.

Merry Christmas!
Love,
Gin

Previous Books by Warren F. Kimball

*Allies at War: The Soviet, American, and British Experience,
1939–1945* (co-ed.)
*America Unbound: World War II and the
Making of a Superpower* (ed.)
The Juggler: Franklin Roosevelt as Wartime Statesman
Churchill and Roosevelt, the Complete Correspondence (3 vols.,
ed. with comments)
American Diplomacy in the Twentieth Century (ed.)
*Swords or Ploughshares? The Morgenthau Plan for Defeated
Nazi Germany, 1943–1946*
The Most Unsordid Act: Lend-Lease, 1939–1941

FORGED IN WAR

Roosevelt, Churchill, and the Second World War

WARREN F. KIMBALL

William Morrow and Company, Inc.
New York

Paula prodded;
Tom teased;
Donna laughed;

but this is Jackie's book.

Copyright © 1997 by Warren F. Kimball

It is the policy of William Morrow and Company, Inc., and its imprints and affiliates, recognizing the importance of preserving what has been written, to print the books we publish on acid-free paper, and we exert our best efforts to that end.

Library of Congress Cataloging-in-Publication Data

Kimball, Warren F.
    Forged in war : Roosevelt, Churchill, and the Second World War / Warren F. Kimball.
    p. cm.
    Includes bibliographical references and index.
    ISBN 0-688-08523-7
    1. Roosevelt, Franklin D. (Franklin Delano), 1882–1945.
2. Churchill, Winston, 1874–1965. 3. World War, 1939–1945—
Diplomatic history. 4. World War, 1939–1945—Diplomatic history.
5. United States—Foreign relations—Great Britain. 6. Great
Britain—Foreign relations—United States. I. Title.
D753.K48 1996
940.53'2241—dc20   96-28633
                                              CIP

Printed in the United States of America

First Edition

1 2 3 4 5 6 7 8 9 10

BOOK DESIGN BY PAUL CHEVANNES

CONTENTS

The prerogative of making war is a very sublime one, its exercise is so utterly unscrutable. A British war is like an earthquake; it occurs, and when we have recovered our presence of mind we sit down and ask how it came to pass and what were the first indications. Whether in earthquake or in war the question is equally fruitless. . . . Doubtless there are those who know it, but the British public do not, and never will; nor to the end of time will any historian know it, for historians know about as much of real cause and consequence as postmen, porters and footmen do of their masters' private affairs.

–*The* Times of London,
editorial, October 14, 1856

A democracy is peace-loving. It does not like to go to war. . . . But I sometimes wonder whether in this respect a democracy is not uncomfortably similar to one of those prehistoric monsters . . . you practically have to whack his tail off to make him aware that his interests are being disturbed; but once he grasps this, he lays about him with such blind determination that he not only destroys his adversary but largely wrecks his native habitat.

—GEORGE C. KENNAN,
American Diplomacy, 1900–1950

FORGED IN WAR

The *"pugnacious looking b[astard]"*

The *seductive artist*

CHAPTER 1

———●———

The Players:
"A Pugnacious Looking
B[astard]" and "This Artist,
This Seducer"

Never were there two less likely-looking warriors. Winston Spencer Churchill was, to be candid, short and fat; "very pink and cuddly," commented one journalist's wife upon her first close encounter. His round red cheeks invariably prompted the description "cherubic," though nothing could be further from the truth. He waddled rather than walked and lectured rather than listened, talking endlessly about everything, the opposite of the virile, strong, silent leader that fiction idealized and John Wayne and Hollywood popularized. Much of his working time was spent lying abed, and when he did get up, it was often to prance around in soft slippers and pink bathrobe or his "siren suit" (designed to be pulled on easily in the event of an air raid), getups that brought derision from more than a few diarists. "A marvellous garment [Churchill's dressing gown], rather like Joseph's many-coloured robe," General Alan Brooke, the chief of the Imperial General Staff, acidly commented, going on to describe a typical evening's work with the prime minister:

Finally at 2:15 A.M. he suggested we should proceed to the hall to have some sandwiches, and I hoped this might at least mean bed. But, no! We went on till ten to three before he made a move for bed. He had the gramophone turned on, and in the many-coloured dressing

1

gown, with a sandwich in one hand and watercress in the other, he
trotted round and round the hall, giving occasional little skips to the
tune of the gramophone.

On each lap near the fireplace he stopped to release some priceless
quotation or thought. For instance he quoted a saying that a man's
life is similar to a walk down a long passage with closed windows on
either side. As you reach each window, an unknown hand opens it and
the light it lets in only increases by contrast the darkness at the end
of the passage.[1]

That image of English eccentricity must be balanced against the
description of Churchill from a soldier in the ranks during a formal
inspection: "He's a pugnacious looking b[astard]."[2] But as Adolf
Hitler found out, it was more than just looks.

A search committee working in 1939, or even 1940, to hire a
wartime leader would have carefully examined Winston Churchill's
résumé. After all, he had attended the British military academy at
Sandhurst, had been first lord of the admiralty during the Great
War of 1914–18, and had called stridently for Britain to rearm as
Germany became more belligerent in the 1930s.

But those assets were more than offset by performance. Whatever Churchill's fascination with things military, his academic performance at Sandhurst was undistinguished, and his military service
uneventful and brief. His mother, the former Jennie Jerome and
an American debutante from Baltimore when she married Randolph Churchill, once cautioned her son not to come home from
India on leave early in his short army career. Though her real motive was to save money—always in short supply for a woman with
champagne tastes—she hit on a truth when she warned young
Winston: "They will say & with some reason that you can't stick
to anything. You have only been out six months. . . ."[3] His tenure
during the First World War as civilian head of the British navy (first
lord of the admiralty) was best remembered for the bloody debacle
at Gallipoli in Turkey, where bad planning and worse execution
cost thousands of lives. He had alienated the labor movement with
his vocal opposition to socialism at home and bolshevism in Russia
and had widened the gap by leaving the Liberal party in 1922,

when it supported a Labour government. His vigorous public support for strong action against the general strike in 1926 only added to his reputation as being unsympathetic to the working class, though Churchill's response was that his quarrel was with the socialist intellectuals who had captured the trade unions.[4]

Nor were his new colleagues in the Conservative party happy with him. During the 1930s he had infuriated Tory leaders by condemning even the very mild steps toward home rule in India they had proposed. His method and style of predicting confrontation with Germany had angered and alienated many of the very people upon whom any prime minister would have to depend. By the winter of 1937–38 "his propensity for self-inflicted injuries . . . had left his reputation in shreds."[5]

Whatever Churchill's dramatic personal style, the search committee, initially intrigued, would have looked suspiciously at the candidate's preference for knights in shining armor and cavalry charges—despite his equal fascination with aircraft and technology. It would have shaken its collective head at his lack of political correctness and then slipped Churchill's application into the stack marked "Routine Rejection" (just as a majority of Conservative party MPs would have done in May 1940 had they voted on a leader to replace then Prime Minister Neville Chamberlain).[6]

Franklin Delano Roosevelt had once the lean, lithe, athletic body and handsomeness of a Hollywood leading man. But all that remained after the ravages of polio in 1921 (then called infantile paralysis) and subsequent confinement to a wheelchair for twenty years was a leonine head and broad torso attached in incongruous fashion to a pair of wasted, completely useless legs. He could not walk or stand unaided. Benito Mussolini, leader of Fascist Italy, privately mocked Roosevelt as "that cripple" and described FDR's speech in 1938 as either demented or a result of sickness of the brain. But outward appearances were not all that made Roosevelt, as well as Churchill, an improbable warlord.

The same hiring committee that had examined Churchill's credentials would have found even less to commend Franklin Roosevelt's candidacy for the job of American war leader. Family prominence—he was from the American equivalent of the landed gentry and a cousin of President Theodore Roosevelt—had gotten him into Columbia Law School, but a mediocre academic record was followed by a desultory and unsuccessful fling at the practice of law. He ran for office as a Democrat before the First World War because, he told a young woman, there were already too many Roosevelts in the Republican party trying to capitalize on Theodore's name. ("The most calculating, unprincipled thing she'd ever heard," was the woman's later comment.[7]) Childish vices had continued into manhood; "vain," "superficial," and "spoiled" were the words used by contemporaries and biographers, though his affable charm struck all who met him, anticipating the later assessment of Supreme Court Justice Oliver Wendell Holmes: "A second-class intellect. But a first-class temperament!"[8]

Before contracting polio in 1921, Roosevelt seemed content to live in a comfortable cocoon of upper-class security and respectability. His love of sailing and a few years as Woodrow Wilson's assistant secretary of the navy during the First World War gave him a parochial acquaintance with naval affairs; he was fascinated by great warships and naval lore but knew little about the army and its air force and displayed no interest in military strategy of any kind. Any letters of reference from that era would have pictured an ambitious conniver who, with an eye on his own political career, disloyally failed to support his boss, Josephus Daniels, before a congressional committee. Character references would have hinted at an extramarital affair, though no one would have known that Eleanor, his wife, had given him an ultimatum: She would file for divorce unless he gave up the other woman (Lucy Mercer). Divorce in that era meant the end of a political career, and FDR made the practical choice.

But his response to polio demonstrated a new grit and patience. The crippling disease either brought out or created an inner strength, which, added to his always breezy, optimistic style, made for a formidable public persona. At the same time the illness provided Eleanor Roosevelt a chance to develop her own sense of confidence and self-worth as she helped nurse him back to not only physical but political health. That strength of purpose was to serve them, and the nation, well during the two major crises of FDR's presidency: the Great Depression and the Second World War.

Those assets brought him to the governor's mansion in Albany, New York, in 1928 and to the White House in the election of 1932. But his election as president came with a mandate for dealing with domestic crisis, the Great Depression. Roosevelt had little interest or experience in international affairs. His few forays into that arena, in the form of speeches and articles, combined belligerence with ignorance.[9] Whatever his political credentials, the search committee once again would have sent him the standard rejection letter.

But the Second World War leaders for Great Britain and the United States were not chosen by committee. Both Winston Churchill and Franklin Roosevelt rose to wartime power through the political process.

If British voters had been asked to pass judgment on Churchill the individual, as Americans do every four years on their presidents, his election could have come only at the moment of deepest British despair, when France collapsed in June 1940 after only token resistance. Appeasement had failed; its successor—Chamberlain's postponement policy, predicated on the ability of the French to hold out—seemed to have left Britain at Hitler's mercy. The situation demanded a new leader with new policies and a new sense of purpose.

When war had broken out nine months earlier, Chamberlain had tried to co-opt Churchill by bringing the government's most vocal foreign policy critic into the Cabinet as first lord of the admiralty. But the very fact of having to go to war had discredited Chamberlain's policies, and his ineffective public leadership in the months that followed left him vulnerable to any failure. Then came Norway, a disaster for all concerned. "The Norwegians lost their independence, the British their government, and the Germans most of their surface fleet—at least for the time being" and perhaps long enough to have interfered with German plans for an invasion of Britain. More immediately the bumbling Anglo-French response to Hitler's violation of Norway's neutrality (he took Denmark en route) made Britain—and the Chamberlain government—look weak and foolish. Even Churchill admitted that Hitler had "completely outwitted" them.

On May 9, 1940, following an all-too-slim victory on a vote of confidence in the House, Chamberlain decided to resign. He hesitated the next day, when the Germans began their roll westward through the Low Countries (prompting one Churchill supporter to complain, "It's like trying to get a limpet off a corpse"), but could not delay any longer.

Change was inevitable, but Winston Churchill was not—at least not until Foreign Secretary Lord Halifax took himself out of the running. That left the king, George VI, with the reality that, in his own words, "there was only one person I could send for to form a Government who had the confidence of the country, & that was Winston." No matter that Churchill had supported Chamberlain's appeasement of Italy, the invasion of Norway, and the rest of the government's policies after war had begun. Churchill promised action, and action was what Parliament and the public demanded.[10]

Roosevelt's path to war leader was even more a matter of chance than Churchill's. The Englishman had actively involved himself in foreign and defense policy issues throughout the 1930s, whereas FDR was reelected president in 1936 as a domestic problem solver. Yet in the years that followed the international crisis demanded increasing attention. The silly argument that FDR welcomed and even exacerbated the problems with Germany and Japan in order to distract attention away from his domestic failures is belied by the fact that those crises were initiated by the Germans and Japanese, not by the United States. Nor is there persuasive evidence that Roosevelt had lost faith in the New Deal, even if he worried that the public might not share his view.

In one sense American voters did choose Roosevelt as their war leader. Although the United States did not enter the fray formally until the Japanese attack on Pearl Harbor in December 1941— two years and three months after the war in Europe had begun and four and one-half years after Japan's all-out assault on China—

Roosevelt's reelection in November 1940 was a choice of a war leader, or at least a leader most Americans thought or hoped would keep the nation out of all-out war without letting that war be "lost." No one *wanted* to go to war, yet no one *wanted* Hitler to win. At the same time a growing number (a majority by mid-1940) believed that defeating Germany would *require* that the United States join the fighting.[11]

Roosevelt played to the numbers. Whatever his own beliefs about entering the war, he avoided that black-and-white issue like the plague. His "private" lobbying effort (what in the 1990s is called a political action committee) was led by the Committee to Defend America by Aiding the Allies. The name alone illustrated the strategy. His major aid program before the election was a swap of old, decrepit World War I–vintage destroyers for valuable base rights in seven British territories in the Western Hemisphere, and in October 1940, just before the election, FDR pandered to national fears by promising that "your boys are not going to be sent into any foreign wars," never raising the question of how American support for the Allies might force war on the nation.[12]

Did he believe, before the election of 1940, that the United States should and would enter the war? Who knows? He quickly dropped his initial prediction in 1939 of a very short war resulting from either a quick German victory or the collapse of the Nazi regime. Within a few months he had moved firmly, and publicly, toward a neutrality that favored the Allies. But no evidence has surfaced to demonstrate that he lied actively and consistently to the American people about his ultimate intentions, and there are good reasons to conclude that he hoped that the United States could (or would have to) fight a limited war—with only naval and air forces engaged against the Germans. Even after his reelection Roosevelt told his secretary of state, Cordell Hull, and the American military chiefs in mid-January 1941 that the United States should be prepared to fight a defensive war in the Pacific, while the Navy should prepare to convoy supplies to Britain. But the Army should follow "a very conservative" approach, he said, focusing on protecting Latin America.[13]

But not lying is not the same as telling the truth. Clearly Roosevelt did not take the public into his confidence during the election campaign of 1940. He avoided and evaded answering awkward questions about how the United States could be neutral and still provide naval vessels and war supplies to one of the belligerents. The usual justification for such actions has been that FDR, wary of being told no if he asked the public to endorse greater assistance to Britain, needed time to "educate" Americans and their congressional representatives.[14]

But the public, the president, and politicians in general follow conventions—accepted usages that provide what reporters call plausible deniability for all parties. They use an adult version of the children's taunt "Ask me no questions; I'll tell you no lies." Even the unsophisticated polls of that era (FDR occasionally suggested questions for the pollsters to ask)[15] demonstrate that by mid-1940 those questioned understood quite well what was at stake but refused to ratify the hard decisions. That only illustrates the role leaders are expected to play: to make unpleasant choices and then to take the blame. What Americans wanted to hear in 1940 (and in subsequent crises) was not what they knew was the truth but what they wished were the truth. In a sense they wanted to be lied to.

The international crisis created by Hitler's conquest of Western Europe forced the Republican party to nominate Wendell Willkie, an avowed supporter of aid to Britain. Old-line leaders like Senator Robert Taft of Ohio, who had expressed a preference for a German victory over American involvement in the war, stood no chance of nomination (or election). Public opinion, expressed in polls and Congress, saw Hitler as a threat, and someone had to deal with that. However much the two presidential candidates avoided public candor, both Roosevelt and Willkie would give Americans exactly the foreign policy they believed they needed (according to the polls), leaving the electorate to vote its predictions, which were in fact its wishes.[16]

Before the collapse of France in June 1940 and the successful German conquest of Western Europe, Americans, including their president, tended to think complacently that the British and French would at least stop Hitler even if they could not defeat his forces.

But Hitler's successes changed all that—and guaranteed the re-election of Franklin Roosevelt, thus helping select America's war leader.

———————

A half century after the end of the Second World War, Anglo-American images of that struggle remain dominated by the Battle of Britain, the desert war in North Africa, and the Normandy invasion, along with an endless stream of television reruns of, in the United States, John Wayne winning the Pacific war single-handedly or, in Britain, Jack Hawkins cleverly outwitting the Germans. A deluge of books, motion pictures, and television docudramas, often set in wartime Britain, constantly reinforces that historical memory. But astride those nostalgic and heroic images are Winston Churchill and Franklin Roosevelt.

From the time Churchill became prime minister, he was, in the words of one of his biographers, "a genuine Superstar." Always surrounded by press and photographers, he was a "splendid, irrepressible showman," who "did not disappoint his fans," delighting Britons with his V for victory gesture, universally translated as an "up yours" to Hitler. They devotedly followed his actions through newsreels and radio, seeing Churchill as what every Briton should be: resilient, principled, self-reliant, and dogged.[17]

The sweep of war, horrible and inhuman as it is, has long seized human imagination, but the Second World War occupies a special place in our minds. At the root of that hypnotic spell, in both Britain and the United States, is a perception of the conflict as an unambiguous, just war against evident evil. That patriotic, idealized, romanticized image makes many Britons and Americans recoil, even fifty years later, from evidence of selfish British and American war aims, nasty quarrels between Churchill and Roosevelt, or even Anglo-American discord or competition for wartime glory and postwar advantage. Any challenge to the memory of World War II as the "good war" brings immediate outrage, and books that discuss tensions between British and American leaders get front-page treatment as if they were truly newsworthy.[18]

Equally important for public memory of the Second World War

is the heroic depiction of the link between the two national leaders. The postwar generation of American politicians has regularly exploited the public's veneration for the Churchill legend. His 1946 Iron Curtain speech became an unchallenged scripture that American leaders cited to justify their policies. Historians took to blaming or praising Churchill for leading the United States into the Cold War. Presidents from Kennedy to Bush quoted him regularly, most often when their own actions forced them to look for some kind of historical imprimatur. Even one of those convicted in the Watergate affair during the Nixon years adopted as his public motto a Churchill admonition not to give way "in things great or small, large or petty."[19]

FDR likewise has his fans, from John Kennedy, Bill Clinton, and Ronald Reagan to Newt Gingrich. The Churchill and the Roosevelt images each receive constant burnishing from such organizations as the Franklin and Eleanor Roosevelt Institute and the International Churchill Society, which promote both debates among scholars and less critical observances and celebrations of the major events in their heroes' lives. Studies of the two men evoke powerful pictures of a special personal partnership operating within the already special Anglo-American relationship, "The Partnership That Saved the West" was the late Joseph Lash's label. Whatever the problems caused by America's growth and Britain's decline, whatever the tensions created by the clash of empire and anticolonialism, whatever the differences between Churchill's "realism" and FDR's "idealism," whatever the conflict between Churchill's distrust of bolshevism and Roosevelt's desire to cooperate with the Soviets—all that pales, goes the popular view, alongside the singular and personal relationship between the two men that made possible victory against Germany, Italy, and Japan.[20]

Churchill's memoir-history of the war, immodestly titled *The Second World War*, set the parameters for the histories that followed during the next twenty years. "The Churchill legend is a powerful one," writes one historian, "and has been lovingly tended by Churchill himself in his memoirs." The prime minister drew a much-exaggerated portrait of himself as the wise and prescient leader who foresaw Soviet expansion, while Roosevelt comes off as a naive, well-meaning neophyte, unwilling to accept the facts of geopolitical power. The overall impression gained of his relationship with Roosevelt was ambiguous, as Churchill sought to create an image of equality and, at the time, account for his inability to change American policy. History, at least Churchill's history, has (in the words of Roosevelt speechwriter Robert Sherwood) created a sacred tradition that "when an American statesman and a British statesman meet, the former will be plain, blunt, down to earth, ingenuous to a fault, while the latter will be sly, subtle, devious and eventually triumphant." Sherwood went on to try, in vain, to correct that impression: "In the cases of Roosevelt and Churchill, this formula became somewhat confused. If either of them could be called a student of Machiavelli, it was Roosevelt; if either was a bull in a china shop, it was Churchill." In the bitter, admiring assessment of Roosevelt by Charles de Gaulle, "It was difficult to contradict this artist, this seducer. . . ."[21]

But Britons (and continental Europeans) held on to their depiction of Roosevelt and the Americans as shortsighted and "unrealistic"—the ultimate insult. Britain's wartime foreign secretary, Anthony Eden, warned a colleague not to "regard R[oosevelt] as either 'simple or naif,' " but the belief persisted. Nor has that assumption been restricted to the east side of the Atlantic. One student of international affairs, who by 1990 had become a regular contributor to the op-ed page of *The New York Times*, writes in his 1988 dissertation: "Washington and London came into the post-war world as Tom Sawyer and Perfidious Albion. Tom was full of faith in reason, in the ability of man to solve things. . . ." But Britain "knew how games were played and knew what its interests were." British historian A. J. P. Taylor's barb—"Of the great men at the top, Roosevelt was the only one who knew what he was doing: he made the United States the greatest power in the world at virtually no cost"—had little effect.[22]

There are other cautions to consider before we deal with the Roosevelt-Churchill pairing. Should we look at the wartime experience from just the vantage of those two leaders? There is ample evidence that Great Power policies were often influenced by the localized and even domestic policies of less powerful nations. The actions of the Polish government-in-exile and the effect of Chinese internal disputes—the civil war between Chiang and Mao—are but two obvious examples. Even more pressing is the need to incorporate Soviet and Stalin's perspectives and actions into any study of the war, lest we make the Second World War "appear like an Anglo-American film with occasional Russian subtitles." But that is more easily said than done in the absence of full access for all, including Russians, to Soviet archives.[23]

Yet both the Anglo-American relationship and the Churchill-Roosevelt link were different from the tripartite connection with the Soviet Union and Stalin. Part of that difference flowed from broad dissimilarities—those of language, history, and ideology—but those deep divergences were accentuated by more immediate geopolitical influences. Foremost among these was Stalin's unwillingness to join in the war against Japan until the complete defeat of Germany. Beginning with his refusal to send a Soviet representative to a proposed four-party meeting in Chungking, China, shortly after the Pearl Harbor attack, Stalin stubbornly rejected any involvement with the Pacific war. That policy made sense early on, when the Soviets had to avoid a two-front war in order to concentrate all their resources against Hitler's attack. But the Soviet stance did not change, even in 1944, when Germany's defeat had become certain—perhaps for military reasons, perhaps as "revenge for their [the Anglo-Americans'] dragging their feet on the second front."[24] Whatever the reasons, it was an opportunity lost, for it made the Soviets "associates" rather than partners in the wartime coalition and made efforts to perpetuate the wartime alliance even more difficult.

Churchill and Roosevelt met eleven times without Stalin. On most of those occasions they held discussions of extraordinary candor, the exceptions being the short meetings they held preceding and following the Big Three conferences at Teheran and Yalta.[25] Churchill did meet twice just with Stalin, and the second of those meetings, the so-called Tolstoy Conference, found the two bargaining with remarkable directness as they agreed to a crude geopolitical division of Eastern Europe. Even so, that Stalin-Churchill relationship never threatened to become anything more than opportunism, in either reality or myth.[26] Anglo-American strategy and intelligence were "combined," whereas they merely intersected between the Anglo-Americans and the Soviets. Britain and America shared the atomic secret, while agreeing to exclude everyone else, including their Soviet associate. Roosevelt planned and worked for the tripartite wartime coalition to develop into a close postwar association, but during the Second World War the "Grand Alliance" was fundamentally an Anglo-American partnership that included the Soviet Union primarily because they had a common enemy.

At the center of that Grand Alliance were Roosevelt and Churchill. The two war leaders, who worked together with remarkable closeness for more than five years, were drawn together by circumstances, not personalities. However much they alternately "cussed each other out" and expressed mutual affection and admiration, the reality of differing views, interests, and goals kept creeping in.[27]

Even before the two held their first conference, the president expressed concern about the Englishman's antiquated, "Victorian" views and his excessive drinking—hardly expressions of confidence or closeness. To be fair, Churchill expressed concern—"horror" might be a better word—about Roosevelt's drinking habits as well, though in this case it was the president's custom of concocting what he called martinis—a mixture of gin with both dry and sweet vermouth, stirred vigorously by FDR himself. Churchill loathed such mixed drinks, once going so far as to spit out a mouthful of what FDR's cousin Polly Delano called a Tom Collins.[28]

More substantive were Roosevelt's concerns about Churchill's old-fashioned nineteenth-century views. The prime minister ruefully admitted that "in the White House, I'm taken for a Victorian Tory." Fittingly, when he stayed in the White House, he slept in a room decorated with prints of the court of Queen Victoria. New Dealers and Roosevelt himself frequently spoke critically about Churchill's unsympathetic attitude toward the progressive reforms they believed were necessary in the United States—and throughout the world. According to Harry Hopkins, Roosevelt's closest adviser, the president "loves Winston as a man for the war, but is horrified at his reactionary attitude for after the war." Even though Roosevelt balanced that apprehension with the comment "Isn't he a wonderful old Tory to have on our side?" the unmistakable conclusion was that Churchill posed a barrier to the kind of postwar world sought by FDR. That certainly was the belief of Eleanor Roosevelt, who told their daughter, Anna, "I like Mr. Churchill, he's lovable and emotional and very human but I don't want him to write the peace or carry it out." But then Eleanor Roosevelt thought that Franklin was also "much in the nineteenth century."[29]

When FDR wheeled into the prime minister's room to find a naked and dripping wet Churchill finishing a dictation he had begun while in his bath, the Englishman may have quipped that "the Prime Minister of Great Britain has nothing to conceal from the President of the United States."[30] But that claim of total candor between Churchill and Roosevelt is belied by the visit of Hopkins to a meeting of the British Cabinet in 1941, shortly after the German attack on the Soviet Union. It was a carefully orchestrated charade. Once the American heard what he was supposed to hear, he was told the meeting was over, then escorted out while the Cabinet took up the touchy issue of the United States and Japan.[31] And more serious questions of candor remain. Doubts have not yet been laid to rest concerning still-closed British files that may relate to the Japanese attack on Pearl Harbor, leading to speculation that Churchill may have chosen not to pass certain information on to the Americans in the hope such an attack would draw the United States into the war.[32]

Similarly, the fact that both men were proud that they represented democracies must be balanced against the remarkable ignorance each displayed about the political system in the other's country. Each was jealous of what he saw as his counterpart's ability to wield political power. Churchill often claimed that being half American, he understood Americans and their political system. But that was a conceit. He mistakenly thought the presidential system left FDR free to do virtually as he pleased, while Roosevelt had no appreciation for Churchill's difficulties with and responsibilities to both the Cabinet and domestic politics.[33]

Their only meeting prior to the war had been fleeting and offered no hint of a special relationship. In 1918 Assistant Secretary of the Navy Franklin Roosevelt spoke at a dinner at Gray's Inn, one of London's ancient, traditional legal associations. Also present was Winston Churchill, a member and a far better-known public figure than Roosevelt. Joseph P. Kennedy later claimed that FDR told him the Englishman had been rude and a "stinker, . . . lording it all over us." Whether or not that injury occurred, insult followed, for when next they met, in August 1941 at the Atlantic Conference, Churchill did not recall having been introduced to the young Roosevelt, something that chagrined FDR enough to prompt him to mention it to his cronies. That tells us a good deal about Roosevelt's ego but also illustrates that no immediate sparks of friendship and admiration were struck when they first came face-to-face—whatever embellishment Churchill later put in his memoirs about remembering Roosevelt's "magnificent presence in all his youth and strength."[34]

Roosevelt ignored attempts by Churchill's publishers in the mid-twenties to arrange for him to review the Englishman's book *The World Crisis*, and in autumn 1929 FDR evaded Churchill's attempts to set up a meeting during a visit to New York. With Roosevelt's election to the presidency, Churchill followed his routine practice of cultivating contacts with important people, sending an autographed copy of his biography of Marlborough via Roosevelt's son James. A few years later Churchill used the same messenger to send the president a sketch of the "currency of the future"—a bill with the dollar and pound signs woven together. But none of those politic courtesies could be confused with camaraderie or early signs of a "special relationship."[35] Nor did Roosevelt respond . . . until World War II intervened.

There were some instructive similarities between the two. Certainly each had a flamboyant, public style that he consciously developed and used to provide leadership. But to work, those styles needed a popular sense of crisis and a popular need for direction. Churchill wandered in the political "wilderness" in the 1930s, when the British—leaders and public—viewed him as a threat to politics and to peace. When peace ended, Churchill became necessary as the public and Parliament looked for a forceful leader who promised to answer the hard questions. Even then he nearly failed in his efforts to displace Neville Chamberlain as prime minister.

"All Mr. Churchill needs is the direction in his life of a great idea," a popular British writer suggested in 1923. "He is a Saul on the way to Damascus. . . . That is to say, that to be saved from himself Mr. Churchill must be carried away by enthusiasm for some great ideal. . . ."[36] But the reverse was also true. Churchill's enthusiasm for Britain's well-being in the face of threats from many quarters—Hitler's Germany, the Bolsheviks, Japan, nationalism in the colonies—was not enough to bring him to power. His enthusiasm had to be paralleled by public fear (an equally strong "enthusiasm") that Britain's security was truly threatened by outside forces.

Roosevelt too came to power as a crisis leader. His unruffled, commonsense demeanor made it possible for him to calm a banking crisis in 1933 by merely closing the banks for a few days and then declaring everything was OK. Public faith in the system was restored. Critics and some historians may argue that his New Deal accomplished little, that his reforms were hardly more than sleight of hand. But the electorate disagreed, and in 1936 it returned him to the White House with the largest popular majority in American history to that point. Roosevelt's actions and rhetoric were often at odds—in foreign as well as domestic affairs—but the image of decisiveness and common sense that he cultivated made Americans look to him for leadership. He schemed and maneuvered in 1940 to get renominated as president. But he did not create the international crisis that made the Democratic party, and the public, turn to him for leadership.[37] As a crisis leader Roosevelt had the public's confidence.

Both men were masters of the English language, gaining the extraordinary power that such skill gives its practitioners. Churchill's curiously Victorian constructions neatly "mobilized the English language and sent it into battle," to use the words of the broadcaster Edward R. Murrow, in that period when, in Churchill's words, "the British people held the fort ALONE till those who hitherto had been half blind were half ready." Such grand phrases did not erupt spontaneously—Churchill worked long and hard at his prose and speeches—but he had the knack of talking to the British, and even the Americans, in a way that struck a chord.[38] The American diplomat Dean Acheson described Churchill's (and Roosevelt's) genius for speechmaking, both language and delivery: "[H]is use of all the artifices to get his way, from wooing to cajolery, through powerful advocacy to bluff bullying—all were carefully adjusted to the need. To call this acting is quite inadequate. Acting is a mode infinitely variable and adjustable. What we are speaking of is a transformation, a growth and a permanent change of personality. Napoleon understood this. So did Roosevelt." That from a man who admired Churchill but disliked FDR.[39]

Roosevelt guarded his emotions carefully, but they were there. When Senator Burton Wheeler described the lend-lease bill as "the New Deal's triple A foreign policy: it will plow under every fourth American boy," FDR's anger was palpable: "the most dastardly, unpatriotic thing . . . that has been said in public life in my generation." (Who but FDR and Churchill could call something "dastardly" without seeming archaic and silly?) When the former ambassador and adviser William Bullitt forced the resignation of Undersecretary of State Sumner Welles by releasing information that in that era amounted to character assassination, Roosevelt angrily told Bullitt he should "go to hell" for what he did.[40]

The two leaders generated intense loyalty. The plethora of reminiscences from those who worked with Churchill, from secretaries and bodyguards to Cabinet officers and his own medical doctor, all express an unmistakable genuine affection. They laugh lovingly at his foibles, telling stories about his upper-class ignorance of buses and the London Underground or his puzzlement at why his private secretary could not take his valet with him when he joined the Royal South African Air Force (his poorly paid secretary of course did not have a valet).[41]

Roosevelt also generated deep loyalty, most conspicuously from his wife, Eleanor, whose affection and esteem for him never left her, despite his infidelities and sometimes deprecatory treatment of her and her ideas. There were others: Hopkins, who became FDR's alter ego during the early war years; Henry Morgenthau, Jr., whose admiration for Roosevelt was unshakable; Marguerite "Missy" LeHand, Lucy Mercer, and Daisy Suckley, who loved him. The physician who cared for FDR during the latter part of the war,

Howard Bruenn, remarked "that like all people who work with this man [FDR]—I love him. If he told me to jump out of the window, I would do it, without hesitation."[42]

But that circle of close, loyal Roosevelt admirers and friends was much smaller than that of Churchill. Moreover, the reminiscences of those closest to him less frequently reveal the kind of warm affection that Churchill received—and for good reason. With the exception of family members, toward whom Roosevelt was cheerfully tolerant, and his small group of close women friends, loyalty often seemed a one-way street. In autumn 1943, when Hopkins, the president's most intimate adviser, decided to stop living in the White House—partly for health reasons, partly to save his marriage—Roosevelt acted annoyed, rejected, and puzzled. Hopkins, who became seriously ill a few months later, never regained his role as surrogate for the President.[43] FDR's treatment of Morgenthau, a long-standing friend and loyal treasury secretary, was laced with cruel humor. The president's baiting of Churchill during their meetings with Stalin prompted Averell Harriman (a Churchill fan, to be sure) to conclude that Roosevelt "enjoyed other people's discomfort" and "unquestionably had a sadistic streak."[44]

Churchill worried about detail to the point of distracting his colleagues. He distrusted staff analyses, dismissing them as "a form of collective wisdom." Initially he insisted that *all* Enigma (Ultra) decryptions of secret German messages be sent to him daily without first being "sifted and digested" by intelligence agencies. That was patently impossible—not because the 250 decrypts a day received by winter 1940–41 were too many but because the frequency of code names, technical phrases, and obscure references to places and military units took such extensive research to explain. Amid a crisis during the Battle of the Atlantic, when analysts at Bletchley Park, where the British decrypted signals intelligence, were working frantically to break the German code, Churchill interrupted their work to ask for full details on the trivial matter of six German minisubs that intelligence data reported being transported to the Caspian Sea.[45]

Roosevelt, on the other hand, dismissed detail with a cavalier wave of the hand. With the possible exception of the promotion lists for the U.S. Navy, which he monitored painstakingly, Roosevelt focused on ends, not means. In September 1941, worried that under Hitler's onslaught morale in the Soviet Union would collapse even before its armies, Roosevelt ordered an unenthusiastic Secretary of War Henry Stimson to send the aircraft promised the Russians "right off with a bang next week." That admitted morale-building gesture was followed by orders to set up an effective aid program: "Use a heavy hand—act as a burr under the saddle and get things moving. . . . Step on it!"[46] He left the details to Stimson and the War Department.

That same goal-oriented leadership style surfaced in autumn 1942, when FDR stunned production experts by telling them that they needed to build one hundred thousand combat aircraft in 1943. A few days later he cabled Churchill: "[I] have agreed to reduce it to eighty-two thousand combat planes but . . . I want that many combat planes actually delivered," then left the details about the types to "be decided by the military."[47]

Churchill was an optimist, yet subject to fits and periods of depression—what he himself called his "black dog." He reveled in argumentation and confrontation, which he approached like a feisty bulldog, both combative and stubborn. If FDR became depressed, it is a well-kept secret. He could be angry (witness his reaction to Wheeler's "plow under every fourth American boy" crack), but his breezy optimism and compulsive avoidance of confrontation (he could not bring himself to punish his own children, leaving disciplining them to his wife) combined to make depression either foreign to his nature or unnecessary since problems deferred were problems solved—for the time being.[48]

Churchill was a person of feelings, someone who grappled with a problem by talking it out with anyone who would listen. Roosevelt was more a person of things, someone who kept his own counsel and solved, dismissed, or ignored a problem. Churchill's conception of relaxation was to deliver a lecture on the course of the war to whatever audience he had available. One of his secretaries recalls that after a discussion with the Japanese ambassador in February 1941, Churchill "could remember his own remarks, but found it difficult to recall the other side of the conversation."[49]

The war completely obsessed and possessed him, whatever the occasional stories of bricklaying at his country residence in Chartwell. He completed only a single painting between 1939 and 1945. If Roosevelt's confrontation with polio transformed him, the war did the same for Churchill. In both cases Saul became Paul.

Unlike Churchill, Roosevelt escaped the war whenever he could. His cronies were one diversion, but his favorite relaxation came in chats over tea with his two unmarried cousins, Laura "Polly" Delano and Margaret "Daisy" Suckley, whom he once told: "You're the only people I know that I don't have to entertain." Tête-à-têtes with his onetime mistress, Lucy Mercer Rutherfurd, or the occasional private visit to the polio rehabilitation center he founded at Warm Springs, Georgia, allowed him to limit conversations to gossip and reminiscences about family and friends—no war or politics.[50] Those were problems that he had to solve himself—a characteristic that may have contributed as much to his hypertension and death as his polio and subsequent paralysis. FDR occasionally vented his ideas in rambling monologues,[51] but much less frequently and much less fully than Churchill, who used such occasions as part of his "thinking it out" process. Roosevelt's musings were, contrary to the popular image, broad and almost philosophical (though that imputes too much structure), whereas Churchill tended to focus on practical, immediate problems.

Despite FDR's apparent dislike of introspection and his stubborn refusal to let others know his inner thoughts, he too succumbed to the ruminations on mortality that winter beach walkers, Waldenites, and those watching the sunset from atop tenement roofs have in common. I give you the words of Roosevelt's remarkably sensitive biographer Geoffrey Ward: "His favorite site was Dowdell's Knob, a rocky overhang 1,395 feet above sea level, reached by a dirt track that threaded its precarious way along the crest of nearby Pine Mountain [Georgia]. . . ."

Whenever a polio [sufferer] seemed about to give in to despair, Roosevelt once told a friend, he or she should be brought up to Dowdell's Knob right away: one look at the glorious view would provide them with the will to go on." Ward adds a poignant footnote: "Frail and ashen, FDR himself would spend several hours at

Dowdell's Knob, staring out at the view, on the afternoon of the day before he died in 1945."[52]

That issue of health remains, for later generations, a puzzling parallel between the two men. Both suffered from serious and recurrent health problems throughout the war. (Coincidentally, so did two of Roosevelt's senior advisers. Hopkins, following an operation for stomach cancer in 1937, had very serious digestive problems accentuated by misdiagnosis; Cordell Hull suffered from tuberculosis, worsening diabetes, and intense claustrophobia. Stalin apparently shared that claustrophobia, at least when it came to flying, and he was once found slumped unconscious at his desk.) The health of Churchill and Roosevelt is medical fact. The question to answer is, Did those health problems affect history in any significant way?[53]

Not surprisingly the major wartime conferences apparently occasioned serious health problems for both. Those meetings were periods of extreme stress and tension exacerbated by long travel (especially for Roosevelt) and inadequate rest—a particular problem for FDR, who groused about what he called "the Winston hours," which called for drinking and talking until the wee hours of the morning. FDR invariably returned from such gatherings with elevated blood pressure.[54] Both Churchill and Roosevelt suffered serious illnesses after two major conferences—those at Casablanca and Teheran. Churchill's first major episode of angina pectoris was during the Arcadia Conference in Washington, right after the Pearl Harbor attack. Roosevelt died within a few months of the Yalta Conference.

For the prime minister, pneumonia was the primary problem. Each of the three episodes he experienced—after the conferences at Casablanca and Teheran and again in August 1944—was accompanied by high fever (104°F in the August 1944 attack). The pneumonia that followed the Teheran Conference was possibly the result of a typhoid infection.[55] His physician, Lord Moran, also diagnosed a heart fibrillation and prescribed digitalis (which did not cause Churchill to lose weight, as FDR did). Churchill's health remained uncertain throughout the war. An episode of pneumonia that began in late August 1944 lasted intermittently until after the prime minister's meeting with Stalin in Moscow in October, leaving Churchill tired and worried.[56]

Roosevelt's cigarette smoking had a clear effect on his health. Less clear is the impact of Churchill's alcohol consumption on his health and abilities. No book about Churchill is complete without stories about his drinking, stories he repeated and improved upon. His classic retort was that "I have taken more out of alcohol than alcohol has taken out of me." When his science adviser and crony Lord Cherwell estimated that Churchill's lifetime consumption of champagne, which he drank every day, would fill only one end of a compartment on a railroad car, Churchill appeared visibly disappointed. Late in the war, during a discussion of health, he vigorously asserted that he "could still always sleep well, eat well and especially drink well."

His close aides have called such tales exaggerations and noted (correctly, according to Hopkins) that Churchill watered his whiskey—a weak "mouthwash," according to Jock Colville, one of Churchill's private secretaries during the war, however occasional the *"stiff* whiskey and soda, at 8:45 A.M.," as reported by Eden. But Colville's defense ignores the fact that Churchill drank a great deal more than just whiskey. As White House speechwriter Robert Sherwood put it, Churchill's "consumption of alcohol continued at quite regular intervals through most of his waking hours without visible effect." Offered tea for breakfast at 7:30 A.M. at the Cairo Embassy after an eleven-hour flight from Marrakech, the prime minister declined, asking for some white wine, which he drained in a gulp. He then remarked, "Ah! that is good, but you know I have already had two whiskies and soda and two cigars this morning." A British diplomat observed him at Yalta "drinking buckets of Caucasian champagne which would undermine the health of any ordinary man."

At the same time there is no credible testimony of Churchill's being drunk, in the falling-down slurred-words sense, while he was prime minister. Perhaps, as C. P. Snow quipped, Churchill was no alcoholic, for no alcoholic could drink that much.[57] "Alcohol-dependent" may be the appropriate phrase, which postpones (to the end of this book) any assessment of the effect of Roosevelt's and Churchill's health and habits on their policies and on history.

Regardless of arguments, regardless of tensions, regardless of differences in style, philosophy, and character, what is crystal clear is that Roosevelt and Churchill quickly came to respect and hold affection for each other. They both were national statesmen, ever conscious of their constitutional responsibility to promote the interests of their nations. Yet at the same time they believed that their two societies, whatever the flaws, were moving in much the same direction. FDR had his doubts about Churchill's "progressivism." Churchill had his doubts about Roosevelt's tendency to ignore Britain's interests. But neither had any doubts whatsoever about the other's commitment to winning the war and to making the peace something they would decide together.

—————

That war between Hitler's Germany and most of the rest of Europe came in a series of challenges that began as soon as the Führer came to power in Germany in 1933. Under his leadership Germany broke out in less than a decade from the isolation the other European powers had tried to impose with the Versailles Treaty after the First World War. Hitler had not made it easy for Britain and France to oppose him. During the 1930s he rejected the Versailles peace treaty system in increments, each relatively contained and thus unsettling rather than threatening. Military reoccupation of the Rhineland, rebuilding an air force, negotiating a naval agreement with the British—these all seemed the legitimate province of any independent state. Blatant but unofficial military intervention in the Spanish Civil War was more troubling, but then France and Britain hardly had clean hands in that arena. Union (*Anschluss*) with Austria and demands for union with the Sudeten Germans in western Czechoslovakia masqueraded as corrections to ethnic inequities perpetuated by the World War I peace settlement.

That geopolitical pot of troubles was stirred by two consistent and consistently alarming Nazi policies. First was Germany's selfish and aggressive economic actions—autarkical policies of protectionism and bilateral trade agreements that went directly against both American liberal economics (free markets) and the British imperial system, which was in its own way a worldwide commercial structure. The second was Hitler's increasingly brutal and callous treatment of Jews and his repression of organized Christian churches. Nazi persecution of Jews was and would be far more horrific than the regime's anti-Christian policies—there were no plans for a "final solution" for Christians—but Hitler's treatment of the Christian churches, particularly the Roman Catholic and Lutheran churches, alienated their coreligionists throughout Europe and America, a far larger and politically more influential element than Jews. According to one German diplomat, Americans feared that Hitler was planning to replace Christianity with state-sponsored paganism, and there was "doubt and wavering even among the Lutherans," who, with Catholics, constituted the bulk of German-Americans.

Yet without the threat posed by Hitler's aggressive policies and apparent military strength (grossly overestimated by all in the West), Western leaders would have shaken their heads, made the appropriate public expressions of concern, and then, as Churchill did, claimed they could not intervene in the internal matters of other states.[58]

By 1938, perhaps earlier, Hitler's cautious, step-by-step expansion and rejection of the First World War peace settlement presented the European leaders with a conundrum: The only way to prevent war was to go to war. Neither Britain nor France was willing to do or even think that, nor—to hazard a guess—was the Soviet Union. Memories of the horror of the Great War were too recent and strong, while the Great Depression had reinforced the natural tendency of societies to focus on local, internal problems. At the same time domestic instability made both France and the Soviet Union reluctant to get entangled in external confrontations. In the mid-thirties France had stopped its revolving door of premiers only by settling on a weak coalition led by Socialist Léon Blum. In the Soviet Union Stalin's anxieties had brought on the Great Purge, which crippled political, bureaucratic, and military leadership. In Britain the government of Neville Chamberlain, though far from weak, was until the last equally reluctant even to consider taking a military stance against Hitler.

Supposed American isolationism is a misconception. The passage of legislation like the Neutrality Acts of the mid-1930s was in fact an admission that the United States was, either by choice or by fate, a player on the international scene. Those laws aimed at preventing big business (a ready villain in the midst of the Great Depression) from dragging the United States into the war, as had supposedly happened in 1917. Americans prohibited aid, particularly arms sales and loans, to nations at war lest the United States be pulled into another European war. Underlying those actions was the belief that Europe had rejected American leadership after World War I.

But the Neutrality Acts could not change the course of events outside the United States. Perhaps FDR's intuition was at peak efficiency when, in 1920, he declared: "Every sane man knows that in case of another world-war, America would be drawn in. . . ." Yet the desire to avoid entanglement—what became misleadingly called isolationism—made Americans nostalgic for a time that had never existed, a time when the rest of the world did not matter.[59]

Perhaps British Prime Minister Chamberlain, indelibly associated with "appeasement," was as much an "isolationist" as the Americans. He set a simple and absolutely self-defeating test for U.S. intentions. If the United States was willing to make specific, presumably military commitments, then it was serious. Roosevelt was, apparently, expected to lead in Europe, even though the Europeans had rejected that task and the Chamberlain government had opted for "military isolationism." Actually, American leadership was the last thing in the world an egotistical Chamberlain wanted. (This was, after all, the man who pompously wrote his sister Ida, "[N]ow I have only to raise a finger & the whole face of Europe is changed."[60]) At any rate, anything less than an unequivocal commitment on Roosevelt's part and the prime minister could (and did) label American initiatives as hot air. Chamberlain's test for Hitler was not nearly as rigorous. All the German leader had to do was toss off a few vague promises, cock an eyebrow (or mustache?), and declaim about his desire for peace. Chamberlain immediately responded with suggestions for conferences and optimistic letters to his sisters. As for working with the Soviet Union, the most obvious ally against Hitler, Chamberlain would have no part of it.[61]

Any alliance against Hitler formed in 1938 or after would have had to be willing to force a fight. Yet British and French diplomacy in those years was always guided by the absolute belief that war was worse than its alternatives. Their uninterest in Soviet proposals for a full-fledged military alliance, whether or not those proposals were sincere, highlighted Anglo-French unwillingness to consider such a step. No wonder Franklin Roosevelt repeatedly lectured the British about stiffening their resolve. FDR's support for the Munich agreements of September 1938—the appeasement approach that attempted to assuage Hitler's hunger by feeding him Czechoslovak territory—did not reflect a liking for Chamberlain's excessive accommodation but rather the president's understanding that leadership in Europe had to come from Europeans. Privately he had remarked to one of his ambassadors the previous February that if the police chief makes a deal with gangsters that prevents crime, he "will be called a great man," but if the gangsters break their word, "the Chief of Police will go to jail." Chamberlain seemed to be "taking very long chances."[62]

Perhaps American military commitments to fight in Europe could have prevented war, though deterrence did not prevent the Japanese from attacking Pearl Harbor. But in an era when even the German Army still used horse-drawn wagons to bring supplies to the front, the burden for establishing a deterrent policy in Europe lay primarily with the Europeans—France, Britain, and the Soviet Union—not with a country on the other side of the Atlantic Ocean.

The Munich agreements did not bring "peace for our time," as Chamberlain had predicted. In fact the confrontation that lay behind the arrangement made all aware that they had merely papered over the cracks, not reached a long-term solution. That understanding stimulated increased planning and spending on military preparedness, in Germany as well as among Hitler's future enemies. By December 1938 Roosevelt had assigned his treasury secretary, Henry Morgenthau, Jr., the task of coordinating U.S. aid to the European democracies, as both Britain and France sought to buy aircraft and related equipment.

In January and mid-February 1939, some six months before the war began in Europe, Roosevelt provided senators and news reporters with a remarkably clear picture of the foreign policy he hoped to follow for the next few years.[63] Ostensibly speaking "off the record" (which meant reporters could not quote him), Roosevelt, ever the classic liberal, linked economic and political freedom, telling the journalists: "[T]here are certain nations, about thirty or forty strong . . . whose continued independent political and military and . . . , let's say, their economic independence . . . acts as a protection for this hemisphere.

"Suppose I say," he went on, "that the continued independence, in a political and economic sense, of Finland is of tremendous importance to the safety of the United States?" Then what about the Baltic states, Scandinavia, Greece, and the Middle East? Deftly slipping to more immediate problems, he pointed out that Austria and Czechoslovakia had come off the list of independent nations. The independence of others "acts as a protection for the democracies of this hemisphere," he argued. Some senators accused the president of claiming that America's "frontier" lay on the Rhine River or in France. When the White House's verbatim transcript of that meeting failed to even mention the Rhine, FDR labeled the accusation a "deliberate lie," and gave instructions to install a recording system in the White House (something some later presidents would come to regret). But even Senator Gerald Nye, the father of the neutrality legislation and Roosevelt's archetypal "isolationist," understood that FDR hoped to use Anglo-French power as America's "first line of defense"—a different concept from a "frontier."[64]

Roosevelt had set his agenda. The situation was perilous. The spread of dictatorships threatened democracy, the code word for American political liberty and economic opportunity. Back in 1937, in the wake of the Japanese attack on China, he had spoken of preventing war by quarantining the dictators. He was apparently thinking aloud, for he had no plan and quickly backed away in the face of vocal opposition from what he called the isolationists. Now he advocated helping the British and French to quarantine (without using the word) the European dictators. Quoting Arthur

Krock, the influential *New York Times* writer, the president asked, "Isn't this unneutral?" "Yes," FDR went on, "it might be called that." But, he went on, the policy of this government was to do everything it could to keep arms away from the Axis powers—Germany, Japan, and Italy—and sell as much arms to the "independent nations" as they could pay for.[65]

This was not the military globalism of Cold War America or even the Great Power cooperation that FDR himself came to advocate. Rather it suggested a leader who recognized the limits of American power, limits imposed by domestic attitudes, perceptions of the ability of the United States to influence events, and common sense.

Whatever Roosevelt's reluctance to lead in Europe, the German ambassador to the United States in the late 1930s, Hans Dieckhoff, hit the nail on the head when he warned his superiors in Berlin that "the American Government, should it so desire, will encounter no insuperable difficulties in again pushing this country into the war at the psychological moment, just as in the [First] World War, and perhaps even more quickly." Dieckhoff exaggerated more than a little when he wrote that one could recognize "his master's voice" from London, but the overall point—that the United States was hardly isolationist—proved on the mark.[66] What the German diplomat seems to have recognized was that there was considerable ground between isolation and intervention.

The German occupation of Prague in March 1939, a blatant violation of the Munich Pact, along with Italian Premier Benito Mussolini's move across the Adriatic Sea into Albania, not only prompted increased preparedness efforts on the part of those threatened by Hitler but also pushed Chamberlain to begin, ever so tentatively, discussions with the Soviets about some sort of private, unofficial mutual assistance arrangement. The negotiations never brought agreement. The Soviet Union continually changed its position; fear of Soviet intentions caused the Poles and Balts (Latvia, Lithuania, Estonia) to refuse promises of cooperation; and Chamberlain, who distrusted the Bolsheviks intensely, always found reasons to delay. He remained convinced that the Russians had no choice but to cooperate against Germany, despite reports of contacts between Berlin and Moscow.[67]

Stalin had concluded otherwise. Following World War I, the new Polish state had twice used military force to take territory at the Bolsheviks' expense, while the Baltic states had taken advantage of Soviet weakness to declare their independence after some two hundred years of Russian czarist rule. Fundamental to Stalin's foreign policy was the regaining of those lands. Munich, with its implied invitation to Hitler to move eastward, destroyed any expectation Stalin had of developing collective security against Germany; the desultory British approach toward negotiations merely confirmed that conclusion. Little surprise, then, that Stalin made a virtue out of necessity and agreed to a pact with Hitler, gambling that the short-term benefits—time for the Soviet Union to rearm plus reacquisition of the "lost" territories—seemed a better bet than relying on the British and French both to become effective allies against Germany and to agree to Soviet reabsorption of those lands.[68]

On August 21 rumor became reality when Berlin radio reported that German Foreign Minister Joachim Ribbentrop was on his way to Moscow to sign the Nazi-Soviet nonaggression pact. Ten days later, on September 1, the Germans moved against Poland. Within two days the United Kingdom declared war on Germany. The Soviets—cautious about German intentions, eager to present their actions as a regaining of their legitimate territory, and worried about an ongoing military confrontation with Japan along the Mongolia-Manchuria border—delayed but finally collected on their part of the bargain with Hitler and moved into eastern Poland a few weeks later. "It's the end of the world, the end of everything," despaired the American ambassador in London, Joseph Kennedy.[69] As Roosevelt had predicted, the chief of police would have to go to jail or, the political equivalent, lose his office. The only question was when.

Perhaps, some have argued loudly, Churchill led Britain down the primrose path by placing his faith in an alliance with the Americans. Chamberlain's appeasement policy could have worked, the argument goes, for it would have set the Germans against the Soviet Union and thus have allowed Britain to bargain for the security of its economy, its empire, and itself.[70] Regardless of self-respect, which governments may not have but a people do, regardless of what that would have meant for the peoples of Europe, particularly Western Europe, regardless of how little Britain had to gain and how much it had to lose in such a gamble, regardless of what Britain did lose in the course of the war, it was Neville Chamberlain, not Winston Churchill, who declared war on Nazi Germany.

Britain went to war in September 1939 for the reason nations always go to war: It felt threatened. The threat was cumulative, not direct, although that was to come. Britain did not go to war to save the Jews, although mounting Nazi brutality, especially Kristallnacht in 1938, when Nazi-led Germans destroyed Jewish-owned property all over Germany, raised doubts about working with Hitler. Britain did not go to war to save Czechoslovakia; Hitler had violated that country and the Munich agreements when he occupied Prague in the spring of 1939. Britain did not go to war to save Poland, even though Hitler's invasion of that nation triggered the decision to declare war on Germany. If saving Poland had been Britain's motive, then how could the U.K. still seek an alliance with the Soviet Union, which had occupied eastern Poland like a thief in the night a few weeks after Hitler had taken Warsaw? Chamberlain despised bolshevism, but the Soviet Union posed no threat. He had tried to appease the Nazis, but by September 1939 Germany did pose a threat.

British strategic assumptions were simple—and simply wrong. They assumed that Hitler's gaze was fixed on the Slavs to the east, especially the Ukraine. They also assumed that if the Germans did attack toward the west, France would hold out for a year, even two years, giving Britain time to do what Winston Churchill had persistently advocated: rearm.

Ironically, Soviet and American assumptions were much the same. No one, least of all Stalin, thought the Nazi-Soviet Pact would survive for long, given Hitler's rantings about the inferior Slavs. But analysts in both Washington and Moscow believed that the Germans had to take care of the problem closest to home, France. And France had already demonstrated, they thought, that while it might not be able to win alone, it could not lose. Thus both Stalin and Roosevelt, as well as Chamberlain, believed they had what every politician covets, the time to make tough decisions.

It was there that things stood when Franklin Delano Roosevelt addressed his first communication to Winston Spencer Churchill, the newly appointed first lord of the British admiralty.

PRIVATE

My dear Churchill:—

It is because you and I occupied similar positions in the World War that I want you to know how glad I am that you are back again in the Admiralty. Your problems are, I realize, complicated by new factors but the essential is not very different. What I want you and the Prime Minister to know is that I shall at all times welcome it if you will keep me in touch personally with anything you want me to know about. You can always send sealed letters through your pouch or my pouch.

I am glad you did the Marlboro volumes before this thing started— and I much enjoyed reading them.

With my sincere regards, Faithfully yours,

[signed] *Franklin D. Roosevelt*
September 11, 1939[71]

With those few sentences President Franklin Roosevelt began an extraordinary correspondence, perhaps modern history's most significant. In just over five and one-half years, from September 1939 until FDR's death on April 12, 1945, he and Winston S. Churchill exchanged nearly two thousand letters, memorandums, and messages. The Englishman's messages were longer and more frequent—about three for every two sent by FDR. Most contained an intentionally personal touch: Churchill's were often expressed in the formal niceties that he habitually used ("The Treasurer and Masters of the Bench of Gray's Inn, including Master Winston Churchill, . . . send you their most respectful greetings"); Roosevelt's came as typically American wisecracks ("while your French grammar is better than mine, my accent is more alluring").[72]

But French grammar and mannered invitations merely served as lubricating oil for what was the most crucial wartime alliance of modern times, the Anglo-American alliance against Hitler's Germany. In a way this is a misleading statement because in the broadest sense, the Second World War was three separate but interconnected struggles. Between September 1939 and spring 1941, Great Britain won the first of those contests. *"Not to lose the war"* was the British strategy.[73] The Battle of Britain, what Churchill called his nation's "finest hour," ensured the island nation's survival against the threat of a German invasion. American aid, particularly lend-lease, made it possible for Britain to implement its simple strategy. That defensive victory proved indispensable. It diverted German resources from Hitler's fight against Russia while providing both the psychological prop that kept the United States in the struggle against Germany and then the physical platform for the invasion of German-held Europe. Churchill wrote of the first major British victory of arms, the Battle of El Alamein in late 1942: "Before Alamein we never had a victory. After Alamein we never had a defeat."[74] He was wrong about the victory. Had Britain not won the battle for survival, the United States could not and would not have confronted Hitler unless and until he challenged American security in the Western Hemisphere, a challenge that would not have come until after Germany had taken care of the Soviet Union. Without the Anglo-Americans, Stalin would have sought further accommodation with Hitler.

Yet only the Soviet Union could provide the massive forces and vast geography needed to win the Second War. Defeating the German Army was the prerequisite to winning (as opposed to not losing) the fight against Hitler. The survival of Britain and its fleet made it possible for the United States and the United Kingdom to quarantine Germany within Europe, but only the Red Army had the sheer weight needed to win that war. The difference between quarantine and victory is crucial. Anything less than complete victory would have meant the continuation of Nazi genocide—racial "cleansing"—a horror that exceeded even Stalin at his most barbaric.[75]

The third war, the American campaign against Japan's brutal military expansion in East Asia and the Pacific, pitted the immense strength of the United States against a smaller, less industrialized nation. But the vast watery distances of the Pacific gave Japan an advantage in a war fought far away from America's shores. Had

Britain not survived as a bastion against Germany, and the Soviet Union not committed itself fully to the war against Hitler, then the United States could have found itself facing a hostile and threatening Nazi German Empire allied with Japan.

There were significant differences between the three wars. To begin with, Great Britain's war lasted six and one-half years, the Soviet Union's a little more than four years, and that of the United States only three and two-thirds years—about half the length of Britain's struggle. But the Anglo-American alliance proved both enduring and essential to all three wars. Whatever Anglo-American quarrels persisted over military strategy and European colonial empires, and despite the tensions of an alliance between a nation in relative decline and one rising to superpower status, the British and the Americans maintained a remarkably close, relatively candid, and extraordinarily cooperative relationship throughout the war.

Their wartime alliance was partly a matter of a common purpose: the defeat of Germany and Japan. Partly it derived from their shared historical experience and the advantage of speaking and writing the same language (despite George Bernard Shaw's acid comment that the British and Americans are divided by a common language). Partly the alliance flowed from a set of common values: representative democracy, civic duty, the role and responsibilities of government, individual rights and freedoms.

But the indispensable glue for the wartime alliance was leadership. Without that element the Anglo-American relationship would surely have become a mere coalition, as it was with their military partner, the Soviet Union. Had either Britain or the United States been led by an irresponsible statesman prattling about selfish interests, the alliance could have been overwhelmed by the jealousies and fears that characterize nations. But neither Winston Churchill nor Franklin Roosevelt fell prey to such actions. They made mistakes in judgment, disagreed about how to win and how the postwar world could (and should) look, and looked to their own countries' interests. But time and again, at the most crucial moments, they put their wartime alliance first.

This is their story, a story that is also, inevitably, the story of their nations.

England must survive! . . .

CHAPTER 2

"If Britain Is to Survive"
September 1939–September 1940

Rex Harrison to the arresting officer from Scotland Yard: The world always underestimates the British. How could I have made the same mistake?

—*Midnight Lace* (1960)

The Churchill-Roosevelt relationship, a "special" relationship by virtue of its closeness and significance, did not happen by accident. Nor did inevitability play a role, whatever the historical and geopolitical forces that drove Britain and the United States together. The Anglo-American alliance seems, as of 1939, foreordained, just as the German ambassador to the United States had concluded. But the nature and texture of that alliance, the details that make history what it is, required individuals.

It is hard to imagine any other American president bypassing traditional channels to write a personal letter to a relatively minor, if slightly notorious, member of the British Cabinet. There was some logic to it: Roosevelt remembered having met Churchill in 1918 even if the Englishman had forgotten. That FDR recalled Churchill's being a "stinker" suggests that the president reached a bit for an excuse to contact the man many were predicting would be Britain's next prime minister.[1]

More important were Roosevelt's constant efforts to be in control. Whether or not his physical infirmities strengthened that desire, his administrative style invariably worked to limit the power and authority of any individual or agency he worked with. Those who lasted longest in his inner circle were persons willing to subordinate their own ambitions and egos to the president's. Cantan-

35

kerous, independent-acting people like Harold Ickes and Cordell Hull soon found their freedom of action limited or some of their responsibilities assigned to someone else.

Roosevelt's initial letter to Churchill fitted into that search for control, for it aimed at establishing a personal contact that would allow FDR to evade routine and be in charge. In March 1942, with the Churchill-Roosevelt channel firmly in place, the president claimed that he could "personally handle Stalin better than either your Foreign Office or my State Department." Like Churchill, Roosevelt trusted people, not bureaucracies. Faceless career diplomats, he concluded, reported what the State Department culture demanded.

To get around that problem, Roosevelt constantly sought contacts with foreign leaders and diplomats, partly to get their measure, partly to gain information. He chatted regularly with his personal representatives and even occasionally with American career diplomats. Sometimes he bounced ideas off his visitors, as British Foreign Secretary Anthony Eden learned during a visit to Washington in the spring of 1943. Other times FDR made swift decisions, as George Kennan, then a mid-level diplomat, discovered when he spoke with Roosevelt in autumn of that same year. Kennan, the U.S. chargé d'affaires in Portugal, managed, by luck and persistence, to make an appointment to see the president. Once through the door, Kennan warned that a shopping list of facilities in the Azores that the American military chiefs wanted presented to the Portuguese president, Antonio Salazar, not only would be rejected but would raise suspicions about America's long-term intentions. FDR listened, then told Kennan to do his best and not to "worry about all those *people* over there," a clear reference to the military and the State Department.[2]

More often than not, Roosevelt's conversations were interviews disguised as friendly chats. When the Nationalist Chinese leader, Chiang Kai-shek, failed to measure up during a face-to-face meeting in Cairo in late 1943, the president began looking for alternatives.

That same personal approach extended to Roosevelt's use of diplomatic representatives. Time and again he indicated his preference for the personal touch. He told his major ambassadorial appointees—William Dodd in Berlin, Joseph Kennedy in London, William Bullitt in Paris—to keep in direct touch by personal letters. He understood their shortcomings—labeling Kennedy a defeatist and characterizing Bullitt as too easily influenced by others—but the president felt more comfortable with their reports than with those of the "boys in the striped pants," as he derisively called State Department diplomats. Hopkins named Foreign Service officers "cookie pushers, pansies—and usually isolationists to boot." Both men shared the notion that the State Department was "a professional priesthood" that believed it should have a "priestly monopoly against intervention by members of Congress, journalists, professors, voters, and other lesser breeds." Even those not at the prestigious posts, like the ambassador to the Greek government, Lincoln MacVeagh, received similar instructions and even the occasional presidential visit.

Major foreign issues of wartime policy usually brought a special presidential mission from nonprofessional diplomats like Harry Hopkins, W. Averell Harriman, William Phillips, and Patrick Hurley or Roosevelt's special assistant for intelligence operations, William J. Donovan. All were told to bypass the State Department and go directly to the president whenever they wished. Even foreign diplomats got the "treatment," as the British ambassador in Washington in 1939–40, Lord Lothian (Philip Kerr), quickly found out.

More than once FDR left his personal envoys "twisting in the wind." But then that was what "personal" envoys were for: to represent the president, not to represent the established foreign policy–making bureaucracy. Along with the privilege of floating trial balloons and having direct access to Roosevelt went the knowledge that such a direct relationship was subject to his personal decisions and even whims. Few of these envoys protested, and when they did, like Bullitt, they were exiled to the hedgerows. Most reacted as MacVeagh did when the President expressed displeasure: He defended himself in fawning and embarrassing detail, signing off, "Affectionately yours as always."[3]

There is a certain irony in Roosevelt's search to escape the grasp of big bureaucratic government, given his reputation as the man who brought that kind of government to the United States. But perhaps foreign policy is a different case. The dramatic expansion and increased complexity of America's involvement in international relations in the post-1945 world of near-instant communications would seem to work against micromanagement, but just the opposite is the case. Diplomacy at the summit—meetings between national leaders—so much a special feature of World War II, have become commonplace as presidents try to control the bewildering events they confront.

Roosevelt's first message to Churchill avoided open discourtesy toward Prime Minister Chamberlain by including him in the appeal for a correspondence and by sending him a separate message. But the president's heart was not in the courtesies. Shortly after Chamberlain had taken office in May 1937, he had resisted FDR's efforts to establish personal contact, spurning an invitation to visit the United States and focusing on a European solution to German expansion. Part of that solution was to deter Hitler from further aggression by convincing him that the war was not worth the winning. British rearmament and a weak German economy that would be vulnerable to the traditional British tool of economic blockade would, Chamberlain thought, give the Nazis pause and give the German people time to get rid of Hitler. But more important was Chamberlain's conviction that the Germans would move east—toward the Soviet Union—and as the Czechs soon learned, he did what he could to ensure that Hitler looked in that direction.[4]

Churchill, on the other hand, seemed a better bet. Despite his firm loyalty to Chamberlain, Churchill had managed to appear the apostle of military preparedness and firmness toward Hitler, policies that went against the now-discredited appeasement approach. Moreover, Churchill had long and vocally supported close Anglo-American relations. The title of his multivolume study *A History of the English-Speaking Peoples* reveals his conviction that a common language counted for more than anything else, and geopolitically the United States was the English-speaking nation that counted most, something Churchill had observed firsthand from his position in the British Cabinet during the First World War. To top it off, Roosevelt's schemes for helping Britain resist the Nazis focused on the sea—he had mused about an expanded "neutrality patrol" during King George's visit to the United States in June 1939— and Churchill headed the Admiralty.[5]

Cultivating personal contacts was part of Churchill's style as a longtime public figure. As merely a Cabinet member in 1939 he would not have thought to initiate a private correspondence with a foreign head of state, but given the opening, he quickly seized the opportunity. The day after the president's letter arrived on October 3, Churchill wrote to Chamberlain suggesting that the initiative be taken up. The prime minister agreed and sent a cable of his own to Roosevelt.[6]

Neither Churchill nor Roosevelt could have dreamed of what that correspondence would become, particularly since the early exchanges offered little hint of how the connection would develop. In fact, as historian David Reynolds has reminded us, from the time the war started until Chamberlain resigned as prime minister on May 10, 1940, the Chamberlain-Roosevelt exchanges were more substantive than those between Churchill and the president.[7]

That said, the foundation of the Churchill-Roosevelt relationship was set with the willingness of the two men to communicate from the outset of the war. Churchill's quick recognition of the potential in such exchanges prompted him to insist that the channel remain direct, despite the efforts of the British foreign secretary, then Lord Halifax, to have outgoing messages to Roosevelt first approved by the Foreign Office. Churchill preferred that Joe Kennedy, the pessimistic, even defeatist American ambassador in London, see the messages rather than subject them to prior approval from the British Foreign Office. Moreover, he could undo any damage from Kennedy's comments since British intelligence had long since broken the American diplomatic code. Churchill won the argument, though he agreed to send a copy of his cables to the Foreign Office so that British diplomats in the United States would not be embarrassed.[8]

Fittingly, given both Churchill's and Roosevelt's love of conversation, agreement to keep in touch came by telephone. Even as Chamberlain and his Cabinet were considering how to answer Roosevelt's invitation, the president used the transatlantic telephone cable to contact Churchill with a bizarre story gleaned from the Berlin cocktail party circuit by the American naval attaché: Grand Admiral Erich Raeder, head of the German Navy, claimed the British would sink an American merchant ship, the *Iroquois,* and then accuse Germany of sinking the vessel, thus re-creating the situation that had brought the United States into the First World War.

The story turned out to be unfounded—nothing happened to the *Iroquois*—but it illustrated just how eager FDR was to work with the British. The president himself passed the information to the British government; when the British, with Churchill as spokesman, stood the tale on its head and accused the Germans of planning to sink the ship and then implicating the British, FDR took Churchill's advice and publicized the story.[9]

Churchill wanted to "feed" the president's predisposition to use American naval forces to help the British. The neutrality patrol Roosevelt had mentioned to King George became a reality in autumn 1939, accompanied by a Western Hemisphere foreign ministers' declaration setting up a "safety belt extending outward from 300 to 1000 miles around the hemisphere except for Canada," which had declared war on Germany. This meant American warships would enforce neutrality (that is, suppress German attacks on merchant shipping, including British vessels) in that vast area, freeing the British Navy for other tasks closer to home.

Roosevelt justified the neutrality patrol with the dual-level argument he first used when he spoke to the Senate Military Affairs Committee and to the press at the beginning of the year. That approach continued to be his explanation for the neutral aid policies he adopted, at least until mid-1941. Every move would be to protect "the peace, the integrity, and the safety of the Americas," yet as the president had proclaimed when the European war began, Americans were not expected to ignore their consciences and "remain neutral in thought. . . ."[10] To put it another way, the best defense for the United States against the dictators was to help Britain and France.

He used that same approach in fulfilling his private promise to the British to change what he sarcastically called the "so-called"

Neutrality Laws that prevented Hitler's opponents from purchasing war materials. But that was more easily said than done, particularly done quickly. Even if the administration concluded it had public support, there was the threat of a filibuster in the Senate, and the Allies needed immediately the great "psychological lift" Chamberlain called for. How to do that without evoking American fears that they were being dragged into another unnecessary war?

The trick was to avoid names and speak in generalities. Roosevelt's appeal to Congress stated that the embargo gave "a definite advantage to one belligerent as against another. . . ." No names, no call for aid to Britain and France, but everyone understood.[11] The press, and certainly the anti-interventionists, grasped the purpose: Only the British and French were in a position to make effective use of the new procedures. German, Italian, and Japanese diplomats had ostentatiously boycotted FDR's speech. But he made no mention of that or of aiding the Allies. Why should he? The press, the anti-interventionists, and the isolationists all did their jobs and pointed out the obvious. So did Roosevelt's supporters, including Henry L. Stimson, the most recent Republican secretary of state; Senator George Norris, who had voted against American entry into World War I; and a number of senators and representatives who supported revision of the Neutrality Acts.

The public campaign against revision soon fizzled out, while FDR mounted a countercampaign that included creation of the cleverly named Non-Partisan Committee for Peace Through Revision of the Neutrality Act. (The committee, under the leadership of William Allen White, a nationally known newspaper editor from Kansas, later became the equally cleverly named Committee to Defend America by Aiding the Allies.) Taking congressional advice to require that war materials be purchased only on the basis of "cash and carry" (in non-American ships), the administration got a revised Neutrality Act passed by solid margins on November 3. One columnist summed it up aptly: "What a majority of the American people want is to be as unneutral as possible without getting into war."[12]

Even as the White House fended off domestic opposition to that benevolent neutrality, British efforts to make the British blockade of Germany effective created problems for Roosevelt's campaign. That blockade, formally called contraband control to assuage American sensitivities (the "greatest of all neutrals," Churchill called the United States), aimed at preventing Hitler from conducting any significant trade with the Americas. The system was complicated. Neutral merchant ships had to be certified by a British consul abroad that their cargoes were not intended for Germany, directly or indirectly. Otherwise they were subject to diversion to a British control port. In addition, the British blacklisted any company that traded with Germany—something Americans resented. The entire scheme had all-too-familiar echoes of how Americans thought they had been dragged into the First World War.

Even though the blockade, which formed an essential part of Chamberlain's strategy toward Germany, fell squarely within Churchill's bailiwick, he was slow to seize the opportunity presented by Roosevelt's invitation to correspond. He sent only two messages to the White House before Christmas, signing off cutely as "Naval Person," a careful compromise between his cumbersome formal title (first lord of the admiralty) and the familiarity of a simple "Churchill." One cable accepted the American "neutrality zone" in the Atlantic and pushed for effective neutrality patrols; the other offered a "sea story" about an Anglo-German naval encounter, along with a hint (which FDR ignored) about sharing the much-coveted Norden bombsight in return for British technology for detecting submarines (asdic, what the Americans later developed and called sonar). Ever conscious of the president's position as both head of government and head of state, Churchill couched his cables in very proper terms, calling Roosevelt "sir"—a bit obsequious to American ears. More significant was the Englishman's awareness of FDR's public and personal need to keep "the war out of the Americas."[13] But that was never the same as keeping America out of the war.

Churchill's Christmas message had real substance. Following his own advice to court the Americans, Churchill apologized for British violations of the neutrality zone (usually British warships pursuing German warships—particularly the attack on the German battleship *Graf Spee*, off the coast of Uruguay), then issued a veiled threat: "Hope the burden will not be made too heavy for us to bear. . . . If we should break under the load South American Republics would soon have worse worries than the sound of one day's distant cannonade. And you also, Sir, in quite a short time would have more direct cares."[14] That tactic of apology and threat, dictated by Churchill's conclusion that Britain had to have American help, cropped up time and again in his dealings with Roosevelt.

Churchill ended his Christmas message with a prediction that "war will soon begin now." But that was not the case. What Americans had come to call the Phony War—the failure of Hitler to mount an attack on Western Europe—continued through the winter of 1939–40, leaving Anglo-American relations to focus on the annoyances and inconveniences of the British blockade. Roosevelt's irritation was obvious: "[T]he net benefit to your people and to France is hardly worth the definite annoyance caused to us."[15]

Roosevelt was right, and Churchill knew it. Ambassador Lothian reported in December 1939 of general American sympathy for the Allies combined with a firm resolve to stay out of the war. But he also detected two ideas that could pose problems for Britain. One was a kind of defeatism engendered by the absence of military victories; it was to worsen in 1940. The other, running counter to defeatism, was that Hitler had ensured his own destruction by making a deal with the Soviet Union that brought the two into direct contact, standing over the corpse of Poland. It made a Soviet-German war inevitable, went the argument, a view reinforced by the Soviet attack on Finland. That inclined Americans to think they were not threatened, allowing them to focus on British trade regulations. Old suspicions quickly reasserted themselves, prompting Americans to conclude that the wily British were manipulating the blockade in their own economic interests.[16]

Chamberlain remained convinced the Americans would not come to Britain's aid in time to make a difference. When, in January 1940, Churchill promised that "no American ship should, in any circumstances, be diverted into the combat zone around the British Islands," he went too far. The Chamberlain government, which to Churchill's dismay seemed all too willing to push the

Americans into a corner, quickly forced a modification. At the same time even Churchill underestimated FDR's ability and commitment to stand up to (and Hitler's ability to scare) the so-called isolationists. He pessimistically told Chamberlain that FDR is "our best friend, but I expect he wants to be re-elected and I fear that isolationism is the winning ticket."[17]

FDR, concerned that petty issues might predominate, reached out to Churchill, expressing the desire that they talk face-to-face. But the Phony War had lulled both into thinking they had time to let the relationships, personal and Anglo-American, develop. Roosevelt's message went by letter, not cable.[18]

On February 9 the president announced that "Under Secretary of State Mr. Sumner Welles will proceed shortly to Europe to visit Italy, France, Germany and Great Britain. . . . Mr. Welles will, of course, be authorized to make no proposals or commitments in the name of the Government of the United States." Given Roosevelt's frequent statements to the effect that Hitler was a "nut" and a "wild man" and that his assassination or overthrow by the German people was the only alternative to rearming Britain and France, the Welles mission makes no sense.[19]

Yet, unless Welles, a friend of the Roosevelt family's as well as a career diplomat, violated his instructions, the mission was much more than just a Roosevelt whim or a subterfuge to delay the expected German offensive. Even after visiting Hitler and Mussolini, Welles told the British War Cabinet that the only peace proposals that could work would have to begin with broad disarmament (a favorite Roosevelt proposal) while providing a "sense of security to the Allies" without requiring "the elimination of Herr Hitler." Churchill told Welles that Britain "must and should fight it to a finish," but privately Churchill and the Cabinet were concerned about the possibility of "a patched up peace. . . ."[20]

One explanation for the mission was that with the 1940 nominations and presidential election coming up, FDR wanted to blunt any accusations that he had not done everything reasonable to broker a peace settlement. That seems to contradict Roosevelt's forceful descriptions of Hitler as "mad" and "wild" but leaves open the possibility that hubris had overtaken the president and he had concluded that his continued leadership was essential for the nation—whatever the means.

The other option is to conclude that Roosevelt, despite his misgivings and doubts about Hitler, believed it his responsibility to make every effort to avoid what seemed almost inevitable: all-out war. This latter option fits in with the persistent American belief that Europeans could not resist the inclination to go to war over petty and selfish quarrels. That belief, often associated with "Wilsonianism" though it predates Wilson, prompted Americans to think they could mediate the creation of a new and better international structure; a "new world order" was the phrase of an American President forty-five years after Roosevelt's death.[21]

A wild card in the game was the prevailing belief that the Italians were militarily important and independent of Hitler. That may have been true in the mid-1930s, but by 1940 Mussolini's foolish schemes for an Italian empire had made him heavily reliant on German military strength. Nevertheless, Welles arrived in Europe with the old British notion of weaning the Italians away from Hitler.

Even though Roosevelt told the British ambassador, Lord Lothian, of the proposed mission nine days before it was announced to the press, the British remained desperately worried that it meant the United States would mediate a peace that Britain could not live with. But Welles's conversations with both the Axis and the Allies convinced the American diplomat that neither side would compromise. Moreover, whatever Roosevelt's motives and whatever Welles's diplomacy, FDR's public and private attitude toward the Nazis makes clear that any compromise he would have proposed would have been unacceptable to Hitler.[22]

The Welles mission was not Roosevelt's last attempt to set the rules without intervening. But it was the last serious (if it was serious) attempt to avoid all-out war in Europe. The situation was about to change so drastically that the entire mission became irrelevant.

Up to early April 1940 Chamberlain's strategy of deterrence through delay and diversion seemed to be working. The Soviet invasion of Finland on November 30, 1939—the Winter War—

begun when the foolhardy Finns refused Moscow territorial or political concessions, posed no threat to the West even if it was a public relations and nearly a military disaster for Moscow. Churchill, ever the geopolitician, had pointed out that the Soviets would seize the opportunity to regain territory taken by Finland after the First World War and, reflecting Chamberlain's assumptions, argued that Britain's interests lay with strengthening the Soviet Union. By early March the sheer weight of Soviet force had won out, and the Finns sued for peace. But that was in the East.

In the West, the British prime minister cockily claimed on April 2 that Hitler had "missed the bus."[23] A month later Chamberlain himself would have to take his own bus out of town.

Hitler's invasion of Denmark and Norway on 9 April caught the British—as well as the Danes and Norwegians—by surprise. The Chamberlain government had been on again, off again with moves to deny the Germans access to Swedish iron ore by mining the shipping lanes out of northern Norway and by occupying the Norwegian port of Narvik, thus putting British and French in a position to advance on the Swedish mines. But the Germans attacked first—partly in response to rumors of British schemes, partly in accordance with their own plans to establish naval bases on Norway's coast. The British and French were reluctant but willing to violate Scandinavian neutrality; Hitler never gave it a thought.

Denmark, surprised and unequipped to mount serious resistance, surrendered the same day. In Norway a British force augmented by Polish and French troops landed near Trondheim, but it was too late with too little, accentuated by dubious British military leadership. Belated success at Narvik meant little; Hitler's attack on the Low Countries forced an Allied evacuation early in June. The Phony War—what Churchill called "this prolonged trance"—was over.[24]

The Norway campaign had three unintended effects. First, German naval losses were staggering. Three months later the Germans could still deploy only one heavy and two light cruisers plus a meager four destroyers. Their only two battleships, *Gneisenau* and *Scharnhorst*, both were put out of action for the remainder of 1940 by British torpedoes. As Churchill recalled, "Although many of their ships could be repaired, . . . the German Navy was no factor in the supreme issue of the Invasion of Britain."[25]

Second, the Norwegian debacle broke the back of the Chamberlain ministry, and put Churchill in office as prime minister. Chamberlain's credibility had improved from its nadir after the failure of appeasement, but the German assault again demonstrated his misreading of Hitler. The Norway fiasco tarred Chamberlain, but Churchill somehow escaped blame even though the campaign had largely been his plan.[26]

Third, it brought the war a bit closer to the United States physically and psychologically. Roosevelt remained unwilling to risk getting the wrong answer in a national debate on American policy toward aid to the Allies, but he told newspaper editors on April 18 that Eleanor Roosevelt had, during a lecture trip, noticed "that people were beginning to take their heads out of the sand," asking, " 'What is going to happen *if?*' . . . Before this Denmark episode and the Norway episode, there weren't nearly as many questions by the public." He didn't have an answer to the question, he said, but charged the editors to perform their "very definite duty to start that thing going around the country." Moreover, the possibility of the Nazis' taking over Iceland and Greenland, both under the Danish monarchy, raised questions in the minds of reporters—and presumably Americans. Once again there was need to identify the good guys and the bad guys, but no names were used.[27]

Attempts by the Norwegian Nazi sympathizer Vidkun Quisling to effect a coup and quickly capitulate to the Germans contributed to the myth, promoted by Hitler's propagandists, that pro-Nazi subversives posed a real threat. The real effect was to reinforce the Nazis' unsavory reputation in the United States and to add "quisling" to the English language.

On May 9–10 Hitler's armies violated the neutrality of the Low Countries—Belgium, the Netherlands, and Luxembourg—launching a major offensive that met with rapid success. The Dutch, with heads deep in the same sand FDR worried about, had forlornly counted on neutrality, refusing to coordinate with the Allies. On May 14 the Germans turned to calculated war on civilians with the indiscriminate terror bombing of Rotterdam, forcing a quick

Dutch surrender. The Belgians, with an army larger than British ground forces on the Continent, fought bravely but, outflanked by a swift German move through the supposedly impenetrable Ardennes Forest (a lesson not learned by the Anglo-Americans), were out of the battle by May 18.

That was only the prelude to disaster for the Allies. A deadly combination of incompetent leadership, inadequate planning, lack of coordination, and superior German tactics and strategy brought about the stunningly rapid fall of France. By the time Churchill became prime minister on May 10,[28] the Germans had almost completed their move through the Ardennes. Three days later they broke the French lines at Sedan, crossed the Meuse River, then easily beat off poorly executed French counterattacks. The battle for France was over, although it took another month before Paris fell and organized resistance to the Germans ended.

For that month the Churchill-Roosevelt/British-American relationship focused on the effect of events in France. On May 15, in his first message as "Former Naval Person" (not a code but a shrewd way of maintaining informality in his correspondence with Roosevelt), the new prime minister went through the motions of asking for some sort of American commitment to France, requests he was to repeat until the French capitulated. But his real concern was for Britain's survival and, that accomplished, for victory. "I shall drag the United States in," he responded when his son, Randolph, asked how Britain could expect to defeat Germany.[29] Churchill's appeals to Roosevelt always included requests for immediate aid needed to hurl back any German invasion, then alternated between confident bombast about Britain's resolve and thinly veiled threats picturing an America alone against the dictators—a strategy he followed for the next year. Predicting, correctly, that Mussolini would scurry into the war alongside the Germans "to share the loot," he warned Roosevelt that "the voice and force of the United States may count for nothing if they are withheld too long. You may have a completely subjugated, Nazified Europe established with astonishing swiftness, *and the weight may be more than we can bear.*"[30]

The full message was a typical Churchill *tour d'horizon*. He

passed on rumors of German parachutes seen dropping into southern Ireland, reflecting Cabinet fears that the Irish would follow the
axiom "The enemy of my enemy is my friend." However genuine
the fears, Churchill's solution, a prolonged visit by a U.S. naval
squadron to Irish ports, seemed aimed more at entangling the
Americans than curbing Irish unrest. Even a reference to keeping
"that Japanese dog quiet in the Pacific" contained what Churchill
hoped would tempt the Americans to move toward greater cooperation: an offer to use the great port of Singapore as part of the
overall U.S. strategy to deter further Japanese military aggression
by tightening trade sanctions and stationing the fleet at Pearl
Harbor.

But the crux of Churchill's first message as prime minister was
his shopping list. The key request was political—and impossible:
"All I ask now is that you should proclaim nonbelligerency, which
would mean that you would help us with everything short of actually engaging your armed forces." Requests for submarines, aircraft, antiaircraft equipment, and American raw materials followed.

With the fall of France still a month away, Roosevelt and his
advisers continued to assume that Hitler would get bogged down
in a long struggle that would allow British naval strength to quarantine Germany on the Continent. FDR ignored the plea for a
declaration of nonbelligerency and backed away from anything except facilitating British purchases of war materials. He had put the
loyal Henry Morgenthau in charge of coordinating Allied purchases of war goods and warned those administration officials who
were reluctant to sell military supplies that they thought the United
States needed to comply "in toto." Beyond that, and the assurance
that "I am most happy to continue our private correspondence,"
the president remained noncommittal.[31]

Churchill retorted that he expected a German attack "on the
Dutch model"—heavy bombing followed by a combined airborne
and sea assault—but that Britain would "persevere to the very
end." Still, American assistance "must be available soon" if it was
to be of any help. Again the combination of belligerent bombast
and veiled threats. Then the prime minister dropped the veil and
exposed unsightly reality. Even as he insisted that "under no con-

ceivable circumstances would we consent to surrender," he added that a negotiated settlement with Germany might eventuate should his ministry be replaced. After all, who could blame a government for making the best deal it could under such circumstances? Of course that "nightmare" would not happen while Churchill remained in charge, but . . . The consequence remained unspoken. Little wonder that the president repeatedly brought up the importance of keeping the French and British fleets out of German hands.[32]

Amid this to-ing and fro-ing arose a minor but potentially embarrassing affair. With France about to fall, word reached the two leaders that their secret personal correspondence had been compromised. A code clerk in the American Embassy in London, one Tyler Kent, had taken copies of Churchill-Roosevelt messages out of the embassy, allowing at least one to fall into the hands of Italian agents. Anglo-American communicators switched to different codes, and Kent, whose unsavory personal conduct was accentuated by virulent anti-Semitism, was quickly incarcerated for the duration of the war in a British prison. What is significant were the steps taken to ensure that for most of the war Kent remained unable to reveal the existence of the Churchill-Roosevelt channel. Rightly or wrongly both men concluded that American public opinion, inside and outside Congress, was not ready for what would seem an all-too-cozy relationship.[33]

With France about to fall and a German invasion of Britain seemingly in the cards, the Churchill government made the difficult decision to evacuate the British Expeditionary Force (BEF) from the Continent. Hitler, for reasons that remain unclear, halted his advance, giving the British Navy and a ragtag fleet of private vessels—from fishing smacks to pleasure craft—time to lift more than three hundred thousand British from Dunkirk and neighboring beaches. Only fifty-three thousand French soldiers managed to escape to Britain, bringing angry accusations that the British had deserted their allies.[34]

Churchill warned Parliament on June 4 that "wars are not won by evacuations." But they are won, or at least greatly affected, by morale. The troops that escaped from France did not spell the difference between survival and conquest, but had the entire BEF been captured, the pressure in Britain for a negotiated peace with Hitler would have grown significantly. In that same speech Churchill succeeded in turning a military defeat into a psychological victory. In ringing tones he promised "we shall defend our island, whatever the cost may be, we shall fight on the beaches, we shall fight on the landing-grounds, we shall fight in the fields and in the streets, we shall fight in the hills; we shall never surrender, and even if this Island were subjugated, then our Empire would carry on the struggle until, in God's good time, the New World, with all its power and might, steps forth to the rescue and liberation of the Old [ellipses omitted]." The extraordinary oratory moved listeners in Parliament and when it was rebroadcast on the radio. Churchill's old friend General Louis Spears, listening in France, spoke for most Britons when he wrote that it was as if they had been given "a password, the significance of which only we could grasp, it bound us in a great secret understanding." Remarked one Englishman: "We have got into the final, and it is on the home ground." The message was crystal clear, whatever Churchill's insinuations about possible negotiations: His government would resist, and it placed its faith in the United States.[35]

As the situation in France fell apart, Churchill importuned Roosevelt to make some grand public gesture of support, but the closest the president came was a speech at the University of Virginia commencement exercises in Charlottesville on June 10. Reversing his usual emphasis on avoiding American involvement in the war, FDR promised to extend American aid "full speed ahead." But what Churchill called "the Italian outrage" attracted the most attention. Mussolini, hoping for easy gains, had declared war on Britain and France earlier that day, and Roosevelt caustically condemned the Italians for striking a dagger "into the back of its neighbor."[36]

"Full speed ahead" on aid was a step in the right direction, but Churchill had heard such vague promises before. Now the crisis was squarely on Britain. The war in France—what British leaders had counted on to give them time to prepare—had ended. Film editing by Allied propagandists made Hitler seem to dance an obscene little jig when the French signed the surrender document in the same railroad car at Compiègne used when the Germans had signed the armistice ending World War I.[37] But that contrived image was virtual reality. France, now occupied in the north and west by Germany and governed in the center and south by the collaborationist regime of the now-senile First World War hero Marshal Henri Pétain, no longer stood between Hitler and Great Britain. All that remained was a narrow channel, the Royal Air Force, and the hope that eventually the Americans would join the fight and make Churchill's clarion call worth following.

On June 14, as French veterans of the Marne and Verdun wept, German soldiers goose-stepped through the streets of Paris, the very soul of France. For the rest of that frightening summer Churchill had to focus on preventing or preparing for the invasion he knew the Germans planned. (British intelligence had begun to feed him information gleaned from breaking German encrypted radio traffic, Ultra intercepts.[38]) At the same time he bent every effort to put Roosevelt on record with a major and public step toward involvement.

The Americans did take some immediate steps, but they only provided equipment, not ships and soldiers. Those steps began a flow of supplies that eventually turned the tide of war, but that flow would have no meaning unless Britain won its struggle for survival. Even as the French government moved toward capitulation, Arthur Purvis, the head of the British Purchasing Commission in the United States (set up in November 1939 to coordinate buying war goods), arranged for the transfer to Britain of French contracts for American military supplies, a move that doubled the British dollar debt. As with so many of Roosevelt's moves, encouraging British purchases helped both them and the United States. The revision of the neutrality legislation in autumn 1939 had stimulated a vast increase in orders for military aircraft, particularly by the French, orders that increased American production capabilities fourfold, according to the army's chief of staff, General George Marshall.

Roosevelt, following up his Charlottesville speech, encouraged that transfer of contracts and moved to make his administration more receptive to aiding Britain. Fed up with the lack of cooperation on the part of his secretaries of war and the navy, the president replaced them with two internationalist Republicans who favored aid to Britain, creating an image of bipartisanship, something Churchill had done by establishing a War Cabinet that included Labour party leaders. Frank Knox, the Republican vice presidential candidate in 1936 and owner of the Chicago *Daily News*, became secretary of the navy. Henry Stimson, a respected public servant ("wise man" would be today's term) who had served as President Taft's secretary of war and preceded Hull as secretary of state, became secretary of war. In an era before the creation of the Department of Defense, those positions were crucial to any foreign policy that involved the military. Knox and Stimson had spoken out publicly and forcefully in support of both American preparedness and aid to Britain. The two were tossed out of their party for consorting with the enemy, but polls showed that even Republicans supported the moves 57 to 43 percent.[39]

But the British needed something more than changes in Roosevelt's Cabinet. As the French moved toward an armistice, Churchill continued to raise the specter of British negotiations with Hitler. More aircraft, rifles, and a transfer of American destroyers would help, but German control of both the British and French fleets would, the prime minister threatened, give Hitler "overwhelming sea power" and the ability to bring the war to America's shores. France could continue the fight only from overseas, Churchill admitted, but unless the United States gave some "assurances," he feared the Germans would get their hands on the French fleet. The "assurance" Churchill wanted was U.S. entry into the war, even if no army was dispatched to Europe. The president ignored Churchill's pleas. Privately an angry Roosevelt spoke of not guaranteeing the French a return to their empire if their fleet was lost. To Churchill, the president said nothing.

Perhaps the prime minister, or his advisers, sensed he had pushed too hard too fast. When he drafted a petulant message saying he could not understand why the United States could not extend the "modest aid" of some destroyers to help fight German U-boats, Foreign Secretary Halifax objected to the phrases. Churchill continued to massage Roosevelt's fears about the French fleet, but only indirectly, sending summaries of the Franco-German armistice talks to the White House via Lothian and instructing the ambassador to "be bland and phlegmatic" but to raise the specter of a British surrender. In a mid-July interview with an American newsman, Churchill suggested that a new prime minister might be "a man who could get the best possible terms from Hitler." But for the two months following the French surrender, the Churchill-Roosevelt channel lay unused.[40]

The only exception, hardly of substance, was a belated announcement that the Duke of Windsor had been appointed governor of the Bahamas. The former King Edward VIII, who had abdicated in 1936 in order to marry an American divorcée, had, in Churchill's words, caused "some embarrassment." He apparently thought the Germans would win and therefore had been associated with those who favored negotiating with Hitler. Churchill claimed that the duke's "loyalties are unimpeachable," while the documents available suggest that the duke was obsessed with matters of personal privilege and, like all the Windsors, with the safety of the dynasty. Nevertheless, one plausible tale has the duke sending a message in 1940 via Fulton Oursler, an American journalist who had access to Roosevelt, asking if the president "would consider intervening as a mediator when, as and if the proper time arrives"? The duke would then support the mediation, an action he claimed would initiate a revolution in Britain and force a peace. FDR, who apparently already knew of the proposal (this suggests that British intelligence had been doing its job), contemptuously commented, "When little Windsor says he doesn't think there should be a revolution in Germany, I tell you, Fulton, I would rather have April's [Oursler's teenage daughter] opinion on that than his."[41]

The two-month silence may also have occurred because Roosevelt resented Churchill's prod-and-promise technique and was genuinely concerned that the prime minister's allusions to negotiations with the Germans were more than just gossip. Unbeknownst to the Americans, the British government had tried to determine what terms Hitler might demand and developed a tentative position "that would preserve Britain's 'independence.' " In mid-July Hitler had publicly proposed negotiations with the British government. Officially Churchill ignored the offer. Privately he sought the advice of both Neville Chamberlain and the head of the Labour party, Clement Attlee. Churchill finally decided that he would not "say anything in reply to Herr Hitler's speech, not being on speaking terms with him,"[42] But he did not pass on that reaction to FDR, apparently preferring to let the president continue to worry about the disposition of the British fleet and the possibility of a negotiated Anglo-German armistice.

The drumfire of threats only made Roosevelt more cautious, particularly as he had received reports of interest on the part of some members of the British Cabinet in such Anglo-German talks. Perhaps the Tyler Kent matter also made the two more cautious about communicating, but more likely the prime minister's tactics backfired a bit, raising enough questions about Churchill in Roosevelt's mind to prompt him to work through Lothian for the next two months. Still, the British ambassador thought he had it right when he referred to the "paralysing illusion" that gripped Roosevelt. Would not fear of the Germans' getting the British fleet make the president more inclined to give more aid to Britain?[43]

Lothian had it wrong. However much Roosevelt hoped to keep the United States out of the war, particularly a land war in Europe, he remained convinced that America's best hope lay with Britain's survival. At the same time what he could do to bring about that outcome was limited. A declaration of war, even if he had wanted one, was patently impossible. Direct military involvement under some pretext or another was neither possible nor plausible in summer 1940. American military aid could not have significant impact before the crisis, expected in autumn 1940 or spring 1941. Nor did domestic factors favor dramatic action.

Nineteen-forty was an election year. Whenever Roosevelt decided to run for an unprecedented third term and whether he decided from hubris, overweening ambition, or conviction, by mid-July 1940 it was a done deal.[44] But that decision further restricted FDR's ability to take dramatic action to aid the British. The potential national debate on foreign policy was further submerged when the Republicans, after six raucous ballots, gave its presidential nomination to Indiana-born New York businessman Wendell Willkie, a very recent convert to the party. There were differences between the two on domestic issues, but Willkie shared Roosevelt's conviction that aid to Britain was aid to America. That made it possible for FDR to continue his policies but militated against dramatic change. If White House assessments were correct, the American people agreed that aiding Britain, without going to war, made great good sense. But if Roosevelt moved strongly toward deeper involvement in the conflict, he ran the risk of making Willkie appear more cautious and safer, and that could elect the Hoosier.

On July 3 the British moved to secure their own security and American support. Fearful that the French Navy, commanded by an openly anti-British supporter of the armistice with Germany, Admiral Jean François Darlan, would be allowed to fall into German hands, Churchill authorized British warships to destroy French warships moored at Oran and Mers-el-Kebir, adjacent ports on French Algeria's Mediterranean coast. FDR had already indicated that such an attack should be carried out if it became necessary. Although one battleship and six cruisers escaped, French losses were heavy. The attack was probably not needed to keep French naval forces out of German hands. Warships at Toulon, Alexandria, Martinique, and Casablanca sat out the war. The political fallout created by erstwhile allies killing each other clouded Anglo-French relations for a decade. But the incident helped convince the Americans that backing Britain was a good bet. At least that was Churchill's conclusion.[45]

The question of how best to bolster and sustain the British remained for Churchill and Roosevelt to work out. Effective American military assistance was out of the question. Boosting morale and hope was not. Since taking office, the prime minister had repeatedly begged Roosevelt for destroyers to combat German U-boats and surface raiders that threatened the supply lifelines into the British Isles. Churchill himself had indirectly and perhaps unintentionally implied his real motives when while denying that he expected an American expeditionary force to save France, he wrote to Roosevelt of "the tremendous moral effect" American entry into the war would have "in all the democratic countries. . . ."[46]

The deal—"arrangement" was the official euphemism—was simple and, as things turned out, militarily unimportant: fifty over-age American destroyers in return for long-term authority to build and operate bases on eight British colonies in the Western Hemisphere, ranging from British Guiana through the Caribbean to Bermuda and on north to Newfoundland, and a commitment from Churchill that if Britain were forced to surrender, the fleet would be sent abroad "for the defence of other parts of the Empire."[47] But the tortured negotiations needed to put the deal together illustrated the minefields of law and politics that Churchill and particularly Roosevelt had to get through.

FDR had long had his eye on Bermuda and assorted British possessions in the Caribbean as sites for American military bases. After all, the British (and other European empires) had no business being there anyway. He had negotiated, though never implemented, a general agreement for such bases back in June 1939. Predictably he brought up the same idea in the summer of 1940 as he cast about for ways to "sell" the American people, and his own military, on aid to Britain.[48]

Churchill wanted a long-term American commitment to the war, but the immediate need was equipment needed to fight off a German invasion. Aircraft were in the supply pipeline, particularly with the acquisition of French aircraft orders. But if Britain were to survive, destroyers were needed to ward off Nazi submarines that threatened the Atlantic supply lanes. In the way stood a U.S. law forbidding the sale of military equipment needed for the defense of the United States, and Roosevelt's military chiefs saw no way around that requirement. What FDR needed was an arrangement that made it clear that the transfer of those destroyers benefited the nation's defenses more than keeping them did.

The price Roosevelt set for Churchill was straightforward and reasonable. The destroyers would be transferred in return for "leases" (an important word) to base rights. That was the key to persuading the American public, already alerted to the talks by the press, that the nation was getting a "good deal." For the president, the key was a public commitment by Churchill that the British fleet would be neither scuttled nor surrendered should the British Isles be taken by the Germans. That fulfilled Roosevelt's very real commitment to defend the United States. He had already initiated establishment of a Canadian-American Joint Defense Board to ensure U.S. leverage over the use of any elements of the British fleet sent to Canada, a clear indication of his deep concern that Britain might fall, despite cautious reports that given enough aid, it might well fend off any German invasion.[49]

Whatever the conflicting concerns in Roosevelt's mind, he went ahead. The negotiations, which took place over late July and most of August, were routed through Roosevelt's aides and British Ambassador Lothian, purposefully bypassing the defeatist, anti-British American ambassador in London, Joe Kennedy.

The course of the talks was not smooth. Understandably suspicious that American anticolonialism masked a desire to displace Britain, Lothian asked Roosevelt if suggestions in the Chicago *Tribune* for a swap of British colonies for aid was in the wind. Roosevelt airily dismissed the notion: "See here, Philip, you may as well get this straight once and for all: I'm not purchasing any headaches for the United States. We don't want your colonies."[50] But FDR did want their bases.

More important was distress felt by the British, particularly Churchill, that the kind of formal, public deal that Roosevelt insisted on was humiliating. "Empires just don't bargain," the prime minister told Roosevelt's attorney general, Robert Jackson, during a phone conversation between London and the White House. Jackson shot back: "Republics do."[51]

The president had his own problems, what with anti-interventionist (invariably labeled "isolationist") protests, complaints from his own military that the destroyers were needed for American defense, and arguments that he was violating the law and even the Constitution to make such a deal. He told his secretary, Grace Tully, that "Congress is going to raise hell about this but even another day's delay may mean the end of civilization . . . but if Britain is to survive, we must act."[52] And he did.

On September 3, Labor Day, Roosevelt informed Congress of

the terms. He treated it as a fait accompli, citing his attorney general's opinion regarding the law. Mutterings were heard in the expected quarters: Senator Nye, the anti-interventionist America First Committee, Robert McCormick's Chicago *Tribune*. But the firestorm that even FDR expected never appeared. When it came time to pass appropriations to implement the agreement, Congress did just that.

Why? Perhaps it was FDR's cleverness. Perhaps it was the distraction of the upcoming presidential election. Perhaps it was Churchill's élan and persuasiveness. But more likely it was just plain common sense, in Congress and among the public. The German bombing campaigns on the Continent and over Britain had driven home the arrival of the air age; the security provided by distance and the Atlantic Ocean had eroded. The swap was a good deal for America in every sense of the phrase. The nation's security was enhanced, Britain's ability to resist a common threat was strengthened, and by besting their long-standing rival and colonial progenitor, Americans could grin a bit.

But what about the president's torturous avoidance of the law, and of Congress, by using an executive agreement, the legality of which depended to a degree on the placement of a comma?[53] What could or should Roosevelt have done in the summer of 1940? By every calculus and calculation, a declaration of war would not have passed Congress. A premature public debate would almost certainly have brought the wrong answer—wrong as far as Roosevelt was concerned, wrong as far as Britain was concerned, wrong as far as history is concerned. The British felt alone and isolated. Americans liked to argue that Britain ought to handle its own problems; it was, after all, the world's greatest empire and, moreover, bore a heavy responsibility for the situation it found itself in.

Opponents of presidential action in foreign policy have always complained that the White House exceeded its authority. That argument was a staple of the contemporary and later historical debates over Roosevelt's policies from September 1939 through the Pearl Harbor attack more than two years later. Given the American political system, the alternative to presidential leadership lies at the other end of Pennsylvania Avenue: Capitol Hill. That alternative became elevated during the anti–Vietnam War debates into an accepted truth. But arguments that the destroyer-bases deal led inevitably to the imperial presidency ignore the way Congress plays the game. Since sheer practicality places the making of foreign policy primarily with the executive branch, Congress is able to sit back and play dog in the manger, carping, criticizing, and playing to the voters. Congress reflects public perceptions far more accurately and broadly than any opinion poll or pundit. Yet for the crucial stages of America's "neutrality," whether before Pearl Harbor or, for that matter, before the mid-1960s "intervention" in Indochina, Congress felt no overwhelming public pressure to restrain presidential actions or change U.S. foreign policy.

One critic of Roosevelt's disingenuousness quotes the Book of Psalms: "Put not your trust in princes."[54] That is always good advice, but it begs the question. Where should trust be placed? The psalmist meant God, but that too begs the question. In the American democratic republic the alternatives are Congress and the courts. No one in Congress introduced legislation to nullify the destroyer-bases deal. No one filed charges against the president or his Cabinet for violating the law. Public opinion—created and expressed in polls, print, and radio—supported the arrangement, as did the bulk of White House mail, to Roosevelt's surprise. One hundred and seventy-five years earlier James Madison had argued that the prince, in this case the president, could be restrained only by politics, not by law. Perhaps the reason FDR could manipulate the politics and even dissemble and lie is that the "people" did not disagree. That is how politics works.

Regardless of the debate, the destroyer-bases deal constituted a major move by the United States toward an alliance with Great Britain. The two nations were more than just "somewhat mixed up together," as Churchill told the House of Commons when the arrangement was coming together. The United States had come a long way from where it had stood a year earlier, when Hitler invaded Poland and broke the peace of Europe. And the prime mover was Franklin Roosevelt.

Had FDR not pushed the deal, it likely would never have happened. Had he not been running for a third term, he would have deferred to the wishes of the Democratic nominee, either the legalistic and cautious Cordell Hull or perhaps the ward heeler James Farley, neither of whom would have brooked the wrath of anti-interventionist outcries lest it cripple his chance to win. The Republican nominee, Wendell Willkie, had a certain reckless courage and was more of an interventionist than either Hull or Farley, but the destroyer-bases deal, which he endorsed in advance, came before the 1940 election.[55]

A clear indicator of public concern for the nation's security came shortly after the destroyer-bases deal when, on September 16, Roosevelt signed into law the first peacetime draft in American history. Even though the legislation forbade using draftees outside the Western Hemisphere or U.S. possessions, anti-interventionists and peace groups (again labeled "isolationists") mounted a campaign against it, arguing it was a step toward militarism at home and intervention abroad. But it passed Congress with solid margins.

The Roosevelt administration and the bulk of the American public, according to every indicator at the time, supported aid to Britain—but always short of war—even if such aid set the United States on the slippery slope toward full involvement. But aid is not alliance, and supplies are not armies. Great Britain—its people, its air forces, its spirit, its geography, and its leaders—won the first and indispensable victory of the Second World War and, in doing so, made it possible for others to win the rest of the war.

That first battle was about to begin in earnest.

America wants to help—but how?

CHAPTER 3

———◆———

"A Year of Indecision"
October 1940–June 1941

The Battle of Britain, so christened by Churchill, had begun with the French surrender in June 1940. The Nazi leader of the German Air Force (Luftwaffe), Hermann Göring, had made flamboyant promises about bringing the British to their knees with a massive bombing campaign that would gain the air superiority over southern England needed for an invasion of Britain. "The defence of Southern England will last four days and the Royal Air Force four weeks. We can guarantee invasion for the Fuehrer within a month," he bragged. That campaign reached its peak in August with a sustained two-week attack on RAF (Royal Air Force) fields and aircraft. It failed, though in Wellington's phrase, it was a "close-run thing." A combination of better strategy, better leadership, better technology (including radar), and better intelligence gave the British the edge. The Battle of Britain proved militarily far more important, if less famous, than the blitz, the indiscriminate bombing of London and other British cities that followed. By September the inability of the Luftwaffe to sweep the RAF from the skies made the German invasion of Britain, Operation Sealion, impossible. Never "was so much owed to so few by so many" was Churchill's accurate appraisal.[1] Had that invasion taken place, the blitz would not have happened.

But it did, and in the process had a profound effect on Americans. The blitz made exciting and emotional copy for reporters. Edward R. Murrow, the American radio commentator, launched a career on broadcasts from London describing in sonorous tones the tension, the destruction, and the resilience of the British. It was, in the words of a later era, a public relations disaster for Hitler. The night attack on Coventry, which devastated the central city, including its striking fourteenth-century cathedral, became a prime exhibit of German brutality, even though twelve armament factories were also destroyed.[2] The blitz went on from September 1940 until spring 1941, when Hitler found another use for his air force (this time in Russia). It killed 43,000 civilians, while an additional 139,000 were injured. From June through October 1940—the height of the Battle of Britain and the blitz—the Luftwaffe lost more than twelve hundred aircraft, including at least six hundred bombers, while the RAF lost nearly eight hundred fighters. More important, Britain survived, and Americans—from FDR to the people on the street—were persuaded that backing Britain would not be throwing good money after bad.

Britain's struggle for survival is curiously absent from the Churchill-Roosevelt exchanges, at least on the surface. The two leaders appeared focused on the destroyer-bases deal, important for the development of the alliance and for the war against U-boats but trivial compared with the crucial and destructive air battle in which the war's outcome hung in the balance. The Battle of Britain was hardly mentioned and never discussed.

That was in part because there was nothing the president could do to help, short of the impossible task of bringing America into the war. Production in the United States could not even meet existing American and British contracts for aircraft. Churchill, for his part, said little because details about losses in the air war over Britain could feed defeatist fears in the United States.[3]

Defeatism was a major problem for Roosevelt as well. He sent Churchill a note complimenting the RAF on "the fine job" being done, and he included a letter addressed to FDR in which Alexander Kirk, the chargé d'affaires at the American Embassy in Berlin, expressed the "profound conviction that any concession on the part of the British government would destroy forever the chance of eradicating the forces which are threatening our civilization." The entire message went through Joe Kennedy, giving a clear, if indirect, warning to the ambassador about his continued defeatist remarks.[4]

Sunday, September 22, 1940, was a wet, windy day on the English Channel. Secretary of State for War Anthony Eden, spending the weekend at his country home on the south coast of England, received word that Roosevelt had sent a warning that "zero hour for the German invasion" was at three that afternoon. A quick walk to the hill overlooking the Channel prompted a message to Churchill suggesting that seasickness would be the reward for any Germans who attempted to cross. No invasion of Britain took place, but the warning was not without foundation. The garbled text had somehow substituted Britain for French Indochina. On that day the Japanese, with the acquiescence of the Vichy French regime, occupied the northern portion of that French colony.[5]

The Japanese move, which further threatened China and Southeast Asia, brought little response from Washington. The administration, which had not broken diplomatic relations with the Vichy French government, remained committed to its policy of stiffening that regime to ensure it did not allow the Germans to make use of French colonies, particularly those in the Caribbean. But the Indochina situation raised the issue of overall United States policy toward Japanese military expansion in East Asia.

American sympathies, official and unofficial, lay with China in its efforts to resist the Japanese invasion that had begun in 1937. Yet the first principle of American policy was to stay out of war. That left only diplomatic and economic measures to help China and deter Japan. Worried that the West might turn to military actions yet convinced that East Asia was too distant—physically and culturally—from the European war to allow such a response, Japanese leaders concluded by 1940 that their "security" required more than just controlling China. They counted on the European situation to keep the United States away from a confrontation in the Pacific and allow creation of what Japan disingenuously designated its Greater East Asian Co-Prosperity Sphere. Garbed in anticolonial rhetoric, the scheme was window dressing for an expanded Japanese Empire. The occupation of French Indochina was but an initial step toward military expansion into the rest of resource-rich Southeast Asia.

Committed to nurturing Vichy neutrality, the State Department offered only mild protests, but the occupation of northern Indochina lent strength to the arguments of those in Washington who believed a tough stance would deter Japan from further expansion. At the time Roosevelt halved the difference and set up a loose, partial embargo. But the hard-liners eventually won out.[6]

A few days later, on September 27, Germany, Japan, and Italy made a serious miscalculation by signing the Tripartite Pact. Aimed at discouraging the United States from intervening in either Europe or the Pacific by raising the prospect of a two-front conflict, the pact served as the only formal political agreement binding the three Axis powers together during the war.

Hitler advanced the pact once he concluded that Sealion could not be launched that autumn. Eager to switch his attention to the east, he assumed that after German armies had crushed the Soviet Union and he commanded the resources of all Europe, Britain would have to negotiate on his terms. But a military alliance between the United States and Britain could thwart that prospect. As he wrote to his ally, Mussolini, in mid-September, "close cooperation with Japan is the best way either to keep America entirely out of the picture or to render her entry into the war ineffective." Hitler's fool for an ally thought the Americans afraid of Japanese naval strength, while the ex-champagne salesman who served as German foreign minister, Joachim Ribbentrop, thought the odds on a Japanese victory over the American Navy were two to one in Japan's favor. Hitler may have agreed but preferred not to take chances. He had ordered his U-boat commanders to avoid incidents with American vessels and to stay out of the Western Hemisphere neutrality zone, and now he looked to the Japanese to distract the Americans.

It turned out to be a strategy that guaranteed that fourteen months later the United States would enter the European war by the back door in the Pacific—not because of a plot on FDR's part but because both Germany and Japan mistakenly believed that the Americans did not have the stomach for a long, costly two-front war. Moreover, the pact from the outset worked against Axis interests by providing the Roosevelt administration with a convincing argument that the nation was truly threatened with encirclement. Equally important, it prompted the president to choose the grand strategy of Germany first that ultimately spelled defeat for the Axis. The ripple effect of the pact pushed the British and Americans closer together, prompting one historian to title a book chapter "Reactions to the Tripartite Pact; or, Staff Conversations Anyone?"[7]

But as leaders in every walk of life so often complain, details threaten to overwhelm events. In the autumn of 1940 staff conversations and selection of a grand strategy took a backseat to the immediate issues of Britain's survival and everyday matters of challenging the Axis.

Stimulated by the destroyer-bases deal and the new Axis lineup they faced in common, the Churchill-Roosevelt channel became more active as the prime minister chatted about things great and small, though Roosevelt, ever more cautious, tended to acknowledge receipt with only a few comments. Churchill worried about arrangements for the transfer of rifles to Britain as part of the destroyer-bases deal. He gave forewarning of British plans for what he hoped would be an unopposed occupation of the Vichy French port of Dakar, in French West Africa (now Senegal), a scheme FDR supported to the point of mentioning the possibility of sending American warships to the area, "purely as a friendly move."[8] The operation was aborted when the Vichy regime resisted, but Churchill and Roosevelt continued to voice deep concern about the French fleet, particularly two battleships, *Jean Bart* and *Richelieu*, falling into German hands. Churchill passed on reports of British carrier aircraft successfully attacking the Italian navy at Taranto on the southeast coast of Italy, an attack that foreshadowed the end of the battleship era (though it took the Pearl Harbor attack and a few more naval disasters in the Pacific to convince the admirals).

Rumors of a Spanish-German alliance, which would close access to the Mediterranean through the Strait of Gibraltar and move the Germans uncomfortably close to the Western Hemisphere by giving them bases in the Canary Islands, prompted Churchill to suggest that the United States send food to Spain. Although the Spanish dictator, Generalissimo Francisco Franco, had no liking for the Allies, who had vocally, though not militarily, opposed his cause during Spain's bloody civil war, he proved too shrewd to involve Spain in a war that would only have further devastated his country. Even though the Germans and Italians had intervened on Franco's side, using that civil war as a training ground for their forces, no matter what Hitler offered as terms of alliance, Franco always upped the ante. His tactics prompted Churchill to write sarcastically in his war memoir: "It is fashionable at the present time to dwell on the vices of General Franco, and I am, therefore, glad to place on record this testimony to the duplicity and ingratitude of his dealings with Hitler and Mussolini."[9]

Roosevelt's victory in the 1940 election put the Anglo-American team together for the duration of the war. Like Woodrow Wilson in 1916, FDR played his version of the peace card, arguing that his aid to Britain policy was the best chance of keeping the nation out of war. He felt confident enough of support for his aid policy to tell reporters on October 4 that the government was "speeding things up all we possibly can."[10] Both candidates supported such aid; both had promised they would not send American boys to war; both had unspoken doubts about that promise. Willkie differed little from the president beyond style and general criticism of the Democrats' New Deal programs. But the war in Europe overrode domestic politics. Polls had suggested a Willkie victory without the war; instead FDR won easily, even if by a margin reduced from his record-setting 1936 victory. His electoral college majority was impressive, 449 to 82, with twenty-seven million to twenty-two million in the popular vote.[11]

Quick to seize an opportunity to cement their relationship, Churchill sent off an ingratiating message claiming he had "prayed" FDR would win. Roosevelt never acknowledged the congratulations. Perhaps, as the White House claimed, the message was forgotten in the after-election confusion, or perhaps the president remained a bit piqued that the Willkie campaign could find some statements made earlier by Churchill that criticized the New Deal. The episode revealed Churchill's uncertainty about his relationship with the president, for he nervously prodded the Foreign Office to find out why FDR failed to reply. Four years later FDR denied having "forgotten" the 1940 message when Churchill resent it following Roosevelt's victory in the 1944 election.[12]

As the end of 1940 approached, Britain and Churchill faced more serious problems than whether or not Roosevelt answered his mail. The real question was, would he and the United States answer Britain's call for help? FDR's reelection brought on a brief euphoria in London. Even Churchill spoke, probably wishfully, of how Roosevelt's reelection would mean American entry into the war.[13] But November passed with FDR seemingly interested only in preventing the French battleships from falling into German hands.

If Britain could not count on speedy American entry into the war, it had to be able to count on getting the goods needed to help hold out against whatever Hitler planned for the spring. The German leader had, in fact, issued on December 18 the directive calling for an attack on the Soviet Union: Operation Barbarossa. But the British Cabinet and military chiefs of staff remained convinced that Germany would not turn toward the Soviet Union until it had eliminated Britain from the war.[14] That put a priority on obtaining war materials, something the Roosevelt administration was eager to facilitate.

In late November British Ambassador Lothian, returning to the United States from talks with Churchill and the Cabinet, let reporters know that financial problems were "becoming urgent." Whether or not he told them, "Britain's bust," or, "Britain's broke; it's your money we want," the press grasped Lothian's point.[15] The cash-and-carry revision to the Neutrality Act had forced Britain to use its ready money—"the hobble that cramped medieval kings," Churchill once wrote. Britain was far from broke, but it was running short of dollars. It was just that problem that had brought Lothian back to England for talks.

Wearied by the election campaign, the president left Washington on December 2, for a two-week cruise aboard the USS *Tuscaloosa*. Had Lothian not dropped his bombshell, Roosevelt would have given little thought to the finance issue during a voyage dedicated to rest and relaxation, which in his case meant "fishing, basking in the sun and spoofing with cronies."[16] He knew the money issue was coming to a head but did not share Lothian's sense of urgency. Before he left, Roosevelt had authorized a large quantity of British orders for military goods, orders he knew Britain could not pay for, at least not in cash. Briefly tempted by the vision of British imperial opulence, Roosevelt suggested they first sell their Western Hemisphere assets. But when Morgenthau argued that such a demand was meanspirited and would not raise enough cash, FDR discarded the idea. That left the money problem unsolved.

While Roosevelt fished, his Cabinet scrambled to find a solution. Everything it looked at required congressional approval—and promised a long battle for votes. Merely revising the Neutrality Act again was not enough since loans and credits to Britain were illegal under the Johnson Debt Default Act of 1934, passed when the European nations were defaulting on their First World War debts. Navy Secretary Knox put his finger on the issue, asking rhetorically, "We are going to pay for the war from now on, are we?," then answered his own question, "Got to. No question about it."[17]

A week later Roosevelt's junket was interrupted by a letter from Churchill, cabled from London and flown out to the *Tuscaloosa*. The prime minister later called it "one of the most important I ever wrote." Certainly it was one of the most carefully written, going through multiple drafts once Lothian convinced Churchill the letter was needed. The prime minister offered one of his classic surveys of the state of the war, summarizing in powerful phrases the nature of the threat and what Britain needed in order to continue the fight effectively. Ever conscious of the crucial nature of maritime strategy for Britain and its empire (a word he added at one point) and of Germany's superior ground forces, Churchill focused on shipping and supply. "The decision for 1941 lies upon the seas," he wrote. "It is therefore in shipping and in the power to transport across the ocean, particularly the Atlantic Ocean, that in 1941 the crunch of the whole war will be found." Britain needed more warships; vast numbers of merchant ships had to be constructed; supply ships crossing the Atlantic needed the protection of American escorts. "The industrial energy of the Republic" was also needed for "a further 2,000 combat aircraft a month"— a dramatic increase in British orders that they could not pay for in cash.

Only one paragraph of the nineteen in the four-thousand-word message addressed the issue that had to be solved, and solved quickly: ready money. "The moment approaches," warned Churchill, "when we shall no longer be able to pay cash for shipping and other supplies." To force Britain to sell its assets would be "wrong in principle . . . after victory was won with our blood, civilisation saved and time gained for the United States. . . ."[18]

Apprised of the letter, British representatives in Washington finally acceded to relentless pressure from Morgenthau and disclosed Britain's dollar assets. There were $6.9 billion (over 75 billion in 1995 dollars) of new orders in the pipeline, and Britain already had a dollar deficit of $8.5 billion that grew every month. It was a gloomy picture.[19]

Churchill's dramatic plea alone would not have carried the day. The calculated public tactics of Lothian, British financial disclosures, Morgenthau's efforts, and, perhaps most of all, a period for Roosevelt away from the everyday fires he had to fight in Washington—all these created a chain of events that led directly to the president's press conference on December 17, the day after he got back from his cruise.

Roosevelt was finally ready to act. Sealion had been postponed, rumors had surfaced of a German move toward the Balkans and the Soviet Union (despite British insistence that the United Kingdom was Hitler's primary target), and full American aid held out the promise of success without the United States' having to send its troops to fight in Europe. At a carefully planned press conference FDR suggested a way to give the British what they needed without calling it loans, credits, or subsidies. A few months earlier one of Roosevelt's Cabinet officers had complained that "Americans are like the householder who refuses to lend or sell his fire extinguisher to help put out the fire in the house that is right next door." Now the extinguisher became a fire hose that, according to the president, should be lent to the neighbor to put out the fire. If the hose were damaged and unreturnable, then there would be "a gentleman's obligation to repay in kind" rather than a bill for the dollar amount. That would, according to Roosevelt, "get rid of the silly, foolish old dollar sign."[20]

Twelve days later the president laid out the rest of the package in one of his regular radio broadcasts, the fireside chats. He warned that "the Nazi masters of Germany," who sought "to enslave the whole of Europe," and their Axis partners could "dominate the rest of the world" if Britain fell. Rather than live "at the point of a gun," the United States would be the "arsenal of democracy."

That powerful phrase probably came from Jean Monnet, who later became the political father of the European Common Market, but whatever its genesis, the commitment was astounding. FDR had, in typically vague terms, promised to provide those who opposed the Axis with whatever they needed to win the struggle. Henry Stimson, uncomfortable with Roosevelt's insistence that "this was not a fireside chat on war" but a talk about how to keep out of the war, confided to his diary that the United States "cannot permanently be in the position of toolmakers for other nations which fight." But he admitted that the issue of American intervention could not yet be broached. The reaction in Congress and the press suggested that Americans were comfortable with the idea of protecting their security without going to war.[21] When FDR followed up with his inaugural address on January 6 calling for a postwar world based on what he labeled the Four Freedoms— freedom of speech, freedom to worship, freedom from want, freedom from fear—the reaction in Congress and the press suggested he had wide popular support.

Only the "isolationists" raised the awkward question of whether or not the British could ever muster the military strength to defeat Hitler, but FDR continued his campaign to marginalize such voices by picturing them as Hitler's dupes. During his arsenal of democracy speech, Roosevelt described fifth column agents operating in Latin America and the United States, then tarred the anti-interventionists by denouncing those "American citizens, many of them in high places, who unwittingly in most cases are aiding and abetting the work of these [Nazi] agents." The insinuation was unfair, but FDR's tactics of painting his opponents as extreme isolationists, combined with Hitler's actions, had succeeded in discrediting those who opposed aiding those fighting the Axis. Moreover, the leading anti-interventionist organization, the America First Committee, seemed blatantly partisan to many, dominated as it was by Republicans and conservative opponents of the administration.[22]

Putting the fire hose idea into practice required congressional approval, and Henry Morgenthau's Treasury Department got the job of drafting the legislation. The president provided two broad guidelines: First, the debate in and out of Congress was to appear full and unrestricted, although that did not mean full candor. Broad questions about the implications of the bill were out of bounds; for example, would it mean American warships convoying supply ships across the Atlantic? Roosevelt wanted the appearance of a great debate without turning it into a dialogue on overall foreign policy. The second guideline was the president's insistence that the legislation provide the widest possible latitude for him to decide which nations to aid, what goods to send, and what to ask as repayment.

He got largely what he wanted. The debate inside and outside Congress was long and loud, offering the administration a golden opportunity to make Americans aware of the geopolitical threat. Congress attached a few conditions to the bill (popularly known as H.R. 1776, a number assigned by the House parliamentarian to give it a patriotic ring). Annual appropriations and year-end reports provided a modicum of congressional oversight, but the bill's supporters held out against an amendment prohibiting convoying.

Aware of the increasing likelihood of an attack on the Soviet Union by Hitler, the administration fought off attempts to forbid the extension of aid to Russia. Roosevelt broke his own no-comment rule after one senator proposed an amendment saying nothing in the bill gave the president "additional powers" to send military forces outside the Western Hemisphere or American possessions. FDR called it a matter of geography and gave reporters an extraordinarily expansive definition of the Western Hemisphere. His advisers feared the rider would sound a go-ahead signal for Japan, but since the amendment only repeated Roosevelt's own promises, it passed with minor changes. When all was said and done, Democrats gave solid support to the bill, and the few Republican crossovers ensured an overwhelming victory, suggesting the mandate the president hoped for.[23]

Churchill later termed lend-lease, as it came to be known, "the most unsordid act in the history of any nation."[24] That may be accurate, given the infrequency of "unsordid" actions by nations. But the bill gained the support of Congress and, by all indicators, the American public because it served the nation's purposes. Just as the British left the French to face the Germans alone in June 1940, just as the Anglo-Americans delayed the second front while the Soviet Union held off the bulk of the German Army, just as the Soviet Union carefully avoided entering the Pacific war until Japan was virtually defeated, so the United States, including Roosevelt, was happy to let Great Britain fight the war without sending American ground forces overseas.

Sordid or unsordid, lend-lease was an extraordinary program. Allied victory in the Second World War was a product of many factors, but harnessing the economic strength of the United States was indispensable to success. Over the course of the war lend-lease provided between forty-two and fifty billion dollars' worth of aid (in World War II dollars) to those fighting the Axis, without creating the bad aftertaste of war debts and recriminations.

More striking, lend-lease constituted a declaration of economic warfare. Hitler understood that lend-lease made the United States exactly what Churchill had asked for months before, what he called nonbelligerency, helping with "everything short of actually engaging armed forces." But the Germans did not want to see a repeat of what had happened in the First World War, when their military persuaded the government that the German Navy could sink every troopship heading for France while the army was breaking through the Anglo-French lines. The German submarine warfare campaign that followed had so alienated Americans that entering the war in April 1917 became politically feasible. Hitler did not want that to happen in 1941.[25]

Unbeknownst to the German leader, the issue of engaging American armed forces was under very serious consideration. Even while Congress debated economic warfare against Germany, high-level British and American military officers were meeting in Washington to discuss broad joint strategy in the event the United States joined the war. American naval planners had already concluded that Britain's survival was essential to the United States and in late 1940 proposed taking a Germany first approach should the Japanese enter the war (Plan Dog). But Roosevelt had neither endorsed nor rejected the proposal. He agreed to military staff talks but, still unwilling to put his military commitments to a public test, insisted that they be secret, particularly since the lend-lease debate was under way.

Those talks concluded that the defeat of the most powerful of the Axis powers, Germany, was the first priority. But the participants could not agree on how to deal with Japan's challenge. The British, following Churchill's tactic of involving the United States in the defense of the British Empire, argued for a forward strategy against Japan: moving the U.S. fleet to the Philippines and to Singapore. But the Americans insisted on neither confrontation nor retreat and opted for leaving the fleet at Pearl Harbor in Hawaii and for continued negotiations, particularly with the new Japanese ambassador in Washington, Admiral Kichisaburo Nomura, an old acquaintance of the president's. The ABC-1 (American-British conversations) report of March 29 subscribed to the Germany first strategy, a commitment that Roosevelt consistently implemented but never formally endorsed until after the United States had entered the war.

ABC-1 was a major commitment, though it did not have the

public sanction gained by lend-lease, which had congressional approval. It is easy to raise valid questions about the lack of candor on the part of Roosevelt, hiding from Congress and the public a most significant strategic commitment. But Roosevelt was not prepared to debate the question of war or peace. Nor is there any indication that he had made a choice. For FDR, war meant ground forces in Europe; air and naval units could fight Hitler under a different rubric. In fact, shortly before the ABC-1 talks, the president had expressed concern to General Marshall that although there was only a one-in-five chance of Germany and Japan's waging a joint war against the Anglo-Americans, such an action could bring the collapse of British resistance and a German attack on the Western Hemisphere. Hardly the musings of someone contemplating an offensive war against Hitler.[26]

Lend-lease and ABC-1 were not the only aspects of remarkably close Anglo-American collaboration. In February, while Congress considered a declaration of economic warfare (though not in those candid terms) and Anglo-American military officers developed a joint strategy, American Army intelligence personnel brought a complex machine to British code breakers at Bletchley Park, a country home north of London. It was the now-famous Purple machine, the equipment used to decipher Japanese diplomatic messages (called Magic). There is no deeper trust between nations than sharing important intelligence assets. But that trust did not, at this stage, go both ways. The British, still dubious about their American quasi allies, did not share their incredible breakthrough, the Enigma machine, used to decipher German military traffic (called Ultra by the British).[27]

While the lend-lease bill was being developed in the Treasury Department, a key step in the evolution of the Churchill-Roosevelt relationship took place. There had been some hints of testiness when Churchill drafted a message complaining that American demands for cash payments right up to the implementation of the Lend-Lease Act (the so-called interim commitments) had the appearance of the "sheriff collecting the last assets of a helpless debtor."[28] Churchill also expressed, in draft form, "anxiety" and some anger that the president expected Britain to transfer some of its gold reserve from South Africa to Washington. Sandwiched in between was a petulant complaint that the destroyers sent to Britain as part of the destroyer-bases deal were so decrepit as to be of little help. All three messages were toned down lest they alienate the Americans, but the resentment was clear.[29]

On January 9 the points of friction in the Churchill-Roosevelt relationship got some much-needed lubrication. On that day Harry Hopkins arrived in London for a monthlong visit. Hopkins was an unusual man on an unusual mission; "to be a catalytic agent between two prima donnas" was his own description. He had impressed Roosevelt by effectively administering two New Deal relief programs. His candor and practicality prompted Churchill to name him "Lord Root of the Matter." FDR commented that "Harry is the perfect Ambassador for my purposes. He doesn't even know the meaning of the word 'protocol.' When he sees a piece of red tape, he just pulls out those old garden shears of his and snips it. And when he's talking to some foreign dignitary, he knows how to slump back in his chair and put his feet up on the conference table and say, 'Oh, yeah?' " After Hopkins had the experience of a January stay at Chequers, the prime minister's country house, one of Churchill's private secretaries recalled the American's effectively cutting through British reserve by promising that central heating would be his *victory* present.[30]

Roosevelt's confidence in Hopkins was much more than a matter of style. He somehow managed to be on the same wavelength as FDR. He anticipated Roosevelt's questions and concerns, sensed when to make decisions and when to refer them to "the Boss," and, above all, demonstrated unfailing loyalty. As one journalist put it with hyperbolic accuracy, "Should the President on a dull day suggest casually to his friend and confidant, Harry L. Hopkins, that the national welfare would be served if Mr. Hopkins would jump off the Washington Monument, the appointed hour would find Mr. Hopkins poised for the plunge. Whether with or without parachute would depend on what the President seemed to have in mind."[31] During the time Hopkins actually lived in the White

House, from May 1940 until New Year's Day 1944, when his serious chronic illness and a new wife forced him to leave, he acted as Roosevelt's alter ego. All the Cabinet members quickly came to understand that the path to the president ran through Hopkins. He was, between 1941 and 1943, the first national security adviser—before the post was invented—and without needing a huge staff and bureaucracy.

His effectiveness in that role and as a person is testified to by the thoughtful, sincere endorsements of three leaders, each of great integrity. Henry Stimson, hardly a New Dealer, believed it "a Godsend that he [Hopkins] should be at the White House." Churchill (who underestimated Hopkins's suspicions of British intentions) wrote that the American "was a true leader of men" whose "love for the causes of the weak and poor was matched by his passion against tyranny, especially when tyranny was, for the time, triumphant." General George Marshall, hardly noted for effusiveness, wrote Hopkins birthday greetings in 1944, saying, "I missed you much and sadly during the recent period of your indisposition. . . . You have rendered a great service to your country . . . you will be of great importance to what comes next in our international and war problems." The austere general's affection for Hopkins shone through as he closed the letter: "I ask you to be careful, to conserve your energies and not to overdo and I am also prepared to damn you for your cigarettes, your drinks and your late hours. Confine your excesses to gin rummy."[32]

Hopkins's visit to London, which he had proposed as a means of getting the measure of Winston Churchill, reshaped the relationship between the prime minister and the president. Churchill, uncomfortable in the role of petitioner, found Hopkins a breath of fresh air. At one point during the visit the prime minister waxed poetic about British goals: "We seek only the right of man to be free. . . . We seek government with the consent of the people, man's freedom to say what he will. . . . But war aims other than these we have none." He asked Hopkins how Roosevelt would react to such sentiments. "I don't think the President will give a dam' for all that," Hopkins replied laconically. "You see, we're only interested in seeing that that Goddam sonofabitch, Hitler, gets licked." However disingenuous that claim may have been, one of those present commented that "there was loud laughter, and at that moment a friendship was cemented which no convulsion ever undermined."[33] For most of the war Hopkins acted as a special channel between Churchill and Roosevelt, particularly when the prime minister was uncertain of the president's reaction to a proposal or complaint.

At the same time Hopkins was in London, other players who were to play important wartime roles in the Anglo-American equation were put in place. Lord Lothian had died suddenly on December 11. Churchill considered sending David Lloyd George, who had been prime minister during World War I but had later supported appeasement and spoke often in defeatist tones. Roosevelt was unenthusiastic but acquiesced. Foreign Office and Commonwealth opposition, plus Lloyd George's own doubts, caused Churchill to instead nominate Foreign Secretary Lord Halifax, who had refused the opportunity to be prime minister. Hopkins accurately predicted that FDR would like Halifax's honesty, religious views, and style. Halifax was at first baffled by the casual American political scene, which he likened to "a disorderly line of beaters out shooting; they do put the rabbits out of the bracken, but they don't come out where you expect." But he quickly became effective with government officials and with the press.[34] When he arrived on January 24 off Annapolis in the Chesapeake Bay aboard the battleship *King George V*, FDR went out on the presidential yacht to meet the new ambassador, a public gesture of support for Britain as well as a grand opportunity to see the great warship close up.

Likewise, a new American ambassador to the United Kingdom came on the scene, though for a different reason. Joseph Kennedy, anti-British, anti-interventionist, and by then anti-Roosevelt, had returned to the United States before the November elections and, in accordance with protocol, handed in his resignation the day after Roosevelt's reelection. But Kennedy meant it, and FDR meant to accept, telling Eleanor in November 1940 (according to one story), "I never want to see that son of a bitch again as long as I live. Take his resignation and get him out of here!" To the disappointment of anti-interventionists and various Roosevelt haters, Kennedy never launched an attack on FDR. His widely anticipated testimony during the lend-lease hearing proved uninteresting. There is much speculation on why, including stories of threats from Roosevelt to ruin the political career of Kennedy's son Joe, Jr. But it seems more likely that Kennedy chose not to burn his own personal political bridges to the Democratic party.[35]

Kennedy's replacement, John Winant, a liberal Republican, had served the Roosevelt administration in various posts, particularly with the International Labor Organization. Roosevelt's penchant for sending personal emissaries to London—Hopkins and Averell Harriman particularly—limited Winant's role, but he acted as an important interpreter when Churchill or Roosevelt misunderstood the other's intentions.

But such appointments, the crucial ABC-1 agreement, and lend-lease all would be meaningless if Britain's military situation deteriorated, a distinct possibility in mid-1941. For most of that spring Britain's war in southern Europe and Africa commanded Churchill's attention. He and FDR fenced a little over implementation of the destroyer-bases deal: The destroyers were old and not immediately available for service; the Americans wanted more economic concessions at the base sites than Britain wished to give. But arguments over the use of valuable beachfront in Bermuda and duty-free cigarettes for American servicemen (an item perhaps only a smoker like FDR would have noticed) were trivial, and the president passed the dispute on to subordinates with the comment that he did not want to make mountains out of molehills.[36]

Shortly after the new year had begun, Churchill relayed some unusual news: a British victory. Ground forces had routed the Italian Army in what Churchill invariably called Cyrenaica (eastern Libya, which had been coupled with Tripolitania to the west in 1934 to form a single Italian colony). Huge numbers of Italian soldiers were taken prisoner (forty thousand alone at Bardia); then the fortress of Tobruk fell to the British, and the Italians fled westward to Tripolitania, where the Germans helped them hold the line.[37]

But the comfort of that victory was short-lived. Bulgaria, helpless before the overwhelming power of both Germany and the Soviet Union, allowed German troops to enter without opposition. Then, in late March, the Yugoslav government gave in to German pressure and signed the Tripartite Pact. A coup d'etat, led by nationalist Serbs, replaced the regent, Prince Paul, with the eighteen-year-old King Peter II, and the British and Americans responded immediately with congratulations and promises of aid. But such promises did not prevent Hitler from launching an indiscriminate air attack on Belgrade and invading from Bulgaria, which had joined the Tripartite Pact on March 1 in hopes of gaining both security and territory. That attack, combined with the refusal of Croats to support King Peter, brought a quick capitulation by the Yugoslav government on April 17.

At the same time German forces came to the aid of the Italians in Greece, which Mussolini had once again invaded, after failing in October 1940. Despite the misgivings of the British chiefs of staff, Churchill dispatched British and Commonwealth forces from North Africa and the Middle East to join the Greek defense. It was, he admitted a few months later, the government's "one error in judgment" up to that point. The Germans outflanked the Greek and British forces and forced their evacuation to Crete and Egypt. When the new German commander in Libya, General Erwin Rommel, learned through signals intelligence of Churchill's decision to reinforce Greece, he launched a successful offensive in the so-called Western Desert (that is, west of Cairo). Rommel's advance was spectacularly successful (to the consternation of the British and of the German high command, which was focused on the pending attack on the Soviet Union). He retook most of Libya by the end of May, threatening Egypt and the Suez Canal.[38]

The Germans quickly took the logical next step and attacked the island of Crete, nearly two hundred miles south of Athens and three hundred miles northwest of Alexandria, Egypt. In the only large-scale airborne invasion of the war, German paratroops suffered staggering losses but managed to gain control of key airfields—in good measure because of poor British generalship. That allowed reinforcements to come by air and forced the British to evacuate over the rugged mountains to the south coast. German tactics were a microcosm of the excesses and atrocities they used elsewhere: terror bombing of the lovely old Venetian city of Chania; executions of hostages; reprisals against villages where Greek resistance proved stubborn. The Royal Navy, exhausted by the evacuation of Greece and without effective carrier or land-based air support, initially managed to prevent the Italians and Germans from landing seaborne reinforcements of their invasion force, but it suffered such heavy losses to German air attack that its commander, Admiral Sir Andrew Cunningham, brooked Churchill's displeasure and recalled his fleet to Alexandria. The American military attaché in Cairo offered a prescient warning: "It was the first engagement of a first-rate fleet without air support with a first-rate air power. The battle ended in a complete and undeniable air victory. . . ."[39] Neither the British nor the Americans would learn that lesson until after the attack on the American fleet at Pearl Harbor and, a few days later, the sinking of two British capital ships, *Prince of Wales* and *Repulse*, off the Dutch East Indies.

Thus, by the beginning of summer 1941, British military fortunes in the Mediterranean looked grim. Rommel had gained control of everything along the North African coast, west of the Vichy French colonies, except Tobruk; the devastating (though eventually unsuccessful) three-year siege of the British island of Malta, strategically located between Sicily and Tunisia, had intensified, with invasion expected; Greece, Crete, and the Aegean were Axis-controlled. The only bright spots were pinpoints: A German-sponsored revolt in Iraq had collapsed; the Italians had been forced out of East Africa (Somalia, Ethiopia, Eritrea) by early April, thus keeping the Red Sea in British hands; the Spanish maintained a dubious neutrality; and the French fleet remained out of German hands, despite rumors to the contrary.[40]

The Mediterranean setbacks paled in comparison with the growing crisis in the Atlantic. Britain's ability to resist depended on convoys of merchant ships getting through the German U-boat gauntlet. Britain had begun to restructure its own production to mesh with supplies from overseas of war materials, food, and basic consumer items, making safe delivery of those goods crucial. The Battle of Britain could have been in vain, and that was what Churchill had in mind when he dubbed the supply struggle the Battle of the Atlantic.[41] It became the forgotten war, with heavy losses of ships and of men whose deaths were somehow treated, then and after the war, as less heroic than those on the front lines. Losses were (and are) invariably cited in "tons of merchant ships," an appalling statistic in its own right. In 1941 German attacks, mostly by submarines, sank 3.6 million tons of shipping, peaking in the March–June period, when Churchill raised the crisis with the president. The sinking in late May of the German battleship *Bismarck*, spotted by a U.S. Naval Reserve "observer" flying with the British, provided an exciting interlude but, for Roosevelt, did not change things.[42] On May 27 he declared an unlimited national emergency in response to what he regarded as Hitler's threat to the Western Hemisphere.

Part of the answer to the Battle of the Atlantic and to Churchill's ever-constant efforts to get the Americans more and more involved was the escorting of merchant ships, the issue that FDR had told his subordinates to avoid during the lend-lease debate. The president continued to avoid that decision until April 1941, when he extended the "security zone" farther east to 25 degrees west longitude—putting Greenland and the Azores inside the patrol zone; he subsequently issued his own papal Bull by assigning "most of the Azores" and Iceland to the Western Hemisphere! But cautious as ever, he told Churchill he thought it "advisable that when this new policy is adopted here no statement be issued on your end. . . . I may decide to . . . let time bring out the existence of the new patrol area."[43] Churchill regularly warned Roosevelt of possible German actions that would threaten the United States. What about a Turkish arrangement with the Axis? What would happen if the Spanish made an agreement with Hitler and gave the Germans access to the Canary Islands? Would not Portugal have to make a deal giving Hitler control of the Azores and the Cape Verde Islands—adjacent to the bulge of Brazil?[44]

Roosevelt's response was scary. He reiterated his commitment to extend the American naval patrol zone but connected that with a warning against a British occupation of the Portuguese Azores lest it suggest imperialism. Then, in one of his rare surveys of the geopolitical scene, FDR took a very pessimistic tone, suggesting that Britain might well withdraw from the eastern Mediterranean and the Near East after destroying the oil facilities there. Returning to his typically American focus on sea defenses, Roosevelt concluded that "in the last analysis the Naval control of the Indian Ocean and the Atlantic Ocean will in time win the war."

Churchill, ever sensitive to the dangers of pessimism on Roosevelt's part, told Anthony Eden (who had replaced Halifax as foreign secretary) that "quite unconsciously we are being left very much to our fate," then did what he could to dispel Roosevelt's doubts. He thanked the president for assuring Britain "that no temporary reverses, however heavy, can shake your resolution to support us until we gain the final victory"—a clause that had originally read "I am depressed by your message." Likewise, a prediction that the loss of Egypt and the Middle East would be "mortal" or "overwhelming" became "grave." But the thrust of the prime minister's argument was that if all Europe and much of Africa and Asia were incorporated in "the Axis system," then the war would be a "hard, long, and bleak proposition." A week later Roosevelt backed off, promising to expedite shipments to the Middle East. But American concern about fighting the war for Britain's empire soon resurfaced.[45]

The Western Hemisphere, at least as demarcated by Roosevelt, was a different matter. In June he authorized American forces to relieve the British garrison that had taken on the defense of Iceland. Admiral Harold "Betty" Stark, head of the American Navy and a staunch supporter of aid to Britain, admitted the move was a virtual act of war, but FDR went ahead.[46] But that was small potatoes compared with the world situation.

Germany astride Europe. The Suez Canal and the Middle East

under the gun. U-boats threatening delivery of lend-lease goods. Japan in control of northern Indochina and refusing to consider any compromise in China. Roosevelt either still waiting for the right moment or immobilized by fear that Britain would collapse.

Then on June 22, the first day of summer, Russia's war began.

You and I know who started this war.

CHAPTER 4

———◦❮❯◦———

"History Has Recorded Who Fired the First Shot": The Soviet Union and the United States Enter the War June 1941–December 1941

On June 22, 1941, the entire geopolitical and ideological nature of the Second World War changed dramatically. Before dawn German forces attacked in strength all along the new Soviet-German border. Hitler's long-rumored offensive against the Soviet Union, Operation Barbarossa, became a reality. Despite warnings passed on as early as March 1941 from both American and British diplomats and even earlier from Soviet intelligence, Stalin had apparently remained convinced that the Western powers were trying to provoke a Nazi-Soviet war. Whatever his reasons, the Red Army was caught unprepared. But then so was Churchill, who on May 20 had commented that a German attack was not worth worrying about and two days later said that "either war or showdown is near."[1]

Like Roosevelt, Stalin had counted on having enough time to prepare. But France had failed to hold out (little wonder that throughout the war both Roosevelt and Stalin looked with contempt on the French), and Hitler had surprised Moscow by swinging to the East without first subduing the British. Stalin had learned nothing from Chamberlain's failure and hoped his own form of appeasement would delay Hitler. He rigorously met his commitments to Germany for shipments of raw materials and carefully avoided any provocative actions or statements. But to no avail.

A week before the German attack, with clear intelligence indication of what was about to happen, Churchill and Roosevelt had agreed on how to respond. In Churchill's words, "We shall of course give all encouragement and any help we can spare to the Russians, following the principle that Hitler is the foe we have to beat." He assured the president that there would be no "class political reactions" in Britain and trusted the matter would not cause Roosevelt "any embarrassment." FDR responded through Winant that he would publicly endorse any such announcement.[2]

Those statements came as planned, but there was little that vague promises of aid could accomplish as German tanks and troops (along with some six hundred thousand horses used to transport supplies!) quickly occupied eastern Poland, the Baltic states, Byelorussia, and western Ukraine, capturing more than six hundred thousand Soviet soldiers along the way. German Army grand strategy was reminiscent of Napoleon's a century and a quarter earlier: Eliminate the Russian Army as a fighting force; then take Moscow, and force the government to capitulate. One senior German general predicted having to "fight fierce battles for eight to fourteen days and after this we won't have to wait long for successes." The chief of staff of the German Army, General Franz Halder, concluded in early July that "the campaign against Russia has been won within two weeks." As late as the end of August such predictions seemed accurate, with the Wehrmacht approaching Leningrad and Kiev and only three hundred miles from Moscow. Nevertheless, by then the German military had begun to worry that too much of the Red Army had evaded the encirclement strategy and escaped to the east. Moreover, Hitler did not make taking Moscow his main priority until October. Nor, the Germans concluded, would they be able in 1941 to take either the Caucasus and its oil resources or the ice-free northern port of Murmansk.[3]

But the British and Americans had no knowledge of growing German misgivings. For Churchill and Roosevelt, Barbarossa was as much a threat as a blessing. The kind of blitzkrieg that Hitler had planned and that seemed to be happening in Russia meant only a temporary respite for Britain—and therefore for the United States. The thought of a triumphant Hitler with all the resources of Eastern Europe and the Soviet Union behind him was truly frightening. Perhaps the difficulty of controlling a vast antagonistic population would prove an albatross around the Führer's neck, though he understood that danger, providing a functional excuse for his schemes for "ethnic cleansing." But even if a hostile populace could distract and cripple Germany, that would take time, and the war in the West might be over.

In the United States Harry Hopkins, ever practical, worried that Soviet requests for supplies would interfere with aid to Britain. Stimson and Knox both recommended an increase in naval support to the United Kingdom. William Bullitt, once one of FDR's personal emissaries and an anti-Soviet crusader since his tour as ambassador in Moscow in the mid-1930s, as well as George Kennan, a young State Department Russian expert, took an ideological stance. Bullitt predicted a quick Soviet collapse and irrelevantly warned against Communist subversion at home, while Kennan, who was willing to use the Soviets against the Nazis, admonished against calling the USSR an ally, lest that lend moral legitimacy to the Soviet regime—an ideological approach that would only have encouraged Stalin to seek a negotiated peace with Hitler and poisoned the wartime alliance. Even the American ambassador in London, John Winant, suspicious of another Nazi-Soviet deal, accused Stalin and Hitler of a "put up job," though Churchill found that laughable. Senator Harry Truman quipped that the United States should help Germany if the Russians were winning and Russia if Germany was winning, though he added that he would not want Hitler victorious under any circumstances. That comment reflected the mood swings of Americans toward the Soviet Union, ranging from admiration in the mid-thirties (when the USSR seemed to be correcting the excesses of capitalism) to anger and revulsion (following Stalin's purges and the Nazi-Soviet Pact) and then to cautious collaboration during the Second World War. Despite American suspicions about Soviet intentions, Truman's gambit never became a serious possibility; disgust for the Nazis may not have been enough to bring America into the war, but it was much too strong to allow such cynical aloofness.[4]

The American military was initially pessimistic about Soviet chances, and Roosevelt's first reaction to panicky Soviet requests for aid was caution, deftly dodging questions from the press about extending lend-lease to Russia, particularly with polls showing Americans opposed. With the fall of France still fresh in their minds, Americans asked if they should risk wasting such aid. Long-term Soviet intentions raised concerns, and reports were full of references to secret agents and suspicious requests from the Soviets for secret military technology.[5]

But FDR often played his hunches, and he had a hunch that backing the Soviets might be worth the gamble. After a long evening's conversation on July 11 with Hopkins, the president sent his trusted adviser to London to discuss two related issues: the American aid program and the effect of the German-Soviet war on broad strategy. Hopkins's discussions focused on the Battle of the Atlantic, preparations for a Churchill-Roosevelt meeting that would take place in mid-August, and British strategy in the Middle East. When the American said that he doubted the wisdom of deepening Britain's commitment in the Middle East, the British replied that the likely Soviet collapse made a stronger defense in that region even more important. It was during this visit that the prime minister, eager to present the image of openness, invited Hopkins to attend a Cabinet meeting. The playacting ended when Hopkins left, after being told the Cabinet would take up dull domestic matters. The British then went on to discuss the delicate issue of United States policy regarding Japan.[6]

But the battle in Russia was the real reason for Hopkins's visit to London, so it seems preordained, if not planned, that he should suggest a visit to Moscow to assess the situation for himself and FDR. It is hard to read Churchill's reaction to the proposal. He endorsed it to Roosevelt and certainly supported anything that would cause Hitler problems. The prime minister had predicted that the Soviets would "assuredly be defeated" but then quickly promised to "go all out to help Russia." That prompted his loyal private secretary, Jock Colville, to wonder if Churchill was not condoning immorality; "bowing down in the House of Rimmon" was Colville's colorful phrase. The prime minister's response put ideology in the perspective of survival: "If Hitler invaded Hell he

[Churchill] would at least make a favourable reference to the Devil." Nevertheless, as one Labour leader commented, the Soviets were hardly fighting for the principles that Britons held dear.[7]

The maxim "The enemy of my enemy is my friend" controlled Churchill's rhetoric, but he never forgot for a moment that each gun, tank, and airplane that might go to Russia had to come out of those Britain needed. Why should he forget that? Every military appraisal predicted a quick, decisive German victory on the Russian front. Little wonder that he focused on Britain's needs, particularly in the Middle East, which would be threatened if Rommel continued to march east toward Egypt and Suez or if the Germans moved into the Caucasus just north of Iran. No surprise that Churchill's promises of quick aid to the Soviets never fully materialized.[8]

The British were torn between the hope that the Russians would inflict heavy losses on the Germans and the fear that the Red Army would be quickly defeated and British matériel would fall into German hands, but Churchill could not risk alienating the Americans by disparaging the Hopkins proposal. Always eager to act as broker for Soviet-American relations, he sent Stalin a bombastic explanation of why Britain could do little, then another commending Hopkins as someone with "a flame . . . for democracy and to beat Hitler"—a curious choice of words to use with the Soviet dictator.[9]

Significant aid could not arrive in time to help the Red Army get through the crisis of summer–autumn 1941, while immediate military intervention was impossible. Stalin seized on idle and foolish suggestions of some British officers and wishfully called for second fronts in France and the Arctic, an issue that became overpowering in the months to come. More realistically he admitted to a British general in late September that "he quite understood why we [Great Britain] could not at the moment establish a Western Front." But the second front was not yet the issue. To ensure that Winant's "put up job" did not become a reality, what mattered was the believable promise of future assistance—just as when Churchill combated British defeatism in the autumn of 1940.[10]

Hopkins set off for Moscow wearing one of Churchill's gray

homburgs and carrying a hastily handwritten visa from the Soviet ambassador in London along with a message to Stalin from Roosevelt. It was a long and arduous journey, especially for someone with serious health problems. His condition had distressed Clementine Churchill, and one observer at the Cabinet meeting Hopkins attended commented that he looked "more dead than alive."[11] But then, as throughout most of the war, he pushed himself to the limit—and beyond. He got VIP treatment in Moscow, managing to go places and talk to people denied to the American ambassador, Laurence Steinhardt. When Hopkins was assigned a bomb shelter during a German air raid (which did not destroy Moscow buildings like "matchsticks," as some had predicted), the disgruntled Steinhardt complained that he had never before been given a bomb shelter. Hopkins laughed.

Hopkins found more than the red-carpet treatment. He also found confidence, high morale, and "unbounded determination to win." Time and again Stalin promised to continue the fight from the Ural Mountains even if Moscow fell. "The Russians are confident," and so was he, were Hopkins's first words to FDR a week later. Hopkins recognized that Stalin was a dictator who had intimidated his subordinates (something Roosevelt and Churchill sometimes seemed to forget) but concluded that all-out aid to Russia was a good bet. At worst it would prolong the war and give the United States time to prepare. At best it could accomplish what the U.S. chiefs of staffs hoped for: "the maintenance of an active front in Russia [which] offers by far the best opportunity for a successful land offensive against Germany. . . ."[12] To put it another way, if the power of the Wehrmacht was to be broken, the Red Army had to do it. Anything less meant the Anglo-Americans would have to settle for the long haul: for quarantining Germany on the Continent and leaving Western Europe to Hitler's cruelties.

The message to Stalin from FDR made it clear that the president hoped for the best. He promised that the United States would do what it could "within the next three months" but, more important, that a "great amount of matériel" would be forthcoming after that crucial three-month span. Survive, implied Roosevelt, and like Britain, you will receive American largess. As Hopkins told Stafford

Cripps, the British ambassador to the Soviet Union, FDR would go "all out to help . . . even if the Army and Navy authorities in America did not like it."[13]

Roosevelt's message to Stalin also reflected a deep concern that the Soviet leader might, *in extremis,* make a settlement with Hitler. Joseph Davies, who had been a most sympathetic American ambassador to the Soviet regime in the mid-thirties and whose reputation as an analyst of the Soviet scene had been greatly enhanced when he predicted the signing of the Nazi-Soviet Pact, had suggested that the ability of the Red Army to resist would surprise everyone. Nevertheless, he warned, Stalin "might even again 'fall' for Hitler's peace as the lesser of two evils." After all, Davies argued, it made little sense for Stalin to pull " 'chestnuts out of the fire' for allies who have no use for him."[14]

That explains why, even as German forces threatened the heart of European Russia, Stalin sought political bona fides from Churchill and Roosevelt. What the Soviet leader proposed was recognition of what he had regained in the Nazi-Soviet Pact: a boundary with Poland along the so-called Curzon Line, which returned the Baltic states and eastern Poland to Soviet control. Both the Soviet and Polish government had rejected the frontier proposed by British Foreign Secretary Lord Curzon during the Paris Peace Conference in 1919, but Stalin now found it acceptable.[15] His preoccupation with geopolitical security was no different from that of his potential partners. Government leaders invariably consider the preservation of the state and "nation" an overriding goal. Churchill had concerned himself from the start with imperial considerations. Marshal Pétain had justified the French armistice with Hitler on those same grounds. British leaders like Lord Halifax and R. A. Butler had given serious thought to some sort of settlement with Hitler in June 1940 for just those reasons. Roosevelt had wrapped the Western Hemisphere in a protective military and economic cocoon, although the Americans never faced a clear choice between fighting on and compromise. Even so, some elements in the anti-interventionist coalition seemed ready to live with an Axis-dominated world. Why should Stalin be expected to act or think differently?

Moreover, Stalin thought he had reason to worry that he might be left twisting in the wind as the British negotiated a separate settlement with Hitler. Chamberlain's unsubtle encouragements for Hitler to look to the East were not forgotten in Moscow. More immediately, on May 10, 1941, Nazi Deputy Führer Rudolf Hess landed by parachute near Glasgow, Scotland. Ostensibly he came to suggest the outlines of an Anglo-German settlement and to prompt negotiations. Soviet intelligence, specifically via the British spy Kim Philby, learned quickly of the Hess flight and reports that the Nazi had brought some kind of peace proposals with him. The implication was that the proposals came from Hitler and that the so-called British Peace Party was a political force to reckon with.

The Peace Party in May 1941 was hardly a significant factor, but there was, it appears, something for the British to hide. When Roosevelt queried Churchill about Hess, the prime minister lied to or misled FDR, saying Hess denied rumors of a planned German attack on Russia. In fact Hess had warned of Barbarossa, although the Americans did not learn that until six months later. Stalin, presumably aware of that warning, had every reason to suspect that British government officials knew in advance of the Hess mission. What did they have up their sleeves: genuine negotiations with Hitler? An attempt to convince Hitler he had tacit British support for an attack on the Soviet Union? Or was Hess a pawn in a British disinformation scheme aimed at threatening the Russians with a separate peace? Whatever the truth, such lies and disingenuousness only fueled Stalin's strong suspicions about British, and Western, long-term intentions.[16] Within the context of past suspicions and the Hess affair, Stalin's attempts to commit his new partners to his political agenda make sense.

The British responded ambivalently to Stalin's political proposals, perhaps prompting Roosevelt's warning to Churchill, repeated through Hopkins, not to make "trades or deals" regarding "some of the [German] occupied nations."[17] But there was more to the American position than just idealistic concern about sordid bargains. Throughout the war Roosevelt had to try to reconcile practicality and ideals, often while resisting attempts by others to impose ideological imperatives on him. Those imperatives came most often in the form of the self-righteous Wilsonianism that "chilled" Anthony Eden by raising the "spectacle of an American President talking at large on European frontiers," as Woodrow Wilson had done about the World War I settlement.[18] Frequently, that Wilsonian perfectionism masked other motives, as when Bullitt warned of the evil immorality of both the Soviet Union and of a rival in the State Department. But whatever ideal seemed at stake, Roosevelt had also to deal with the politics of alliance and a postwar settlement.

In the summer of 1941 Stalin's irreducible political minimum was acceptance of his reabsorption of the Baltic states into the empire, now Soviet instead of Russian. FDR saw no choice but to put off such discussions. It was more than just trying to avoid the mistakes of the First World War, when the secret treaties had destroyed Wilson's credibility with his own public. Roosevelt likewise hoped to broker a fair and lasting peace and worried openly about lashing hostile ethnic groups together into a single state. He presciently questioned Churchill "whether it is advisable . . . to keep the Croats away from the throats of the Serbs, and vice versa."[19] Putting together a wartime coalition took priority, particularly since Hitler's defeat (as opposed to mere quarantining) required the Red Army. Still, agreeing to Stalin's territorial claims would jeopardize domestic support for such a coalition, and the United States was not even in the war. Nor could such an agreement be kept secret.

Leaks had always been a way of life in official Washington. Consider, for example, Cordell Hull, Roosevelt's secretary of state. Hull was a zealous Wilsonian already bitter at not having been asked to be the Democratic candidate for president in 1940. He had no qualms about using his contact at *The New York Times*, Arthur Krock, to get front-page coverage of what the secretary considered violations of Wilsonian ideals or even personal morality, as Sumner Welles and Henry Morgenthau later learned. White House recognition of Soviet claims to the Baltic states would have been headline news the next day.[20]

Truman's gambit had pointed to a political probability: Whichever state emerged victorious from the Russo-German war would

be a major political power in the postwar world. Roosevelt's working assumption (more a wish to start with) was that the Soviet
Union would be that power. He believed Wilson's admirable attempt after the First World War to achieve a worldwide settlement
had failed in good part because the Great Powers would not cooperate, with either Wilson or one another. FDR intended to temper Wilson's liberalism with practicality, something Wilsonians and
conservative nationalists would and did condemn as the corrupting
of American ideals through compromise. Even in 1941 Roosevelt
called for plebiscites—"one of the few successful outcomes of the
Versailles Treaty"—to cloak territorial shifts. It was but one of his
attempts to find a middle ground between the two diametrically
opposed idealisms, Wilsonian and conservative nationalism. "Economic or territorial deals—NO," he instructed Hopkins before the
latter left to talk to Churchill—and Stalin.[21]

Roosevelt saw no alternative but to defer consideration of the
Soviet political docket until he could exercise better control over
the situation. More to the point, it made no sense to make politically embarrassing agreements with a government that might not
exist six months hence, so long as that delay did not prompt
another Nazi-Soviet deal. Hopkins's Moscow trip provided the assurances FDR needed—the Russians would fight, not parley—
which meant that Stalin would not get the guarantees he wanted,
at least not in 1941. Stalin, ever practical, told Molotov to drop
the demand for Western recognition of the 1941 frontiers with the
comment that force, not treaties, would decide such matters.[22]

Hopkins had also gone to London to work on arrangements for
getting his two "prima donnas" together for their initial conference, the first in a series of summit meetings that were materially
to shape the progress of the war and the peace that followed.[23]
Both Churchill and Roosevelt had mused frequently about the
benefits of a face-to-face meeting, and Hopkins had tried to set
one up when he visited London in January 1941. Lend-lease and
the British military crisis in the spring had pushed the meeting
back, but during his second visit in July the three spoke by telephone and arranged an August meeting.

Hopkins returned from Russia just in time to clamber aboard the ill-fated battleship *Prince of Wales*, taking Churchill and his party to meet Roosevelt aboard warships anchored in Placentia Bay, Newfoundland, within sight of Argentia, one of the sites leased to the Americans in the destroyer-bases deal. Roosevelt had proceeded in great secrecy aboard the cruiser USS *Augusta*, after arranging for a double to sail on the presidential yacht *Potomac* along the Cape Cod Canal in plain sight, deceiving news cameras and reporters.

Both Churchill and Roosevelt later testified to their own personal and emotional reactions to their meeting. That was not unusual for the Englishman, all of whose biographers point to his tendency to romanticize. He was, after all, someone who quoted poets to express his own deep hopes for a true alliance with the United States, as he did in April 1941:

> For while the tired waves, vainly breaking,
> Seem here no painful inch to gain,
> Far back, through creeks and inlets making,
> Comes silent, flooding in, the main.

> And not by eastern windows only,
> When daylight comes, comes in the light;
> In front the sun climbs slow, how slowly!
> But westward, look, the land is bright!

Roosevelt's easy affability provided effective cover for his honest feelings, but he too could resort to poets to verbalize his hopes, as he had in January 1941, when he scrawled a stanza from Longfellow and asked Wendell Willkie to give it to Churchill:

> Sail on, Oh Ship of State!
> Sail on, Oh Union strong and great.
> Humanity with all its fears
> With all the hope of future years
> Is hanging breathless on thy fate.[24]

Fittingly Churchill brought to Newfoundland two illuminated copies of the Longfellow verse to be signed—one for himself and one
for the president.

That personal relationship, however "official" it always remained, was the most important result of the conference. A joint
church service on Sunday aboard the *Prince of Wales*, carefully re-
hearsed by the British, provided, in Churchill's phrasing, "a deeply
moving expression of the unity of faith of our two peoples." FDR,
more tersely, called it the "keynote" for the conference. On August 12, even as the two leaders debated the wording of what was
to be called the Atlantic Charter, Churchill cabled Clement Attlee,
head of the Labour party and a member of the War Cabinet as
lord privy seal: "I am sure I have established warm and deep personal relations with our great friend." Churchill was right, despite
his failure to recall his earlier meeting with FDR.[25]

Whatever their faith in God, Roosevelt and Churchill were there
for more than prayer. The issues they faced fell into two broad
categories: the war and the postwar world. Roosevelt had told
Hopkins before his London trip not to discuss American participation in the war, an instruction that reflected the president's dogged refusal to consider anything beyond U.S. naval and air
involvement.[26] But the Battle of the Atlantic remained critical, and
that meant confronting the issue of U.S. warships escorting vessels
carrying lend-lease, a problem bound to intensify as the Arsenal of
Democracy extended aid to the Soviet Union. Moreover, escorting
was an issue that revived memories of events that had brought
America into the First World War. But the shipping situation could
not be ignored.

The British had experienced some success against German submarines in the Atlantic following the deciphering of the German
submarine command code (offset slightly by German breaking of
the British merchant shipping codes). The British achievement
came from hard work and the lucky capture of the *U-110* in May
1941, complete with the ship's code books and an Enigma type of
cipher machine.[27] But that was not enough. At the Atlantic Conference naval staff officers from both countries quickly worked out
arrangements for the Americans to provide escort cover for all ship-

ping, not just their own, as far as Iceland (now "defended" by the United States). FDR gave his approval, and the order took effect on September 16, signaling the start of undeclared war with Germany. As one historian put it, "U-boat commanders would find it impossible to distinguish between the national origins of threatening warships. On some dark, foggy night, a German torpedo would smash into an American destroyer's hull. The British understandably looked forward to such an occurrence."[28]

The "keynote" of the Atlantic Conference may have been the cementing of the Churchill-Roosevelt relationship, but the meeting accomplished much more. The two leaders insisted that their military chiefs "work it out" and not bring every little dispute to the top, a directive that created an atmosphere of teamwork that lasted throughout the war. British and American staffs could and did argue and disagree, but only broad issues of grand strategy were expected to require decisions by Churchill and/or Roosevelt.

The key substantive issue for Roosevelt was a statement on broad, general postwar aims, the Atlantic Charter (so named by a London newspaper[29]). What FDR intended was a preemptive statement about the fundamental issues that had caused Wilson's postwar settlement to founder. But he would avoid Wilson's mistake of failing to obtain Great Power agreement *before* the peace conference that would follow the war. No accident, then, that FDR "suggested" that Churchill draft such a statement; why not start with principles the British could accept? No accident, either, that Roosevelt and his advisers spent a great deal of time revising that British draft. No accident as well that the Atlantic Charter was sent to Stalin for his comments. The president had repeatedly professed a desire to postpone such discussions of postwar arrangements, but it was he who tried to take the high ground by initiating just such talks. Whatever Churchill's input, the charter was a classic statement of American liberalism; Americanism would be the appropriate label.[30]

The charter's eight paragraphs fell into four broad categories. *Basic freedoms* were offered as goals. Freedom from want and freedom from fear were specifically mentioned. Freedom of worship and freedom of speech/information, mentioned in FDR's earlier

Four Freedoms address, were soon added; FDR said they were implied all along.[31] A commitment to a *postwar international "system"* was kept vague, despite Churchill's efforts to strengthen it. FDR not only feared the reaction of his domestic enemies, the isolationists, but believed Great Power collaboration had to take precedence.

The other two elements, *self-determination* and *economic liberalism*, posed greater problems for the British and the Soviets. The phrase "self-determination" became shorthand for the pledge that territorial changes required "the freely expressed wishes of the peoples concerned," along with "the right of all peoples to choose the[ir] form of government." In each instance democratic choice was part of the process. For FDR, that included European colonies. Churchill, his attention focused on getting the Americans into the war, had assumed that self-determination referred to nations under Hitler's yoke. But he quickly exempted the British Empire, even if Attlee said the charter applied to "coloured peoples, as well as white." Stalin, recognizing the threat that self-determination posed to his territorial aspirations, likewise excluded the Soviet Union.[32] The president was reluctant to let go so easily, but self-determination raised issues that could not be reconciled with Great Power harmony. Roosevelt was perilously close to creating the kind of credibility gap with the public that Woodrow Wilson had faced when professed ideals and the realities of Great Power relations proved so different. FDR was to raise the issue of self-determination for European empires consistently throughout the war, and he scrambled for ways to make Soviet claims in Eastern Europe palatable to the public, but in each case preserving Great Power collaboration came first.

Finally, and to the annoyance of the British, the charter referred to *economic liberalism*—promises to seek freedom of the seas, international economic cooperation, and "access, on equal terms, to the trade and the raw materials of the world." During the discussions the British managed to get the Americans to take out phrases that called for the elimination of discriminatory trade restrictions. But that only postponed the issue.

A few months before Churchill and Roosevelt met in Placentia

Bay, the brilliant British economist John Maynard Keynes had come across the Atlantic to negotiate a master agreement governing how Britain's lend-lease accounts would be settled. U.S. Treasury officials argued for simple, straightforward trade-offs; for example, American defense information would be paid for by raw materials. Hull and the State Department opposed any sort of accounting that could curtail Britain's ability to buy American goods after the war. Moreover, the secretary of state and his economic liberals had bigger fish to fry. In return for cancellations of the bulk of Britain's lend-lease debt, London would have to drop its preferential ("discriminatory" was the loaded American word) trade system within the empire—imperial preference (the Ottawa agreements). "The lunatic proposals of Mr. Hull," as one British official called them, were a by-product of the secretary's dogged fixation on reciprocal trade agreements as the road to international peace.[33]

Later, at the Atlantic Conference talks, Churchill hit the Achilles' heel of economic liberalism as practiced by the United States, despite American preachments. During discussions about phrasing that called for access to trade and raw materials "without discrimination," the prime minister complained, with a good deal of accuracy, that British trade concessions to the Americans over the past eighty years had gotten "in reciprocation only successive doses of American Protection."[34]

The Americans, accustomed to careful deference and fulsome praise for their benevolence and altruism, brushed away any suggestion by the British that lowering trade barriers and moving toward "free trade" was a two-way street. Hull and his allies in the State Department knew who the sinner was, and eliminating imperial preference had become a neoreligious quest. The specific issue, negotiation of a master lend-lease agreement, was not resolved until 1942, when State Department persistence, with firm support from FDR, brought Keynes and British politicians to conclude that postwar cooperation with the United States was far more important than the largely symbolic benefits of imperial preference. That agreement included a clause calling for "the elimination of all forms of discriminatory treatment in international commerce."

Churchill drafted a bitter message to Roosevelt in which he referred to Britain as "a client receiving help from a generous patron," softened that to "a combatant receiving help from a generous sympathiser," and then decided not to send the message directly to the president. As James Meade, a British economic adviser and later Nobel Prize winner, put it, "The Americans are obviously playing quite genuinely on the construction of a unilateral commercial convention."[35]

Churchill, perhaps making a silk purse out of that sow's ear, commented to Lord Halifax that freedom of trade would generate "a great increase in wealth," presumably including that of Britain.[36] But the broader issue was the curiously American belief (often masquerading as anticolonialism) that the way to peace and prosperity was unrestricted commercial access, what Americans historically called free trade or, in reverent tones during the 1980s and 1990s, the free market. It was an issue that would not be settled so quickly.

The British were willing to ignore points in the charter that later proved embarrassing because they put agreement with Americans as the highest priority. Sir Alexander Cadogan, permanent undersecretary in the Foreign Office, later responded to complaints about the charter by asking if those who were upset had "reflected that it [the charter] had its genesis in an offer by the President? And at that time a joint declaration of any kind went beyond our wildest dreams?"[37]

Another of Churchill's "dreams" was further ensnaring the United States in a web of connections and commitments that would ultimately bring the Americans into the war. The prime minister returned to London from Newfoundland to a Cabinet, Parliament, and public that expected news of an American declaration of war—or at least something close to that. He had written his queen before the meeting that FDR would not have asked for such a meeting "unless he had in mind some further forward step."[38] But the president obeyed his own instruction to Hopkins—"No talk about war"—forcing Churchill to present the Cabinet with what he called his "*impression* of the President's attitude." FDR "was obviously determined," concluded the prime minister, that the United States should enter the war, but as the close vote on the extension of the draft demonstrated, the president had to be careful. Churchill described Roosevelt as saying "he would wage war, but not declare it, and that he would become more and more provocative." The prime minister went on to explain that they had worked out the details of an escorting system and that Roosevelt had ordered the U.S. Navy to attack German submarines on sight, thus forcing, in the president's word, an "incident."[39]

Churchill, pressured to meet the high expectations of the British War Cabinet, had read more into Roosevelt's comments than the president intended. Presidential speechwriter Robert Sherwood later wrote that the British assumed that Churchill had obtained some secret assurances during the Atlantic Conference in August 1941, and "it is improbable that Churchill did much to discourage this hopeful assumption." As one British participant later remarked, "We wished to God there *had* been!"[40]

The U.S. Navy did not issue a shoot-on-sight order. But American naval policy in the Atlantic did become increasingly belligerent, and FDR's references to an "incident" suggest he was thinking about what had happened in World War I, when such events as the sinking of the *Lusitania* and the German declaration of unrestricted submarine warfare had brought the United States into the conflict. Hitler, who also remembered, had already ordered his U-boat commanders to avoid any incidents with the Americans.

When an incident did occur—a submarine attack on the destroyer USS *Greer* on September 4—FDR made no call for escalation or even retaliation (nor did he explain that the American ship had been trailing the submarine for hours, providing tracking data for British patrol planes). Instead he used it to edge another step closer to Britain by authorizing American warships to escort foreign shipping between the United States and Iceland.

When Harry Hopkins, just returned from Moscow, opened a tub of Russian caviar while he and Churchill were sailing toward Newfoundland, the prime minister expressed pleasure at getting such a treat, "even though it meant fighting with the Russians to get it." The immediate effect of the German-Soviet war was as ambiguous as Churchill's comment. Not only did the British regret, even resent the loss of any American supplies, but they also worried that the Americans would enter so late that Britain would be too devastated to recover, whatever the benefits the Red Army might bring in the long run. Churchill, feeling a good deal less confident than he let on before the War Cabinet, wrote his son, Randolph, shortly after the Atlantic Conference, "[O]ne is deeply perplexed to know how the deadlock is to be broken and the United States brought boldly and honourably into the war. There is a dangerous feeling in America that they need not worry now as all will be well."[41]

The German-Soviet war certainly gave Roosevelt some breathing space and even heightened his increasingly wishful hope that the United States could avoid all-out participation in the war. But that could go too far. The anti-interventionist group America First issued a press release arguing that Hitler could not invade the Western Hemisphere as long as Britain survived, and any invasion of Britain was indefinitely postponed by the war in Russia. The "defense" of America for FDR meant victory over Hitler, while anti-interventionists spoke only of preventing a German attack on the United States.[42]

The context for Roosevelt's caution was the debate in Congress over the extension of the Selective Service Act, the draft. Presidential advisers like Stimson, Knox, Morgenthau, and Ickes encouraged FDR to act boldly, to confront the anti-interventionists and move toward the direct involvement those advisers thought necessary. But "FDR's political antennae were more sensitively tuned than theirs were." The extension of the draft, with its implications of American soldiers fighting overseas in Europe, passed the House of Representatives on August 12, the final day of the Atlantic Conference, by a single vote, 203–202.[43]

Hindsight suggests that the vote was not indicative of national sentiment. Perhaps Roosevelt could and should have moved more decisively and openly toward American entry into the war. But in 1941 there was no emotional issue as there had been in 1917—no open submarine warfare on neutral American merchant ships or a Zimmermann Telegram implying a German-Mexican alliance against the United States. Those events had so inflamed Americans that Wilson felt pressured enough by events, the public, and Congress to ask for a declaration of war, which passed by overwhelming margins in both houses. That was not the case in 1941. Even if FDR had wanted U.S. entry into the conflict, as Churchill claimed the president had said at the Atlantic Conference, a Congress that only narrowly passed an extension of the draft would not have approved a declaration of war. This was not a case of FDR's being cowed by a misreading of public opinion or of a president's being "unwilling to confront the risks that accompany aggressive leadership."[44] Nor was it the maneuverings of someone who thought the United States could limit its involvement to naval and air forces. It was just plain political common sense.

Churchill's other entanglement ploy was far more hazardous. Japanese-American relations had seemingly reached a dangerous stalemate. The Roosevelt administration had concluded, wrongly, as it turned out, that the Japanese were too "smart" to risk war with the United States, a nation with vastly greater resources. "Notorious bluffers" was Stimson's assessment, while Stanley K. Hornbeck, the primary architect of the hard-line American policy, defied his State Department colleagues to find "one case in history when a nation went to war out of desperation." Moreover, the Americans believed that their new superweapon, the B-17 Flying Fortress bombers being sent to the Philippines, would deter Japan from any hasty military action. Then there was the powerful American fleet, stationed at Pearl Harbor, Hawaii.[45] The Japanese, with equal wrongheadedness, concluded that American interests and commitments in East Asia were not intense enough to support a war in that part of the world. Hitler's victories, concluded Tokyo, would continue to divert American and European attention and military forces away from the Pacific. Those miscalculations were a recipe for trouble—and the basis for Churchill's gamble.

Britain, already stretched to the breaking point, did not want a war in East Asia. Its forces would have to be transferred to the Pacific area, and Australia and New Zealand might well demand the recall of their troops from the North African campaign. Moreover, war with Japan would complicate relations with restive nationalist movements in India and Southeast Asia—particularly with the Japanese claiming they were defending Asians against the racist imperialism of Europe. (Admiral William Leahy, Roosevelt's ambassador to the Vichy French, upon hearing of that government's surrender of sovereignty to Japan in Indochina, noted in his diary: "Here endeth the French colonies in Asia."[46])

Yet Churchill was tempted to use the Pacific to snare the Americans in an ever-tighter alliance. His romanticized image of the fortress-port of Singapore—an image that came back to haunt him—provided something concrete to offer Roosevelt. Time and again Churchill had welcomed American naval forces to make use of the "impregnable" port. Time and again Roosevelt had indicated he intended to leave the fleet at Pearl Harbor in the Hawaiian Islands, close enough to "deter" the Japanese without being provocative.[47]

By the time of the Argentia meeting Churchill had bought in to the American hard-line strategy and advocated sending the Japanese a harsh, unequivocal warning. Japan had taken advantage of the German attack on the Soviet Union to occupy southern Indochina, and Churchill wanted to warn Tokyo that further movement toward British and Dutch colonies in Southeast Asia could be considered an act of war. Only tortured logic could conclude that Churchill hoped to drag the United States into the European conflict via the "back door" of a Pacific war. Even though he could not anticipate the shock of the Pearl Harbor attack, the prime minister understood that Roosevelt's commitment to dealing with Germany first was only as firm as American willingness to follow that strategy. War in the Pacific could not only drain British and British Empire military assets and threaten access to critical natural resources in Southeast Asia, but also fatally distract the United States.

Roosevelt and Welles were tempted to go along with the stern warning approach, but the secretary of state adamantly opposed any ultimatum. Hull's reasoning was, as ever, opaque. He argued that he did not want to cut off any opportunity for negotiations, yet he had supported the hard-line strategy. Perhaps his reaction came from petty jealousy; he had been excluded from the Atlantic Conference while his rival, Sumner Welles, had sat at the president's elbow.[48] Perhaps his desire to avoid war was sincere, although a few months later he washed his hands of attempts to negotiate. Perhaps, with his political ambitions on hold following Roosevelt's decision for a third term, Hull sought to insulate himself against any subsequent accusation that he had led the nation into war—plausible deniability, in the phrase of later American leaders. In any event, Roosevelt—himself ambivalent about what policy to pursue, advised by his military to give the nation more time to prepare for war, and worried about anti-interventionist criticism—deferred to Hull's wishes. The message that went to Tokyo via the Japanese ambassador was as vague and convoluted as was Roosevelt's explanation to Churchill.[49]

Early in July 1941, as the initial German surge rolled over Soviet defenses, the Japanese leadership, dominated by the military, met to determine how to respond to the new geopolitical situation. The initial Japanese temptation was to ignore their neutrality pact with the Soviet Union, signed on April 13, 1941, and to take advantage of the war in Russia and move into eastern Siberia, an area they had long considered a legitimate target for expansion.

But Japanese leaders, as eager as the Soviets to avoid a two-front war, concluded that Siberia should come later. The steady enlargement of U.S. trade embargoes on the sale of strategic materials focused Japanese attention on Southeast Asia. Those expanded embargoes were due in large part to rearmament efforts in the United States. But the steady tightening of such restrictions within the tense political climate of the Tripartite Pact and the war in China lent credence to the Japanese military's insistence that its ability to wage war and hence Japan's security required control of the land and resources that lay to the south—in the jungles of Indochina, Malaya, and the Netherlands East Indies (today's Indonesia). Once Southeast Asia came within the Japanese Empire, the pretentious-sounding Greater East Asian Co-Prosperity Sphere became very real. India, Australia, and eventually Siberia all lay within reach.

American intelligence decrypts of Magic intercepts revealed the Japanese decision to move into southern Indochina, made at an imperial conference on July 2, leaving American policy makers convinced that an attack on Malaya and the Dutch East Indies was imminent. No one in Washington, then or for the next six months, thought seriously about a Japanese attack on the United States—in the Philippines or elsewhere. Roosevelt's response to the occupation of southern Indochina—an embargo on high-octane petroleum and the freezing of Japanese assets, which virtually cut off trade—followed the Japanese decision to expand into Southeast Asia, a decision that guaranteed war unless the militarists in Tokyo were willing to back off.[50]

That decision came because Germany seemed to have presented Japan with an opportunity to win its objectives without winning a war, perhaps without even having to fight much more than a skirmish! Britain, and particularly its fleet, were distracted by the war in the Mediterranean and the Battle of the Atlantic. The Soviet Union, defending itself against the full power of the German Army, had become more a potential target for Japanese expansion than a potential restraining force. China—decentralized, lacking modern industry, and weakened by ongoing civil conflict among traditional warlords and between Chiang Kai-shek's Nationalists (Kuomintang) and Mao Tse-tung's Communists—seemed unable to withstand Japan's demands for economic concessions and political security without outside help. Only the Americans stood in the way, and they were focused on Europe and the German threat. What better time for Japan to force a confrontation? The Americans' hearts, minds, and military, fixed on the German menace, would quickly lose interest in a long, arduous struggle fought in Asia, some ten thousand miles from California, a struggle that offered the Americans little reward for victory. If at the outset that struggle seemed long, costly, and difficult, the Americans would be even more inclined to negotiate.

Roosevelt and Hull knew none of that when, after the Atlantic Conference, they toned down the warning that Churchill had intended to deter Japan. But that statement, toned down or not, had little to do with the coming of the Pacific war. The decision for war would be made by the Japanese, whether or not the United States might or might not negotiate. Whether the statement was the near ultimatum that Churchill wished or the ambiguous declaration that Hull successfully insisted on, it could have no effect on the outcome.[51]

The secret Japanese decision in September to wage war as soon as possible on the United States, preferably within a month (subsequently extended to late November), came because the military depended completely on imported oil, most of it from the United States and Southeast Asia. If Japan waited too long, it would not have the fuel reserves its aircraft and warships needed to operate. Oil did not cause the Japanese-American confrontation. That was the product of a half century of growing economic and political tensions and the vast cultural disconnect between the Japanese and the Americans that had worked against the kind of accommodation the United States had reached with the European powers.[52]

Nor did oil cause the war that was about to erupt. Japan had embarked on a war of conquest and expansion during the 1930s, and the United States found that a threat to its interests and sensibilities. However much Tokyo argued that its expansion was merely doing what the "Europeans" (including the Americans) had done decades earlier, its resort to naked military force violated what Americans considered the norms of acceptable international conduct. More important, Japan had made the overtly hostile move of joining the Tripartite Pact. The story of Japanese-American relations from the Atlantic Conference to Pearl Harbor was not about diplomatic failure; that had come earlier. It was merely a countdown to war. By autumn 1941 the Japanese were interested not in negotiations but only in concessions, while the Americans, even as they began to assume the inevitability of war in the Pacific, found it difficult to take a Japanese military threat seriously. Moreover, Washington officials drew an analogy between the Munich Conference deals and Japan's demands, concluding that concessions only encouraged expansionists to ask for more.

More crucial to the outcome of the Second World War were events in Russia. As the crisis mounted there, with German armies advancing steadily on Moscow and the Finns and Romanians seizing what seemed an opportunity to regain territory, Stalin resorted to the same pressure tactics Churchill had used so well in the summer of 1940. The Soviet leader asked for aid—supplies and "a second front this year somewhere in the Balkans or in France"—and then, like his British counterpart, laid out a worst-case scenario. For Churchill in 1940 that had been the British fleet falling into the hands of the Germans. For Stalin in 1941 the threat was that "without these two kinds of aid the Soviet Union will be either defeated or weakened to the extent that it will lose for a long time the ability to help its Allies . . . against Hitlerism."[53] Churchill had been even more blunt, threatening a new British government that would sue for peace, but the message was fundamentally the same.

Roosevelt, while en route to Washington after the Atlantic Conference, had received a report based on a "reliable source" of German-Soviet negotiations. The message was delivered by one Adlai Stevenson, a young special assistant to the secretary of the navy. "I don't believe it," the president commented. "I'm not worried at all. Are you worried, Adlai?" Stevenson, the future Democratic party presidential candidate in 1952 and 1956, mumbled agreement and departed.[54] However wishful Roosevelt's remark, his commitment to support the Russians was evident.

But that commitment required more than words. Lend-lease was the logical answer, but FDR was not quite ready to face the firestorm that would ensue. The virulent anticapitalist, antireligion, antibourgeois rhetoric of the Bolsheviks, added to the Nazi-Soviet Pact and the Russo-Finnish War, made Americans leery of alliance with the USSR. Instead Roosevelt ordered the secretaries of war and the navy, Stimson and Knox, to treat aid to Russia as "of paramount importance for the safety and security of America." The military remained reluctant to comply. When Stimson passed on army objections to the transfer of aircraft with the comment that the planes were needed to train pilots in Texas, Roosevelt's emissary, Wayne Coy, shot back that the war was not being fought in Texas. Stimson gave in, but the scene repeated itself in various forms.

Washington was not the only place where aid problems existed. With American defense production only beginning to develop, supplies were limited. Not only did the U.S. military jealously guard its share, but so did the British. General Marshall complained that the Soviets would "take everything we own" if they could and contended that additional aid for Russia had to come from British allocations. To deal with the crucial issue of the politics of priorities, Roosevelt and Churchill had agreed at the Atlantic Conference to ask Stalin if they could send representatives to Moscow to discuss Soviet supply requirements within the context of Anglo-American requirements. Moreover, thought Hopkins, such talks might force the British to do more than just promise aid to Russia.

The Soviet leader quickly agreed. Roosevelt sent pro–New Deal businessman W. Averell Harriman, who had been in Britain as Roosevelt's lend-lease administrator. Harriman had during the 1920s met Leon Trotsky and tried to set up business ventures in the Soviet Union. Churchill dispatched his confidant and political ally Lord Beaverbook (Max Aitken), who staunchly advocated unconditional aid to the Russians.

Those talks were a milestone in the Soviet Union's relations with the Anglo-Americans. Beaverbrook and Harriman were met with national anthems and the unique sight of the American and British flags flying in their honor. Stalin's requests were extensive and often impossible to meet, nor were the Anglo-Americans willing to share military technology (the Americans had not even given the Norden bombsight to the British), but when the conference ended, the Soviet leader did not "conceal his enthusiasm." Beaverbrook, despite Churchill's warning to ensure that aid to Russia come from American stocks lest Britain be "bled white in the process," pushed hard for aid without strings. Harriman, following Roosevelt's lead, went along.

From the inception of the aid to Russia program, Roosevelt used it for more than just military purposes. It would be two years before he had to confront the reality of Soviet power in the postwar world, but FDR instinctively recognized from the outset that a Soviet Union that survived Hitler's onslaught would be a key actor in both the war and the peace. The president promised not only aid but also legitimacy for Stalin's regime. That fitted neatly with Roosevelt's earlier actions and statements. He had extended recognition to the Soviet Union, had predicted the short life of the

Nazi-Soviet Pact, had avoided any break in diplomatic relations over the Soviet invasion of Finland, and had generally restricted his comments to phrases that would not antagonize the Kremlin. Far from being a prisoner of congressional and public opinion, FDR moved quickly to send aid to Russia, then chose his time carefully to announce the extension of lend-lease to the Soviets. Roosevelt's wartime policy of making civilized Soviets out of belligerent Bolsheviks, his effort to create a cooperative relationship that would continue into the postwar period began with the aid to Russia program.

For Churchill, aid to Russia was a way to fight Hitler—little more. The prime minister, who drew no fine distinctions between empires, rarely referred to the Soviet Union. With the perspective of a long Anglo-Russian history of mutual suspicion from a distance, he spoke of Russians when the issues were geopolitical and of Bolsheviks or Communists when ideology lay at the root of an issue. He spent the entire war without reconciling those two ways of viewing the Soviet Union, and he never answered—for himself or anyone else—whether geopolitical accommodation could or should be reached with an ideological foe.

Stalin, whatever his satisfaction with the Beaverbrook-Harriman mission, surely put the immediate survival of his regime ahead of all else. There are stories of an offer to Hitler of a settlement in November 1941, when Moscow seemed about to fall, although Soviet archives have not yielded any proof for such rumors. Nor did Stalin have any reason to believe he and his regime would survive such a deal, given Hitler's betrayal in June 1941.[55] Gratitude has little place in international relations. Within a month Stalin was to return to his political agenda, asking the British to agree to Soviet incorporation of the Baltic states. But the image of Roosevelt as someone who tried to create a better Soviet-American relationship, a depiction that appeared in the pages of all the official Soviet histories of World War II, got its start with the aid to Russia program.

By autumn 1941 Roosevelt was again a man with a conception but without a plan. He wanted Hitler to lose. He wanted the

United States to play an appropriate role in that loss and to be a major player in the restructuring of the postwar world. But he did not want to join the war against Hitler in the full, participatory sense—with American ground forces used to the fullest. Nor did he want to fight the Japanese. What he wanted was to gain victory and global political influence without paying the price. He had followed that course since 1939, and there is every indication he would have continued that ambivalence until events overtook the policy. Britain had survived, even if things looked bleak in the Western Desert of North Africa. The Battle of the Atlantic was going reasonably well (though that soon changed for the worse). Would the success of the Red Army outside Moscow have prompted Roosevelt to ask for a declaration of war, or would the increased chance that the Soviets could survive have made him even more reluctant to take such a step? The latter seems more likely, particularly since his advisers were telling him that the Red Army, not the American Army, was the instrument of defeat for Germany.

Perhaps, in the quiet of his mind, Roosevelt thought back to the First World War and the way in which American troops came in at the crucial moment and tipped the balance, gaining maximum leverage at minimal expense. Could that balance point again surface some twenty-five years later? As for the Japanese, he seems to have been convinced that a smaller, less developed nation that was imitating the Europeans would not be so stupid as to take on the United States. He worried that Japan might bypass the line in the water he had drawn at the Philippines, but that was concern over a Japanese conquest of British and Dutch resources—natural and military—in Southeast Asia, not a desire to go to all-out war. Nor is there any reasonable or even suggestive *evidence* that FDR viewed a war with Japan as a "back door" to war with Hitler. ABC-1 and Plan Dog were common sense, not self-fulfilling prophecies. (There were, after all, contingency plans developed during the 1920s in Britain and the United States for armed conflict against each other. That is what military planners do in their spare time.)

During the last half of October Roosevelt tried to move the United States toward a more active anti-German position. On October 17 the destroyer USS *Kearny* had to limp back to port after being struck by a torpedo. The president announced that "history has recorded who fired the first shot," without mentioning that the *Kearny* had been helping British corvettes escort a convoy near Iceland. Ten days later Roosevelt, apparently duped by fraudulent documents provided by British intelligence, told a Navy Day audience at the Hotel Mayflower that he had proof that the Nazis intended to conquer Latin America and eliminate religion. Then, on October 31, a German submarine sank the USS *Reuben James*, with the loss of more than one hundred lives, while the destroyer was escorting a North Atlantic convoy. The attack took place at daybreak, so the German submarine commander probably knew he was firing at an American ship. The events of October evoked only a mild reaction from the American press and public, leaving FDR little choice but to do what came naturally: wait. He managed to get the existing neutrality legislation, already emasculated, revised to allow American merchant ships to sail into war zones and to be armed, but by a margin of only 50–37 in the Senate.[56]

Churchill, on the other hand, knew what he wanted. "Better she [the United States] come in now and give us no supplies for six months than stay out and double her supplies," he told a dinner party that included the American ambassador, John Winant. When the ambassador predicted American entry into the war by March 1942, the prime minister seemed disappointed it would take so long. That disgruntlement only deepened when a British offensive in Libya ground to an inconclusive halt in late November, although the British held Tobruk while General Rommel suffered irreplaceable losses in tanks and equipment.[57]

Amid the gloom created by uncertainty on the Russian front, by German occupation of most of Europe, by the stalemate in North Africa, and by the deteriorating situation in the Pacific, there was no reason to imagine that what seemed a small footnote in the 1941 Churchill-Roosevelt correspondence would develop into a force that seemed to have potential for geopolitical leverage beyond their wildest dreams. On October 11 the president proposed, in a letter addressed "Dear Winston," that they "correspond or converse concerning the subject which is under study by your MAUD committee. . . ." Churchill quickly agreed. The subject "under study" was the atomic bomb.[58] But before that weapon could make its dark appearance over Nagasaki and Hiroshima, a war had to begin and be fought.

Which way do we go from here, Franklin?

CHAPTER 5

"It Is Fun to Be in the Same Decade with You" December 1941–July 1942

In the parochial view of many Americans, the Second World War began only when the United States entered the conflict in December 1941, two years and three months after Great Britain had declared war on Germany and nearly six months after Hitler had attacked the Soviet Union. Roosevelt seemed committed to some sort of involvement in the war against Hitler but could not figure out how to pull the trigger. No one planned that Japan should bring the United States into the European war, but that was what happened.

By mid-November 1941 Roosevelt and his advisers had become resigned to Japan's refusal to back down. Even preliminary discussions were impossible from the American point of view unless the Japanese agreed to withdraw from southern Indochina. A temporary working agreement, what diplomats call a modus vivendi, offered by the Japanese on November 20, brought a moment of hope, but six days later that bubble burst when Magic (decrypts of Japanese radio messages) revealed the dispatch of additional Japanese troops to Southeast Asia and, a few days later, the deadline Japan had set for action unless the Americans made vast concessions. What Tokyo required—acceptance of its occupation of Indochina, guaranteed access to Southeast Asian resources, and recognition of its "special" position in China—not only amounted to an American diplomatic surrender but, with the Tripartite Pact in the background, constituted a threat to the effort against Hitler. The American military was ill prepared for a war in the Pacific, but it made no sense to buy time by giving away the very things the United States was going to fight about.

Roosevelt and his Cabinet toyed with various counterproposals but ended up speculating about a surprise attack by Japan and worrying not about preserving peace but about "how we should maneuver them into the position of firing the first shot without allowing too much danger to ourselves." As Hull told Henry Stimson, the secretary of war, "it is now in the hands of you and Knox—the Army and the Navy." A flamboyant proposal written by Treasury Department official Harry Dexter White called for a mutual withdrawal: The United States would focus on Europe and normalize trade with Japan; the Japanese would pull out of China and play a peaceful role in East Asia. But that flew in the face of history and required a degree of mutual trust that had long since vanished. Even with revisions, the plan never stood a chance of being offered to Tokyo.[1]

Both Churchill and China's leader Chiang Kai-shek looked askance at the modus vivendi. Chiang, fearing he would be deserted, protested vigorously in a message to Roosevelt that the British ambassador to China, Clark Kerr, claimed to have written. Churchill, worried that withdrawing full American support might prompt the Chinese to embrace the pan-Asianism preached by Japan, wondered, in a message to FDR, if Chiang was not being put on "a very thin diet."[2] The prime minister also remained concerned that a Japanese attack into Southeast Asia might bypass the Philippines and not bring the United States into the war. British policy therefore was to delay any confrontation without encouraging the Japanese to think they could expand with impunity. All the while Churchill worked to get the Americans into the war. He had repeatedly promised that a Japanese attack on the United States would bring British military support. He never spoke of the Pacific as a "back door" to war, but his policies indicated that he thought of it.[3]

But Britain did not bring the United States into war with Japan, nor was Churchill's concern about Chiang Kai-shek's "thin diet"—lack of political support—what stiffened the Americans' resolve when the modus vivendi made its appearance. Throughout November Roosevelt had looked for ways to "baby Japan along" since he didn't have "enough Navy to go around." Stimson and Knox argued for firmness, but the president persisted in his search for some way to delay what seemed increasingly inevitable. As late as December 6 he rejected requests for a strong warning to Tokyo because he had not received an answer to his direct appeal to the emperor for a cooling-off period.[4]

But Japanese intransigence and information provided by Magic decrypts forced FDR to conclude there was no benefit in waiting. Any U.S. counterproposal required Japanese withdrawal from southern Indochina and a three-month waiting period, during which time Japan and the United States *might* initiate talks, all of which served only the interests of the Americans. Such proposals would gain the United States time to prepare without fully opening the petroleum spigot and allowing the Japanese to build up oil reserves. The countdown to war moved ahead regardless of whatever Churchill did.[5]

On December 1 Roosevelt casually commented to Ambassador Halifax that if Japan attacked Malaya or the Dutch East Indies, Britain could count on American support, although it would "take a short time" to take care of the politics. Two days later Halifax followed instructions and asked the president if that meant "armed support." Yes, Roosevelt replied, although he could not predict if Congress would go along. FDR was a master of misdirection who routinely let his listeners think he had agreed with them when in reality he was only indicating that he had understood what they said. But Halifax was no fool, and his reports of Roosevelt's comment on December 3 indicated that the ambassador believed he had gotten a firm commitment. Still, Churchill's assessment to the War Cabinet was worded cautiously. He had "every confidence," he said, that the Americans would aid the Dutch if they were attacked. No British record claims that FDR uttered the simple key words: I will ask for a declaration of war on Japan if it invades British or Dutch colonies.[6]

Nor would the deterrent measures Churchill continued to recommend have been of any use. All the while he and Roosevelt fretted, a Japanese strike force of six aircraft carriers, two battleships, two cruisers, plus destroyers and support ships, was steaming east across the North Pacific. The ships had begun leaving Kure on the Inland Sea on November 10, even before the Japanese offered their modus vivendi. The warships rendezvoused in the Kurile Islands north of Japan's main islands, then, with even the facade of diplomacy destroyed, set out on November 26 for Hawaii. The fleet's movements were masked by a combination of radio silence, deceptive movement signals sent from other stations, and the accident of a weather front full of clouds and rain that moved eastward at the same speed as the strike force. On December 2 Rear Admiral Husband Kimmel, stationed in Pearl Harbor as commander in chief of the U.S. Pacific Fleet, told that his intelligence staff did not know the location of the Japanese carriers, responded sarcastically, "Do you mean to say they could be rounding Diamond Head and you wouldn't know it?" Little did he know how close he came to the truth.

The Army-Navy football game program for November 29, 1941, showed a picture of a battleship with the caption "A bow on view of the U.S.S. *Arizona* as she plows into a huge swell. It is significant that despite the claims of air enthusiasts no battleship has yet been sunk by bombs."[7] Eight days later the *Arizona* lay at the bottom of Pearl Harbor, sunk by bombs dropped from aircraft.

The Japanese air attack on Hawaii began at 7:49 on the morning of Sunday, December 7, 1941. The military goal was the destruction of the U.S. Pacific Fleet. Japanese bombers and torpedo planes sank six battleships and damaged two others. Three light cruisers, four destroyers, and four other ships were damaged or sunk. Some three hundred American military aircraft were damaged or destroyed, while casualties were about twenty-four hundred killed and nearly twelve hundred wounded. In just two hours the great battleships, the foundation of the U.S. Pacific Fleet and of American naval strategy, disappeared beneath the oily waters of Pearl Harbor.

With that disaster came two myths. One was the conspiracy myth, an emotional combining of partisan politics, innuendo, and ex post facto reasoning, all buttressed by FDR's congenital inability to be candid, and resulting in the thesis that Roosevelt (and perhaps Churchill) had set up the American fleet for destruction at Pearl Harbor to get into the European war by the "back door." That argument, which generated conspiracy books for the half century that followed, is unsupported by facts, ignores contrary evidence, and flies in the face of common sense. Magic provided political, not military, intelligence; no one in Washington knew the location or destination of the Japanese strike force, partly because American procedures for intelligence analysis were incredibly cumbersome and played to ridiculous rivalries between the army and the navy. Virtually every American military and political leader, including the army and navy commanders at Pearl Harbor, expected an attack, but they believed it would come in Southeast Asia— possibly in the Philippines, more likely in British Malaya. Most of all, Franklin Roosevelt—long caught up in his romanticized image of the navy—could never have sacrificed his beloved battleships.[8]

Moreover, hindsight misleads us into thinking the American victory in the war against Japan was, even in December 1941, a foregone conclusion. That was not at all the case. With Hitler controlling Europe and the Soviet Union on the verge of collapse, the Americans—military men and politicians—wondered if they could win such a vast two-front war. Why would the president want to start a long, hard struggle in the Pacific by allowing the destruction of the key element in his military strength? This was, after all, the man who referred to the navy as "we" and the army as "they," to General Marshall's dismay.[9]

The other Pearl Harbor myth is the one that makes the attack immoral, unethical, disgusting, evil, debased (use your thesaurus to add to the list). How is Pearl Harbor a "day that will live in infamy" any more than, say, Custer's Last Stand or other defeats in which Americans were caught by surprise? War is, by definition, the collapse of law and order, and the Americans fully expected war. Why should the Japanese be obliged to announce their attack?

FDR's self-righteous rhetoric aimed at mobilizing public opinion. It succeeded well—perhaps much too well or at least for too long. The uncomfortable question that arises is what effect did that

stab-in-the-back stereotype have on subsequent American decisions—in particular, on the internment of American citizens of Japanese descent and the eagerness of Truman to drop the bomb on
Japanese cities? Cordell Hull abdicated his role as diplomat when
he relegated the war to the army and the navy. But diplomacy
should not end with war; rather, war should be merely the beginning of renewed diplomacy. FDR's "day that will live in infamy"
label worked against that.

But that must be seen in the context of the Japanese Empire's
appalling record of brutality and oppression wherever it spread outside the home islands. Koreans, Manchurians, and Chinese all had
experienced the murderous practices of the Japanese military. Humiliation, harsh treatment, economic exploitation, and a rigid social structure that assumed Japanese ethnic and cultural superiority
characterized Tokyo's rule. Rape and forced labor were routine.
For the Japanese to present their conquests as beneficial "liberation" from the oppression of European colonialism was ludicrous,
as Filipinos, Malays, and Indonesians soon came to realize.

Churchill recalled that after hearing the news of the Japanese attack, he "went to bed and slept the sleep of the saved and thankful."[10]
The Pacific war fulfilled his sweetest dream—American entry into the
war—but the new war brought with it two threatening nightmares.
The first was the deep fear that American outrage over Pearl Harbor
would force Roosevelt to focus on fighting Japan, despite the Germany first agreements made at ABC-1 and echoed repeatedly by the
president. The second nightmare was all too real: the frightening ease
with which the Japanese attack in Southeast Asia overcame British and
American defenses, something that added to the danger that the
Americans would concentrate on the Pacific since those victories
made Japan seem a greater and more direct threat.

The prime minister learned of the Pearl Harbor attack via a radio
news broadcast and immediately telephoned Roosevelt at the
White House to verify the report. FDR assured him "we are all in
the same boat now," but Churchill was unconvinced. Perhaps it
was during that call that the anxious British leader proposed a
meeting. At any rate within twenty-four hours the prime minister
sent a message suggesting that he and a small group of advisers

could leave almost immediately and sail to Annapolis or Baltimore by warship. The purpose of the visit, Churchill told Roosevelt, was to "review the whole war plan," but the prime minister's real purpose was to ensure that the president stuck to Germany first.[11]

Churchill had good reason to fear the Americans might rethink their grand strategy. Before FDR amiably agreed to the meeting, he had twice considered sending a message that delayed any summit conference. The excuse was the need to gain a better understanding of where things stood in the Pacific. The reality was that Roosevelt and his advisers did not want to be influenced, or appear to be influenced, by the British. Appearances prompted FDR to ask, too late, that Churchill delay any declaration of war on Japan until after the president had made his war request to Congress. That ingrained combination of suspicion and concern about appearances characterized American reactions to British political and military initiatives throughout the war.[12]

Even if Roosevelt and his Cabinet remained committed to a Germany first strategy, the fact remained that the United States and Germany were not at war. Churchill predicted that Hitler and Mussolini would hold to their agreements with Japan and go to war with the Americans, but until that happened—if it happened—no one in the White House thought Congress would be willing to do anything except wreak revenge on Japan.[13]

Yet the president hesitated only briefly before beginning a public campaign to equate the European and Pacific conflicts. Hitler and Mussolini already "consider themselves at war with the United States," he told his listeners in a fireside chat on December 9. "Japanese successes against the United States in the Pacific are helpful to German operations in Libya; . . . German success against the Caucasus is inevitably an assistance to Japan. . . ."

On December 11, as the smoke still billowed from the remnants of the U.S. battle fleet sunk at Pearl Harbor, Adolf Hitler opened the way for Roosevelt to dispel Churchill's first nightmare. On that day the German dictator, speaking to his adoring Reichstag, declared war in the form of a personal attack on Roosevelt. He "is the main culprit of this war . . ." shouted Hitler. "I consider him mad," a rich elitist surrounded by Jews. Mussolini quickly followed suit. The Führer had chafed under the restrictions he had imposed on his U-boat commanders and relished the opportunity to take the fight to the Americans. Moreover, as his underlings later testified, "it would not befit the Master Race to sit and wait supinely. The Master Race must demonstrate its vigor and courage. . . ."[14]

But Hitler's declaration of war was not simply a gratuitous, impulsive move, as historians have often suggested. Although Nazi officials recognized the difficulty Roosevelt might have getting a declaration of war on Germany from Congress, Hitler also was convinced (rightly at the time) that the Americans were already doing all they could to aid the British. He overestimated Japan's strength and, like the Japanese, assumed the Americans would not want to conduct a two-front war. But the German leader drew the opposite conclusion from that of his Japanese ally. Hitler believed the United States would respond as he would have responded to the Pearl Harbor attack—with rage and fury. The day after Hitler's declaration of war, he rhetorically asked his navy chief, Admiral Erich Raeder, if the Americans might take a defensive posture in the Pacific and concentrate on Germany. Raeder's answer—he assured Hitler the United States would focus on the Japanese—was irrelevant; the question came too late. If the German leader knew of a report in the Chicago *Tribune* of December 4 that had summarized the ABC-1 agreements, he paid it no heed. He ignored a strategy proposal drawn up by his staff that would have delayed further offensives in Russia while Germany focused on preventing the United States from delivering men and equipment across the Atlantic. Perhaps Hitler recalled the empty promises of the German military in 1917, when they had assured the kaiser that U-boats would prevent American reinforcements from ever setting foot in France, but more likely he thought that a declaration of war on the United States was a low-risk way to live up to his commitment to the Japanese emperor.[15]

Even then FDR chose not to ask Congress for a declaration of war against Germany and Italy lest that precipitate an open debate about whether Europe or the Pacific should be the priority for American military efforts. Instead he merely requested that Congress recognize the state of war that already existed. Realizing that many America Firsters would revert to what many had been all along, "Asia firsters,"[16] Roosevelt acted as if there were nothing to debate. He was to continue that pose until American soldiers went into combat against German and Italian forces in North Africa, ten months later.

Churchill's only comment to Roosevelt about Hitler's declaration of war was indirect. "I am enormously relieved at turn world events have taken," he cabled the President from London on December 12.[17]

That comment certainly did not reflect the prime minister's assessment of the military situation on the other side of the world. The Pacific war actually began a few hours before the attack on Pearl Harbor when Imperial Japanese warships jumped the gun by bombarding Kota Bharu in northern Malaya (just south of the Thai border) prior to conducting a diversionary amphibious landing.[18] The Japanese went on to take most of Malaya in two weeks, then moved deeply into Burma. Hong Kong, helpless against Japanese armies moving in from China, fell immediately. That accomplished, the Japanese focused their attention on Singapore.

British planners had expected early losses to the Japanese offensive but, hoping to maintain access to the vital raw materials of the Dutch East Indies, envisaged setting up a successful defense perimeter based on British naval strength and what Churchill viewed as "Fortress Singapore." On December 10 that strategy collapsed along with what remained of the doctrine that great warships could control the seas. That morning Japanese aircraft sank two great British warships, the battleship *Prince of Wales* and the battle cruiser *Repulse*, which had just arrived from the Atlantic. The ships should have had air cover, but the aircraft carrier *Illustrious* had stayed in Ceylon for repairs. Then the force commander, Admiral Tom Phillips, unwisely chose to steam out of range of land-based aircraft. The elimination of British naval strength from the area left Singapore as the useless linchpin for a broken strategy.

Nor were things better for Churchill's new ally, the Americans. Control of the sea-lanes lay behind the Japanese decision to invade the Philippines, a sprawling collection of countless islands that lay astride the ocean routes between Japan and Southeast Asia. From the time the United States acquired the Philippines in 1899 following the Spanish-American War, it had been unwilling to make the military commitments needed to defend the islands. When Japan took the path of overt military expansion, it was too late for the United States to catch up. In mid-1941 Roosevelt recalled General Douglas MacArthur from retirement to command U.S. Army forces in the region, but attempts to build up Philippine defenses could not undo forty years of neglect—neglect the Roosevelt administration had failed to consider when it adopted its hard-line deterrence policy.

The initial Japanese air attacks on the Philippines, which found MacArthur largely unprepared despite a ten-hour advance warning following the Pearl Harbor bombing, gave Japan control of the air, thus forcing the evacuation of U.S. naval forces. That left the islands open for the amphibious landings that soon followed. The B-17 bombers, the American superdeterrent, were caught helpless on the ground when Japanese planes bombed the airfields. Elsewhere, in the Central Pacific, the Japanese took the defenseless American colony of Guam without significant resistance. Construction workers and marines resisted bravely but briefly on the tiny atoll outpost of Wake Island—without being so silly as to say, "Send us more Japs," regardless of wartime propaganda.[19]

An ignorant cultural stereotype of physically inferior Japanese whose poor eyesight made them bad pilots and inaccurate bombardiers contributed to both Pearl Harbor and the sinking of the two British battleships. Churchill had called the Japanese the "Wops of the Pacific" and "little yellow men," a combination of contempt and a diminutive that betrayed his belief that they could not measure up to Northern Europeans—or at least no better than could Italians. MacArthur, upon hearing of the attack on his airfields, argued that the pilots must have been white mercenaries since Japanese fliers could not have accomplished such a feat.[20] But whatever the reasons, the sinking of those warships and the Pearl Harbor disaster gave Japan naval superiority from Hawaii to Ceylon in the Indian Ocean.

On December 12, even as Anglo-American defenses in the Pacific were collapsing, Churchill left London for the United States, less than forty-eight hours after Roosevelt had agreed to a meeting (code-named Arcadia). But in 1941 the London-to-Washington ocean voyage took ten days, even aboard a battleship (the *Duke of York*, sister ship to the *Prince of Wales*) that left her destroyer escorts behind in the heavy seas. Despite his impatience at the delay, Churchill used the time to compose four long papers, addressed to his chiefs of staff but written for Roosevelt, designed to fold the American war effort into British strategy. The abiding focus of Churchill's arguments was to get the United States to participate in operations in West and North Africa, thus drawing the Americans into the western Mediterranean. Churchill characterized the Russian front as "the prime fact in the war," then deftly dismissed it as a place where "neither Great Britain nor the United States have any part to play," other than living up to their supply commitments.[21] He disingenuously assumed that the United States would not overreact to Pearl Harbor by concentrating on the Pacific, then played to what he had known, ever since the Atlantic Conference, were the preferences of American Army leaders by recommending a series of invasions of German-held Europe starting in 1943.

That strategy of wearing down the Germans by attacking at various points on the periphery of German-held Europe made sense for the British. Churchill always insisted that Anglo-American forces liberate Western Europe. Honor and duty, if nothing else, demanded it. Moreover, as early as February 1942 British officials pointed to geopolitical reasons for Britain to return militarily to the Continent. Should Stalin conclude a truce, however temporary, with Hitler, the "Western Democracies" might exhaust themselves defeating Germany (Stalin's version of the Truman gambit). Then, went the Foreign Office argument, Anglo-American participation in the peace would depend on Soviet goodwill, Moscow's need for economic assistance, and "the presence on the continent of British and U.S. forces." Another official added that his hope was that the Soviets would continue to fight, "with erosion of further manpower and material and not *too* great a geographical advance." (Again the Truman gambit.)[22]

But Britain lacked manpower to defeat the Germans on the

ground, particularly with the empire under siege by Japan. The Soviet Union, which had an ample supply of ground forces, might collapse or, as the Foreign Office feared, demand too high a price for an alliance. The Americans had the troops needed, if too many were not sent off to the Pacific war, and their price would be far less threatening than that of the Bolsheviks. But any all-out land war against Hitler would be long, bloody, and by no means a sure thing, and even the American military worried that its public might not support such a costly conflict being fought in that foreign place Europe.

Churchill, to his relief, quickly found that FDR and his advisers would stick to the Germany first strategy. But that required getting the American public "involved" in the war against Hitler. Propaganda, gift programs like Bundles for Britain, war bond campaigns, rationing, and industrial mobilization were not enough to make the home front feel part of the war. Roosevelt could present Germany as the greater threat, but doing nothing against either Hitler or the Japanese after the Pearl Harbor humiliation might force the president to take the offensive in the Pacific. That made operations in Northwest Africa extremely appealing.[23]

Roosevelt had long been concerned about the Axis presence in West and Northwest Africa. His pessimistic appraisal of British chances in the Mediterranean in mid-1941 prompted references to Dakar, a port city on the tip of the westernmost portion of Africa, as vital to the security of the Western Hemisphere. He had toyed with occupying the Azores and the Cape Verde Islands and repeatedly brought up the idea of sending American forces to West Africa, even mentioning the notion to British Deputy Prime Minister Attlee. By September William Bullitt and the Navy Department had hatched a scheme for dispatching an expeditionary force to Casablanca. Churchill, learning in late October of the proposal, quickly ordered that plans be drawn up for such a campaign in the hope of getting the Americans militarily involved. Stimson, with Marshall's support, had managed to talk the president out of the idea, but only temporarily.[24]

General Marshall, convinced that only a major, concentrated invasion of Western Europe would bring victory, adamantly opposed anything he considered a diversion, and the invasion of North Africa (Gymnast), which had been tentatively agreed on at the Arcadia talks, was just such a sideshow, even with local French cooperation. It took Marshall and Stimson until March 1942 to get Gymnast postponed, but it proved a short-lived victory. The Americans offered criticisms of Churchill's overall peripheral strategy, but all agreed to postpone any decision on the best way to invade German-held Europe.

Depressing discussions about various military actions around the world—North Africa, the Philippines, Hong Kong, Malaya—could not change what was happening, but the Americans had proposals that would change how the Anglo-Americans fought. Marshall and his army colleagues, with FDR's firm support (though not that of the fiercely parochial U.S. Navy chief Admiral Ernest King), proposed that each theater of operations should have an integrated command structure. This unity of command could, they argued, avoid the poor coordination of land, sea, and air operations that had plagued the British in Crete and Libya. Churchill resented the criticism and had strongly resisted the concept when he first heard of it two months earlier, but faced with FDR's insistence and offered the inducement that a Briton would get the Southwest Pacific command, he reluctantly agreed.[25]

In principle, unity of command allowed a British commander to give orders to American forces, and vice versa. Marshall, with justifiable pride, viewed unity of command as one of his major accomplishments. But in practice Churchill and Roosevelt took great care throughout the war to create balanced command structures wherever both nations had significant military involvement. Sometimes political concerns resulted in special arrangements, as in China, where Chiang Kai-shek refused to give the British any significant role. What Chiang's policies point out is that the indispensable glue needed for unity of command to work was the unique Anglo-American relationship.

Unity of command at the theater level required unified strategic direction. Building on the insistence of Churchill and Roosevelt, expressed during the Atlantic Conference, that they should not act as umpires between quarreling generals and admirals, the Americans proposed creation of a central military committee (eventually the Combined Chiefs of Staff Committee—CCSC) in Washington to coordinate military strategy and logistics. The British tried to hold on to some measure of control by calling for an equivalent organization in London, but the Americans argued that two committees would hinder rather than help coordination. A one-month trial period for a single committee that met in Washington became permanent. Like unity of command, the CCSC tied the Anglo-American war effort together in a way no amount of good intentions could have done, particularly as it set the precedent for other combined boards that coordinated acquiring, shipping, and allocating various war materials. But the growing personal relationship between Churchill and Roosevelt created the atmosphere of cooperation and common purpose that made unity of command and the CCSC relationship possible.[26]

More often than not, that relationship was, and would be, on American terms. Churchill had come to Washington convinced that Britain no longer needed "to strike attitudes to win United States' sympathy." He told one adviser that they no longer had to woo the United States; "now that she is in the harem, we talk to her quite differently."[27] The unity of command and CCSC issues were instances in which logic prevailed, but more likely Churchill and the British gave in because they had no choice. In 1942 the Americans were not really ready to fight a war. Training, equipping, and positioning troops took a great deal of time. They needed the British as much as, if not more than, the Brits needed the Yanks. But that would change, and Churchill knew it.

Even with the lackluster British military performance through early 1942, it was nearly eighteen months before the American military role predominated. But the political leverage the United States could exercise did not depend on how many soldiers it had fighting Hitler or how many ships it had facing the Japanese. By 1942 Britain had become dependent on American supplies. That only foreshadowed what was coming, as Churchill and the British Cabinet well recognized. Eden's secretary detected the concern: "AE [Anthony Eden] rather isolationist where Americans coming into Europe is concerned. He wants us, not them to be the predominant partner." In October 1941 Eden had authorized planning for the postwar lest FDR show up and pull a treaty out of his pocket. British leaders did not propose to sell their inheritance of British leadership and interests and assume that the Americans would be kind and gentle. But they had no acceptable choice, as Halifax and others had concluded eighteen months earlier, when things looked much darker for Britain. They suspected, rightly, that this time the United States would not come to save Europe (as the Americans would put it) and then withdraw, leaving Britain in charge.[28] Roosevelt's long and eventually successful campaign against isolationism would not let history repeat itself.

When Churchill addressed Congress in December 1941, he criticized the failure, "five or six years ago," of Great Britain and the United States to enforce German disarmament.[29] Senators and representatives sat silent, but such chastisement fitted perfectly with the campaign Roosevelt and Hull continued to conduct against any resurgence of isolationism after the war. Their key argument was that the refusal of the United States to cooperate in international peacekeeping (Hull used the phrase "collective security"; Roosevelt preferred vaguer language) had allowed Hitler and World War II to happen. It would be a war-long but successful campaign. The Americans were coming to Europe and coming to stay.

The Anglo-American wartime relationship also worked because Churchill charmed the Americans, beginning with the Arcadia Conference. He worked at his public image from the outset, standing on a chair at a press conference so reporters could see him, speaking at the White House Christmas tree–lighting ceremony about how much at home he felt in the United States, teasing Congress that had his American mother been his father, "I might have got here on my own." That public relations campaign continued, and by war's end he had become the popular figure in the United States that he remained for the rest of the century.[30]

Churchill's stay in the White House prompted one of the more repeated stories about his engagingly eccentric behavior. He more than occasionally dictated while he lay in the tub, submerging and rising as the mood struck him. On one occasion he continued that dictation while walking around his room, long after losing the towel he had draped over himself. At that point Roosevelt wheeled into the room to face the naked prime minister of Great Britain. Without hesitating, Churchill quipped, "You see, Mr President, I have nothing to conceal from you. . . ." That was of course not true, nor did the story get out until after the war, but it typified the image Americans had of Churchill.[31]

Just before Christmas, even as Roosevelt and Churchill were discussing wartime grand strategy, the Japanese invasion of the Philippines began in earnest. Filipino and American troops, after retreating to the Bataan Peninsula west of Manila, resisted for four months, but MacArthur's flawed defensive strategy and Washington's inability and unwillingness to send reinforcements forced the ill-equipped, starving, disease-ridden defenders of Bataan to surrender, despite MacArthur's orders that they attack—an empty sacrifice of lives that Churchill repeated regarding Singapore, and Hitler about Stalingrad. The island fortress of Corregidor, at the mouth of Manila Harbor, succumbed in early May. The infamous Bataan Death March, a sixty-five-mile forced evacuation of the captured troops, resulted in the deaths of five to ten thousand Filipinos and more than six hundred Americans, as Japanese troops clubbed and bayoneted the prisoners with an angry inhumanity.[32]

In early February 1942, while Filipinos and Americans on Bataan held out against increasing odds, a Japanese force half the size of the army defending Singapore negated that fort's defenses, which presumed an attack from the sea, by approaching through what British planners believed was impenetrable jungle (this might be called the Ardennes Forest analogy, the supposed barrier to German attacks in both world wars). The Japanese breached the island's defense perimeter, forcing the surrender of the garrison of thirty-two thousand Indian, sixteen thousand British, and fourteen thousand Australian troops. The Australians had been embarked on American transports en route to India and been rerouted when Churchill asked FDR for permission to divert the convoy to Singapore. Tragically they arrived just in time to surrender on February 15.[33]

Churchill, himself partly responsible for Singapore's plight, called it the "worst disaster and largest capitulation of British history."[34] That embarrassment was accentuated in early March, when

Rangoon and most of Burma fell into Japanese hands. The Japanese victory was more than military; it constituted a challenge to the mythology of Western supremacy that had allowed dominance of Asian societies by a small number of administrators backed up by a warship or two and a few troops. That challenge in turn threatened the entire structure of European colonialism in Asia. If the Japanese could defeat the Europeans, what about other Asians?

Although the atrocities on Bataan and subsequent Japanese mistreatment of prisoners of war did not become public knowledge until 1944, Roosevelt and General Marshall, with a good deal of help from MacArthur's coterie of publicity experts, managed to turn the Philippine fiasco into a public relations victory akin to Churchill's manipulation of the Dunkirk evacuation. MacArthur ended up a hero, partly through his own self-promotion, partly because at a time of national humiliation Americans desperately wanted a military hero. General Edwin "Pa" Watson, the president's military aide, claimed that MacArthur as hero of Bataan was "worth five army corps." Hollywood and Washington worked successfully to create folk heroes out of the "battling bastards of Bataan," the "heroic doctors and nurses of Corregidor," and Douglas MacArthur. Motion pictures like *Bataan* (1943) and *Wake Island* (1942) helped create three strong images: American heroism, Japanese cruelty, and the American military as, in the words of the Office of War Information (OWI), "A people's army, fighting a people's war."[35]

How different it was for Churchill and the British after the rapid conquest of the British Empire in Malaya and the stunning loss of the Singapore fortress to the Japanese. "Rangoon and Singapore are great names in the British eastern world," Churchill later told British General Hastings "Pug" Ismay, "and it will be an ill day for Britain if the war ends without our having made a stroke to regain these places. . . ."[36]

The American-British-Dutch-Australian Command (ABDACOM), the first Anglo-American unified command, draws the adjective "ill-fated" in nearly every description of its short, unhappy life. When Churchill and Roosevelt agreed during Arcadia to establish the ABDA theater, neither thought defending the Southwest Pacific—Malaya and Singapore, the Philippines, the Dutch East Indies, New Guinea, and the approaches to Australia—would be easy. But the Japanese conquered the region faster than the Allies could organize. There was no time to deal with command problems created by individual egos (MacArthur and Dutch Admiral C. E. L. Helfrich), disputes between the U.S. Army and Navy, differing strategies, and the growing apprehension of the Australians that they were next. Superior Japanese air power eliminated the ABDA ability to resist. A Japanese force of twenty-three fighters, the famous Zeros, shot down forty Allied fighter planes during a single raid on February 19; a week later Japanese planes played a key role in the Battle of the Java Sea, where four Allied cruisers and numerous destroyers were sunk by air and naval action.

ABDACOM, unable to act as a unified organization, disintegrated, reappearing in short order as the Southwest Pacific Area under the command of Douglas MacArthur, headquartered in Australia after he had fled the Philippines on orders from the president. Roosevelt had proposed at the Arcadia Conference that the entire Pacific theater be an American theater, with operational decisions made in Washington. Now, with British military strength eliminated from the Pacific and the United States assuming responsibility for the defense of Australia and New Zealand, that proposal was put into place. The United States would set the strategy, although a Pacific War Council (PWC) in Washington, composed of British, Chinese, Australian, and New Zealand representatives, would provide political guidance. FDR made himself chair of the PWC and treated it as a body created to talk, not act, leaving the Americans in full control. Churchill tried to maintain some degree of British influence in the region by insisting on a Pacific War Council that met in London as well, but that group was stillborn. Australian Prime Minister John Curtin, in a New Year's message, put into words the effect of Britain's failure to mount a defense in strength of the Southwest Pacific: "Australia looks to America, free of any pangs as to our traditional links with the United Kingdom." The statement referred specifically to defense against Japan, but the Australian nationalism it represented continued beyond the war.[37]

Pearl Harbor and the entire Japanese offensive in the Southwest

Pacific and Southeast Asia were a tactical success. But Pearl Harbor also forced the tradition-bound American Navy to adopt the very tactics and military strategies that spelled defeat for the Japanese Empire. The aircraft carriers of the U.S. Pacific Fleet, which had all been at sea, escaped unscathed, as did the American submarine force. The vast repair and fuel storage facilities as well as the submarine pens suffered light damage. With the battle fleet lying at the bottom of the harbor, the United States could not fight the naval war its admirals had expected. Instead of traditional clashes between huge warships, the proponents of carrier warfare won the day by default. Naval actions were left to the submariners, who quickly turned to unrestricted warfare on nonmilitary shipping (something the United States had condemned as illegal and immoral ever since the First World War) and eventually closed the sea-lanes around Japan.[38]

Pearl Harbor also guaranteed the failure of the Japanese political strategy. That strategy had assumed that an overwhelming military victory would confront Americans with the reality of a long, costly war in East Asia and the Pacific when their primary concerns and interests lay in dealing with the European crisis. Initial Japanese successes did seem overwhelming, and Americans might well have backed away from a war over the Philippines. But the "day that will live in Infamy" allowed the Roosevelt administration to present the entire Japanese offensive as a threat to the United States and a threat to civilization. The Tripartite Pact had seemed to join Hitler's Germany with Imperial Japan. Pearl Harbor confirmed those suspicions.

Joseph Stalin, breathing a sigh of relief that Japan had not attacked the Soviet Far East, waited ten days before laconically cabling Roosevelt: "I wish you success in the struggle against aggression in the Pacific."[39] He said nothing more. By that time things looked a bit better on the Russian fronts. The Germans had postponed any move into the Caucasus, and they had isolated but failed to take Leningrad, beginning that city's incredible nine-hundred-day siege. As for Moscow, the German offensive had stalled in late October, when the autumn rains and mud made roads and fields impassable. Stalin took advantage of that pause as well as intelligence that the

Japanese would not attack in the Far East to move well-trained, well-equipped Siberian divisions to the front. When the Germans resumed the attack in mid-November, they made little progress. Then deep winter arrived on December 4, earlier than usual, with temperatures plummeting to $-40°C$ ($-40°F$) by the next night. The Wehrmacht, its winter equipment still stored in Poland, lost the initiative to Red Army and partisan forces that were prepared for the bitter cold. When the Soviet counterattack began on December 5, a German panzer division stood only about twelve miles from the Kremlin, just outside the city suburbs. It was the closest Hitler's forces ever got to Moscow. The Battle of Moscow meant that the Soviet Union had survived—at least until spring. That kept alive the possibility of a complete victory over Hitler, and alliance politics thus took on a whole new meaning.

That new meaning did not include trust. American proposals for a Supreme War Council that would include the Soviets went nowhere. That was in part because the immediate situation worked against such close cooperation. Stalin could not get involved in anything that might provoke a Japanese attack in the Soviet Far East. In addition, in 1942 the Soviet and Anglo-American war efforts against Germany were widely separated by geography and by differences in the type of warfare: a vast land war in Russia versus a complex mix of sea, air, and land warfare in the West.

But at another level proposals to give Stalin equality did not have the advantage of a Churchill-Roosevelt relationship (even if FDR had had a special system to ensure quick and private delivery of Stalin's messages).[40] A lack of urgency might have prevented creation of a Supreme War Council in 1942, yet even in the absence of memorandums explaining why the two Western leaders hesitated, one detects the presence of the long-standing distrust between the Soviet Union and the Anglo-Americans. Distance, cultural misunderstanding, and even old Anglo-Russian enmities dating back to czarist times played a role. But ideology remained the constant cause of mutual uneasiness and suspicion. Balance of power politics does not explain the consistent Anglo-American appeals to democracy, Western style, and the just as persistent Soviet calls for democracy, Soviet style. Stalin acknowledged the pervasive atmosphere, commenting in December 1941 that "there has been much talk in Europe of our intentions to Bolshevise Europe. . . ." When FDR vaguely suggested preliminary conferences that might lead to "more permanent joint planning," Stalin mocked him, then guardedly asked British Foreign Minister Eden, at the time in Moscow, for more details. None were sent, and a small window for Soviet-Western confidence building slid shut.[41]

Eden was in Moscow in response to some testy Stalin-Churchill exchanges that boiled down to the Soviet leader's insistence that an Anglo-Soviet agreement was needed "on war aims and plans for post-war organisation" as well as "on mutual military assistance in Europe." That did not mean bargaining over getting the Soviet Union into the war against Japan, as Churchill thought, although the subject came up; it was a renewal of demands that the British recognize the Soviet frontiers that existed just before Hitler invaded Russia—what Stalin called the "old frontiers, the frontiers of 1941." He made other proposals, in particular a call for the dismemberment of Germany (which Soviet historians later denied), but his basic concern was his western boundaries.[42]

Eden had, from the outset of the war, inclined toward a territorial settlement based on spheres of influence that offered the Soviets security while keeping them fenced off in East and East-Central Europe—the old cordon sanitaire approach, though Eden denied it. The British foreign secretary could not argue against Stalin's logic: How could there be an alliance if they did not have agreed-upon war aims? But recognizing Stalin's claims, even if the Polish question could be left until later, was unacceptable to Churchill, who suddenly found the self-determination principles of the Atlantic Charter convenient, using them to chastise Eden for even proposing such a "forcible transfer of large populations." Moreover, Churchill lectured Eden, "President Roosevelt holds this view as strongly as I do. . . ."[43]

Shortly after the Arcadia meeting, one of Churchill's favorites, Lord Beaverbrook, called the Baltic states "the Ireland of Russia," an analogy full of hints of disloyalty. The Irish government, to Churchill's fury, had consistently rejected his overtures to join the war against Hitler, and rumors abounded of German spies and plots in Ireland. With that in mind, Beaverbrook argued that the "strict application" of the Atlantic Charter "would be a menace to our own safety as well as to that of Russia," perhaps even forcing the "surrender of Gibraltar to the Spaniards," a reference to a government Churchill loathed almost as much as the one in Dublin.[44] By early March 1942 Churchill had shifted his position. Perhaps persuaded by Beaverbrook, perhaps concerned about Britain's military position, perhaps worried about the ever-present rumors of a Soviet-German deal, the prime minister told Roosevelt on March 7 that the Atlantic Charter should not be interpreted to deny the Soviet Union the boundaries it had when Germany attacked since that was the understanding when Stalin accepted the charter. Beaverbrook's analogy may have worked, for Churchill, in the final paragraph of his cable, mentioned with seeming casualness his problems with India.[45] The joining of the two themes was neither new nor accidental.

During the Arcadia talks Roosevelt directly confronted Churchill about Indian independence. We have only Churchill's cryptic comment on the substance of the remarks: "The President . . . discussed the Indian problem with me, on the usual American lines. . . . I reacted so strongly and at such length that he never raised it verbally again."[46] But it is easy to make a plausible reconstruction of the discussion. When Americans spoke of anticolonialism, they referred to European colonial empires, where European powers ruled politically as well as dominated economically. The United States had practiced its own imperialism, but that did not stop Americans—particularly Roosevelt—from believing that colonialism, with its closed economic systems and political repression, would generate future wars. By 1941 the United States, goaded by Japanese anticolonial propaganda and self-righteous about having set the proper example by promising independence for the Philippines, had begun to push Britain on the issue. In the spring Hull had suggested self-government for India, and the Atlantic Charter with its promise of self-determination indirectly raised the issue a few months later. Now, only two weeks after the Pearl Harbor disaster, Roosevelt apparently suggested that Britain promise India independence and establish some sort of timetable for that to happen. Churchill claims to have responded as he did whenever such proposals surfaced, with angry arguments that the Americans did not understand the bitter Muslim-Hindu feud, that only the Muslims (the minority) had proved effective as soldiers, and that he would resign before he would "yield an inch of the territory that was under the British flag."[47]

At times Churchill played the British bulldog more as a terrier, using angry barking and bravado in an attempt to cover weakness. The president may not have raised Indian independence again with Churchill face-to-face—FDR later told Stalin that discussing India with the Englishman was a waste of time—but Roosevelt, convinced that colonialism's day was over, never quit trying to push and persuade the British to beat the inevitable to the punch, to choose devolution over revolution. He insisted in January 1942 that India sign the wartime alliance pact, grandly titled the Declaration by the United Nations, a title that FDR took credit for, particularly once it became the name for the United Nations Organization.[48] Shortly after the Arcadia meeting in Washington, Roosevelt unleashed Chiang Kai-shek, who visited India, where he suggested that the Indians would fight effectively against Japan if Britain promised independence. At the same time the president opened a second front against colonialism by instructing Harriman and Winant, both in London, to "get a slant" on Churchill's thinking about a changed relationship between India and Britain. All this in the wake of the humiliating British defeat at Singapore—to an army of "little yellow men."[49]

Churchill responded to the pressure as he did throughout the war. He presented Britain as the defender of minorities—in this case one hundred million Muslims and "thirty to forty million Untouchables"—then warned against throwing "India into chaos on the eve of invasion."[50] To placate the Americans as well as some at home, Churchill sent Sir Stafford Cripps, an outspoken Labour party critic of British colonial rule, to India in mid-March to offer a proposal for postwar independence. Roosevelt, eager to move the process along and to get credit for helping, sent one of his ever-ready personal emissaries, Louis Johnson, as an observer. The British, following their time-honored policy of setting Hindu against

Muslim, offered solutions neither group would accept. Exhilarated by the news that the talks had failed, Churchill "danced around the Cabinet room. No tea with treason [he said], no truck with American or British Labour sentimentality, but back to the solemn—and exciting—business of war."[51]

Churchill's celebration was premature. He managed to live up to his famous statement—"I have not become the King's First Minister to preside over the liquidation of the British Empire"—but he did preside over the events that made the end of that empire inevitable. A few weeks later Harry Hopkins listened to a "string of cuss words" as Churchill reacted to another suggestion from FDR, this one to allow India to begin the process of developing its own institutions by establishing a "nationalist government similar in essence to our own form of government under the Articles of Confederation. . . ."[52]

Neither then nor later in the war could Churchill or Roosevelt solve, or dismiss, the twin dilemmas of self-determination: Eastern Europe and colonial empires. Even postponement had its perils. But the bleak military situation they and their Soviet partner faced in the first quarter of 1942 allowed them to put such issues on the back burner.

The Japanese had taken most of the western Pacific, Italo-German forces threatened to close the Mediterranean, and the Russians awaited a renewed German offensive in the spring. The best the Anglo-Americans could do was stalemate the Germans in North Africa and try to keep the Atlantic sea-lanes open so American war materials could reach Britain and the Soviet Union. That struggle against the U-boats took a major turn for the worse in February 1942, when the Allies lost their ability to decipher German submarine radio traffic, a crisis that did not abate until well into 1943, when code breakers solved the new German Enigma system and ships and aircraft were equipped with high-frequency direction finders (the "ten-centimeter" radar). Yet there was nothing contrived about Roosevelt's telling Churchill, "Trust me to the bitter end," then cheerfully scrawling in late January, at the end of a long message to Churchill about the unhappy mess in the ABDA theater, "It is fun to be in the same decade with you."[53]

But Roosevelt's optimism would not solve the political and strategic problems he and Churchill faced. Primary among them was the Soviet Union. When Churchill remarked that while allies were always difficult, it was better to fight a war with them than without, he should have had the Soviet Union in mind. When, early in March, he had expressed willingness to go along with Stalin's boundary claims, Churchill had also touched on the crucial question of a second front. In a paragraph not included in his memoirs, he wrote that he would consider an attack designed to take the pressure off the Russians when the Germans renewed their offensive in the spring, an idea that Eden seconded a few weeks later.[54] That was more than just a military proposal. Soviet demands for territorial concessions made the British edgy, but they were boxed in by their dependence on the Red Army and fears that Stalin might negotiate with Hitler—something he had done once before. Soviet Ambassador I. M. Maisky had bluntly, and honestly, laid out the alternative: If Britain left it to the USSR to fight and beat the Germans in summer 1942, then the postwar settlement would be done by Moscow, and Britain would not have much of a share. That may have been bravado in 1942, but not in 1945.[55]

With classic British understatement, Eden wrote in his memoirs that at this point "our discussions with the Americans about the Russian treaty became tangled." The president, who had intimated to both the British and Soviet ambassadors that he might accept an agreement recognizing the 1941 boundaries of the Soviet Union, now played a different card. Concerned that making territorial arrangements could imperil his domestic support for the war and his postwar peace efforts, Roosevelt held out a promise of a second front—vaguely at first, then in so many words when Molotov visited Washington in late May–early June. The unspoken understanding ("deal" implies much too much precision) was that in return for that promise Stalin would drop his demands for public recognition of his 1941 frontiers. Roosevelt spoke to the British and to Soviet Ambassador Maksim Litvinov about the certainty that regardless of any treaty, the Red Army would occupy the Baltic states at the end of the war and hinted to Litvinov that a deal with the British about frontiers was acceptable, so long as it was informal and secret. Even with Eleanor Roosevelt's warning (to Churchill) that "when Franklin says yes, yes, yes it doesn't mean he agrees. . . . It means he's listening," Litvinov's report of the conversation has the ring of authenticity.[56]

Roosevelt's arrangement also reflected the pressure he felt from his most trusted military adviser, General George Marshall, the army chief of staff. Marshall and his planners were wedded to the military strategy of a large-scale invasion of Western Europe, believing that the quickest and ultimately the best and least costly way to defeat Hitler was to attack Germany directly. Not only did that follow American military doctrine, but Marshall, eerily echoing the Japanese strategists who planned Pearl Harbor, feared that the American public would not support a long, drawn-out war on foreign shores.[57]

Despite Marshall's position, Roosevelt had long flirted with Churchill's notion of a peripheral strategy of small raids and air action in Western Europe, and that flirtation continued. On April 1 the president himself wrote out a message informing Churchill that Hopkins and Marshall were headed for London to discuss a plan "which I hope Russia will greet with great enthusiasm. . . ." In a letter he sent with Hopkins and Marshall, Roosevelt elaborated: "Your people and mine demand the establishment of a front to draw off pressure on the Russians . . . [who] are today killing more Germans . . . than you and I put together."[58]

But FDR and his army chief of staff had different things in mind. Marshall went to London to get British agreement for Bolero and Roundup—the first a buildup of troops and supplies in Britain preparatory to a massive invasion across the English Channel; the second the actual invasion, with spring 1943 as the target date. Roosevelt was more interested in Sledgehammer—what the U.S. Army had developed as an emergency plan for a small-scale (five divisions), diversionary invasion of France in 1942, to be carried out only if a German offensive seemed on the verge of forcing a Soviet collapse. As the army planners put it, Sledgehammer "should be considered a sacrifice for the common good."[59]

The Marshall-Hopkins talks with the British were a disaster, though the Americans did not know it right away. Churchill and his military staff firmly opposed any Anglo-American invasion in 1942 (Sledgehammer), knowing full well it would be more Anglo than American, even if Soviet resistance seemed to be disintegrating. Nor were they convinced by Marshall's arguments for a massive, cross-channel invasion (Roundup). But as Pug Ismay lamented; "Our American friends went happily homewards under the mistaken impression that we had committed ourselves to both ROUNDUP and SLEDGEHAMMER. . . . When we had to tell them . . . that we were absolutely opposed to it [Sledgehammer], they felt that we had broken faith with them." Even Churchill later admitted, grudgingly, to a lack of candor with the Americans.[60]

Into the midst of this growing confusion came Soviet Foreign Minister V. M. Molotov, his distrust of the Westerners (and perhaps everyone) displayed by the pistol he kept under his pillow at night. Molotov traveled directly to London, despite FDR's attempt to get him to shift his itinerary and visit Washington first. The talks in London went nowhere. Molotov began with demands for a second front that could divert forty German divisions from the Russian front. Churchill hemmed and hawed but refused to endorse either a 1942 second front or Soviet territorial demands, which now included portions of Finland and Romania as well as what the Soviets had (re)occupied in eastern Poland. Molotov left London for Washington, carrying a nice-to-have Anglo-Soviet Treaty of Alliance that Stalin believed gave the USSR "a free hand" and knowing there would be no second front in 1942 unless Roosevelt were willing to twist Churchill's arm.[61]

FDR might have done just that if his own military advisers had pushed him, but as Harry Hopkins (who had returned from London in near collapse after trying to keep up with Churchill's Falstaffian lifestyle) privately warned Molotov late one evening, the American generals did not share the president's belief in the immediate and "acute necessity of a second front." Roosevelt's open mockery of British claims that they supported a second front may have been intended to make Molotov think the Americans would force the British to go along, but as Molotov recalled after the war, neither he nor Stalin believed FDR, despite a public communiqué that announced a "full understanding was reached with regard to

the urgent tasks of creating a Second Front in Europe in 1942."
The Soviet records of the talks show that endorsements by Roosevelt and Hopkins of a second front by autumn were invariably
followed by expressions of doubt. "The question arises: can we do
it?" the president wondered. Please tell Stalin, Roosevelt requested, "that we were hoping to open a second front in 1942."
At the same time Stalin's messages back to Molotov indicate that
the Soviet leader well understood that Roosevelt considered a 1942
second front highly desirable but far from a promise. In the words
of one Russian historian, "Roosevelt's agreement to the wording
of the communiqué, suggested by Molotov [but following Stalin's
instructions], was intended to reassure the Soviet Union and misinform the Germans. . . ." For Molotov, either not understanding
or ignoring the distinction between Sledgehammer and Roundup,
the "promise" only gave the Soviets additional leverage in their
requests for more war supplies.[62]

Roosevelt's optimism—refusal to face reality, others might say—
often prompted him to hope that things would work out. In this
case perhaps the British could be persuaded to support a second
front in 1942. Perhaps the president had truly talked himself into
believing Sledgehammer in 1942 could work because of the need
to bolster Soviet morale. But whether he believed in the strategy
or not, Roosevelt knew the Soviets were "a bit down in the
mouth" and was "anxious that he [Molotov] carry back some real
results. . . ." Marshall talked the president out of setting August as
the target date for Sledgehammer, but FDR wrote that he was
"more than ever anxious" for the invasion to take place in 1942.[63]

That was not to be. However sincere Roosevelt was about Sledgehammer, opposition from the British and increasing lack of support
from his own generals made it impossible. Molotov, who had earlier
told the British that he knew the burden of a second front in 1942
would fall on them, read the tea leaves correctly, reporting to Stalin:
". . . the British Government does not accept an obligation upon itself to establish a second front this year. . . ."[64]

The great debate over a second front (attacks in North Africa
and Italy would qualify for that name) and *the* second front, as
defined by Molotov, delineated two other major issues. The first

was military. Roosevelt insisted on engaging American soldiers against the Germans as soon as possible, something Churchill learned, this time to his pleasure, when he rushed to Washington to smooth down the American feathers ruffled by the second front misunderstandings.

The second issue was the president's insistence that relations with the Soviet Union were best handled in direct Roosevelt-Stalin negotiations. FDR had tried earlier that spring to arrange a one-on-one talk with Stalin. The talks did not materialize, and Roosevelt never told Churchill about the attempt, although the president did write in a letter to the prime minister: "I know you will not mind my being brutally frank when I tell you that I think I personally handle Stalin better than either your Foreign Office or my State Department. Stalin hates the guts of all your top people. He thinks he likes me better. . . ."[65] That casual arrogance did not sit well with either Churchill or Eden. To the prime minister, it smacked of relegating Great Britain to something less than Great Power status. To the foreign secretary, Europe was Britain's business since the Americans could not be trusted to abandon isolationism and make a permanent political commitment to the region. Moreover, British leaders believed they understood the Russians (though perhaps not the Bolsheviks) better than the Americans. It was an issue that was to nettle Anglo-American relations throughout the war.

There was also the issue of Soviet territorial claims, which would not go away for the next fifty years—if even then. Had those who opposed appeasing Hitler "become wartime appeasers of Stalin," as angry, after-the-fact accusations would have it?[66] True, the Atlantic Charter principle of self-determination, particularly when applied to the Baltic states, seemed honored largely in the breach. But antiappeasers of the 1930s like Churchill came to that position only after they had concluded appeasement would not work. No one was certain if Stalin was primarily a geopolitician seeking physical security or a dedicated revolutionary seeking to impose communism on the world. Nor was that the only dilemma. Historical claims to land and independence are all too frequently a case of *reductio ad absurdum*, particularly in Europe, where boundaries

had changed and populations moved regularly over the centuries—
something that bedeviled Woodrow Wilson during the Paris peace
talks in 1919.

Eden would, by war's end, change his mind about territorial
concessions, but Churchill changed his mind for a second time in
1942, as he did a number of times on the matter. He recounted
to Roosevelt his talks with Molotov in London and proudly explained that he had avoided any territorial concessions. The proposals for an Anglo-Soviet treaty "are entirely compatible with our
Atlantic Charter."[67] But an issue that Stalin said was "really what
the whole war is about" would not go away that easily. Perhaps
the question to ask is, how many enemies can a nation fight at one
time? The moral high ground is always easy to see once the fog of
war lifts. In the winter of 1941–42 Eden thought a bargain with
the Soviets made sense for Britain. After all, he argued, "if we won
the war, Russian forces would probably penetrate Germany, and
. . . at a later day she might well want more than her 1941 frontiers." A trenchant prediction. Defeating Hitler's Germany remained the priority.[68]

Roosevelt seems never to have viewed repossession of the Baltic
states by the Soviet Union as a critical moral or ethical issue. In the
spring of 1942 he revealed what turned out to be his true feelings,
telling a State Department adviser that "he would not particularly
mind about the Russians taking quite a chunk of territory," specifically mentioning the Baltic states and eastern Poland, matching
what he had intimated two weeks earlier to Litvinov.[69]

In the wake of the second front debates, both Churchill and
Roosevelt thought another meeting a good idea. Those talks, ap-
propriately code-named Argonaut since Churchill chose to cross
the Atlantic by seaplane (flying boat, as it was then called)—quicker
than by warship but still a dangerous twenty-six-hour trip—began
on June 19 at the President's country home in Hyde Park, New
York, overlooking the Hudson River. Their talks there focused on
Anglo-American cooperation over Tube Alloys, the atomic bomb
project. They concurred on unrestricted sharing of information,
but their agreement was not reduced to writing. As the British
ruefully learned, that allowed the Americans in charge of the proj-

ect to be, or pretend to be, ignorant of the sharing policy. After two pleasant days at the president's home the two joined their military staffs in Washington to continue discussions.[70] As with all the wartime summits, the military situation provided the backdrop for politics, and in mid-1942 that military backdrop continued to be gloomy.

The war in the Soviet Union had been quiet, but Roosevelt's concern that the Soviets were "a bit down in the mouth" would have been seconded by Stalin. The Soviet leader's calls for a second front came from information (some provided by the British) that with the failure of his winter offensive to cut German supply lines, a major German summer offensive was in the making. Anglo-American intelligence had reported on the impending offensive, making rather pessimistic estimates, but when Roosevelt and Churchill met, the Russian front remained ominously quiet.[71]

Not so in Libya and Egypt—what the British called the Western Desert—where German General Rommel had preempted slowly developing British plans for an offensive by launching his own. A week before Churchill left England to meet the president, Free French forces—military units that had rejected the Vichy government's authority and had joined the Allies—had been dislodged from positions at Bir Hakeim, south of Tobruk, despite a stubborn resistance that established the credibility of the Free French army. Rommel, making good use of German intelligence that revealed his enemy's plans, devised daring tactics that, abetted by British caution, forced Anglo-French-Polish forces to retreat. By the time Churchill arrived in the United States, the Germans threatened the seaport fortress of Tobruk, in western Libya, a symbol of British fortunes in the desert war ever since it had withstood Rommel's siege in 1941.

The less glamorous supply war—the struggle to deliver war goods from the United States to Britain and the Soviet Union—had worsened. The blackout of intelligence about U-boat activities in the Atlantic continued (as it would until just after Christmas 1942), while German air and naval forces in Norway were threatening supply convoys sent around Norway's North Cape headed for the Soviet port of Murmansk. Malta, which lay astride the Axis supply lanes through the Mediterranean to North Africa, had come under an incredibly intense bombing attack. In March and April 1942 alone, *twice* the tonnage of bombs fell on Malta as had fallen on London during the blitz, and an invasion of the island seemed around the corner.[72]

The Pacific war, on the other hand, had seen some improvement since the dreary days after Pearl Harbor. The Americans, burdened by the rivalry between the army and navy, had divided the Pacific into two theaters: the Southwest Pacific, with MacArthur in command, and all the rest of the vast ocean entrusted to Admiral Chester Nimitz. That parochialism later caused delays and cost lives, but in spring 1942 the army and navy had the same goal: Stop the Japanese advance.[73]

Success breeds greater expectations. Thus it was with the Japanese, who, flushed with victory in Southeast Asia, tried to pursue their advantage by military force. The Imperial Navy remained committed to ending the war by forcing Britain and the United States into accepting Japan's suzerainty in the Western Pacific. To that end they took advantage of British naval weakness to conduct raids against Ceylon and India, raids that destroyed shipping but took no territory. Then, in early May 1942, the Japanese Navy chose to threaten Australia by attacking toward Port Moresby, on the southeast quadrant of the huge island of New Guinea (the Japanese Army considered China and the Soviet Union its primary task). The bloody, now-forgotten ground war for New Guinea took two more years to resolve, but intercepts of Japanese military communications (Japanese Ultra intelligence) prompted the dispatch of two American carriers to challenge the Japanese invasion force. The ensuing Battle of the Coral Sea was fought entirely by carrier aircraft, with American and Australian cruisers never sighting their enemy. The Japanese won the naval battle, sinking one American carrier and damaging the other. But it was a pyrrhic victory. The invasion force withdrew, while the Japanese had one carrier sunk and two others temporarily put out of service. Not only was the threat to Australia ended, permanently as it turned out, but the Japanese were three carriers short for the next—and most crucial—naval battle of the Pacific war.

That battle came a month later off Midway, a tiny island at the far western end of the Hawaiian island chain, nearly fifteen hundred miles from Pearl Harbor. The bombing of Tokyo on April 18 by Army Air Force bombers flying off carriers may have embarrassed the Japanese and prompted offensive action. But the Battle of Midway fitted the broad strategy the Japanese Navy had adopted before Pearl Harbor. The plan called for a decisive victory over the American fleet that would, the Japanese reasoned, force the United States to negotiate. To draw out the Americans, the Japanese naval commander, Admiral Isoroku Yamamoto, sent 145 warships to invade Midway. At the same time he hoped to divert some American forces by sending a small force to invade the western Aleutian Islands of Alaska.

The effect of intelligence, both accurate and faulty, at Midway was greater than for any other major battle in World War II. Faulty intelligence misled the Japanese on the size of the American force and failed to detect the fleet gathered at Pearl Harbor. Accurate intelligence and the decision of Admiral Nimitz to trust those assessments allowed the Americans to fathom Yamamoto's plan and to position their forces. After a series of devastating carrier air attacks by each side, the Japanese withdrew when they were unable to engage their three battleships against the American fleet. What mattered were the aircraft carriers. The Japanese lost all four they had committed; the Americans lost one, and that in the aftermath, when the *Yorktown*, repaired in record time after the Coral Sea Battle, was sunk by a submarine torpedo.

The Japanese Navy never recovered. It shifted the focus of naval construction from battleships to carriers, but the decision came too late. Although the Americans did not immediately recognize the significance of their victory, the Midway defeat spelled the end of Japan's carrier-based air superiority in the Pacific and prevented or hampered offensives planned in the Southwest Pacific. As of June 1942, only six months after the Pearl Harbor attack, the Japanese advance had been halted and the balance of sea power in the Pacific had shifted to the United States—all done without the British Navy, which was nowhere to be found.

Churchill's desire to "flip over" for a weekend with Roosevelt came, in large part, from the prime minister's concern that the entire second front issue, particularly American misperceptions of British opposition to Sledgehammer, needed to be talked out at the highest level.[74] But the victories by the United States in the Pacific once again raised the issue of the "Pacific alternative," the threat that the Americans, frustrated by British policy on the second front, would turn to the Pacific war as their priority.

Churchill need not have worried. Secretary of War Henry Stimson understood where the president was headed, telling his diary: "It looked as if he [Roosevelt] was going to jump the traces . . . in regard to BOLERO [preparations for an invasion of France]. . . . He wants to take up the case of GYMNAST [the invasion of North Africa] again, thinking that he can bring additional pressure to save Russia."

At the same time another embarrassing British defeat, this one at Tobruk, may have further inclined the president to favor the North African campaign as a way of taking pressure off the British in the Western Desert. Just as the prime minister arrived at the White House on June 21, Roosevelt handed him word that some thirty-three thousand experienced troops had surrendered to a German force half that size—a humiliation nearly as great as the one at Singapore. As Churchill put it in his memoirs, eight years later, "Defeat is one thing; disgrace is another." Roosevelt's immediate response was spare and straightforward: "What can we do to help?" "Sherman tanks," replied Churchill—a request that the Americans immediately agreed to. The gesture caught the Churchill-Roosevelt relationship at its best, and the prime minister never forgot it. Nearly three years later, when both were caught up in attempts to cope with the Soviet Union as a major power in Europe, Churchill called their friendship "the rock on which I build for the future," then recalled "those tremendous days when you devised Lend-Lease . . . and when you comforted me for the loss of Tobruk by giving me the 300 Shermans [tanks]. . . ."[75]

Marshall bitterly regarded Roosevelt's forays into military planning as "cigarette holder" strategy. But despite the president's willingness during the meetings to float impractical schemes like sending a large American force to protect Suez and the Middle

East, he kept returning to one theme: U.S. forces had to engage the German Army. During Argonaut, Roosevelt and Churchill did not decide on the North African campaign, at least not publicly, but by the time the talks ended on June 25, they had agreed, for different motives, that American forces had to get involved in Europe or Africa in 1942. Roosevelt wanted to reassure the Soviets and even divert at least some German forces from the Russian front as well as to protect against the Pacific alternative. Churchill likewise recognized the dangerous lure of the Pacific and wanted to get the American Army engaged against Germany and Italy, but without committing Britain to the massive, all-or-nothing cross-Channel invasion that General Marshall wanted.

Three days after Churchill left Washington, Hitler launched his summer offensive on the Russian front. Operation Blue aimed at breaking Soviet resistance in the south and gaining access to the oil fields of the Caucasus. By July 6 Stalin had ordered a strategic retreat (the only time he did so during the war), and by mid-July German forces had taken Rostov-on-Don and moved to within one hundred miles of Stalingrad. At the same time the Crimean port city of Sevastopol fell after a four-month siege. The collapse of Soviet resistance, the prospect that had prompted Roosevelt to insist on either Sledgehammer or Gymnast, seemed all too possible.

For a few weeks after the Argonaut Conference, Roosevelt had maneuvered to get around the objections of his military chiefs without having to override them bluntly and directly. Using Hopkins to bypass Marshall, the president maintained the appearance of an open mind until, in mid-July, when Marshall, with Stimson's blessing, threatened to switch his support to the Pacific alternative rather than accept Gymnast. Even Japanese intelligence eventually managed to get wind of the argument, though it missed the point. The Japanese Embassy in Madrid, reporting on information gathered in London, told Tokyo: "The Americans, by the way, want to take precedence over the British in everything. There are even indications that, if a Second Front is not actually opened, they will do their best to have this General-Staff organ moved to the UNITED STATES."

An angry FDR faced Marshall down when the general lamely

claimed the suggestion was merely designed to get the British to back away from their opposition to an invasion of France. The president called that like "taking up your dishes and going away." His written memo was forceful: Focusing on the Pacific was just what Hitler hoped the United States would do, it had U.S. forces fighting for islands that "will not affect the world situation this year or next," and it failed to help either the Russians or in the Near East. FDR then sent Marshall and Admiral King, along with Hopkins as watchdog, to London with strict orders: If the British would not support a 1942 invasion of France (Sledgehammer), then FDR insisted on invading North Africa in 1942 (Gymnast) and planning for a cross-Channel invasion in 1943 (Roundup), despite warnings from American Army planners that a North African invasion would delay Roundup until 1944. But even when the Americans proposed to make Sledgehammer an operation aimed at gaining a permanent foothold in France, the British declined, as Hopkins and Roosevelt knew they would. Marshall and King talked to the British military, but Hopkins talked to Churchill. Germany first meant keeping the Soviets in the war, not slipping off into the Pacific. And Roosevelt and Churchill refused to budge from Germany first.[76]

Marshall and other American generals repeatedly denigrated Roosevelt's decision for a North African invasion as "political." They were committed to the principle of concentration of forces and viewed Churchill's peripheral strategy as inherently flawed. An invasion of North African did not go in the direction of Germany or the major elements of the German Army; hence it would act as a "suction pump," drawing Anglo-American strength away from where it ultimately had to go. Though the accusation was never hurled, the Americans clearly thought the British were "afraid" to take on the German Army. As Secretary of War Stimson later put it, "The shadows of Passchendale and Dunkerque still hang too heavily over the imagination of his [Churchill's] government." But the British Army was not the key to victory over Germany. Stimson and Marshall had told Roosevelt that their hope was "keeping the Russian Army in the war and thus ultimately defeating Hitler."[77] Quarantining Hitler within the European continent might be possible using Anglo-American naval and air forces, but defeating the Wehrmacht demanded an army much bigger than Britain had or the United States would (or did) ever send to Europe.

Most historians have defended the strategic wisdom of Roosevelt's decision. Of course Marshall may have been right. But those who argue that a 1943 invasion of Western Europe, made impossible by Gymnast, might have shortened the war and forestalled Soviet "liberation" of much of Central Europe ignore the pull of the Pacific. As Roosevelt and Hopkins understood, prolonged inaction against Germany could have created enough congressional and domestic pressure to force a shift of resources to the war against Japan. The president worried about "finding a place where the soldiers thought they could fight" and concluded that only bloodying American troops in combat against the Germans would solve the problem.[78] Since the strategy of winners is justified by victory, we will never get beyond conjecture. Moreover, that misses the point.

General Marshall, still petulant years later, commented that the debate taught him that "the politicians must do *something* every year" during a war. True, Roosevelt's decision, however wise or unwise, was made largely for political, not military, reasons. But those political reasons were substantial—not trivial, selfish, or opportunistic, as Marshall implied. The decision to concentrate on the war against Germany was military in that the sensible thing to do was defeat the strongest enemy first. But it was also a crucial political statement that Roosevelt's schemes for postwar collaboration with Britain and the Soviet Union, the Great Powers, demanded a Europe first strategy. If the United States left its Allies alone in Europe, how could it hope to lead in the postwar world? After all, politics, claims Clausewitz, is what war is all about.

Nine months later Roosevelt revealed himself to Marshall: "Just between ourselves, if I had not considered the European and African fields of action in their broadest geographic sense, you and I know we would not be in North Africa today—in fact we would not have landed in either Africa or Europe."[79]

OK, Winston, no Second Front this year—but we need the Soviets, now and later.

CHAPTER 6

———◆◗———

"The End of the Beginning"— and the "Beginning of the End" August 1942–February 1943

By the end of 1942 the fortunes of war would begin to shift. In Russia, Northwest Africa, the desert west of Egypt, and the Pacific, the Axis would be stopped and the Allies would go on the offensive. But nothing was foreordained. That shift from defense to offense required that the members of the Grand Alliance work together. For Churchill and Roosevelt, that meant reconciling their own differences in grand strategy and persuading Stalin that they were not planning to betray him. The decision for the invasion of North Africa, renamed Operation Torch to avoid confusion with the variants of Gymnast that had been offered, resolved Anglo-American strategy—at least for the moment.

But the same decision inevitably meant a delay in the second front that Stalin kept calling for. Roosevelt had balked at that postponement, eagerly embracing Churchill's argument that Torch would in fact allow an invasion of Europe in 1943 from both North Africa and Great Britain. The prime minister had blithely ignored the vast difference between his proposal for two attacks, which moved toward his peripheral strategy, and the Stimson-Marshall commitment to a massive cross-Channel invasion. The issue would not be settled until early 1943, but in the meantime Stalin had to be told, in the words of the "Ballad of the Second

Front"—a piece of doggerel penned by one British general—"No Second Front in 1942."[1]

Churchill's bombast always reached its heights when he could not deliver the goods. His nearly one-thousand-word message of July 18 to Stalin focused on the suspension of the Arctic supply convoys to northern Russia—the main supply route to the Soviet Union—because of staggering losses from German attacks by aircraft, submarines, and surface raiders based in Norway. FDR had disingenuously suggested that a cutback in the Arctic convoys to Russia would hasten the creation of a second front; now he "reluctantly" agreed to holding up the sailings. But the convoys were British, and Churchill took the brunt of Stalin's ire.[2] The British leader tried to mollify Stalin by emphasizing Allied efforts to expand the supply route to Russia through the Persian Gulf and wrote favorably of some small joint military projects that might help Stalin's southern flank in the Caucasus, failing to mention that such schemes would protect Britain's position in the Middle East should the Germans break through. Churchill did not have to remind the Communist dictator that Britain had supported anti-Soviet Muslims in the Caucasus in 1918 and that secessionist sentiments there remained strong; Moscow had recently dispatched Soviet secret police forces to prevent collaboration with the Germans. Not surprisingly Stalin reacted suspiciously and eventually lost interest in such proposals.[3]

The Soviet leader quickly spotted what Churchill had not said. There was no mention of the 1942 second front. That was, Stalin warned, something "the Soviet Government cannot tolerate," particularly with a major German offensive under way. His angry reaction, combined with reports on the possibility of a German peace offer to Russia, prompted Churchill to accept the recommendation of his ambassador in Moscow, Sir Archibald Clark Kerr, to suggest a meeting with Stalin to discuss the second front.[4]

Churchill likened his trip to Moscow, where Stalin had proposed they meet, to "carrying a large lump of ice to the North Pole." He had "a somewhat raw job," he told Roosevelt, asking for Averell Harriman to go along so that "we all seemed to be together." Contrarily, and unbeknownst to the prime minister, Harriman took the opportunity to renew FDR's proposal for one-on-one talks with Stalin. But Churchill also believed in personal diplomacy and relished the "raw job," as his Cabinet colleagues well understood when they concluded there was no sense in speaking of the dangers of the trip since that would only whet the prime minister's appetite.[5]

The talks of August 12–16, 1942, began well. If Churchill and Harriman read Stalin correctly, Torch came as a great relief to the Soviets. Stalin was visibly depressed and angered by the failure to mount a second front in 1942, though the news came as no surprise. But his enthusiastic reaction to the North African invasion suggests that he was as worried about the Allies leaving him to confront Hitler—the Truman gambit—as the Anglo-Americans were that the USSR would negotiate a separate peace. Churchill cleverly drew a sketch that presented Torch as the first step toward an attack on both the "soft belly" and the "hard snout" of the crocodile (Hitler's Europe), an image he had not shared with the Americans. Even with that hint of the Englishman's preference for a Mediterranean strategy, Torch was enough of a second front to convince Stalin that the Anglo-Americans would stay the course, although the Soviet leader would not admit it lest he lose his bargaining advantage.

But Churchill purposefully left vague the matter of when the cross-Channel invasion—a true second front—would take place. Not only were the Anglo-Americans themselves uncertain, but the prime minister still preferred that the second front not be the all-or-nothing campaign the American military wanted. The final verse of the "Ballad of the Second Front" caught the atmosphere:

> Prince of the Kremlin, here's a fond farewell;
> I've had to deal with many worse than you.
> You took it though you hated it like hell;
> No Second Front in 1942.

But as Soviet and British records and memoirs make clear, nothing was said to discourage Stalin from inferring that "No Second Front in 1942" meant that the second front would come in 1943.[6]

Stalin's relief intermingled with insult and abuse. With crude frankness, he unknowingly echoed Churchill's feelings during the dark days of summer 1940, when the United States was so slow to provide aid. As Churchill had put it, the Americans were "very good in applauding the valiant deeds done by others."[7] Stalin's imputation of British cowardice and bad faith for their failure to fight the Germans caused Churchill to erupt in anger. It was bad enough that his government had to rely so heavily on the Americans, but at least they were kin. Kowtowing to the Bolsheviks was more than he could stomach without at least a verbal response. His explosion left Soviet interpreters unwilling to translate, lest Stalin retaliate against the messengers.

Harriman had passed a note to Churchill cautioning him that Stalin often adopted a good cop, bad cop tactic in negotiations, and the Soviet leader lived up to the prediction. He responded, perhaps falsely, that he did not understand Churchill's remarks but that, "by God, I like your sentiment!" Later, when Churchill remained sullen and angry, Stalin displayed his own trust in personal diplomacy by asking the prime minister to join him for drinks.

That invitation brought a six-hour, far-ranging, rambling late-night conversation of the kind to which Churchill routinely treated his dinner guests. Shortly after the meeting broke up at 2:30 A.M., the prime minister returned to his apartment a few miles outside Moscow in a completely different mood. As the chapter title in his memoirs suggests, he thought the result was "A Relationship Established." Perhaps remembering Roosevelt's claim that Stalin "hates the guts" of British leaders, Churchill boasted to the president that "I have established a personal relationship which will be helpful." The exchange of insults with Stalin rankled, but, he wrote, "on the whole I am definitely encouraged. . . . Now they know the worst, and having made their protest are entirely friendly. . . . Moreover Monsieur Stalin is entirely convinced of the great advantages of TORCH and I do trust that it is being driven forward with super-human energy on both sides of the ocean."[8]

Churchill had reason to worry about Torch, for he had not managed to bring the Americans into his soft-underbelly concept, an approach that fitted his preference for a peripheral strategy and protected British interests in the Mediterranean. (Not until 1944, during the debate over the invasion of southern France, would he claim that the soft-underbelly strategy would forestall Soviet expansion into Eastern Europe. Even then the Americans concluded that British interests in Greece, not fear of Soviet expansion, lay behind the proposal.) When Churchill returned to London from Moscow on August 24, he found what he called a (expletive deleted by Churchill's aides) bombshell awaiting. The Americans, fearful of being caught in the Mediterranean "suction pump" and thus becoming ensnared in a war designed to serve British postwar interests, insisted that Torch focus on the Atlantic coast of the French protectorate (a euphemism for colony) of Morocco, arguing that the Germans would move through Spain and cut off sea communications through the Strait of Gibraltar. General Dwight Eisenhower, the American selected to command Torch, called what followed the Churchill-Roosevelt "transatlantic essay contest."

For the next two weeks Churchill bombarded the president with messages pressing for a full commitment to British strategy. To show concern for Stalin's needs, the prime minister included his proposal for an invasion of Norway (Operation Jupiter) that would, he argued, eliminate German land-based air attacks on convoys heading for northern Russia.[9] Both the British and American chiefs of staff found Jupiter implausible, and Roosevelt simply ignored it. As for Torch, the president followed Marshall's advice, insisting on an invasion on Morocco's Atlantic coast at Casablanca (despite accurate warnings from the navy that the surf at those beaches ran dangerously high), while opposing any attack east of Oran, the westernmost Mediterranean port in French Algeria. At the same time FDR pushed for Torch to take place as soon as possible— preferably before the November congressional elections. The "essay contest" finally ended when, early in September, Roosevelt compromised by accepting a third assault, this one at Algiers, some 250 miles east of Oran, while Churchill agreed to the landings at Casablanca. "Hurrah!" FDR cabled the prime minister. "Okay full blast," came the quick response. A bit more ruefully Churchill told Harriman, "I am the President's loyal lieutenant."[10]

Even as Churchill and Roosevelt wrote their essays, events on the Russian front threatened to make their debate irrelevant. Perhaps Stalin concluded that neither the British nor the Americans would jeopardize their chances against Germany just to save the Soviet Union, but that actually reversed the military reality. It was failing to "save" the Soviet Union, and the Red Army, that would jeopardize Anglo-American chances against Germany. Even the British chiefs of staff agreed, rejecting for the moment Churchill's peripheral strategy, by bluntly declaring in October that "the Russian army is, today, the only force capable of defeating the German army or, indeed, of containing it." Churchill scrawled on the report, "I hope Stalin will not see this," but he could not argue the point. In the summer and fall of 1942 Britain's Mediterranean strategy depended on events in Russia, regardless of whether or not Torch succeeded.[11]

Those events in Russia were not promising in late summer 1942. By late July the German offensive toward the south seemed irresistible, with Soviet forces on the verge of losing all discipline. In late September German troops entered parts of Stalingrad (formerly Tsaritsyn and now Volgograd, the city had been renamed for the Soviet dictator after he had consolidated his control in 1925), on the great bend of the Volga River, and by early October they appeared about to break through the Russian defenses. Stalin did not exaggerate when he told his two counterparts that the situation had "deteriorated." At the same time he protested to Wendell Willkie, then visiting Moscow on an "unofficial" worldwide tour, about inadequate deliveries of fighter aircraft—complaints that soon reached the American press. He also accused the British of having "stolen" lend-lease goods when they off-loaded some merchant ships scheduled to go to Russia in order to make them available for Torch. Churchill's message that no convoy would sail to Russia until January 1943 received only a curt acknowledgment from Stalin. Two days later, on October 15, old Soviet suspicions about being left alone to fight the Germans resurfaced when Molotov publicly demanded that Rudolf Hess, still held in a British jail, be tried immediately as a war criminal. Even though Stalin had indicated his intention to fight on by discussing lend-lease requests for the next twelve months, his complaints only reinforced rumors in Washington that he would soon threaten a separate peace unless more aid was forthcoming.[12]

Roosevelt and Churchill reacted quickly. The prime minister proposed sending ten merchant ships, sailing individually, with war supplies for Russia. Roosevelt found that insufficient. His immediate response was to scrawl across the message, "I do not agree," and to set up a meeting with Admiral King. The admiral apparently convinced the president that a convoy was the wrong answer, and FDR agreed to the British proposal, even adding some American merchant ships. Churchill hoped the long Arctic night would give the ships cover, but of the thirteen finally dispatched, only five arrived safely. In addition, Roosevelt and Churchill offered various formulas for sending a British-American air force to the Caucasus (Operation Velvet), but that came under the category of too little, too late. Churchill, with understandable myopia, insisted that Velvet could not be implemented "before the battle in Egypt."[13]

When Churchill griped to Roosevelt about Stalin's surliness, the president's response caught the essence of his long-range approach to the Soviet Union. In the early 1930s FDR had extended diplomatic recognition to the Communist regime primarily on the grounds of practicality. The Soviet government existed; why not recognize that fact? Trade might increase, and perhaps the Soviets would help restrain the Japanese in Northeast Asia, but fundamentally it made no sense not to recognize reality. During the Second World War Roosevelt again ignored ideology and applied common sense, hoping the wartime relationship would turn into a lasting one. But that, he believed, required convincing the Soviets that the United States could be trusted. "I am not unduly disturbed about our respective responses or lack of responses from Moscow," he told Churchill. "I have decided they do not use speech for the same purposes that we do. . . . I want to be able to say to Mr. Stalin that we have carried out our obligations one hundred percent."[14]

Hitler's fixation on symbolic victories at Stalingrad and Leningrad eventually betrayed him, but by August 1942 the Soviet situation was bleak, made a bit bleaker by the continued suspension of the Arctic convoys. One sailed in September with grim results;

twelve of thirty-nine merchant vessels were sunk. A few supply ships sailed individually, but fear of heavy losses and shipping requirements for Torch prevented another convoy until December. Stalin had recognized that a North African invasion offered strategic relief, but that would be meaningless unless the Soviet Union survived.

American Army planners warned that a Soviet collapse would be a "catastrophe" that would put the United States in a "desperate" situation whereby it might have to confront the Axis powers alone. That would force the United States "to adopt the strategic defensive in the European Theater of War and to conduct the strategic offensive in the Japanese theater." Joint staff planners, asked to evaluate the impact of the invasion of North Africa, responded that even if Torch were successful, a Soviet defeat would keep the Allies on the defensive in Europe. Great Britain's security could be maintained, but an invasion of the Continent would be impossible. A dismal prospect indeed for Roosevelt and Churchill.[15]

Nor, as autumn approached, had the situation improved much in the other theaters. The renewed effectiveness in 1942 of the German U-boat campaign in the Atlantic slowed supply preparations for Torch and threatened Bolero, the buildup for a cross-Channel invasion. In the Mediterranean five of fourteen merchant ships, including the American tanker *Ohio*, did manage to run a gauntlet of Axis air and submarine attacks to deliver supplies to Malta. British losses were heavy—a carrier, two cruisers, and a destroyer were sunk, and numerous warships damaged—but the operation prevented starvation from doing what the Axis could not do: force a surrender. In Churchill's inimitable phrasing, "Revictualled and replenished with ammunition and vital stores, the strength of Malta was revived." But the siege continued.[16]

In the Western Desert the German victory at Tobruk had left the British demoralized. "The whole attitude of Eighth Army was that of having one foot in the stirrup," bleakly commented one New Zealand officer.[17] Ultra intelligence reported Rommel's proposals to move "into the heart of Egypt," and by July the British fleet had left Alexandria for safer waters. But, as Churchill later wrote, "Rommel's communications were indeed strained . . . and his troops exhausted," and by midsummer the German offensive had stalled. Still, the threat remained.[18]

An Anglo-Canadian raid ("reconnaissance in force" became the official euphemism) in mid-August on Dieppe, on the French coast north of the Seine River, did nothing to lighten the gloom. A vain attempt to gain a bit of military glory and perhaps to reassure the Soviets, the landing was an unmitigated disaster, fatally flawed in conception, planning, and preparation, regardless of dubious claims that "lessons learned" about amphibious invasions were invaluable. Nor could the Soviets have been impressed that the only invasion of Europe until D-Day in June 1944 involved only a handful of troops, a little more than six thousand, even if getting them across the English Channel and ashore required 237 warships and landing craft. Churchill defensively claimed the raid made "the Germans conscious of the danger" of invasion, taking some of "the weight off Russia" by forcing Hitler "to hold troops and resources in the West." Robert Sherwood had a more plausible evaluation: ". . . it was a deplorable venture from the propaganda viewpoint, for it seemed to confirm all Hitler's boasts about the impregnability of the European Fortress and it put a fearful damper on the Russians' hopes for a Second Front."[19]

Amid all this bad news came the horrifying reports in August 1942 of German plans (actually already in operation for some eight months) to exterminate systematically the European Jews, Hitler's Final Solution.[20]

The situation outside Europe seemed no more promising. The China-Burma-India theater completely lacked any unified command structure, regardless of the Churchill-Roosevelt commitment to that concept. India, which remained a British responsibility, remained in turmoil as the Indian national leader Mohandas Gandhi continued to demand a promise of independence. The Japanese conquest of Burma had cut off the only land supply route to Chiang Kai-shek's forces in China, making that reluctant warrior even less inclined to risk offensive action against the Japanese. Chiang, ostensibly the supreme commander in China but dependent on outside aid and internal alliances with warlords, remained preoccupied with the threat to his rule posed by Communist forces led by Mao Tse-tung. Attempts by the Americans to promote effective Chinese action against Japan fell afoul of arguments between Chiang's two American Army advisers, Generals Joseph Stilwell and Claire Chennault. The former wanted to build up the Chinese Army, while the latter, an army air force officer, advocated air power.[21] All the while, Chiang played the British against the Americans and then one American against the other in order to keep the reins of control in his own hands.

In the Pacific, on August 7, the United States landed nineteen thousand Marines on Guadalcanal, in the Solomon Islands east of New Guinea, hoping to prevent the Japanese from any further advance southward. Naval battles to bring supplies and reinforcements determined the outcome as much as fighting in the tropical jungles, the "domain of giant ants, three-inch wasps, spiders, leeches, and above all, the malarial mosquito." So many ships were sunk in the waters just north of the island that the area was christened Ironbottom Sound. The psychological importance of the battle prompted Roosevelt, in October, to instruct his military chiefs "to make sure that every possible weapon gets into that area to hold Guadalcanal."[22]

Not until November did naval battles decide who would control the island. Then, in a series of engagements that included exchanges of fire between battleships—a rarity during World War II—the Japanese suffered staggering losses: Six warships, including two battleships, were sunk; three cruisers were damaged; eleven troopships bringing reinforcements went down. Only four managed to off-load their troops, and then only after they had run aground intentionally. U.S. naval forces lost nine warships and had a battleship damaged, but in the words of one American general, the "Tokyo Express [the Japanese naval supply line] no longer has terminus on Guadalcanal."[23] In early February 1943, even as the U.S. Army forces that had replaced the marines launched an offensive, the Japanese evacuated nearly thirteen thousand troops by barges to destroyers waiting offshore. The withdrawal was a brilliant maneuver, with overtones of the British at Dunkirk although, like most of the actions in the Pacific, on a much smaller scale.

In fact, despite popular perceptions in the United States, during the war and ever since, ground actions in the Pacific war involved relatively small numbers of troops, even if the logistics of sea communications and amphibious attacks were complex and demanding. The Americans never had more than fifty thousand troops on Guadalcanal, and most of the time between ten and twenty-five thousand marines were on the island. Japanese forces never exceeded thirty thousand. To provide some perspective, in October 1942 at the Battle of El Alamein in the Western Desert, Montgomery and Rommel had about two hundred thousand and one hundred thousand men respectively. The British amassed about one thousand tanks to some five hundred for the Germans. That despite the fact that the Western Desert was a secondary campaign, particularly for the Germans.

The forces involved in China dwarfed the Pacific and North African campaigns. Although little large-scale fighting went on in 1942, the very existence of a vast, if disorganized, Chinese Army— 5.7 million men and growing in 1941—tied down a half million or more Japanese soldiers for most of the war.

On the Russian front the numbers were equally immense and more active. At the same time as the battles at El Alamein and Guadalcanal, Germany and its allies had some five million troops facing the five and one-half million men Stalin had in action, while the Red Army held ten field armies and a tank army in reserve. At the Battle of Kursk, a year later, the Germans had twenty-four hundred tanks to thirty-four hundred for the Soviets—more than three times the number that fought in the Western Desert.

Statistics on the size of Soviet military forces vary widely. German sources claimed that the Red Army alone approached thirteen million men by the beginning of 1943. At the same time the grand total (army, navy, marines, coast guard) of women and men serving in all branches of the U.S. military was seven million, and in Great Britain some four million. That disparity of sheer numbers compared with the Soviet Union continued to the end of the war, with the Anglo-Americans never facing more than 20 percent of Hitler's military strength. For the British, with a smaller population to draw on, the gap grew throughout the war.

For the United States the difference was in part a conscious choice. The nation never fully mobilized its population for military service. The president, along with Stimson and Marshall, worried about adverse public reaction to more extensive conscription. With the luxury of no threat of invasion and the knowledge that the Red Army faced the bulk of the enemy's ground forces, the administration gambled that "an air war plus the Russians" meant that ninety army divisions would be sufficient for its military—and political—needs. That decision only heightened Washington's concern over the prospect of either a Soviet defeat or a separate Soviet-German peace.

The U.S. industrial sector had not yet reached the levels that it was to achieve in 1943, when it produced 60 percent of the total Allied war matériel, truly making it the Arsenal of Democracy. But even in 1942 American production played a significant role. The Soviet Union produced an impressive total of some twenty-five thousand tanks that year, while American lend-lease supplied about fifty-four thousand tanks to the Russians. But given Soviet losses (some thirteen thousand tanks destroyed), lend-lease supplies in 1942 may well have been critical. Certainly Stalin's impassioned concern about the convoys was more than pro forma. But American economic strength did not give the Allies much political leverage in 1942 and 1943, a time when the war could be lost before that strength was brought fully to bear.[24]

The ominous state of the war in the autumn of 1942 made the success of Torch that much more critical for the Anglo-Americans. For Roosevelt, failure could force him to adopt the Pacific alternative; for Churchill, failure could mean that the parliamentary no-confidence vote he had easily overcome after the fall of Tobruk would be reintroduced and carry; for both, failure could mean that Stalin would conclude he was left alone to confront the Germans. Initially that offered the frightening prospect of a Soviet-German accommodation. Then, in early November, when reports on the Stalingrad and Caucasus battles began to suggest an opportunity for overwhelming Red Army success, the unsettling image of a Soviet victory *without* Anglo-American assistance loomed larger. (Little wonder that Stalin kept his allies ignorant of Soviet military failures, not just during 1941 and 1942, but afterward. For example, a major offensive in Byelorussia in November 1943 had to be abandoned because of effective German resistance and the onset of winter.[25])

In early December Sumner Welles, echoing the concern expressed by British officials ten months earlier, told Ambassador Halifax that if Germany should collapse "without our two governments having reached any agreement with Russia, we could look forward to the Russian armies following the German armies westward and no one could predict where they would stop, the Baltic states of course, probably Roumania, Finland and what else. It would not be in the power of the United States or Great Britain by any physical pressure to stop them. . . . We could probably get an understanding now that would help to avoid these dangers because we still have much to give Russia of which she stood in need. But if we put it off it might well become too late."[26]

From the outset the Anglo-Americans had recognized the risk of depending on an ally that had been their ideological and political enemy a few years earlier. No one could predict in 1942 the military successes that would make the Soviet Union a great power after the war, but Churchill and Roosevelt understood that if they achieved the victory they sought, their ally would play a major role in the postwar world. Torch was more than an attack on Germany and its allies, more than an attempt to keep the Soviet Union in the war, more than a way to keep focused on the war against Hitler. It was a political declaration of independence—or at least a declaration of Anglo-American intent to escape dependence on the Red Army.

The politics of Torch was more difficult than the military operation and less successful. The North African invasion could not escape the French civil war being waged under cover of the broader struggle against Hitler. When France surrendered in June 1940 and declared its neutrality, Charles de Gaulle, just promoted to brigadier general, rejected Vichy's authority and escaped to Great Britain. Churchill, eager to rally forces in the French colonies to the Allied side, designated de Gaulle the "leader of all free Frenchmen, wherever they may be" and arranged for Britain to provide military and financial aid. By the end of 1940 de Gaulle had rejected the Vichy government and asserted his own legitimacy as leader of the true France. The British became prisoners of their own policy. They had rejected Vichy by accepting the Free French, and de Gaulle worked hard to ensure that no other practical alternative appeared.

Despite de Gaulle's dependence on British assistance, his haughty style and unswerving dedication to what he considered French rights and responsibilities brought him into conflict with Churchill, particularly on issues related to the French Empire. In Syria, a French protectorate since World War I, Britain encouraged the Free French to make commitments to independence so as to prevent popular uprisings and to promote Syrian opposition to German schemes. De Gaulle rejected British interference and accused the British of having designs on the French Empire. When Free French officials arrested Syrian nationalists elected to office on an independence platform, Churchill piously told FDR that "there is no doubt in my mind that this is a foretaste of what de Gaulle's leadership of France means. It is certainly contrary to the Atlantic Charter and much else that we have declared."[27] One French historian puts the dispute in words that could have come from the general himself: "Even after Free French administrations were installed in French territories like Syria, Lebanon or North Africa, relations with the British were less than cordial. This was not only because local would-be Lawrences harboured secret designs of supplanting the French, or even because the British military . . . never quite understood de Gaulle's political importance. . . . It was above all because. . . . it could well be necessary to thwart the French in order to propitiate the natives."[28]

De Gaulle's contemptuous rejection of all Vichy authority soon brought him into conflict with American policy. The Vichy regime had richly earned the pejorative "collaborationist" by following Nazi guidance in persecuting its own citizens, particularly Jews, and by willingly providing forced labor for Germany. But in 1940 Roosevelt had maintained diplomatic relations with the Vichy government, hoping initially to keep the French fleet out of German hands and then to gain nonresistance, if not cooperation, from Vichy authorities in the French Empire.

De Gaulle refused to allow that compromise with Hitler to go unchallenged. On Christmas Eve 1941 Free French forces had occupied St. Pierre and Miquelon, two tiny Vichy-controlled islands located some 180 miles west of Placentia Bay, Newfoundland, the birthplace of the Atlantic Charter. The islands' names had a familiar ring in the United States since they had provided safe havens for liquor smuggling during the only period of prosperity in their history, the *temps du whisky*—Prohibition. Immediately after the Free French moved in, residents of the islands held a plebiscite that resulted in a near-unanimous vote for affiliation with de Gaulle's organization. The occupation, which amounted to the Free French's thumbing their collective nose at the Western Hemisphere's guardian, despite prior assurances that no military action would take place, infuriated and embarrassed the State Department. Hull, now wishing that Congress had succeeded during the late 1930s in its efforts to annex the islands as part payment for France's First World War debts, protested the actions of what he termed the so-called Free French, particularly after newspaper reports generated enthusiastic public support among Americans for de Gaulle's actions. "Why," asked a typical American newspaper editorial, "is it considered vital policy to give these islands back to Vichy, after their people have voted democratically for Free France? How does that agree with the Four Freedoms proclaimed by Mr. Roosevelt?"[29] In public Roosevelt treated the matter casually, taking Churchill's advice to allow the two barren islands to "relapse into the obscurity from which they have more than once emerged since the Treaty of Utrecht." But the affair seems to have convinced him that de Gaulle could not be trusted.[30]

In September 1940 Vichy French units in Dakar had resisted a British invasion that included Free French units. That prompted Churchill to conclude that fear of Gaullist reprisals had caused the Vichy forces to obey orders to resist the Allied invasion. After all, reasoned the British, de Gaulle offered military officers loyal to Vichy little comfort. They had to face the choice of violating their oath of loyalty to the government or of being labeled traitors should de Gaulle win out. But the reluctance of the French military to lay down its arms and welcome an Allied occupation, with or without the Free French, was more a matter of stubborn pride and perceptions of honor than fear of de Gaulle.

Eighteen months later the British learned from Magic intercepts that the Germans had requested a Japanese attack on the Vichy-controlled French colony of Madagascar off Africa's east coast. Since that would threaten British control of the Indian Ocean, Churchill and his military chiefs became preoccupied with mounting a preemptive invasion of the island that took place in May 1942. This time Churchill rejected de Gaulle's offer of Free French units, but again the Vichy forces resisted, stubbornly for a change, holding out in the southern part of the island until November.[31]

Those events reinforced Roosevelt's belief that British attacks in 1940 on the French fleet in Toulon and Algeria had embittered French officers, prompting him to insist that Torch take on the appearance of being primarily an American show. That was in part because the president wanted Torch to involve the American public and Congress in the war. But the more immediate reason was the hope that French military forces in North Africa could be persuaded not to resist. Even Churchill thought that "the danger of offensive action by the French Fleet in the Mediterranean would be markedly reduced by the showing of the American flag" and at one point offered to have British troops making the initial assault wear American uniforms if FDR found that "convenient."[32] Press releases and messages to other governments all emphasized the Americanization of the operation. Plans even called for a small American assault force to land at Algiers before the British invasion force could launch the main attack. Harriman told the president that Churchill "understands fully that he is to play second fiddle in all scores, and then only as you direct." Given such indignities, one understands the tinge of bitter sarcasm in a letter from the prime minister to FDR on the eve of the invasion: "I pray that this great American enterprise, in which I am your lieutenant and in which we have the honour to play an important part, may be crowned by the success it deserves."[33] In the harem or not, the Americans were still being wooed by Churchill.

Even as the Anglo-Americans made their final preparations for Torch, British forces prepared for a confrontation in the Western

Desert with Rommel's Panzer Group Afrika—the German Afrika Corps plus the Italian 21st Corps. The Axis campaign in North Africa had never been a high strategic priority for Hitler, and by autumn 1942 the situation on the Russian front had forced him to cut back support for Rommel even further. For the British, the defeat of Rommel offered an opportunity to recoup some degree of military credibility and regain prestige within the Grand Alliance, while eliminating a secondary but nonetheless dangerous threat.

Intelligence had a great deal more to do with the famous British victory at El Alamein than Churchill's decision to install General Bernard Montgomery as commander of the Eighth Army. As at the Battle of Midway, information about the enemy's intentions provided the winning edge. During most of the desert war Rommel had enjoyed a distinct intelligence advantage, particularly the ability to decipher messages sent by an American military attaché in Cairo back to Washington (the so-called Good Source). But by autumn the Good Source had dried up while British code breakers provided increasingly detailed information on Rommel's plans and capabilities. At the same time Ultra allowed the British to intercept German supply convoys sailing across the Mediterranean from Italy, even if that necessitated going to near-ludicrous lengths to protect the source of the intelligence. (For example, upon learning of a convoy, the British sometimes sent out a reconnaissance plane that took great care to be sighted by the enemy so that the bombers that quickly appeared were assumed to have found the target because of the bad luck of a visual sighting.)[34] Whatever the subterfuges, cutting off those Axis convoys and the demands from the Russian front meant that Rommel was overmatched in manpower, weapons, and supplies—especially the gasoline crucial for his tanks. That forced him to turn to static defense in place of the aggressive, mobile tactics that had made his previous successes possible, spelling victory for the British.

Near the insignificant railroad rest stop of El Alamein, about sixty miles west of Alexandria and some twenty-five hundred miles east across the North African coast from where Torch would soon take place, General Montgomery finally got the set piece battle he had sought against Rommel's army. The relatively moderate size of the forces involved—fewer than 200,000 British versus 104,000 Italian and German troops—belied the significance of the battle. With overwhelming British superiority in men, tanks, aircraft, and intelligence, the battle was much closer than it should have been. Finally, making good use of concentrated artillery and air attacks, the British Eighth Army broke through during the first few days of November, sending Rommel in a westward retreat that did not end until he joined Italo-German forces in Tunisia in February. On November 6, two days before Torch began, General Harold Alexander, British commander in chief Middle East, reminded the prime minister of his promise to unwrap Britain's church bells on news of a military victory. "I decided on second thoughts," wrote Churchill, "not to ring the bells till after TORCH, now on the verge, had begun successfully." As he hoped, Churchill was able to ring the bells "within the week."[35]

Just before dawn on Sunday, November 8, 1942, Operation Torch put some sixty-five thousand Allied troops ashore at Algiers and Oran on Algeria's Mediterranean coast and at Casablanca and two other locations on Morocco's Atlantic coast. The Germans did not think the Allies would do anything to drive Vichy into an open alliance with Germany and had therefore assumed that the convoy approaching North Africa was another attempt to send supplies to Malta, a belief encouraged by British deception measures. The Moroccan invasion, an exclusively American affair, proved the most difficult. The surf ran, in Churchill's understatement, "less severe than had been feared," but French resistance proved tenacious. In fact the French resisted at all the landing sites despite widespread sympathy for the Allies among many of the senior French military officers on the scene. Nevertheless, the invasion was a success, and as the next Sunday dawned, church bells rang throughout Britain.[36]

A small sidebar: Torch took place five days after American elections that significantly diminished the support FDR had in Congress for his leadership and programs. "Jesus Christ! Why couldn't the Army have done this just before [the] election!" exclaimed Steve Early, a White House aide. Hopkins had pushed the president to launch the invasion before the voting, and Roosevelt had thrown out the idea to General Marshall. But when Eisenhower set a date only five days after the election, FDR said nothing.[37]

Stalin had foreseen the political mess surrounding Torch, telling Churchill during their August 1942 talks that de Gaulle should be included in the operation. But the Anglo-Americans had placed their bets on Henri Giraud, an austere French general suggested by Churchill, back in April, as a possible alternative to de Gaulle. Giraud's main claim to fame seemed to be that he had escaped German prison camps during both world wars (no one seemed interested in why he had been twice captured), but he was untainted by Vichy (he had already been captured when France surrendered), not associated with de Gaulle, and well respected by his military colleagues. That made Giraud attractive to Roosevelt and Churchill, who had placed great hopes on persuading French commanders in North Africa not to resist the invasion.

But Giraud, as Roosevelt and Churchill should have immediately realized, was as prickly as de Gaulle and not as smart. Asked to meet with General Eisenhower at Gibraltar, the Frenchman flatly refused to travel on any British ship. Since only the British submarine *Seraph* was available to pick up Giraud at his hideaway on the coast of southern France and take him to the meeting, an American naval officer took nominal command while the crew dressed in American uniforms. The farce succeeded when Giraud pompously stayed in his cabin for the entire trip, refusing to talk to anyone but the supposed captain.[38]

Giraud proved neither charismatic nor effective. Instead of working to persuade his comrades to join the Allies, he focused on gaining recognition as the leader of France, a preoccupation like that of Chiang regarding Mao in China, and with similar military nonresults. Secret negotiations between Roosevelt's agent Robert Murphy and Vichy officials in North Africa proved equally ineffective because French Admiral Jean Darlan, the Anglophobic head of the French Navy and the onetime leader of the Vichy government, happened to be in Algiers on the day of the invasion. Darlan, following Vichy orders, at first refused to command French forces to lay down their arms.

It was Hitler who released Darlan from his oath of loyalty to the French government—if that is what motivated the admiral, who also seemed very aware that the fortunes of war had begun to shift toward the Allies. Even before the North African invasion Darlan had hinted to various Americans at Vichy that he might be persuaded to shift his support.[39] Once the success of Torch became clear, Darlan and Eisenhower's deputy on the scene, General Mark Clark, worked out a deal: The Americans would designate Darlan the high commissioner of French North Africa, and in return he would bring French forces in on the side of the Allies. Two days after Torch began, and too late to prevent casualties, Darlan ordered that French forces in North Africa cease fire. When news of the invasion prompted the Germans to end the sham of an independent French government at Vichy by occupying the remainder of France as well as French military facilities in Tunisia, Eisenhower carried out the next part of the deal by appointing Darlan high commissioner and designating Giraud commander of French military forces. De Gaulle was muzzled (Churchill would not let him deliver a speech on the BBC "denouncing the maintenance of the Vichy regime in North Africa") and ignored.[40]

Nearly twenty-five hundred French military personnel died in North Africa fighting the very nations that intended to liberate France. Pétain, or someone who signed the senile old marshal's name, called the invasion "aggression," claiming that whatever the "pretexts" invoked by Roosevelt, "France and her honor are at stake." In Robert Sherwood's pungent phrase, "Thus, for the 'honor' of the Vichy Government, was enacted the sordid spectacle of Frenchmen shooting at and killing Americans and Americans shooting at and killing Frenchmen."[41]

Eisenhower displayed careful sensitivity to the Roosevelt administration's Vichy policy, even though his immediate concern was to get French ground troops to join the fight and to persuade the French fleet to sail from Toulon and other ports before the Germans took over. "It isn't this operation that's wearing me down," he complained; "it's the petty intrigue and the necessity of dealing with little, selfish conceited worms that call themselves men."[42] The French Army did join the Allies in the fighting, but most of

the French fleet was scuttled when commanders on the scene refused orders from both Darlan and the Germans.

Public reaction to the Darlan deal caused both Churchill and
Roosevelt to run for cover. Churchill had been unenthusiastic, but
fully informed, and his protests came after the fact. In a secret
session speech before the Commons on December 10, 1942, he
intimated that it was all an American idea, then defended the arrangement on grounds of military necessity. At the end of the
statement he offered a trenchant criticism of de Gaulle and effectively associated himself with Roosevelt's policy toward France. "I
cannot feel that de Gaulle is France," he told the House. "Like
the President . . . , we seek to base ourselves on the will of the
entire French nation. . . ." That segment of the speech remained
unpublished even as late as 1976.[43]

The president had initially opposed working with any ex-Vichy
officials in North Africa, but Eisenhower persuaded him that Darlan could be controlled. More persuasive was Giraud's ineffectiveness and the fact that de Gaulle was waiting in the wings. As with
the British, the United States had become the prisoner of its own
French policy.[44]

That did not answer the outraged protests coming from the
British press and Parliament about dealing with so unsavory a politician, protests echoed in the American press, though a little less
stridently since American lives were supposedly being saved by the
Darlan deal. FDR resented the implication that he had collaborated
with fascism. Hopkins, ever the politician, drafted a Roosevelt to
Eisenhower message that was called "very important for the record," suggesting that FDR was more involved with the Darlan deal
than he let on. Although the cable was never sent, it repudiated
Darlan and stated that only the "military situation" warranted the
deal.[45] Roosevelt and Hopkins never mentioned Woodrow Wilson,
but the Darlan deal had all the appearance of the compromises
with principle Wilson had made in 1919. Not until the Casablanca
Conference a few months later did FDR find a way to reclaim the
moral high ground by proclaiming that the only peace term for
the Axis was "unconditional surrender."

Darlan's assassination on Christmas Eve 1942 took Roosevelt and Churchill off the hook publicly, but what might be called the War of the French Succession, every bit as bitter as its namesakes in Spain and Austria two centuries earlier, did not end until de Gaulle received an imprimatur from an ecstatic French crowd assembled outside the Hôtel de Ville in Paris nearly two months after the Normandy invasion in June 1944.[46]

Perhaps Churchill should have held off ringing the church bells in celebration of Torch for just a few more days so they could give thanks for the most important victory. On November 19, with the autumn mud in southern Russia finally hardened by the deepening cold, the Red Army launched a major counteroffensive around Stalingrad, Operation Uranus. The Germans and their allies occupied about two thirds of the city, with their supply and communications lines coming in from the west. The Soviet attack aimed at cutting that supply and escape route and thus isolating Axis forces in Stalingrad.

To picture the operation, imagine a drawing of a man's profile facing to your right, the head tilted very slightly upward. Soviet forces were positioned at the top (north) along the hairline and then on the right (east) along the entire profile. German armies were on the left (west), holding all the head below the hairline. At the tip of the nose—a salient, in military terms—lay Stalingrad. The Soviet maneuver called for two thrusts—again picture a profile—one coming down some seventy-five miles from the eyes, the other up some sixty miles from the mouth, with the two meeting just behind the nose, pinching it off, as it were.

The attacks were a surprise and a success. The ill-equipped armies of Romania (an Axis ally with twenty army divisions on the Russian front) that stood in the way collapsed immediately, allowing the Red Army to close the pincers and cut off twenty divisions of German troops at Stalingrad. Hitler had refused permission for the German Sixth Army to withdraw when that was still possible. Now those troops, some 250,000 Germans plus tens of thousands of Romanians and anti-Communist volunteers from various Soviet ethnic groups, were "entombed in the ruins" of the city.[47]

As the Stalingrad victory became obvious, coalition politics reared its head. How would this broad victory affect Soviet plans and policies? Analysts in the American Office of Strategic Services (OSS) warned that Soviet military operations in 1943 would "depend to a great extent on the attitude of its Allies and on the requirements of coalition warfare." After all, they pointed out, Stalin had continued to call for a second front, even after he knew about plans for Torch, thus demonstrating his dissatisfaction with his Anglo-American partners. The analysts went on to predict that while the Soviets would "commit their ultimate reserves" to defeat Hitler, "mutual skepticism" would be "the major problem of the war—and of the peace to follow."[48]

The Red Army had stopped the Germans; Hitler's armies could no longer win in the East. But Stalingrad and the stabilization of the Russian front did not generate confidence and a sense of security in London, Washington, or Moscow. To the contrary, the victory seemed to stimulate even greater suspicion and concern about mutual intentions. Stalin apparently suspected the Anglo-Americans would delay the second front and let the German and Soviet armies savage each other—the Truman gambit. At the same time the Anglo-Americans worried that the Soviet leader, his state's territory secure, might cut his future losses and pursue a favorable settlement with Germany, leaving his Allies to deal with Hitler. On the other hand, the Red Army might break through and threaten to defeat the Germans before the Anglo-Americans could put their forces into western France.[49]

Rumors of a separate peace between Hitler and Stalin persisted. They were nothing new; there was, after all, the precedent of 1939. Such reports had cropped up frequently in mid-1942, when it appeared that the Germans would break through on the Russian front and when the Soviet offensive stalled.[50] The rumors continued until the second front became a reality in June 1944.

The "indefatigable" Eleanor Roosevelt went to Britain during November 1942, in what turned out to be a remarkably popular visit that exhausted reporters and Clementine Churchill, puzzled Winston (who was not used to having women argue with him), and brought rave reviews in the American press.[51] She could not have picked a better time, for November was the best month so far in the entire war for the Grand Alliance. The Americans had secured Guadalcanal and engaged in a larger-scale campaign on New Guinea, enough to quiet those arguing for the Pacific alternative. It would be another year before they were ready to seize the offensive against Japan's island bases in the Central Pacific, but the war of attrition against Japan—an ironic reversal of Japan's own strategy—would pay off. New Guinea, Midway, Coral Sea, Guadalcanal—these and some smaller actions had, by year's end, worn down Japan's military forces to the point that they would no longer be able to hold everything they had gained in the early months of the war. The struggle would be long and bloody, but the tide had turned.

As for the British, they had refurbished their self-esteem with the satisfying, if strategically secondary, victory against Rommel at El Alamein in the Western Desert. And the massive battle at Stalingrad ensured that military events would not cause the Anglo-Americans to have to face Hitler alone.

On November 10, 1942, two days after the successful Anglo-American invasion of North Africa, Churchill told an audience at the Lord Mayor's Luncheon at Mansion House in London: "Now this is not the end. It is not even the beginning of the end. But it is, perhaps, the end of the beginning." In that same speech he proclaimed that he had "not become the King's First Minister in order to preside over the liquidation of the British Empire."[52] Whatever doubts that latter statement raises about Churchill as seer, hindsight tells us that by the time winter arrived in 1942 the military turning points in the war had taken place. It was clearly "the end of the beginning," if not a bit more. El Alamein, Guadalcanal, North Africa, Stalingrad—each was a vital piece in the mosaic of victory that the Allied coalition was putting together; each signaled the beginning of the alliance's shift from retreat and defense to offense and victory. The Churchills' greeting to President and Mrs. Roosevelt on Christmas Day 1942 called it a "brighter day than we have yet seen." A few hours later FDR replied with "warm Christmas greetings" and an optimistic observation: "The old teamwork is grand."[53]

But that Anglo-American teamwork was to become more difficult in the months to come. The military victories of that autumn and winter created a "strategic paradox." The Soviet Union seemed about to take the offensive. That made a massive cross-Channel invasion of Europe militarily logical and politically prudent for the Anglo-Americans. At the same time the Allied offensive in North Africa, if as successful as the Anglo-Americans hoped, almost demanded that they use North Africa as the "springboard," in Churchill's word, for further operations in the Mediterranean. Churchill and Roosevelt would not resolve, or at least postpone that paradox, until they met at Casablanca in January 1943, by which time military events left them few options.

General Marshall as well as the combined and British chiefs of staff had expected a quick victory in North Africa—Tunis by Christmas, the general thought. Reflecting the optimism, Roosevelt suggested to Churchill, only three days after Torch began, that they should consider "additional steps that should be taken when and if" the Axis was cleared from Africa. Three days later the president modified that proposal by recommending staff talks with the Russians about any "operations springing from the Eastern Mediterranean." The politics of the Grand Alliance remained troublesome.[54]

All this put Churchill in an awkward position. Like FDR, he worried that Stalin might not prosecute the war after Stalingrad but instead negotiate a German withdrawal from the USSR. In late November the prime minister again sent one of his words-in-lieu-of-action messages to the Soviet leader. But colorful descriptions about bringing "the war home to Mussolini and his Fascist gang with an intensity not yet possible" could do very little to divert German forces from the Russian front, while pledges of "continuous preparations" that would "keep the Germans pinned down" in France and bombers "blasting Germany with ever increasing violence" hardly qualified as the second front that Stalin seemed to demand as a bona fide.[55]

Yet Churchill recoiled from a massive cross-Channel assault in 1943 (or later), even while the Americans assumed it was already joint Anglo-American strategy. His oft-expressed support for Roundup referred to the smaller version that fitted his and General Brooke's peripheral strategy, a distinction made as early as May

1942, when he referred to "SUPER-ROUND-UP" to distinguish the massive attack from the smaller Sledgehammer attack on Western Europe. But Churchill never explained that in clear terms— either to Roosevelt during the war or to the readers of his war memoirs later on. One of his express purposes in writing that history, he said, was to "dispose of the many American legends that I was inveterately opposed to the plan of a large-scale Channel crossing."[56]

The reality was that Churchill did not want to clarify the distinction between his and the Americans' conception of a cross-Channel invasion because he wanted to steer the Americans toward further operations in the Mediterranean, just as Marshall had feared. If Churchill argued for some sort of "semi" Round-up, he ran the risk of presenting the European strategy as one of attrition, which would almost certainly reinvigorate American support for the Pacific first option. He finally presented his soft-underbelly strategy to Roosevelt in mid-November 1942, when it still seemed that the North African campaign might stay on schedule and see the Axis tossed out by Christmas. Torch was not a defensive operation, the prime minister told his chiefs of staff. "It is a springboard and not a sofa. . . ."[57] A week later he warned Roosevelt that "it would be a most grievous decision to abandon ROUND-UP," raising fears among the British chiefs that Churchill had swung over to a "Western Front" strategy. But he meant his own smaller version; in the event that the Stalingrad battle created "widespread demoralization" among German forces, he wrote Roosevelt, "we must be ready to profit by any opportunity which offers."[58]

Like Churchill, Roosevelt seemed unwilling to face up to the effect of Torch: an enormous drain on manpower, shipping, and matériel. The president quickly reaffirmed his commitment to Bolero (the buildup for the cross-Channel attack) and proposed a military staff conference in either Moscow or Cairo. But that firmness was misleading. The Americans were also engaged in their own debate about how to follow up the expected victory in North Africa. General Marshall opposed any expansion of operations in the Mediterranean lest that take away from Bolero and the cross-Channel invasion, Admiral King continued to argue for greater emphasis on the Pacific, and Roosevelt seemed most concerned about keeping Anglo-American forces engaged against the Germans.

Hitler decided the issue. The refusal of Vichy representatives in Tunisia to obey Darlan's orders had given the Germans an opportunity to reinforce North Africa through the port of Tunis. That reinforcement (seventeen thousand troops) ensured that Marshall's optimistic timetable could not be met. Then the additional forces brought by Rommel as he retreated from Libya (pursued with less than imaginative vigor by Montgomery), and some faulty Anglo-American tactics, pushed victory even further back. In fact, had the Italian high command (which had Axis military authority in Tunisia) not foolishly sent Rommel in the wrong direction after the Americans had been defeated at the Kasserine Pass in February 1943, the Axis might have overwhelmed Allied forces. In any event, operations in North Africa demanded many more resources than the Anglo-Americans had anticipated.[59] Whatever Churchill's enthusiasm, or lack thereof, for Roundup, the North African campaign guaranteed that no cross-Channel invasion, massive or not, could take place in 1943.

Churchill's awareness of that hard reality underpinned his description, in late December, of his notion of a dual attack on Germany—one from Britain, the other from North Africa—an approach that guaranteed a good deal less than what the Americans wanted in the way of a cross-Channel invasion. In fact the tone of Churchill's minute suggests there were proposals from the British military chiefs (General Brooke, for one) to give up completely the idea of an attack on Western Europe.[60]

The postponement of Roundup (or, more accurately, of a "superroundup") would be a bitter pill for Stalin to swallow, and Roosevelt and Churchill knew it. The two equivocated on the decision but in early December agreed on the need to meet and work out strategy for 1943, even if, as they still assumed, Tunisia would be "cleared up" by mid-January.[61] The pattern of the Churchill-

Roosevelt haggling over those talks was repeated whenever the need arose to talk to Stalin and the Soviet leadership about major issues.

Roosevelt began by suggesting Anglo-American military staff talks, then quickly amended his proposal to include Soviet military representatives. Churchill belittled any talks with Soviet military men who could not say anything without first asking Stalin. Moreover, the prime minister said with a sneer, all they would do was ask about the second front. Why "queer the pitch"? he asked. Instead, he suggested, let us take Stalin up on his mention of a Big Three meeting in Iceland or England. Such discussions should of course be preceded by Anglo-American staff talks so they could arrive at an agreed-upon position before talking to the Russians.

Great idea, replied Roosevelt, although Iceland and Alaska were "impossible" in winter. "I don't like mosquitoes," he quipped, but what about a "comfortable oasis" like Khartoum in the Sudan or someplace south of Algiers? By the way, added the president, "I do not want to give Stalin the impression that we are settling everything between ourselves before we meet him," so let us not schedule staff conferences in England beforehand. After all, Roosevelt added seductively, "I think that you and I understand each other so well that prior conferences between us are unnecessary. . . ." The polite phrases notwithstanding, Roosevelt had told Churchill that Soviet-American relations were the key issue; Anglo-American relations could be taken for granted. Churchill dangled the "prospect of attack in Europe in 1943," warning that it "depends on early decision." But "Europe" was a vague description that fitted every size—from Sicily to Greece to Norway—and did not necessarily mean the invasion of France or Western Europe that the Americans wanted.[62]

One small but not irrelevant note: Churchill proposed a meeting in "England" (his politically incorrect term for Britain). FDR transmogrified that into Alaska, illustrating another pattern. The prime minister repeatedly tried to get the president to visit England, and FDR just as invariably found reasons not to. While Eleanor Roosevelt was in Britain in November 1942, she worked with King George to sketch out accommodations that would meet the needs of someone confined to a wheelchair. But nothing came of it. Whenever the enticement of such a visit tempted Roosevelt (an easy thing since he loved to travel), Harry Hopkins or some other adviser whispered that it would lose votes or could restrict the president's ability to be the impartial mediator in Anglo-Soviet squabbles. Whatever the nature of the "special relationship," it had to be modified by the realities of American politics and Soviet power.[63]

But a summit gathering would happen with or without a visit to Britain from FDR. Churchill had pushed for a meeting in Marrakech, a favorite spot of his, located in southern Morocco at the foot of the Atlas Mountains. But once Stalin declined the invitation to meet, the Americans insisted on Casablanca, close to American troops, but a hot, dusty city on Morocco's Atlantic coast, even if the conferees would be comfortably ensconced in the exotic, if slightly seedy, resort of Anfa on the city's outskirts. Bergman and Bogart had been there first—FDR viewed the film *Casablanca* a few weeks before the conference—and now Churchill and Roosevelt were coming.[64] He would be "Don Quixote" and Hopkins "Sancho Panza," Roosevelt cabled Churchill. The prime minister, perhaps fearing that the trip would be labeled "quixotic," suggested that to "make it even harder for the enemy and to discourage irreverent guess work [I] propose Admiral Q. and Mr. P. (NB) We must mind our P's and Q's." Should FDR bring Willkie along (a notion that only demonstrated Churchill's ignorance of American politics), FDR's Republican opponent could be designated "Windmill," one label both the president and conservative Republicans could agree upon. The meeting, code-named Symbol, would begin on January 14.

Churchill's apparent concern for security (he scheduled his flight under Averell Harriman's name) was belied by his evening arrival at an airport near Oxford at the head of a caravan that could be spotted for miles: headlights shining (despite the blackout) and sirens wailing. "No one could make that much noise except the prime minister," complained the local commander. Churchill then compromised the secrecy of the conference site when, after arriving in Casablanca on January 12, he stood on the tarmac in plain view, outfitted in his Royal Air Force uniform, until the plane carrying his military chiefs landed. Pug Ismay, upon seeing Churchill, remarked acidly, "Any fool can see that is an air commander disguised as the Prime Minister."[65]

In the post–World War II era American presidents jetting all over the world for summit talks, casual visits, celebrations, and funerals became commonplace. Not so in 1943. Wilson had gone to Paris by ship. No other American president had visited Europe while in office, much less left the country in an airplane—and crossed the Atlantic Ocean to Africa at that! And what awaited FDR were massed ranks of American GIs and news photographers at Camp Anfa and nearby Rabat, ready for a presidential inspection. FDR had a flair for and love of the dramatic, along with a keen appreciation of how to play public opinion. What better image than that of the president, his cigarette at the usual jaunty angle, riding in a jeep as he reviewed American troops, apparently right there on the front?

Roosevelt complained "of the Winston hours" during the conference, with dinners lasting "to an average of 2 A.M." That average was a bit high. The long night that prompted that remark was when FDR was with his two sons Elliott and Franklin, Jr., both of whom were in the army and in North Africa. On that occasion the Roosevelts and a small group that included Harry Hopkins dined with five officers serving with the U.S. Women's Army Auxiliary Corps (WAAC). As the trip log put it, after dinner the president invited Churchill and others to join "what was now an after-dinner party," which did not break up until two in the morning. But the Casablanca Conference was much more than just a public relations venture or a pleasant visit to a comfortable "oasis." Churchill conferred with the president most evenings until about 1:00 A.M., and one night (January 23, after FDR had written his complaint), the prime minister and his son, Randolph, kept FDR up until 2:30 A.M. working on a joint communiqué and a message to Stalin.[66]

That concern with Stalin and the Soviet Union lay beneath much of the president's actions at Casablanca. A few months earlier, during the Thanksgiving weekend, Roosevelt had told Daisy

Suckley, during a picnic lunch at their special rendezvous at Top Hill Cottage in Hyde Park, that he wanted an opportunity to work on a "definite agreement with Churchill, Stalin & Chiang Kai-shek." There was, he believed, "a growing demand for a definite statement about our intentions after the war." Stalin's failure to attend the conference effectively removed postwar matters from the agenda. The president thought Stalin would "understand" the concept of a disarmed world, an international police force run by the Big Four, and self-determination for colonies worked out "over a period of years" but had doubts that Churchill would go along.[67]

Stalin's absence was his own choice—and mistake. Both Roosevelt and Churchill tried to persuade the Soviet leader to attend, but he pleaded that the press of military operations made that impossible, a plausible explanation given his close management of the Stalingrad battle, even though Churchill and Roosevelt suspected he was pouting about Anglo-American delays in launching the second front. Whatever Stalin's reasons—military operations, his fear of flying, the need to maintain political control in the Kremlin, annoyance about the second front—he missed a chance to influence the very strategies he criticized. Moreover, he could have gained leverage by bringing firsthand news of the Red Army's victory at Stalingrad. That battle, and its implications, were never formally discussed during the Casablanca talks. The expected Soviet victory was already labeled a turning point in the war by intelligence analysts, but Roosevelt, Churchill, and their staffs preferred to work in the sheltered, old-fashioned atmosphere of an Anglo-American world where victories on the Russian front were less important than squabbles over which Frenchman should govern North Africa or whether the Anglo-Americans should invade Sardinia or Sicily.[68]

Events on the Russian front did mean that the Anglo-Americans no longer needed to guard against the possibility of a German victory over the Soviet Union. That in turn meant that Roosevelt, Churchill, and their military chiefs could focus on offensive actions against the Axis in Europe. From the perspective of the successful Normandy invasion, the choice seems obvious, but in early 1943 agreement on joint strategy proved elusive. The Americans believed the time had come to concentrate on a major cross-Channel attack in 1943. The British wanted to follow up the successes and expected successes of the campaigns in Egypt and Northwest Africa by moving against Italy and then, with the Turks as allies, drive Italo-German forces out of Greece and the Aegean.[69]

Despite their differences, Anglo-American discussions on strategy proved deceptively free of acrimony. The key was General Marshall's conclusion that Torch and the delay in achieving victory in Tunisia necessitated pushing the cross-Channel invasion back until spring 1944. That position was reinforced when Admiral King, to the surprise of all, stated that because the Pacific offensive could not begin right away, he could provide sufficient landing craft in 1943 for invasions of both Sicily, which the British (and Roosevelt) advocated, and Burma, which Marshall wanted.

But there were suspicions on both sides. Churchill feared that the Americans would give the Pacific "prime place." That was true for Admiral King and his navy but not for Roosevelt and Marshall. The Americans harbored doubts about British enthusiasm for a cross-Channel attack, and Churchill and his military chiefs shrewdly avoided any specific commitments on the timing and scope of such an operation. Nor did they reveal their desire to focus future efforts on Italy and the Aegean Sea, with General Brooke disingenuously telling the American military chiefs that he "did not believe we could undertake any further operations in Italy from Sicily in 1943, unless Italy collapsed completely."

The Americans, blinded by their commitment to an invasion of France and satisfied by the agreement to establish a planning command for the cross-Channel invasion, failed to raise the obvious question: Once we take Sicily, where do we go from there? When the British made the sensible suggestion for a protracted bombing campaign against the submarine pens built by the Germans along France's Atlantic coast, the Americans did not point out that an early invasion of France would do the job even better, as history demonstrated when the bombing campaign completely failed to damage the massive structures, concrete monuments to the Battle of the Atlantic that still stood undamaged fifty years later in St-

Nazaire (whatever the damage done by the single bomb that, in a fluke, penetrated the concrete bunkers).[70] Nor did the Americans recognize Churchill's continued desire to limit the cross-Channel assault, revealed when he suggested a small-scale invasion (Operation Hadrian) of the Cotentin Peninsula (Cherbourg) and the Channel Islands. No wonder that Marshall subsequently vowed that never again would the Americans be outplanned and outstaffed by the British.[71]

One joint program both agreed upon was the continuation of the strategic bombing campaign against Germany, Operation Pointblank. For Churchill, strategic bombing fitted neatly into his preferred strategy of a war of attrition in Europe, delaying any move in force onto the Continent until the Germans were on the verge of collapse. For the Americans, strategic bombing promised lower battlefield losses—important for Marshall, given his conviction that the American public would not tolerate massive casualties. The premise of strategic bombing was that heavy attacks could be accurate and damaging enough to destroy the enemy's industrial and transportation facilities, as well as to undermine "the morale of the German people," a clear reference to both the incidental and purposeful bombing of civilian targets, with Berlin specifically mentioned as a "political" objective. Moreover, strategic bombing provided "the chief method" for directly attacking the Germans at a time when "the enemy's attention is focussed on Russia," illustrating Anglo-American sensitivity to the reality that the Russians were doing the bulk of the fighting against Germany.[72]

Strategic bombing had begun in May 1940 with a limited British campaign, but lacking fighter resources, they were forced to conduct raids at night. Given the difficulty of hitting targets in the dark, such attacks were directed at the center of small cities and euphemistically termed area bombing. American B-17 Flying Fortress bombers made their first high-altitude daylight raid on August 17, 1942, when they bombed railway yards in Rouen, France, but as the raids extended farther east into Germany, beyond the range of protective cover from fighter aircraft, losses became prohibitive. Moreover, ground and naval commanders constantly requested the use of bomber assets for tactical purposes. The cross-Channel invasion in June 1944 provided fighter bases closer to Germany and brought a drop in tactical requests. That, combined with ever-increasing American aircraft production, finally allowed the full implementation of the strategic bombing campaign in autumn 1944.

Neither Churchill nor Roosevelt could plug into his strategic or political equations at Casablanca what happened at the University of Chicago on December 2, even as the Stalingrad battle turned in the Soviets' favor. On that date scientists induced a chain reaction. The atomic bomb had been proved possible.

The Casablanca meeting is best known as the venue for Roosevelt's statement that the only terms for the Axis powers were "unconditional surrender." A series of persistent myths has grown up about that declaration. To start with, Churchill himself claimed shortly after the war that he had never heard the words until the president spoke them. Churchill carefully corrected that in his memoirs but still managed to give the impression that the policy had not been agreed to in advance. In fact he had already consulted his Cabinet about such a declaration, in part to reassure the Americans that Britain would join the war against Japan once Germany was defeated. The president's decision to make the statement to reporters on January 24, the day the conference concluded, may have surprised the prime minister, but the policy had been developed jointly, with the British Cabinet even adding that the proclamation should apply to Italy as well as Germany.[73]

The other myths relate to whether or not the unconditional surrender policy lengthened the war by strengthening the German will to resist. There is no credible evidence that unconditional surrender played any significant role in buttressing German morale. That is echoed by U.S. intelligence reports written during the war, which concluded that German military fortunes were what affected morale.[74] A variant on that myth is the notion that unconditional surrender discouraged Germans from assassinating Hitler. Such speculation warrants counterspeculation. Had Hitler been eliminated, what would have resulted? A quick and complete surrender of German armies? That is unlikely, and anything less would have been as unacceptable to Stalin as it was to FDR. Significant opposition to Hitler came from the German military fears of defeat, not out of differing geopolitical goals or some kind of moral rectitude. After all, where were the assassins in the late 1930s and early 1940s? Moreover, as one top German commander noted in his diary, even had the famous July 1944 assassination attempt succeeded, the coup would have failed when the military refused to follow orders from the conspirators.[75]

Then there is the charge that Roosevelt's belief that German character had been corrupted was "morally regrettable." By the time FDR made the unconditional surrender statement, he had begun to learn of the inhuman acts we now subsume under the phrase "the Holocaust," although the worst was yet to come. That knowledge only verified his belief that the German character had been Prussianized and Nazified and that fundamental reforms had to be imposed on the Germans. However that was to be done (specific proposals were to come later in the war), unconditional surrender would ensure that the Allies had a free hand to restructure German economics, politics, and society. At the same time the utter defeat and surrender of the German Army would prevent any repeat of the "stab in the back" legend that had allowed the German military to retain public respect by claiming they had been betrayed by the socialist politicians, not defeated, in World War I.

What lies at the root of the supposed "tragedy" of unconditional surrender is an old canard: that a strong Germany at the end of the Second World War would have somehow prevented Soviet occupation of Eastern Europe and won the Cold War even before it started. That was just what the world needed: a strong, armed Germany led by the same wonderful cast of military leaders that had destroyed peace and stability in Central Europe since the 1860s. What "piffle"! (A favorite Roosevelt word.) The most obvious results would have been either Europe engulfed by a Soviet-German war or a Soviet-German alliance. To blame unconditional surrender for prolonging the war and to imply that it prevented an uprising against Hitler and eliminated an opportunity to win/prevent the Cold War are, simply put, fiction.

"Unconditional surrender" aimed at more than just the Axis powers. Stalin's absence from the talks in Casablanca did not mean that he and the Soviet Union were forgotten. British diplomat Har-

old Macmillan caustically named Churchill and Roosevelt the em-
perors of the East and West, then commented perceptively that
only the Red emperor was missing. (Churchill "ate and drank
enormously all the time," wrote Macmillan, "settled huge problems, played bagatelle and bezique by the hour, and generally enjoyed himself.") Growing Soviet power, epitomized by the
Stalingrad victory, was like a ghost in the attic—hidden from view
but always in the back of one's mind. Roosevelt and Churchill did
not worry openly about Stalin's intentions, but their premonitions
are evident.[76]

With the war on the Russian front turning in favor of the Soviets, unconditional surrender offered another bona fide to Stalin
that the Germans and Soviets would not be left to grind each other
down (the Truman gambit) while the Anglo-Americans concentrated on less costly campaigns. With the second front likely to be
postponed until 1944 (something no one wanted to tell Stalin),
Roosevelt had worried about explaining to Stalin that "the United
Nations were to continue on until they reach Berlin, and that their
only terms were to be unconditional surrender," eventually proposing to send General Marshall to Moscow. The unstated fact was
that unconditional surrender was an impossible goal for the Anglo-
Americans without the Red Army. No wonder, then, that they
promised to search for some way to continue the convoys to Russia, even with the drain on shipping resources caused by Husky,
the invasion of Sicily. Churchill understood: "Nothing in the
world will be accepted by Stalin as an alternative to our placing 50
or 60 Divisions in France by the spring of this year."[77]

The unconditional surrender commitment was, for Roosevelt,
neither cynical nor disingenuous. He firmly believed that Germany
needed reforming, and he never wavered from his commitment not
to negotiate a separate peace. He had laced his Pearl Harbor speech
with phrases that said the same thing: "the United States could
accept no result but victory, final and complete." Robert Sherwood
correctly pointed out that the president "refused all suggestions
that he retract the statement or soften it and continued refusal to
the day of his death."[78]

For Churchill it was a bit different. He had told the Cabinet that unconditional surrender was a guarantee to the Americans about the Pacific war. He failed to mention the Soviets perhaps because he remained unable to reconcile his desire for victory against Germany with his fears of Soviet expansion. Certainly British imperial fortunes required that German expansionism be destroyed, but Churchill's rhetoric during the Battle of Britain notwithstanding, the complete defeat of Germany on the battlefield had never been a British goal. The very concept was foreign to a generation of British leaders brought up on "splendid isolation" and a commitment to preventing any single power from dominating Europe. And Soviet expansion could pose a similar threat to British interests. By war's end Churchill was toying with notions of leaving the Germans armed so they could act as a bulwark against the Soviet Union.[79]

Perhaps Stalin's absence is what prompted Churchill and Roosevelt to spend so much time on the question of the French succession. Both Roosevelt and Churchill had developed an active, personal dislike for General de Gaulle, whom they found arrogant, unreasonable, and bent on policies that created problems for the Anglo-American alliance. This was not a case of Churchill's ignoring his better judgment and following Roosevelt's lead because relations with the United States took precedence. The Anglo-American leaders reinforced each other's sense of annoyance (lese majesty?) over de Gaulle's refusals to accede docilely to their wishes.

But Roosevelt and Churchill regularly worked with people they disliked and disagreed with when it suited their purposes. Despite the self-justifying, whistling-past-the-cemetery kind of remarks that both made about how much they liked Stalin, neither did like him—either as a man or as a leader. Churchill had to find General Sir Alan Brooke, whose caustic tongue spared no one, as unbearable as de Gaulle; FDR could not abide General MacArthur. But in each case usefulness outweighed personality; respect, grudging as it may have been, counted for more than aggravation.[80]

Anglo-American planning for postwar France was based on interests and realities, not personalities. Roosevelt not only believed France was a second-class power but remained convinced that

Franco-German quarrels lay at the root of much of Europe's inability to maintain peace. Churchill tended to agree but also had to
face the firm conviction of Eden and the Foreign Office that an
Anglo-French entente was necessary if Britain was to play its proper
role in Europe. The matter of recognition of a French provisional
regime was in itself minor. But the role of France as part of a power
structure that would not only restrain Germany but also balance
the Soviet Union was, for Eden, crucial.[81]

All the negotiations over France during the Casablanca talks
ended with a scene reminiscent of a Gilbert and Sullivan operetta.
De Gaulle, present only under threats from Churchill to cut off his
funding, and Giraud, who thought he had been anointed as the
French leader, unsmilingly obeyed a Churchill-Roosevelt request
that they shake hands at the final press conference, as cameras
clicked like an army of crickets. The two Frenchmen were ostensibly to work together, but privately Roosevelt tried to ensure that
Giraud would win out in the obvious power struggle. "I take it
that your bride and my bridegroom have not yet started throwing
the crockery," wrote FDR to Churchill. "I trust the marriage will
be consummated." But de Gaulle's popularity with the military and
Giraud's political ineptness (called "residual Vichyism" by one perceptive historian) ensured a quick annulment—with de Gaulle winning the property settlement.[82]

Churchill, when writing of the Casablanca Conference, passed
over a dinner FDR had arranged with the sultan of Morocco without a mention.[83] Harry Hopkins described a "glum" prime minister, "bored" and looking for excuses to get away. That may have
been because the dinner was, in deference to Islamic practice,
"Dry, alas!" as Churchill put it, requiring an after-dinner "recovery." But more likely, the evening's discussion was one Churchill
preferred to forget. The president's son Elliott provided the most
detailed recollection of the dinner conversation.

> Father, balancing his fork, remarked cheerfully enough that the post-
> war scene and the prewar scene would, of course, differ sharply, es-
> pecially as they related to the colonial question.

Churchill coughed and again plunged into conversation along different lines.

Politely, the Sultan inquired more specifically, what did Father mean, "differ sharply"?

Father, dropping in a remark about the past relationship between French and British financiers combined into self-perpetuating syndicates for the purpose of dredging riches out of colonies, went on to raise the question of possible oil deposits in French Morocco.

As FDR and the sultan pursued the subject, Elliott Roosevelt records Churchill shifting "uneasily in his chair," then snorting and trying "not to listen." As the dinner ended, the sultan exclaimed, "A new future for my country!" Churchill, "glowering, biting at his cigar, . . . followed the Sultan out of the dining room."[84] Churchill well understood that protecting the British colonial empire meant defending that of France. He would follow that path for the remainder of the war.

Perhaps Roosevelt's prodding was a result of his tour of Bathurst, capital of the British colony of Gambia, which he visited during a refueling stop en route to Casablanca (as well as on his way home). An "awful, pestiferous hole" was his description, one he elaborated on repeatedly after the conference when condemning British colonialism.[85] Certainly the dinner was no accident, nor were Harry Hopkins's discussions along the same line with the grand vizier (prime minister) of Morocco. Each meeting provided an opportunity for the Americans to preach a sermon against old-style European colonialism while promising the benefits of trade and commerce with the United States. De Gaulle later contemptuously asked the sultan, "When President Roosevelt jingled the marvels of independence before your Majesty at Anfa, what did he offer you beyond the cash and a place among his customers?" The sultan apparently refrained from making the logical response: And what else does French rule offer?[86]

That challenge to colonialism was part of the consistent pressure Roosevelt applied to Churchill. Even as the Americans were encouraging the sultan of Morocco to think of breaking away from

French control, Roosevelt was pushing Britain to commit to independence for India. Indian nationalists, led by the charismatic Gandhi, demanded that Britain "quit India," with a timetable for independence as the price of continued Indian support for the war. Churchill, whose contempt for the Indians was palpable, could now, with Japanese forces in Burma threatening eastern India, condemn the Quit India movement for endangering the war effort and have its leaders arrested.

Amid this crisis, another of the president's ubiquitous "personal representatives," William Phillips, arrived in New Delhi on January 8. On instructions from London, the viceroy (the British government official in charge of India) rejected offers from Phillips to mediate between British authorities and advocates of independence. When Gandhi went on a highly publicized fast, the viceroy, Lord Linlithgow, forbade Phillips to visit the Indian leader or to make any public statements about the crisis. Reports of the deterioration of Gandhi's health prompted the U.S. State Department to warn Britain that his death in prison could paralyze India with protests. Phillips, on instructions from Roosevelt and Hull, continued to pressure British authorities to compromise, a move that British officials mistakenly attributed to the influence of Eleanor Roosevelt and Madame Chiang Kai-shek, the Chinese leader's American-educated wife, then visiting the United States.[87]

In mid-February Churchill passed the word to the White House, diplomatically using Halifax and Hull as intermediaries, that he would not compromise with Gandhi and the Indian nationalists and that American interference with British policy would create "great embarrassment between the two Governments." When the viceroy's advisory council, which included a few "representative Indians," recommended discharging Gandhi from prison, Churchill said the British Cabinet should force Linlithgow to override his Council. "What did it matter," he commented derisively, "if a few blackamoors resigned!" Roosevelt could not change British policy, and the crisis abated when Gandhi ended his fast after three weeks. But FDR hardly paused in his relentless campaign to convince the Europeans that colonialism's day was over. By March he was talking to Eden and to the Pacific War Council about postwar trusteeships for European colonies. Roosevelt had placed colonial empires "in the dock," in Churchill's later words.[88]

The conference ended with Churchill persuading FDR to drive south to Marrakech for a brief bit of R&R. They stayed amid the exotic surroundings and equally exotic dinner guests at Flower Villa, which the two rechristened "Pansy Palace," and viewed the shifting colors on the snowcapped Atlas Mountains at sunset. Perhaps Churchill hoped for a seduction of his own. The excursion was clearly an attempt by him to get Roosevelt away from his military advisers and into a more intimate setting. It offered a chance to paint word pictures of British tanks rolling across the Western Desert and of Anglo-American forces pouring across the Mediterranean to take Italy and defeat the Germans, a last chance for the two to daydream about an Anglo-American world. But the Americans, perhaps influenced by being "in splendor befitting a Sultan," held on to their image of the prime minister as an incurable and old-fashioned romantic, living in the era of the Raj. Another stop at Bathurst, "that hell-hole of yours" Roosevelt later told Churchill, only reconfirmed American convictions. As for the prime minister, who had continued to trot around the British world, he sent Roosevelt a message from Cairo that drew a seductive picture of an Anglo-American world: "It is believed that the United States will cooperate with her [Great Britain] and possible even take the lead of the world. . . ."[89]

The crisis of colonialism was to reshape the postwar world, but the Anglo-American decisions at Casablanca had a more immediate effect. The invasion of Sicily would take place once the Axis was expelled from Tunisia. That would lead, ineluctably, to what looked like an easy assault on a weak and demoralized Italy. If Italy collapsed quickly, a cross-Channel invasion in autumn 1943 remained a possibility.

But Adolf Hitler had other plans.

Poor Wilson, he never quite understood.

CHAPTER 7

———◆◆———

"I Am Not a Wilsonian Idealist, I Have Problems to Resolve" March–December 1943

Nineteen forty-two was the year of the generals for the Grand Alliance, the year when averting defeat and starting to take the offensive took precedence over politics. Nineteen forty-three was the year when politics reared its head and began to reassert its primacy. Military victory remained the immediate priority for the Anglo-Americans, but with their survival assured and the eventual defeat of the Axis more likely (so long as the alliance remained intact), visions of the postwar world began a sugarplum dance in their heads.

Military events continued to define political opportunities and choices. Churchill preferred Mediterranean operations that would avoid any massive and costly cross-Channel invasion and, at the same time, protect traditional British interests from Italy to Greece, Egypt, and the Levant. To implement that strategy, he had to win over two opponents. First, he needed the concurrence of the United States. But the Americans continued to insist that only a cross-Channel invasion could get the job done. Second, Churchill had to overcome continued demands from Moscow for the second front. He told his Cabinet that nothing less than fifty or sixty divisions in France would satisfy the Soviets, but then he returned to his pecking-at-the-periphery strategy by proposing that he and FDR hold out to Stalin the possibility of an August 1943 Sledgehammer invasion that would have a maximum of twenty divisions and a total of fifty thousand men, a far cry from what the Soviet leader demanded.[1]

But such a small Sledgehammer and intensified Mediterranean operations would gain American approval only if they concluded that those moves were the quickest and most effective way to defeat Germany. Hitler had nearly guaranteed Churchill's frustration by reinforcing Tunisia and delaying the Allied timetable for the liberation of North Africa. But an attack on Italy and a quick capitulation by the Italians could give Churchill's strategy new life.

At the same time Stalin failed to capitalize on the Stalingrad victory. He launched a massive offensive along the entire Russian front, but it lacked clear objectives and dissipated Red Army strength.[2] Whatever dreams or designs Soviet leaders may have had for liberating more than just the USSR and parts of Eastern Europe, that failed offensive ensured that the massive Soviet march westward would not take place until 1944, just as the Allies were themselves launching their cross-Channel invasion, although the Soviets did establish a deep bulge around the city of Kursk, some five hundred miles west-northwest of Stalingrad, a legacy that eventually spelled the end of Germany's offensive hopes in Russia.[3]

Even as those military campaigns were being contested, Churchill and Roosevelt began to maneuver for position in what was to become the campaign to structure the peace. Whatever values their two societies shared, much of that maneuvering came from mutual distrust. The British well understood Roosevelt's desire to propagate Americanism, that version of liberalism set forth broadly in the Atlantic Charter. That thrust threatened British interests and independence, for it challenged colonial empires, "closed" trading systems, and Britain's desire to remain aloof from any entangling system of politics and alliances in Europe. Moreover, Churchill and his colleagues remained convinced that American "isolationism" would reassert itself once the war ended, leaving Britain to look to its own security—particularly in Europe, where, as Churchill liked to put it, little Britain would face the Russian bear all alone. Even more dangerous, the Americans might again adopt what the British saw as in again, out again international practices, intervening impulsively, then withdrawing just as suddenly. If efforts to civilize the Bolsheviks failed, then the Americans might pull back from Europe, as they had after the First World War, leaving Great Britain to work things out with the Soviet Union. British practicality, realism, and experience would be needed to prevent ideological clashes from creating Soviet-American conflicts. Britain as broker between the Soviets and the Americans was the sensible answer. British diplomat Harold Macmillan offered the model: The Greeks had run the later Roman Empire without the Romans' realizing it.[4]

American suspicions were a near mirror image of British distrust. Churchill epitomized old-fashioned imperialism, the predatory policy that had caused the First World War and contributed to the coming of the Second. British insistence on retaining special trading relationships within their empire provided convincing evidence of London's dedication to the kind of economic nationalism that Americans believed unfair, wrongheaded, and dangerous. Moreover, the British consistently pursued spheres of influence, balance of power structures for the postwar world, and Americans believed that approach meant a return to the same tensions and conflicts that had made peace impossible to preserve. Roosevelt also worried about renewed American reluctance to participate in any sort of collective security (an attitude he invariably subsumed under the inaccurate term "isolationism"), but unlike the British, the president worked on the assumption that he could construct a system that Americans would accept.

As for Britain as broker between the Soviet Union and the United States, the German attack on the Russians had prompted Roosevelt to face early on the probability of a major Soviet postwar role, even while Churchill remained focused on British survival. Eleanor Roosevelt caught her husband's feelings when she sent him a memo quoting a passage from Churchill's book *The World Crisis*, published in 1929. Describing Western military actions against the Bolsheviks ten years earlier, Churchill argued that "it is a delusion to suppose that . . . we have been fighting the battles of the anti-Bolshevik Russians. On the contrary, they have been fighting ours; and this truth will become painfully apparent from the moment . . . the Bolshevik armies are supreme over the whole vast territories of the Russian Empire." Mrs. Roosevelt caustically commented: "It is not surprising if Mr. Stalin is slow to forget." Roosevelt had been serious when he told Churchill that Stalin "hated the guts" of British leaders and that the Roosevelt-Stalin relationship was better than the one between the Soviets and the British. The United States as broker between two traditional European enemies seemed the more plausible scenario.[5]

The visit of Foreign Secretary Eden to the United States in March 1943 came with the usual ceremonials that went with such occasions. A three-day trip brought Eden to army bases along the Gulf Coast and then on to Fort Bragg in North Carolina, after which he was briefly shanghaied by the navy. Each stop invariably included the playing of "God Save the King," once prompting a sotto voce whisper behind Eden: "Why the heck do we salute at 'My Country 'Tis of Thee'?" He spoke at the Maryland statehouse in Annapolis, not far from the grave of his ancestor Sir Robert Eden, the last colonial governor of Maryland.[6] But those were the trappings of alliance.

The talks were not intended to reach decisions—after all, Churchill was not there—but they did provide an opportunity for the two governments to get a sense of where each stood on postwar planning. Eden was in close touch with Foreign Office planners, already hard at work on postwar issues, and focused on political matters, unlike Churchill, who much preferred conducting the war to trying to structure the peace. The foreign secretary could not speak for the prime minister, but unlike FDR and the State Department, Churchill could not ignore the recommendations of the Foreign Office, even if his disdain for its officials was evident—so much so that Roosevelt twitted the prime minister that he and Eden were confident of Churchill's ability to handle the Commons (Eden was the government leader in the House), "but both of us are concerned over what you will do with the Foreign Office! We fear that he [Eden] will not recognize it when he gets back."[7]

Bureaucrats in Washington had also begun thinking about how the postwar situation could and should develop (State Department officials may not keep proper minutes, but contrary to European mythology, they did and do try to plan ahead).[8] By early 1943 Roosevelt was involved in "weekly" discussions of postwar problems with State Department planners. One assumption by the president and his advisers was that of Great Britain as rival. Roosevelt repeatedly said he wanted to avoid the appearance of ganging up on the Russians, but he also feared the British Empire would gang up on the United States. American insistence on the four major powers controlling all international committees was in large part designed to prevent the British from dominating those groups by insisting on equality for Canada and Australia. In hindsight, that fear of a powerful London-led combine seems distorted, but it was a very real concern on the part of Americans, inside and outside the government.[9]

Roosevelt had come into the war with vague but what proved to be consistent views on how to restructure international relations. The United States had to work with other nations to preserve peace, but it also had to avoid commitments that would drag it into every little argument and local squabble. Woodrow Wilson's League of Nations concept had fallen into that trap, and the American public and Congress had rejected the scheme, insisting that the United States retain its freedom of action. That experience, and FDR's assessment of the causes of the two world wars, left him convinced that only the Great Powers could maintain the peace. As he had told one of de Gaulle's emissaries a few months earlier, "I am not a Wilsonian idealist, I have problems to resolve."[10]

Like hereditary aristocrats throughout history, Roosevelt assumed that power and responsibility justified each other, a geopolitical version of noblesse oblige. During the Atlantic Conference in August 1941 he had suggested to Churchill that the two Great Powers, the United States and Great Britain, would have to act as policemen after the war, although some sort of international organization might be possible later on. That same month he casually repeated the idea to dinner guests, saying that the two nations would "have to police the entire world—not on a sanction basis but in trust." Only the Great Powers would have arms, and there would be "complete economic and commercial and boundary lib-

erty, but America and England would have to maintain the peace."
Disarmament would be key—"the smaller powers might have rifles
but nothing more dangerous," he once commented—though he
had to make a virtue of vice by entrusting enforcement to the Great
Powers, which would never accept disarmament. Small nations
would have to trust in the Great Powers; "another League of
Nations with 100 different signatories" would mean "simply too
many nations to satisfy." He had spoken similarly to Molotov in
May–June 1942, and the concept received Stalin's strong endorsement. A few months after Eden's visit Roosevelt wondered why
smaller nations needed arms. "Will it be necessary for these states
to defend themselves after this war?" he asked.

The president's notion that security required only political control over "boundaries" separated economic and cultural matters
from what we now call geopolitics. The idea cropped up later when
Roosevelt tried to promote a settlement in Eastern Europe.
Eleanor Roosevelt warned her husband that the concept "is
fraught with danger. You have more faith in human nature than I
have. Even Anglo-Saxon races will become drunk with power and
will use this power to bring economic pressure on the smaller
nations for the things they want." But FDR never abandoned his
belief in the practical necessity for a trusteeship of international
policemen—though the number grew to three and then four.[11]

During the talks with Eden, Roosevelt outlined a postwar security organization that would consist of three bodies: a general
assembly, an executive committee (the Big Four), and an advisory
council that would meet from time to time to provide advice to
the executive committee. The Big Four, which included China,
would have the key responsibility for "all the more important decisions and wield police powers of the United Nations"—a phrase
that described the alliance against the Axis, not the United Nations
Organization that emerged. The general assembly would meet
once a year to let "the smaller powers . . . blow off steam."

With a debate developing in Congress over whether or not the
United States should be involved with any international organization, the president was cautious about public statements, even
though opinion polls indicated widespread public support for join-

ing. The best he could come up with was an interview in which he drew an analogy with his Good Neighbor policy in the Western Hemisphere. Any organization of the United Nations "would markedly resemble the simple . . . and workable body of arrangements under which the American republics manage their collective affairs." Of course only the United States (the responsible regional power) would have arms and bases, something it had made clear to the Canadians back in spring 1941, when Ottawa had suggested it could occupy the Danish colony of Greenland. "For the first time, the Monroe Doctrine has to be implemented militarily on a frontier," wrote Assistant Secretary of State Adolf Berle.[12]

FDR's four policemen would also act as trustees for colonial societies not ready for full independence. The Pacific islands held by the Japanese (usually old League of Nations mandates), Korea (despite its being independent for centuries before the United States existed), and Indochina were his favorite examples, but the idea tended to be Roosevelt's catchall answer for any difficult territorial problem, as in the case of the Croatians and Serbs.[13] When he spoke to Eden of trusteeships for Japan's Pacific island empire, French Indochina, and Portuguese Timor, Eden knew the president meant all European empires. The Englishman listened but said little. He was dubious about Chinese intentions (perhaps with Hong Kong in mind), commenting that "he 'did not much like the idea of the Chinese running up and down the Pacific,' " and raised questions whether Generalissimo Chiang Kai-shek would survive the civil war that would surely follow Japan's defeat.[14] Whatever Eden's skepticism, Roosevelt intended China eventually to be a player in the postwar world.

But the Great Powers were to be much more than trustees for a few problem areas; their fundamental trust was the peace of the entire world. An international forum for "full discussion" made sense, Roosevelt had remarked after the Atlantic Conference, "but for management there seems no reason why the principle of trusteeship in private affairs should not be extended to the international field." That perception of overarching responsibility inevitably translated into full authority for the world's trustees. There was no need for a vast peace conference, he informed State

Department planners, because peace questions would be handled by the heads of the four Great Powers and technical experts.[15] It was a strikingly optimistic and arrogant scenario.

Eden, warned of Roosevelt's ideas by Ambassador Halifax, tried to force the president to confront the practical difficulties they would face in chaotic postwar Europe. The foreign secretary still believed what he had written a year earlier: that Stalin was "a political descendant of Peter the Great rather than of Lenin." Eden did not think Soviet leaders actively planned for the spread of international communism, but even if they did, "if we are to win the war and to maintain the peace, we must work with Stalin and we cannot work with him unless we are successful in allaying some at least of his suspicion." But it would not be easy. The Soviet Union was "our most difficult problem," Eden warned Roosevelt.[16]

That echoed the president's sentiments. His suspicions about British intentions and hopes for cooperation with the Soviet Union did not blind him to the dangers of growing Soviet strength. During his regular meetings with State Department officials drawing up plans for the postwar world, he worried aloud that "he didn't know what to do about Russia. . . ."[17]

The problem of Soviet intentions crystallized around the issue of self-determination. The decolonization of European empires was only one aspect of that principle and problem. Self-determination for European colonies was awkward and menacing to the British but did not threaten the Great Power cooperation that FDR hoped for since Britain's stake in postwar cooperation with the United States was too crucial to jeopardize. Moreover, colonial boundaries seemed clear (even if that proved deceptive). But in 1943, with the Germans stopped and the tide about to turn on the Russian front, European frontiers and self-determination became a major issue. As Woodrow Wilson had found at Paris, Europe's boundary questions came burdened with irreconcilable pieces of historical baggage. At the same time achieving Roosevelt's and Eden's dreams of persuading Stalin to be a cooperative participant in the postwar world required that the Soviet leader feel secure, satisfied, and sure of Anglo-American reliability. But self-determination for Lithuanians, Latvians, and Estonians—not to mention large groups of Poles, Bulgarians, Finns, Hungarians, and Romanians—was quite a different story, for Stalin had made clear from the outset that his minimal territorial demands encompassed many such peoples.

If self-determination meant independence for the Balts and the establishment of an anti-Soviet government in Warsaw, then how to avoid the obvious? Both Roosevelt and Eden had looked to create a good postwar relationship with the Soviet Union even before the Stalingrad battle demonstrated the likelihood of Red Army occupation of the territory Stalin demanded. What recourse was left to London and Washington? Military confrontation was no option, at least not with Anglo-American forces still struggling in North Africa and fifteen months away from an invasion of Western Europe. More to the point, what was the long-term hope for peace if the United States and Britain chose to confront the Russians? The atomic bomb perhaps changed that calculation, but that weapon was two years away. Then there was Japan waiting in the wings.

What Roosevelt and Eden agreed on, despite their significant differences about tactics, was to make the best of the situation. Rather than fruitlessly oppose any expansion of Soviet power in Eastern Europe, they opted to continue to promote long-term cooperation. As Roosevelt and Welles told Eden, "the real decisions should be made by the United States, Great Britain, Russia and China, who would be the powers for many years to come that would have to police the world." Self-determination would obviously be bestowed by the Big Four, if they could agree on the details.[18]

The Atlantic Charter and FDR's subsequent scheme for bringing the Soviets into his group of world policemen have routinely been dismissed as unrealistic "Wilsonian nonsense." And "Wilsonianism," that catchall term for anything less than untrammeled power politics, was supposedly dangerous daydreaming.[19]

But the Americans saw it differently. The Atlantic Charter was more than mere moral posturing. It was a call for reform, for the new world order, a consistent theme in American foreign policy before and since. Economic liberalism may have promised tangible

benefits for the United States, but Americans had pursued economic liberalism since their Revolution; was that merely two centuries of cynicism? The decolonization of European empires could,
and sometimes did, enhance American power and interests. Shall
we then conclude that Franklin Roosevelt and all his predecessors
plotted to "succeed John Bull"? The United Nations Organization
became, for more than a decade after the Second World War, an
instrument of American foreign policy. Does that mean internationalism in the United States was just a ploy?[20]

Eden and the British did not cynically dismiss the charter. A
Foreign Office memorandum, "The United Nations Plan for Organising Peace," distributed a few months after the Eden mission,
opened with a striking endorsement: "The principles embodied in
the Atlantic Charter will be the basis of any international world
order after the war." "Stability" and "world order" were possible
only if "the World Powers are prepared to accept the responsibilities of leadership *within* the United Nations." That would require
Great Power agreement and a willingness "to take joint action to
enforce it." The alternative would be "the World Powers, each
with its circle of client States, facing each other in a rivalry which
may merge imperceptibly into hostility."[21]

Yet there were limits to British internationalism. Even while
Eden was in Washington, Churchill publicly proposed what Harry
Hopkins described as a "purely European Council of Nations."
Roosevelt and his major advisers, particularly Hopkins and Welles,
favored a loose international structure combined with regional responsibilities and leadership for each of the Big Four. Without such
control in their region of greatest national interest, Great Power
cooperation would flounder. Roosevelt implied a delicate distinction between a Great Power (a policeman) with a responsibility to
lead in a particular region and a dominant regional structure that
could lead to dangerous, independent actions. Overemphasizing
regional authority in Europe, as the Americans thought Churchill
had done, could revive the system of military-political alliances that
had initiated the First World War.

The timing of Churchill's proposal, made in a radio speech on
March 21, was hardly accidental. With Eden reporting regularly

from Washington on his discussions about postwar issues, the prime minister wanted to raise the same practical matters that concerned the foreign secretary. It was all well and good to go on about broad international schemes, but in Churchill's words, "it is upon the creation of the Council of Europe and the settlement of Europe that the first practical task will be centred." Roosevelt seemed to be talking about some sort of new system, though no one could grasp precisely what he meant (nor was precision in such things the way FDR operated). Churchill, unpersuaded that international politics could be reformed, intended to reconstruct the old system to Britain's benefit. Any European council had to "harmonize with the high permanent interests of Britain, the United States, and Russia," but the Soviets were sure to read exclusion and cordon sanitaire in the prime minister's suggestion for "groupings of States or Confederations."[22]

Moscow would have been right. A few months earlier the first Foreign Office proposals for an international organization went a long way toward agreeing with Roosevelt's four policemen proposal. Joint Anglo-American control would be better, the Foreign Office noted, but neither the Soviets nor the Americans would go along with that. That prompted Churchill to warn against "speculative studies" made by people with too little to do during the war, a demeaning dismissal of Foreign Office officials. Resorting to the pretense of preoccupation with the military struggle, he sarcastically pointed to "Mrs Glasse's Cookery Book recipe for jugged hare—'first catch your hare.' "

But Churchill's real concern was that he disagreed with Foreign Office thinking. An Anglo-American condominium seemed both sensible and possible. "It would be a measureless disaster," he wrote Eden, "if Russian barbarism overlaid the culture and independence of the ancient States of Europe." What Churchill hoped for was a "United States of Europe" that would presumably include Russia, but a Russia safely neutralized within a "Council consisting of . . . the former Great Powers, with several confederations . . . which would possess an international police and be charged with keeping Prussia disarmed." Rarely did the prime minister so bluntly state his feelings and fears about the Soviets. Normally he was more cautious, putting the burden of any rift on the shoulders of the Bolsheviks. Yet he left the door open to postwar cooperation with the Soviet Union, albeit on careful terms. Like FDR, Churchill was no Wilsonian idealist, for he too had "problems to resolve."[23]

Nor was Churchill prepared to elevate China to world power status. Not only did that fly in the face of reality—China was far from a modern power and faced civil war—but that would provide "a faggot vote on the side of the United States in any attempt to liquidate the overseas British Empire."[24] The mirage of an Anglo-American world that had appeared briefly at Casablanca was fading.

In an eerie coincidence (or, more likely, a commentary on sanitary conditions in North Africa), both Churchill and Roosevelt had to fight off lingering illnesses after the Casablanca meetings; neither was fully recovered when Eden left for the United States. FDR, as biting as ever about British colonialism, speculated that he had "picked up sleeping sickness or Gambia fever or some kindred bug in that hell-hole of yours called Bathurst." Churchill had a bout with pneumonia that left him bedridden for a week in late February and enervated for some time after. But modern war did not take time-outs for harvests or the illnesses of kings. The president, despite his fever, carried on his talks with Eden, and Churchill worked in near-normal fashion, whatever the concerns he expressed to his physician.[25]

Roosevelt and Churchill tried to maintain the camaraderie they had developed during the crisis of 1941–42. FDR, ever politic, massaged British sensibilities with fulsome praise for their documentary film *Desert Victory*. It was, he wrote Churchill, "about the best thing that has been done about the war on either side," praise that to British ears could fit Montgomery and his military successes as well as the motion picture. When the president received a personal letter relating a story that Churchill's mother had brought him to a small New York town when he was still "a baby in a carriage," the prime minister explained that he was a bit too big for a pram when he made his first visit to the United States in 1895 as he was twenty-one years old. FDR wisecracked back: "SOME BABY!" In April 1943 Roosevelt called the news of British advances in Tunisia "grand," then quipped that he hoped General Montgomery "did not destroy all the wherewithal when he took Sousse; you and I still have to celebrate," a clear reference to drink, possibly prompted by a running joke in a popular W. C. Fields comedy film *The Bank Dick* (1940). (Fields played the often inebriated Egbert Sousé, a name the other characters frequently pronounced as "souse." Whenever that happened, Fields would roar: "That's Sousé. Accent grave on the *e*!") Both Churchill and Roosevelt also played the short snorter game. To join the "club," initiates had to have flown the Atlantic Ocean (not the commonplace it became in the age of jet travel) and then get signatures on dollar bills or pound notes attesting to that flight. The key to the game was that members had to carry their "short snorter" bill at all times. Caught without the bill by another member resulted in fines, usually in the form of buying drinks for all other "worthy short snorters" present.

(A short snorter story, of which there are many: While Harriman and Churchill were flying to and from the 1942 Moscow Conference, the American caught one of Churchill's aides, C. R. "Tommy" Thompson, without his short snorter bill. Harriman passed a note [airplanes were too noisy for casual conversation] asking the prime minister, "How many demerits does Tommy get for 'no mustard [no short snorter bill]?' " Churchill scrawled back: "The two pilots asked me if I was one of that bloody club . . . now they want to see mine. I think I left it at Chequers. You *must* go back & [save it?]." Harriman was relentless. "How many?" he again asked.[26])

But cute exchanges could not hide growing Anglo-American tensions. In 1945, when Stalin spelled out his axiom to Yugoslav Communist Milovan Djilas—"whoever occupies a territory imposes on it his own social system"—the Soviet leader expressed what had been both his own fears and his intentions. In the words of his biographer Dmitri Volkogonov, Stalin "was more concerned about governments than borders." Churchill had offered his own cynical contention that "the right to guide the course of history is the noblest prize of victory." Following that epigram, he proposed in April 1943 that Britain be the "senior partner" in the Anglo-

American occupation of "HUSKY-land" (Sicily). Roosevelt responded by insisting that the United States have a major role "in view of the friendly feeling toward America entertained by a great number of the citizens of Italy," as well as the large number of Italian-Americans. He then suggested to Churchill that the occupation be presented to the world as joint and without any "senior partner." Given growing British dependence on American resources, particularly the landing craft needed for any Mediterranean operations, the prime minister could not push the matter further, but his frustration showed through when he ruefully told the president that "perfect equality" in Sicily would not "prejudice" American primacy in North Africa. I will continue "to be your Lieutenant there," Churchill added self-deprecatingly.[27] But such strains in the Anglo-American relationship were part of a long, peaceful commercial and political rivalry that, since the American Civil War, had not threatened to degenerate into military confrontation.

Not so for Anglo-American relations with the Soviet Union. Military engagements had taken place between the Bolsheviks and the West within the memory of the leaders of the Grand Alliance; cooperation and a modicum of trust were very recent developments and then only because of a common enemy in Hitler. Neither Churchill nor Roosevelt (nor Stalin for that matter) wanted the Second World War to become the Third. How to avoid that was the question. Churchill favored creating a balance of power that would restrain the Soviets, but he drew back from abandoning efforts to prolong the Grand Alliance. Roosevelt, halfway around the world from Moscow, reversed the precedence, insisting on working to bring the Grand Alliance into the postwar world, while he drew back from actions that might compromise America's interests or security. The two leaders never considered allowing their difference to split their nations—a demonstration of their "special" relationship—but the dispute affected all major aspects of Anglo-American wartime relations. Decolonization, the fate of France, the establishment of an international organization, occupation and liberation policy, the treatment of Germany and Japan—all took different shape because of divergent views in London and Washington on how to deal with the Soviet Union.

Eden had hardly unpacked his bags when the Anglo-American commitment to work with the Soviets faced the beginning of a test it eventually failed. Although Stalin had temporarily shelved his request for territorial agreements, Soviet-Western relations in spring 1943 were constantly pressured by what had become standard fare: Supply convoys to Russia would again be suspended; shipping requirements for the invasion of Sicily plus the presence of a German battle fleet in Norway made sailings impossible. The stalled Red Army offensive after Stalingrad heightened Soviet concern that the second front remained only a vague promise. Stalin's praise for Anglo-American operations in Tunisia was frequent and full, but he warned the Sicily invasion did not "replace a second front in France."[28]

That was the atmosphere when, on April 13, 1943, the Germans announced discovery of a mass grave in the Katyn Forest near Smolensk, close to the Russian border with the Byelorussian SSR. The ground contained the bodies of some forty-four hundred Polish officers and men, murdered by the Soviet secret police after the Russians had occupied eastern Poland in 1939. Stalin angrily claimed that the Germans had done it themselves and were blaming the Soviet Union in hopes of destroying the Grand Alliance, but even in 1943 the evidence pointed to Moscow. The Polish government in London, which had always viewed the Soviet Union as an enemy equal to the Germans, called for an investigation by the International Red Cross, bringing on the open Soviet-Polish clash Churchill had worked to avoid. The prime minister warned that he had no military leverage over Stalin and continued his efforts to persuade the exiled Polish leaders to accept the compromise offered back in 1942. The Poles, overconfident of American support and seeing an opportunity to gain the moral high ground, persisted. But what exiled Polish leaders interpreted as hints of support from Roosevelt never translated into action. The realities of war, Polish intransigence, and the need to maintain the Grand Alliance and extend it to Japan prevented the Anglo-Americans from giving the Poles anything more than private and empty re-assurances.[29]

Stalin responded by breaking relations with the London Poles and sponsoring a rival regime. Then, in July, General Wladysaw Sikorski, the leader of the Polish government-in-exile, died in an airplane crash at Gibraltar. The accident (whatever the rumors that the Soviets sabotaged the plane) robbed the Poles of the one leader Churchill supported and worked well with. The British prime minister never established a personal relationship with Sikorski's successor, Stanislaw Mikolajczyk, and by the time of the Teheran Conference at the end of the year Churchill was ready to endorse the Soviet definition of the Soviet-Polish boundary, telling Stalin that they were not "very far apart in principle." Of course, Churchill added, Poland would be "friendly to Russia."[30]

But that unsettling crisis quieted, as the politics of war remained focused on Anglo-American maneuverings over offensive strategy in Europe and the Soviet reaction to those maneuverings. After Stalingrad, in the spring and summer of 1943, Soviet-German probes about a separate peace began during meetings of mid-level officials in Stockholm. Soviet motives are unclear. Perhaps they were simply gathering intelligence on intentions, although they did not share what they learned with the Anglo-Americans. Perhaps Soviet participation was stimulated by the German victory at Kharkov in the Ukraine in March 1943, for as American intelligence had surmised, Hitler was far from defeated on the Russian front. Soviet calls for the second front never paused, but Roosevelt and Churchill feared that "Stalin may be building a case—The Allies not opening a second front, etc.—and make a separate peace with Germany."[31]

Moreover, American military planners worried that Churchill's Mediterranean strategy could make the Soviets more "susceptible" to German offers of a separate peace by resurrecting the old Anglo-Russian clash in Southeastern Europe and by reinforcing Soviet suspicions (and those of many American military officers) of British willingness to adopt the gambit proposed by Truman in 1941: Let Germany and Russia bleed each other to death. Yet the Kharkov defeat may have made Stalin aware of his need for allies by driving home the fact that having to fight all the way to Berlin alone could be prohibitively costly.[32]

It was a Hobson's choice that faced Roosevelt and Churchill. As they wrestled with their fears of a separate surrender, knowing they needed the Red Army in order to achieve full victory over Hitler, they also recognized that for the Anglo-Americans to gain (or regain) leverage in Europe, they had to invade Western France, particularly after the Soviet victory at Stalingrad had briefly increased concern about a German collapse and a speedy Soviet occupation/liberation of Europe.[33] Twice in early 1943 Roosevelt, and particularly Hopkins, expressed concern that Anglo-American forces might be no farther than Italy when Hitler's resistance crumpled. They feared chaos and anarchy, but they also worried that Stalin would have an opportunity to impose his system on much of Europe, according to the axiom he later gave Djilas. That concern mirrored a recommendation from former presidential adviser Bullitt that the Anglo-Americans confront the Soviet Union lest it expand into Central Europe and beyond. Hopkins thought that the Russians would cooperate but that there ought to be an Anglo-American plan. Roosevelt was cautious but told Hull to discuss the matter with the British and then with the Russians. Cooperation with the Soviets remained his priority. But just in case, Anglo-American planners in London (COSSAC, or Chief of Staff to the Supreme Allied Commander) drew up the various Rankin plans for a quick insertion of Anglo-American forces onto the European continent in the event of a German collapse. In November, while Roosevelt and his military chiefs were aboard the battleship USS *Iowa* headed for the Big Three meeting at Teheran, he predicted a "race" for Berlin and reviewed Rankin planning.[34]

Hitler had no intention of surrendering, nor was Germany near defeat. The Führer gave his forces in Tunisia his usual "no surrender, no evacuation" order partly out of bravado and partly to prevent the Anglo-Americans from increasing their aid to Russia. But in doing so, he unknowingly helped ensure the cross-Channel invasion. On May 10, 1943, Churchill again ordered that the bells be rung, this time to celebrate the victory in Tunisia.[35] But they rang hollow and months later than he had hoped. Every day of delay had lessened the chances that the assault on Sicily and Italy would succeed in time to convince the Americans that Europe's "soft underbelly" was the best way to defeat Hitler.

Churchill persisted. In mid-May he made his third visit to Washington for talks with FDR. The British objective for the Trident meeting, as it was code-named, was to get the Americans to agree to invade Italy following the expected speedy victory in Sicily. The surrender of Italy, they would argue, would deprive Hitler of an ally and make the central and western Mediterranean an Anglo-American lake. Unspoken was the British hope that a quick Italian surrender could open new options for Anglo-American strategy and perhaps break the American fixation on a cross-Channel attack.

General Marshall and his staff, remembering what had happened at Casablanca, were prepared for the British. Marshall understood that Roosevelt wanted to fight rather than prepare to fight the Nazis. American public opinion and, more important in 1943, Joseph Stalin would not accept a new version of the Phony War. The Americans simply reversed the British emphasis. They insisted that Bolero, the logistical buildup for a cross-Channel attack, take precedence over any other operations, although that did not prevent an invasion of Italy. What the Americans hoped to preclude was any shift in Anglo-American strategy away from an invasion of Western Europe and toward the Mediterranean.

The conferees agreed on early March 1944 (the so-called Trident date) as the target for the long-promised invasion of France, designated Operation Roundhammer, a confusing mix of previous code names that soon gave way to Overlord. They did not commit to an invasion of Italy but told the Allied commander in the North African theater (which then included Italy), General Dwight Eisenhower, to submit proposals for further operations. The message was clear. If the conquest of Sicily went well and quickly, Italy would be next, although Churchill pushed so hard for a formal commitment that Roosevelt got annoyed and, according to Stimson, told the prime minister that he had better "shut up."[36]

As at past conferences, operations in the China-Burma-India (CBI) theater generated more talk than action. Although both Chiang and one of his staunch American supporters, Army Air

Force General Chennault, asked for huge shipments of aircraft, they were not in the cards. As at Casablanca, Churchill and Roosevelt agreed on land operations in Burma, but as before, those never happened. Not only was Europe the priority, but Churchill and Roosevelt could not agree on whether aiding Chiang or forcing the Japanese out of Southeast Asia was the goal.[37]

The documentary record of the Trident talks suggests that the politics of the Manhattan Project—atomic bomb research—received only casual consideration. That misperception is a product of government secrecy. The two leaders continued a vigorous debate that had begun earlier, when Churchill protested American refusal to share information. A number of Roosevelt's advisers opposed revealing atomic secrets to the British, despite early promises and the initial benefits of British cooperation. Hopkins told Halifax that U.S. government officials who would return to jobs in big business after the war were eager to maintain control over the commercial uses of atomic energy. Confronted by the prime minister, Roosevelt agreed, with obvious reluctance, to live up to earlier promises to give Britain access to the results of atomic research. Yet by the time of their next meeting, at Quebec in August, that commitment had not been fulfilled.[38]

But the atom bomb was more than economics. Churchill's science adviser Lord Cherwell had told the Americans that Britain viewed the bomb primarily as a means of restraining the Soviet Union after the war. By agreeing with the British to keep the bomb an Anglo-American monopoly, Roosevelt had succumbed to the temptation of an Anglo-American condominium over the world, perhaps the only time that daydream reappeared after the Casablanca Conference.[39]

Whatever Stalin's spies told him in advance, he responded angrily to the news from the Trident Conference that the second front would again be delayed, this time until spring 1944. He recapitulated the list of promises made by Churchill and Roosevelt, then warned of the "dishearteningly negative impression" the postponement would generate, ending with an ominous refusal to "align" his government with the decision, which, he pointed out, had been adopted without Soviet participation.[40] Hoping to soften the blow, Roosevelt had proposed a meeting between himself and Stalin, without Churchill, using a friendly former ambassador to the Soviet Union, Joseph Davies, to deliver the invitation.

Roosevelt's purpose was to conduct personal diplomacy directly with Stalin, avoiding Britain as broker. But the tactic backfired. Not only did the Soviet premier insist on viewing Britain and the United States as close allies who spoke for each other, but FDR's failure to tell the prime minister in advance marked the beginning of a major shift in the Churchill-Roosevelt relationship. A month after Davies's trip, when Harriman finally told Churchill of the invitation to Stalin, the prime minister reacted bitterly. He exploded at Harriman, criticizing American policy toward France and China and dismissing the second front as a ploy to keep the West out of the Balkans. When Churchill confronted the president directly, Roosevelt lied and claimed the idea had come from Stalin. The prime minister drew back from pointing out FDR's lie, but the damage was done. Not only had Roosevelt implied second-class status for Great Britain and Churchill, but he had betrayed the personal relationship in which the prime minister placed such great stock. Churchill had conducted one-on-one talks with Stalin, and no one in Washington thought they had the whole story from those talks. After all, the president and the prime minister had differing national interests to protect. But the prime minister had not schemed to exclude Roosevelt. In Robert Sherwood's words, "It was fortunate that Hitler did not know how bad the relations were between the Allies at that moment, how close they were to the disruption which was his only hope." The British and Americans had a partnership, but now there was a senior and a junior partner—the very words Harry Hopkins used a few months later to describe the Anglo-American relationship.[41]

Soviet grumblings about supplies and the second front continued throughout the early summer, but Stalin, Churchill, and Roosevelt all were temporarily distracted from politics by military campaigns. The invasion of Sicily (Operation Husky) quickly followed the Anglo-American victory in North Africa. On July 10 the massive amphibious assault, which involved some twenty-six hundred ships, succeeded in landing 180,000 troops. But a cumbersome command structure that allowed Anglo-American rivalries to affect decisions, plus rugged mountainous terrain and fierce German (though not Italian) resistance, slowed the advance. Nonetheless, conquering the large island within a month, only slightly behind schedule, would have been gratifying had not 40,000 German and 62,000 Italian troops, with almost all their equipment, escaped across the Strait of Messina into southern Italy.

That disappointment and the delay were offset a bit by the good news that Mussolini had been arrested by the Italian government on July 25. That opened the door for negotiations with King Victor Emmanuel III and the new prime minister, Marshal Pietro Badoglio, aimed at bringing Italy into the war on the side of the Allies. But that had its downside. A debate between the Americans and British over the terms of surrender delayed the invasion of the mainland, giving the Germans more time to send large-scale reinforcements into Italy, a decision possibly influenced by German intelligence, which intercepted and unscrambled a Churchill-Roosevelt telephone conversation in which the two discussed negotiations with the Italians.[42]

The Anglo-American arguments over surrender terms focused on what seemed trivial detail, but the stakes were high. Roosevelt, ever committed to what he saw as a new world order, demanded unconditional surrender but in truth wanted to commit Italy to democratic postwar elections. Churchill, acting the Victorian Roosevelt thought him to be, hoped to retain the monarchy as the dominant political force in Italy and thus reinforce traditional British interests in the Mediterranean. The prime minister, using the same arguments the president had used during the Darlan deal, said that military necessity should take precedence over postwar matters and that putting the House of Savoy back in charge might be the best way get Italians to support the war. As for any joint Anglo-American statement about elections, he disingenuously wrote that he "should deprecate any pronouncement about self-determination at the present time, beyond what is implicit in the Atlantic Charter."[43]

Sicily was a promising step, and the impending Italian surrender even more so, but the greatest threat that summer to Hitler's survival took place in the vast plains some 500 miles south of Moscow. The Red Army had gained control of a bulge (a salient in military terms), centered on the city of Kursk, extending nearly 120 miles westward beyond the rest of the front. Both sides recognized the opportunity and the temptation. The Russians hoped to use it as a jumping-off point for their summer offensive, while the Germans viewed the bulge as an opportunity to cut off Soviet forces and inflict heavy losses. By the time the Germans attacked in early July, the Red Army was prepared. The armored forces arrayed on both sides were awesome: about thirty-four hundred Russian tanks and motorized guns facing twenty-four hundred for the Germans. In one single encounter on July 12, twelve hundred tanks and self-propelled guns fought in the largest tank battle in history. Even though the Germans inflicted the heaviest damage during the operation, Hitler canceled the offensive, in part lest he lose armored forces needed for the Italian campaign. Thus in one sense the threat of a second front in Italy achieved what Stalin had been asking for since 1941: the diverting of significant German forces away from the Russian front. What Kursk made clear was that while Hitler's armies in the East were far from defeated, they no longer posed an offensive threat.[44]

Churchill had barely returned to Britain from the Trident Conference before he began pushing for another meeting with Roosevelt that would, if possible, include Stalin. But the Soviet leader continued to berate the British, often but not always including the Americans as well, over the postponement of the second front and the cancellation of supply convoys. One particularly sarcastic cable from Stalin prompted Churchill to doubt momentarily even his own skill at personal diplomacy. "I feel that this is probably the end of the Churchill-Stalin correspondence from which I fondly hoped some kind of personal contact might be created between our countries."[45] FDR received the same contentious cable from Moscow, perhaps persuading the British leader that a Roosevelt-Stalin meeting would not take place. In any event, Churchill and the British chiefs of staff were, in the words of Eden's private secretary, "anxious to pin the Americans down before their well-known dislike of European operations except cross-Channel gets the better of them again, and they pull out their landing craft and send their ships off to the Pacific."[46] Stalin's initial agreement on a meeting sometime in July or August faded into no response when FDR attempted to set a date, leaving Roosevelt no choice but to meet with Churchill.

The prime minister headed for North America early in August hoping to persuade the Americans (and some of his own military advisers) to endorse a strategy he had presented to his chiefs of staff a few weeks earlier. Churchill may have assured Eisenhower back in June "that he was not advocating sending any army into the Balkans now or in the near future," and he repeated those assurances to Stimson, but his actions belied his words. The planned transfer of seven British divisions from the Mediterranean back to the U.K. to prepare for Overlord prompted the prime minister to fear that the move would jeopardize the Italian campaign. Keep those divisions where they were, he argued, then drive into northern Italy "with an option to attack westwards in the south of France or north-eastwards towards Vienna." At the same time, make efforts "to procure the expulsion of the enemy from the Balkans and Greece," and launch an attack on northern Norway, using Overlord merely as a diversion. Never was Churchill's opposition to the cross-Channel invasion put more forcefully. No wonder FDR concluded that the British did "not want the Balkans to come under the Russian influence" but wanted "to get to the Balkans first."

The British military chiefs shared their prime minister's concern about the Italian campaign's becoming a war orphan, but they routinely dismissed his oft-repeated calls for a Norwegian expedition. More significant, they remained committed or at least resigned to Overlord, even if General Brooke wrote contemptuously in his diary: "Marshall absolutely fails to understand the strategic treasures that lie at our feet in the Mediterranean. . . ."[47]

Once Anglo-American military leaders understood that they had broad agreement on grand strategy in Europe, the Quebec Conference (Quadrant, August 14–24, 1943) could focus on specific plans. Expeditions in Norway and the Aegean Sea were discarded. They agreed on operations to force the Italians out of the war, to obtain air bases in northern Italy, and to make a diversionary attack on southern France in conjunction with the cross-Channel invasion—but always with one governing principle: "[W]here there is a shortage of resources, available resources will be distributed and employed with the main object of insuring the success of OVER-LORD." The war against Japan again got short shrift, although the combined chiefs agreed to the American Navy's proposals for an island-hopping campaign in the Central and Southwestern Pacific, a historic decision as it turned out.

But the president and the prime minister did not waste their time. Politics kept a low profile at the actual Quadrant talks. Other than a few cautious questions about Soviet postwar intentions, most of the nonmilitary discussions were taken up with the ongoing debates about surrender terms for Italy and whether or not to recognize de Gaulle's Committee of National Liberation as the French government.[48]

On August 12–14, even before the two met at Quebec, they got together at the Roosevelt family home in Hyde Park. Amid hot dogs at Mrs. Roosevelt's cottage and swimming expeditions, Churchill and Roosevelt agreed on what Churchill called "a renewed final offer" for a tripartite meeting with Stalin. If the Soviet leader does not accept, wrote the prime minister in a note to Roosevelt, "we shall be on very strong ground." FDR ignored both the word "final" and Churchill's attempt to gain the moral high ground and agreed on another invitation to Stalin, as well as accepting the suggestion from Moscow for a meeting in the interim of diplomatic representatives of the Big Three.[49]

Even more secret (they hoped) than the Overlord decisions was the agreement reached, for the third time, that the United States would share its atomic research with Great Britain—and no one else. Throughout the summer of 1943 Churchill had complained that Britain had not been given information about the Manhattan Project despite earlier American commitments. The new agreement of August 19 required "mutual consent" to use an atomic bomb or to pass on "any information about Tube Alloys [another code word for the project] to third parties," while Britain and the United States would have "full and effective collaboration."

Whether or not Stalin knew of the agreement is uncertain; the U.S. Congress did not learn of it until 1947. Roosevelt did not know that Stalin had found out about the British atomic bomb research program, the Maud project, back in September 1941, but no later than September 1943 the president knew that Soviet espionage had penetrated the Manhattan Project.[50] Even so, he never mentioned the undertaking to his Soviet ally.

With the meetings dominated by the military, Churchill and Roosevelt found time for other diversions, then and during the prime minister's lengthy stay afterward. A day's fishing near Quebec resulted in their christening the site One Lake after Churchill had caught nothing and FDR had landed only a single fish (the fifty small trout caught by others in the party apparently did not count). The prime minister received an honorary degree from Harvard University (carefully arranged by FDR) and gave an acceptance speech in which he suggested some sort of "common citizenship" between the United States and Great Britain. Churchill visited Hyde Park before the conference (his wife, Clementine, who did not particularly like Roosevelt, remained in Quebec to recuperate from the transatlantic crossing), then spent time in Washington afterward, returning to Hyde Park with Mrs. Churchill to celebrate their thirty-fifth wedding anniversary with FDR and his family.[51]

While Churchill was in North America, the invasion of the Italian mainland took place on September 3, four years to the day after Britain had declared war on Germany. British forces met little resistance in Reggio Calabria (the tip of the toe on the Italian boot), just a few miles across the Strait of Messina. A secondary landing near Taranto (on the heel) was equally successful. That good news was accompanied by word that the Italian military had signed an armistice. The Anglo-American contest over which would sponsor the new Italian government was not over, nor did the so-called short terms for surrender bring the Italians actively into the war against Germany, but it was a promising start.

Then, a week later, Roosevelt and Churchill got a foreshadowing of things to come when an amphibious landing farther north at Salerno, near Naples, bogged down. In what became a pattern for the Italian theater, a combination of insufficient resources, poor command coordination, bad decisions in the field, overconfidence, and tenacious German defense combined to prevent the decisive success Eisenhower had forecast. British intelligence had predicted that the Germans would retreat to defensive positions along the Alps in northern Italy, but the Wehrmacht rushed reinforcements south from Rome and nearly pushed the largely American force back into the sea. Only a diversion of Allied bombers away from their strategic attacks on northern Italy plus reinforcements from North Africa allowed the Allies to hold the beachhead. The Germans finally withdrew after deciding to make a stand a little farther north, but Naples was not occupied (or liberated) until October 1.[52]

Like Churchill, Hitler recognized that his Italian ally had lost its stomach for the war and that, unopposed, the Anglo-Americans could move north rapidly to threaten Germany in the Balkans, Central Europe, or southern France. Unlike Churchill, Hitler and his generals also recognized that the mud and mountains of Italy gave military defenders a huge advantage. The Salerno campaign further persuaded the Germans that they should make the Allies pay for every inch of ground. General Montgomery, the British Eighth Army commander, admitted the impossibility of making progress when "the whole country becomes a sea of mud and nothing on wheels can move off the roads," although General Brooke, the head of the Imperial General Staff, always blamed the Americans and their preoccupation with Overlord.[53]

The political situation in Italy was equally muddy. The king hoped to keep his throne, while Badoglio hoped to stay in power as head of the Italian government. Both presented themselves as the only alternative to a takeover by the Italian Communists, a leading element in the effective anti-German guerrilla activities in northern Italy. Churchill, who had a personal preference for monarchies to begin with, endorsed the anti-Communist arguments of Victor Emmanuel and Badoglio, especially since the two would be more sympathetic to the British than to the Americans. Roosevelt insisted on free elections and had a ready list of antimonarchist Italian politicians, led by ones who had lived in the United States.

Moreover, the president continued to subscribe to his War Department policy that the military should have full political authority in occupied territories. Not only was that a convenient position to take, since the Allied commander was an American (as had been the case in North Africa), but Roosevelt also trusted his top officers to reflect his own broad vision of how to reconstruct the postwar world. After all, he had picked them. Churchill, on the other hand, distrusted his military on political matters and invariably sought to have occupation policy set by political representatives—so much so that he seemed to follow the "traditional" American argument for civilian control over the military more rigorously than did FDR. Harold Macmillan, a junior minister in Churchill's government, had been attached to Eisenhower's headquarters as the British political adviser since the early days of the North African campaign.[54]

Of course being a officer in the U.S. Army did not preclude politics, nor was it intended to. The "boss" of the occupation government in Sicily was Colonel Charles Poletti, an Italian-American who, according to the amused Macmillan, was "Deputy-Governor" of New York State, a product of the Tammany Hall political machine, and "a true American, a 'hundred-per-center.' " They struck it off very well—clearly a case of one politician appreciating another.[55]

Meanwhile Stalin demanded from the wings that the Soviet Union have an equal role in making occupation policy in Italy. Both Churchill and Roosevelt opposed that request, even though they understood the dangers. Back in late July Eden and the American ambassador in London, John Winant, had suggested that Stalin was particularly sensitive about having a role in the Italian settlement. Winant presciently warned FDR and Hull: "When the tide turns and the Russian armies are able to advance we might well want to influence their terms of capitulation and occupancy in Allied and enemy territory." But the Anglo-American leaders also understood Stalin's axiom: Whoever occupies a territory imposes on it his own social system. They would have liked to avoid setting a precedent for exclusion that Stalin could use against them, but the dangers of letting the Russians into Italy seemed too great, particularly with the Italian Communists so strong.[56]

Amid the confusion Eisenhower desperately worked for a commitment from Badoglio that the Italian military would declare war on Germany and actively participate. A few Italian units fought bravely, if briefly, against the Germans, but for the most part the army and air force simply melted away. Hitler's forces occupied Rome in two days and took control of much of northern Italy, although Italian partisans constantly harassed the Germans. A daring raid by glider-borne German troops rescued Mussolini, who had been imprisoned by the Italian military, and transported him to the north, where he established an impotent rival government. Italian garrisons in Corsica, Sardinia, the Balkans, Greece, and the Aegean were quickly neutralized and disarmed by the Germans. The Italian fleet, which managed to escape to North Africa and Malta, eventually became a bone of contention; the Anglo-Americans proposed dividing it between themselves, and the Soviets immediately claimed a share.[57]

The Italians had no interest in rejoining the fighting on anybody's side. The war had been an unmitigated disaster for the nation: Hollow dreams of empire had collapsed; its armies were defeated in North Africa and nearly destroyed during the Stalingrad battle; now Italy was humiliated by a German occupation and divided by civil disarray bordering on warfare. A declaration of war on Germany by the Badoglio regime eventually came about, but only to obtain belligerent status in order to insist (to little avail, as it turned out) that Italian soldiers sent to Germany be treated as prisoners of war, not conscripted laborers. For the Allies, the Italian theater remained for the duration of the war like a teenager—always late, always hungry, and full of unfulfilled promise.

The Italian surrender seemed to offer tempting opportunities in the Mediterranean, at least for the British. The Axis occupation of Yugoslavia, Greece, and the Dodecanese Islands in the Aegean Sea off the Turkish coast all had relied heavily on Italian forces, and the British were eager to replace them. But the Germans were quicker and on the scene. They moved in force against various Yugoslav partisan groups that tried to slip into the place left by the Italians and took firm control in Greece as well. Moreover, in Yugoslavia and Greece (as well as Italy) local groups were distracted by fighting or preparing to fight one another for control of any postwar government. In the Manichaean rhetoric of the Cold War years, that pitted Communists against pro-Western groups, though the situation was far more complicated than that.[58] The Anglo-Americans became ensnared in those civil disputes before war's end, but in autumn 1943 local conflicts combined with German strength to make it impossible for Britain to take advantage of the collapse of Italian authority, whether by fomenting popular uprisings or by sending in British forces.

The Dodecanese Islands, particularly Rhodes, were a different situation. The islands were strategically located off the southwest corner of Turkey and had facilities for aircraft and warships in Rhodes. Mussolini had treated the islands as part of his new Roman Empire and put some effort into building airfields, ports, and administration buildings, even seaside resorts for his senior politicians and bureaucrats.[59] The British had quickly occupied three of the smaller islands—Cos, Leros, and Samos—but could hold them only if they could take Rhodes. The German garrison on that island was relatively small, and the situation uncomplicated by local rivalries. Now, Churchill told General Harold Alexander, the British commander in Italy, "is the moment for intensification of effort and for running small-scale risks audaciously," and the Dodecanese seemed the only possible candidate. The prime minister put it to Roosevelt: "Even if landing craft and assault ships on the scale of a division were withheld from the buildup for OVERLORD for a few weeks without altering the zero date it would be worth while." Moreover, taking Rhodes might bring the Turks into the war against Germany.[60]

General Marshall, in a succinct comment made some years later, caught the American military's concerns and suspicions about such proposals: "I doubt if there was any one thing, except the shortage in LSTs [landing ships], that came to our minds more frequently than the political factors. But we were very careful, exceedingly careful, never to discuss them with the British, and from that they took the count that we didn't observe those things at all."[61] Not only did Churchill want some of those precious LSTs, but postwar politics rather than the expeditious defeat of Hitler seemed the prime minister's motive. The Aegean was a backwater, Turkey's entry into the war was too little and too late, and any diversion of resources threatened Overlord, as the Americans had learned already. Roosevelt's responses were drafted by Marshall and the military chiefs, but it may have been the president who added a brutally frank sentence to one such message: "Strategically, if we get the Aegean Islands, I ask myself where do we go from there. . . ." Marshall, pushed by Churchill, resorted to a rare profanity, telling the prime minister, "Forgive me, but no American soldier is going to die on that goddam beach."[62]

When Eisenhower held a meeting in Tunis on October 9 to allow discussions of strategy for the Mediterranean, none of the British officers supported Churchill's proposal. The prime minister "seemed always to see great and decisive possibilities in the Mediterranean, while the project of invasion across the English Channel left him cold," was Ike's assessment. Back in London General Brooke reflected the attitude of the British chiefs of staff, writing in his diary that the prime minister had "worked himself into a frenzy" and so "magnified" the significance of an attack on Rhodes that he pushed it "even at the expense of endangering his relations with the Americans and the future of the Italian campaign."[63]

As was the case before in the Mediterranean/North African theater, Hitler decided the issue. The German decision to hold the line in Italy forced Eisenhower to insist on no diversion of resources to the Aegean, forcing even Churchill to agree, grudgingly, that the allies might have to cancel any expedition against Rhodes. "I will not waste words in explaining how painful this decision is to me," he cabled Roosevelt, and then complained bitterly to one of his generals that "like you, I feel I have been fighting with my hands tied behind my back."[64]

Churchill's anger perhaps masked his embarrassment. He had insisted on continuing the campaign in the Dodecanese Islands despite military advice to the contrary. Although he authorized British commanders to evacuate Leros (in the northern part of the islands) if they deemed it necessary, the prime minister made his preference clear: Hold on and fight. Whoever made the decision, it was a disaster. The British lost some 4,500 men (1,500 killed, 3,000 captured), 21 warships (cruisers, destroyers, submarines), 11 smaller vessels, 113 aircraft—and the Dodecanese Islands.[65]

Not all the comedies at that time were as tragic as the Dodecanese campaign. The Americans had put steady pressure on Portugal to provide air base facilities in the Azores, Portuguese islands strategically situated in the mid-Atlantic due west of Lisbon. The war against German U-boats was the immediate reason for the request, although U.S. commercial aviation interests hoped to make the islands a postwar way station for transatlantic flights. The Portuguese dictator, Antonio Salazar, played the British against the Americans for as long as he could. Then, when American demands became nearly irresistible, he opted for continuing the historic Anglo-Portuguese relationship. Churchill obviously relished proposing to Roosevelt that American aircrews in the Azores could wear "some badge to indicate that they are temporarily incorporated into the RAF. . . ." After all, he added, "please remember that we were quite ready to put large numbers of troops into American uniforms at the time of Torch. . . ."[66]

Churchill's bitter anger over the Dodecanese campaign, and his amused retaliation during the "occupation" of the Azores, were soon replaced by the next stage in Big Three diplomacy. During October 19–30 the foreign ministers of the Soviet Union, Great Britain, and the United States met in Moscow to discuss postwar planning. Commissar for Foreign Affairs V. M. Molotov represented the USSR, but always with Stalin peering over his shoulder. Foreign Secretary Anthony Eden spoke for Britain, although Churchill insisted on being kept fully informed and regularly sent Eden instructions. Roosevelt, on the other hand, seemed less concerned about control. Even as Secretary of State Cordell Hull was on his way to Moscow, FDR appeared more interested in arrangements to send Churchill a Christmas tree cut from those growing at Hyde Park than in the foreign ministers' conference.[67]

Hull was not Roosevelt's first choice. The president much preferred Undersecretary of State Welles, the family friend and trusted adviser. The undersecretary's special access to the president had embittered Hull, and when Welles was found in some personal indiscretions, the secretary of state and a few confederates had their opportunity to force his resignation. FDR wanted to send him anyway, but Hull, sensing an opportunity to vindicate his tenure as secretary of state, insisted on going to Moscow—his first overseas air journey—despite being seriously afflicted with claustrophobia, diabetes, and tuberculosis.[68]

Having all three conferees either out of the loop or on a very short leash was a recipe for disaster or at least irrelevance. But the Moscow talks proved significant. Eden did in fact share Churchill's views on most of the key issues, particularly the need to create some sort of political barrier to Soviet expansion into Central Europe. Not only did Molotov accept Stalin's leadership unquestioningly, but the Soviet premier himself conferred with Hull and Eden. As for the American secretary of state, he and Roosevelt had differences about how to structure the postwar world, particularly over FDR's four policemen approach, which Hull feared could become little more than a re-creation of spheres of influence.[69] But ego more than substance was what set them apart, and Hull's pride was well stroked by his appointment to head the American delegation. Economic liberalism, decolonization, suspicion of Britain, China as a balance weight in Asia, and postwar cooperation were broad concepts he and the president could agree on, and in autumn 1943 the goal was to get the British and Soviets to agree to the principles, not the details. Moreover, Hull was uninterested in military affairs and would not get enmeshed in the second front or Mediterranean strategy disputes.

Hull and Eden each pursued a pet project. For Eden, that was the establishment of what he called machinery to deal with postwar politics in Europe: occupation policy, boundaries, and the reconstruction of governments. He proposed that the great powers accept a "self-denying" ordinance that would avoid a dangerous struggle to gain control over and/or ally with the smaller states of Europe. Since Britain had historically preferred just such a policy of aloofness, the evident target of self-denial was the Soviet Union.

Eden also echoed Churchill's call for creation of new confederations in Central Europe, ostensibly to reconstruct the economic and political benefits of unity that had theoretically been conferred by the Austro-Hungarian Empire, which had disappeared in the wake of the First World War. Since such confederations would be sponsored by Britain, the proposal tended to contradict his self-denying ordinance. More important, confederations raised images of the old cordon sanitaire, the post–World War I alliance system of France, Britain, and the smaller nations of Central Europe, aimed directly at the Bolsheviks. FDR and Hull thought Eden's proposals "smacked of spheres of influence," a phrase they used in the peculiar American way to describe any form of power politics, whether it formed spheres of influence or not. No one thought to mention that the British "federation" with Scotland and Wales had been accomplished by conquest.[70]

When the British initiatives failed, Eden blamed Hull for refusing to support the proposals. The blame was misplaced; the Soviets, ever sensitive to the re-creation of any cordon sanitaire, would have no part of the scheme. But Hull's lack of interest in the specifics of European political arguments was evident. He labeled the Polish-Soviet boundary question a "Pandora's box of infinite trouble," an accurate appraisal since the Poles claimed territory historically occupied by millions of Byelorussians and Ukrainians, as well as Lithuanians, whose capital, Vilnius, would fall within the expansive boundaries demanded by the London Poles. In the words of one historian, those exiles held "a romantic concept of Polish nationalism which, though just possible to sustain so long as the Soviet Union was prostrate, had become Cloud-Cuckoo-Land in the 1940s." Little wonder that, when the U.S. ambassador in Moscow, Averell Harriman, suggested it was a good time to discuss guarantees of independence for Poland and Eastern Europe, Hull rejected the advice. "I don't want to deal with these piddling little things," he replied. "We must deal with the main issues."

For Hull, and for FDR, the "main issues" revolved around getting the Soviet Union to agree to participate in a worldwide international structure after the war and then defining that structure. Harriman, writing with Cold War hindsight some thirty years later, contemptuously censured Hull for fixating on "his own four-power declaration, a document breathing assurance that the Great

Powers would behave with perfect decorum after the war was won." But at the time Harriman himself was ambivalent on how to deal with the Soviets, pushing Hull to get down to cases while telling Roosevelt that the Soviets seemed "to want to do business with us."[71]

Hull understood, as Roosevelt did, that Poland's relationship with the Soviet Union would be defined largely by Moscow, not by an elitist government-in-exile in London. The Polish boundary and the fate of the other East European states would depend on Stalin's sense of security and his desire for power. If security was the Soviet leader's primary concern, then arrangements were possible. Yet if Stalin's axiom prevailed, the Red Army's impending liberation/occupation of Poland would decide the issue of Polish independence as well as its frontiers. Finding a way to satisfy Stalin's search for security (both personal and national) in the hope of convincing him to act "responsibly" commanded the attention of both Churchill and Roosevelt until the president's death in April 1945.

Hull's pride and joy, the Four-Nations Declaration on General Security, was part of the process of bringing the Soviet Union into the community of nations.[72] He and Eden (and FDR as well) hoped to turn the Grand Alliance into a postwar relationship "for the organization and maintenance of peace and security," although the Englishman much preferred focusing on the specific details of a European settlement, particularly regarding Poland. But whichever agenda dominated, the scheme could work only if the Soviets were convinced that it would be both safe and to their advantage to cooperate with the Anglo-Americans rather than confront them. The declaration embodied FDR's preference for a loose yet firm relationship among the four Great Powers. Molotov did insist on eliminating any requirements for "joint" approval of actions taken to preserve the peace, leaving only the commitment to "consult" the other powers. Eden, either resigned or happy to escape an American veto on British freedom of action, did not protest, and Hull accepted the change. Perhaps the secretary of state understood that limiting American freedom of action by requiring "joint" consent would have raised issues of constitutionality in the

United States and given American "isolationists" the kind of issue that had caused Woodrow Wilson so much trouble.[73]

There were signs that Harriman was right; the Soviets seemed "to want to do business with us." Soviet agreement on creation of a three-power European Advisory Commission that would discuss the specifics of occupation policy for Germany, as well as Stalin's support for dismembering Germany (which Hull did not like but FDR had endorsed), indicated a cooperative approach.[74] When Eden, firmly instructed by Churchill, told Stalin that Overlord might be postponed to early or mid-June, the Soviet leader made no protest. Perhaps he was resigned to Anglo-American postponements. Perhaps recent Soviet victories had diminished the military need for the second front, allowing him to be less interested in the date than in encouraging the Allies to invade Western France rather than get involved in the Balkans. Nor did Molotov fuss much about the effective exclusion of the USSR from occupation policy in Italy, acquiescing to the transparent Allied argument that the military situation required that effective political control rest with the theater commander. But whatever his motive, he gave the impression of being seriously interested in Hull's political proposals and did not adopt his usual pose of berating the Anglo-Americans about the second front. On the contrary, Molotov raised British hopes for their Aegean adventure when he bluntly stated that forcing the Turks to declare war on Germany would serve the interests of both Turkey and the Grand Alliance.[75]

Hull, again reflecting Roosevelt's thinking, tried to get the Europeans to look beyond their regional problems and cooperate on a worldwide basis by insisting that China be included as one of the Great Powers. Molotov nervously demurred, then agreed to have the Chinese sign the declaration, so long as it did not give Japan an excuse to attack the USSR—however implausible that was in autumn 1943, when the momentum had shifted in the Pacific war and Japan had begun to feel the strangling effect of American submarine warfare. Then, to Hull's surprise and Roosevelt's pleasure, Stalin promised without prompting to enter the war against Japan once Germany was defeated. (Stalin's military high command, the Stavka, may not have been quite as surprised. During the summer of 1943 it initiated some very early steps to prepare for future offensive operations in the Far East.) Why that declaration of war had to wait that long, given Japan's inability by 1943 to threaten the Soviet Union, was a question Roosevelt never asked. Nor did Churchill, although he must have wondered since he thought a Soviet break with Japan "possibly near."[76]

Whatever expectations Hull had that his accomplishments at Moscow warranted his being given a major role in policy planning for the postwar world were quickly dashed. Roosevelt met him at the airport but barely listened to the secretary's report. As Hull commented somewhat forlornly in his memoirs, the president "was more interested in discussing the forthcoming conferences at Cairo and at Teheran" than hearing anything more than highlights of the Moscow talks. However much he and the president might agree on broad policy, Roosevelt was caught up in being his own secretary of state.[77]

Hull had managed to avoid the Polish question while in Moscow, but not in the United States. A week after his return, representatives of the Polish government in London, still recognized by the United States, along with the Polish-American press, condemned the Four-Nation Declaration, which Hull had described to a joint session of Congress. His answer was simple and straightforward. "At Moscow," the secretary told the Poles, he had "urged Molotov to find a basis for reestablishing diplomatic relations between the two countries. It is only through this course of friendly discussion and conference that we can possibly get Polish and Russian difficulties worked out."[78] The message to the Poles could not have been more clear. Nor could Hull have reflected Roosevelt's and Churchill's position more precisely. The test over Poland was becoming more difficult.

Arrangements for the first Big Three meeting that so preoccupied Roosevelt proved annoying for both Anglo-American leaders. Stalin had finally agreed to a late November date but refused to stray far from the Soviet Union, despite the president's dubious argument that he needed to be able to sign or veto legislation within ten days and that a Teheran site could make that difficult. "I must carry on a constitutional government more than one hun-

dred fifty years old," Roosevelt pointed out. His alternatives mi-
grated all the way from Alaska to North Africa, Cairo, and even
Baghdad. To no avail. Whether motivated by one-upmanship, his
fear of flying, or concern for his personal safety and political control, Stalin insisted on going no farther than Teheran. Thus the
talks began with his holding a subtle edge.[79]

Roosevelt had played his own game with Churchill. He had insisted earlier to his military chiefs that U.S. participation in Overlord be larger than that of Britain, so that an American could be
put in charge. Although Marshall warned that the U.S. role in the
attack would not exceed that of the British, FDR went ahead and
proposed that an American, presumably General Marshall, become
supreme commander for the entire effort against Germany. Churchill, who had previously insisted on a single commander for North
Africa and Italy, now sensed that Britain was being relegated to
the next level of importance and immediately protested. The issue
was not resolved until January 1944, after the prime minister had
pointed out that a single supreme commander would inevitably
become entangled in political arguments, specifically Anglo-
American disagreement over whether to concentrate the "main effort" in the Mediterranean or on Overlord. Unspoken was his
insistence that Britain have its own theater, where "the laurels
would be all ours." What the prime minister wanted, and eventually got, was a separation of direction of the war against Germany
into two "supreme" commands: a British one in the Mediterranean and the Allied Expeditionary Force (AEF) for Western Europe.[80] The "special relationship" was once again strained and
reshaped.

That is not to say, as some have, that Roosevelt's "hopes for his
brave new world rested largely on the Soviets, not upon the fading
and reactionary power of the British Empire."[81] FDR did not dismiss Britain as some sort of minor player. If Britain was a "junior
partner," it was still a partner in a very limited partnership. All of
FDR's thinking about the postwar world required that the British
exercise the responsibilities of a Great Power. In fact, Roosevelt
and the Americans routinely exaggerated the wealth of Great Britain and its empire. Britain's military image had suffered during the

Second World War, but economic strength and political savvy would be the elements of power in the disarmed world Roosevelt sought.

But Churchill rebelled against junior partner status, even with the Americans. With that in mind, he sought extensive talks with the president in advance of their meeting with the Soviets. FDR never rejected such proposals but kept coming up with flimsy pretexts that prevented a serious Churchill-Roosevelt tête-à-tête. The president agreed to meet at Cairo but sent invitations to Molotov and Chiang as well. When Churchill informed Stalin that the Chinese would be at Cairo (something FDR had somehow failed to do), Molotov and all other Russians became unavailable. But Roosevelt then insisted on waiting in Washington until Hull returned from his journey to Moscow, then took a long ocean journey aboard the USS *Iowa*, visited battlefields and held brief meetings with Eisenhower in Tunis, and did not arrive at Cairo until November 22. The British prime minister was waiting, but so was Chiang, and there were only five days until Churchill and Roosevelt were to leave for Teheran, each in his own aircraft.

The pre-Teheran talks in Cairo (code-named Sextant) were held at the historic Mena House, originally built as a royal lodge for the Ottoman Empire's representative in Egypt. Taking advantage of its location, a half mile or so from the Sphinx and the tomb of Cheops, a British couple had turned Mena House into a hotel that catered to wealthy European travelers. (In 1977 it served as the site for the first meeting between President Anwar el-Sadat of Egypt and Prime Minister Menachem Begin of Israel, talks that proved a great deal more important than those in November 1943.)[82]

The talks at Mena House were far less historic than the locale. Sextant seemed aimed at proving Roosevelt's point that Great Power agreement had to precede any other arrangements for the postwar world. FDR sought Great Power status for Chiang and China for a variety of reasons. His frequent references to his grandfather Warren Delano's involvement in the China trade were both indicative and meaningless.[83] They displayed FDR's romantic predilection to view China as having a special relationship with the

United States. At the same time there was nothing romantic about the role he foresaw for China after the war. Chiang and China were the counterweight to the three powers whose presence Roosevelt sought to eliminate or minimize in postwar East Asia and the Western Pacific. Imperial Japan—the enemy—would lose its place, as the passion to revenge Pearl Harbor demanded. Britain, the colonial power, should not continue its role of exploiter, even if it had the strength to do so, as it did not. That left Soviet expansionist goals in its "Far East." The Russians had long laid claim to territory and privileges in Manchuria and Mongolia, all of which would challenge the legitimacy of Chiang Kai-shek. Chinese nationalism had enraged the Japanese and provoked war back in the 1930s, and Chiang could not openly betray those sentiments, particularly with Mao Tse-tung and his Chinese Communists fighting effectively against the Japanese and proclaiming themselves the only true protectors of China.

Churchill had no interest in talking to Chiang. Not only was he unsure if the Kuomintang leader would survive the civil conflict that seemed bound to come at the end of the war, but the British were uncomfortable about the implications for their empire of the "Asia for the Asians" nationalism that Chiang vocally espoused. Most important, however, was Churchill's conviction that the important theater of operations—political and military—was Europe, not Asia. The Foreign Office hoped that China could emerge independent of both the Americans and the Russians, but whatever would happen to British interests in Asia would be decided by events in Europe. Chiang was irrelevant.

Not for Roosevelt. The Cairo Declaration, a strictly American product, seemed a harmless call for the unconditional surrender of Japan, its expulsion from territories "taken by violence and greed," and the return to China of what Japan had "stolen." But the disposition of the Japanese Empire was not easy. The Soviet Union would demand a say in what happened in Manchuria and northeastern Asia, regardless of China's claims, while restoring Asian territories to former European masters would only prolong the decolonization that FDR believed necessary. Even the American military had begun to put in claims for island bases. The Americans had little understanding of the currents of Asian nationalism un-leashed by the Japanese, but that too would make colonial resto-ration more difficult.[84]

But FDR had also begun to wonder about Chiang's ambitions. A 1942–43 visit to the United States by his shrewd and forceful American-educated wife, Madame Chiang (Soong Mei-ling), had brought great public acclaim but left Roosevelt exasperated. FDR's son Elliott found her manner and aura terrifying. The president recognized that Chiang hoped to replace, not merely displace, the European colonial powers and that he was far from a democratic, popular ruler. Still, "There's just no other leader," Roosevelt con-cluded. "With all their shortcomings, we've got to depend on the Chiangs." FDR later scoffed at Churchill's fears that the Chinese leader would expand into the former European empires but felt it necessary to insist that Chiang promise in the Cairo Declaration not to do so.

At Cairo British dislike for Chiang was obvious—just as obvious as the Chinese leader's anti-British sentiments. General Brooke wrote contemptuously in his diary of Chiang as a "broken reed" and complained that "we were prepared to pander sufficiently to Chiang to affect possible operations in the Aegean against our pri-mary enemy."

Roosevelt, who had hoped Chiang could play a major role, also seemed disappointed. Asked what he thought of the generalissimo, FDR shrugged and replied, "About what I'd expected, I guess. . . . He knows what he wants, and he knows he can't have it all." Not only was the president disappointed with the weak military effort made by China's military forces, but there was no spark, no sense of intimacy—troubling for someone so predisposed to per-sonal diplomacy. FDR had wanted to talk to Chiang "mainly to realize the psychological benefits which would come from such a meeting," but the president left Cairo unsatisfied.[85]

The Americans tried to help Chiang by promoting an amphib-ious invasion of the Japanese-held Andaman Islands off southern Burma (Operation Buccaneer) and the equipping of ninety Chinese divisions, but the British wanted no part of any further diversion of the precious landing craft Churchill hoped to get for operations in the Aegean. Military campaigns to regain the British Empire in Southeast Asia would have to wait. When Marshall and Roosevelt persisted in promoting operations in Burma, even after Churchill's military chiefs had argued that Buccaneer would delay the cross-Channel invasion, the British convinced themselves that the Americans were willing to postpone Overlord.[86]

Both Churchill and Roosevelt had uneventful flights (six and one-half hours for FDR's plane) from Cairo to Teheran, although the prime minister, testy, tired, and plagued by a lingering cold and sore throat, complained of a "bloody bad landing" and "caught the pilot a smack across the ankles with his stick."[87] Roosevelt initially stayed at the American Legation, declining offers from Churchill and Stalin to move into their respective embassies as well as an invitation from the shah of Iran (who had not been told of the conference until the last minute). The next day, however, Molotov passed on reports of an alleged German plot to assassinate one or more of the three leaders, and Averell Harriman, who had joined the conference from Moscow, recommended that Roosevelt accept the Soviet offer. The invitation may have been, as General Ismay surmised, a transparent effort to get the Americans into quarters loaded with microphones and other bugs, although a Soviet counterspy who had penetrated German intelligence apparently did pass on reports of a plot.

Actually Churchill probably prompted the shift. The U.S. Legation lay more than a half mile from the British and Soviet missions, which were next to each other, and the prime minister had expressed doubts to Stalin about "repeated journeys to and fro through the streets of Teheran." Harriman recommended that Roosevelt choose the Soviet over the British Embassy, in part to facilitate talks with Stalin, in part because the quarters offered by the British were small. Churchill made the best of it and pretended to encourage Roosevelt to take up Molotov's offer, but the prime minister's heart could not have been in it. He tried to arrange for private talks with FDR before the first Big Three meeting, but the president chose instead to meet privately with Stalin.[88]

That was, at least in part, as Roosevelt earlier told the prime minister, so that Stalin would not think that the Anglo-Americans "had ganged up on him on military action."[89] Moreover, FDR knew full well what Churchill wanted to talk about—grand strategy in Europe, Overlord versus the Mediterranean—and on that subject there was little new the British could say. The president was far more flexible about such things than his military advisers (witness the decision to carry out the invasion of North Africa), but this time Stalin had to make the call. But there was more to it than that.[90]

Roosevelt had not gone halfway around the world to meet Stalin and Churchill so they could decide military strategy in Europe or Burma or the Pacific. The crippled president did not need to travel nearly nine thousand miles on a long, dangerous journey to decide whether to invade western France or adopt the British Mediterranean strategy. A quick exchange of telegrams among the three leaders would have ended that debate. Roosevelt would have asked if Stalin still wanted the second front or preferred extensive operations in the Aegean, Balkans, and Italy. The Soviet premier would have indicated that the "Soviet people" (in the Gaullian sense of "*L'état c'est moi*") would not accept anything less than *the* second front in northern France. Churchill would have pointed out the potential benefits of a Mediterranean strategy, claimed he had always supported Overlord, and muttered about being Roosevelt's "loyal lieutenant." End of debate!

What Roosevelt actually came to do at Teheran was conduct personal diplomacy, just as he had tried to do five months earlier when he proposed a Stalin-Roosevelt meeting. He needed to take the measure of his Soviet counterpart, "to talk, man to man, with Stalin, & try to establish a constructive relationship," so as to convince him that the United States (that is, FDR as "*L'état c'est moi*") could be trusted to work with the Soviet Union in the postwar world in a way that the interests of both would be protected.[91] FDR wooed Stalin's confidence at every level; refusing to meet privately with Churchill, at Cairo and at Teheran, was just part of the campaign. Given Stalin's intensely personal rule and his unremitting search for his own security, that personal approach by FDR, derided by critics as "unrealistic," was the only hope of preventing or at least lessening the dangers of the later Cold War confrontation and its series of wars by proxy between the Soviet Union and the United States. Even Stalin understood that politics was the primary issue, commenting that he had not expected to discuss technical military questions and had not brought his military staff to Teheran.[92]

Churchill, on the other hand, believed he had to hedge his bets on cooperation much more than did FDR. The war had demonstrated that the English Channel did not effectively separate Britain from the Continent. The Englishman's hatred of bolshevism (the word he preferred to communism) and his inclination to see political and military conflict as the norm rather than the exception all worked to make him uncomfortable with Roosevelt's approach. Since the age of Elizabeth I and Philip of Spain, Britain had worked to prevent any single state or coalition from gaining a preponderance of power in Europe. Now the Soviet Union seemed about to pose just that threat, one that Britain could not combat alone. Hitler's Germany had to be defeated and controlled lest it make another try at dominance. Only the United States could provide the power Britain needed, and the Americans were committed to cooperating with the Soviets. Nor was Churchill certain that such cooperation would not work. He merely wanted to avoid placing all his eggs in that one basket. Hope for the best, plan for the worst. His, and Roosevelt's, dilemma was that planning for the worst could confirm Stalin's suspicions and eliminate any hope for the best.

We've got the whole world in our hands. . . .

CHAPTER 8

———◆———

"A New Heaven and
a New Earth"
December 1943–December 1944

One day during Roosevelt's journey across the Atlantic aboard the USS *Iowa*, the ship conducted an antiaircraft drill using live ammunition in order to show off the "veritable curtain of fire" that would "greet" enemy aircraft. During the drill a torpedo accidentally fired from the tubes on the USS *William D. Porter*, one of the destroyers escorting the president's ship, and headed straight for the *Iowa*. Warned by a radio message, lookouts spotted the torpedo's wake, and the *Iowa* maneuvered to avoid. The torpedo had no primer, but even if it had hit the heavily armored battleship and exploded, there was little chance of a single torpedo's inflicting serious damage or threatening the lives of the president and his party. FDR treated the episode as a lark and breezily ordered that no punitive action be taken, certainly saving the career, if not the life, of the *Porter*'s captain, given Admiral King's volcanic temper.[1]

But what if the torpedo had hit the *Iowa*? What if Franklin Roosevelt had died as a result of the mishap? "If" history is best left to novelists, but a little speculation may illustrate the amount of room to maneuver the Big Three had as they gathered to meet at Teheran in late November 1943. This would have been before the 1944 presidential election, meaning that Vice President Henry A. Wallace, Harry Truman's predecessor, would have become President. Whatever effect a "President" Wallace would have had—and it might have been considerable—FDR's policies had both hemmed in any successor and at the same time failed to provide clear direction.

The second front, already being planned, could be "vetoed," but only by Stalin. Military events on the Russian front and in Italy did not provide the Anglo-Americans with the leverage needed to go against Stalin's wishes—unless they no longer viewed Hitler and Germany as their primary enemy and did not care whether or not the Soviet Union entered that war against Japan. In that theater China's military ineffectiveness had prompted a shift in strategy. Instead of an invasion of Japan from China, planners were assuming an island-hopping campaign, strategic bombing, and invasions of the Philippines and/or Formosa (Taiwan). That military strategy meant that U.S. and British military forces would not be in China at war's end.

As for the postwar world, FDR's policy of promoting cooperation with the Soviet Union and creating a condominium of the four policemen that would restrain both Soviet expansionism and British (European) imperialism could well have died with Roosevelt. His concept was vague, ill defined, and full of distinctions so subtle (or ignored) that even his closest advisers were uncertain about how it would work, and Henry Wallace was far from a close adviser. Even FDR had difficulty describing the difference between a sphere of influence and his notion of regional responsibility. Eleanor Roosevelt's earlier warning that the conception was "fraught with danger" remained on the mark. What would keep the major nations, "drunk with power," from imposing their will on the less powerful?[2] FDR, imprisoned by his own reading of Wilson's actions and too much of an American liberal to opt for untrammeled power politics, had suggested that his Good Neighbor policy in the Western Hemisphere offered an example of regional responsibility without coercive control. The other powers, particularly the British, mocked the notion that the United States did not dominate the region by sheer military and economic power and proposed just such Good Neighbor schemes for Europe as well as the European empires.

But FDR did not die in the cold waters of the Atlantic Ocean, and the talks in Teheran, beginning on November 28 and ending on December 2, laid out the fundamentals of the arrangements that were made fourteen months later (an eternity during war) at Yalta.

Roosevelt had assumed a great peace conference would come after the fighting, just as after the First World War, but it would be a meeting of the Great Powers, not all the United Nations. Like Wilson, Roosevelt was determined that "something 'big' will come out of this war: a new heaven and a new earth."[3] The president was convinced that only the New World—the United States—offered any innovative thinking in international relations. To achieve his goals required not only his presence at the peace table but that the United States have earned on the battlefield a position of at least equality at those talks. In the geopolitical language of international relations that made D-Day and a major American presence on the Continent an imperative. An anonymous U.S. intelligence analyst put it succinctly late in January 1943 in a paper that went to the president: With the survival of the USSR no longer in doubt, the time had come to "start exercising the dominant influence which power properly entitles us."[4]

The discussions at Teheran had an air of cordiality. Churchill offered eloquent lectures on his grand strategy. Roosevelt obviously worked hard to create a good personal relationship with Stalin: "[W]e talked like men and brothers," Roosevelt recalled, chuckling over his audacity in calling Stalin Uncle Joe (although it appears that Stalin was not pleased by the term). The Soviet leader made the most of his bargaining chips but also promised both an offensive timed to assist Overlord and entry into the war against Japan, even toasting lend-lease, without which, he said, "We would lose this war."[5]

But a tension existed that is apparent even in the dry, printed records of the talks. FDR was expansive and optimistic, but he failed in his efforts to get Stalin to preserve at least the appearances of self-determination in Eastern Europe. Nor did the president trust his Soviet counterpart enough to mention the atomic bomb, despite knowing that the Soviet leader already knew about the Manhattan Project. Stalin pushed the Anglo-Americans politely but relentlessly on Overlord, dismissing operations in the Aegean as a diversion, then baiting Churchill and the British during two supposedly festive dinners. Yet he was obviously aware of and uncomfortable with the Soviet Union's dependence on the Anglo-Americans. Churchill, fearful that Britain was being relegated to lesser status, later described "the poor little English donkey," caught between "the great Russian bear" on one side and the "Great American buffalo" on the other. Britain became a "small lion" and America an elephant in a later allusion, but the message was the same: Only little Britain "knew the right way home." When FDR went to meet Stalin privately, Churchill petulantly remarked that "he was glad to obey orders," claimed the right to host a dinner on November 30—his sixty-ninth birthday—and then "said he would get thoroughly drunk and be prepared to leave the next day."[6]

The talks went quickly to the key issues. Overlord was the initial focus and produced the easiest decision of the conference. FDR gave Stalin an opportunity to endorse the British strategy. "One of the questions to be considered here," said the president, was how to use Allied forces in the Mediterranean "to bring the maximum aid to the Soviet armies on the Eastern front." Stalin, assuming that the Americans tied the second front to a commitment to enter the Pacific war,[7] promised to create a "common front" against Japan once Germany surrendered. Next he exploited the advantage of having a victorious army by summarizing the situation on the Russian front. Only then did he casually dismiss the campaign in Italy, where it seemed to him that Hitler had succeeded in tying up a large number of Allied divisions. He was equally dismissive of a Balkans campaign. That would require Turkey's entry into the war, which Stalin repeatedly insisted would not happen. Moreover, "the Balkans were far from the heart of Germany."

Churchill made the proper noises about the cross-Channel attack, then scrambled to justify British campaigns in the Adriatic and eastern Mediterranean, but to no avail. He predicted (inaccurately) that Rome would be taken in January 1944, thus releasing a substantial number of British divisions. Since those forces would be available, the prime minister asked Stalin if any Mediterranean operations warranted a diversion of amphibious shipping and a two-or three-month delay of Overlord. To the relief of both the Soviet and the American military, Stalin disparaged "dispersing allied forces" that had no "direct connection" with one another.[8] Hearing that, FDR chimed in that he opposed any delay in the cross-Channel invasion, and the discussion essentially ended.

When Churchill and General Brooke persisted about the Mediterranean strategy later in the conference, Stalin drove the coffin nail deeper. He warmly endorsed COSSAC plans for an invasion of southern France, even if it meant delaying the capture of Rome, a suggestion that must have made Churchill wince. A promise that the Red Army would also launch an offensive coordinated with the opening of the second front clinched the matter. When Churchill continued to talk of the Aegean and Italian campaigns, Stalin pointedly questioned if "the Prime Minister and the British staffs really believe in Overlord." Churchill replied with his usual bombast—"it will be our stern duty to hurl across the Channel against the Germans every sinew of our strength"—but Stalin had hit the mark. Still suspicious, he asked who would command the invasion, for "nothing would come out of the operation" unless one person were in charge. When the prime minister equivocated on the date for the assault, Stalin rose dramatically, telling Molotov, "Let's not waste our time here. We've got plenty to do at the front."

Stalin's annoyance was likely a tactic, although his translator, still caught some forty years later between orthodoxy and truth, described him as "occasionally irritable," then, with unintended humor, noted that "the slightest objection could provoke a stormy reaction." Roosevelt seemed to take Stalin seriously and quickly suggested they adjourn to prepare for dinner.[9]

Churchill had done his best to look to Britain's postwar interests. Throughout the war he expressed little concern for, and even dislike of, formal postwar planning, but that did not mean he had no postwar goals. He paid little heed to structure but gave much attention to using the war to develop and maintain his nation's interests. Italy might not ever be Great Britain's satellite, but British-led campaigns in the Mediterranean offered one last opportunity to enhance the U.K.'s prestige and protect its influence in the region. It was one last chance to appear like a Great Power.

Because the Americans generally assumed Britain's Great Power status, particularly the opulence of its empire, they interpreted the motives for the Mediterranean option more narrowly. As FDR pointed out to his military chiefs, "the British look upon the Mediterranean as an area under British domination." One American naval attaché expressed the common sentiment: "Now 168 years later [after the American Revolution] we are again being taxed hundreds of thousands of lives and billions of dollars to save the British Empire. . . ."[10]

But it was more than just formal empire. Perhaps the prime minister truly hoped that victory in Italy, military action in the Aegean and Adriatic, and Turkish entry into the war would stimulate uprisings in the Balkans against the Germans, uprisings that could also liberate those countries before Stalin could apply his axiom to their political reconstruction, though Churchill never said so by the time of the Teheran meeting. The Americans viewed Churchill's policy as power politics, not ideological conflict. Elliott Roosevelt recalls his father's claiming that, notwithstanding Churchill's insistence that he had no plan to send any army to the Balkans, the British wanted an "invasion" of the Balkans so as "to keep the Red Army out of Austria and Rumania, even Hungary." The president told his military chiefs that "he personally could not see the logic of this reasoning. He did not believe the Russians would desire to take over the Balkan states. Their wish is to establish kinship with the other Slavic people. In any event, he thought it unwise to plan military strategy based on a gamble as to political results." Neither the joint chiefs nor Stimson commented.[11]

General Marshall, in parallel talks with his military counterparts, General Brooke and Soviet Marshal K. E. Voroshilov, emphasized the shortage of shipping as the ostensible reason for rejecting British proposals for Mediterranean operations, but his deeper reason was the belief that the British were more interested in postwar politics than in defeating Hitler. As for the drain on shipping caused by amphibious operations in the Pacific (Marshall mentioned five invasions and four more planned for January), with Britain unable and the Soviets unwilling to help the Americans in that theater, no one had the temerity to ask whether or not the island-hopping campaign fitted the Germany-first commitment.

Whatever Churchill's motives, Stalin and Roosevelt ended the Balkan pipe dream. Churchill had agreed that Overlord was "top of the hill" but argued that it should not prevent other operations in the Mediterranean. General Brooke's diary entry was, as ever, more pungent, describing Churchill's "masterly statement" on "the dangers of spelling the word OVERLORD with the letters TYRANT." But the decision had been made.[12]

In the aftermath of the second front discussions, Stalin displayed considerable resentment toward Churchill, who responded in kind. Even their dinner toasts were barbed. Churchill sarcastically drank "to the Proletarian masses," while Stalin responded with "to the Conservative Party." Nor did the president come to the prime minister's defense. When Stalin suggested executing fifty thousand Germans at the end of the war, Churchill objected on grounds of honor (though he encouraged killing as many Germans as possible in battle or by the "strategic" bombing campaign). Roosevelt added to the awkwardness by offering the too-cute suggestion that they compromise on forty-nine thousand. The next evening the Soviet leader publicly chastised General Brooke for being "unfriendly toward the Soviet Union" and for adopting "a grim and distrustful attitude." The American note taker detected a "twinkle" in Stalin's eye, but no one else did.[13]

Given Churchill's later attempts to persuade Roosevelt to take a tough line with the Soviets, there is no small irony in the prime minister's stubborn opposition to the American-style second front, for it helped push Roosevelt closer to the Soviets. Stalin had raised the issue out of need but then used it as a lever in his relations with the Anglo-Americans, and Roosevelt reacted to that pressure. Once Allied fears of a Soviet collapse or a negotiated German-Soviet peace dissipated, Roosevelt's desire to gain Soviet cooperation in the postwar world took over. The president had also responded to the insistent prodding of Stimson and his military chiefs for an invasion of western France, but without the pressure from the Soviets, even couched as it was in abrasive and demanding terms, the British might well have been able to ease the Anglo-American alliance away from the second front strategy. But with that strategy settled, Roosevelt and Stalin could take up the issues that really had brought the two together, the postwar world. Churchill, frustrated in his effort to use wartime strategy to buttress Britain's political position, came to that part of the talks with little leverage.

The details of the postwar settlements were not agreed on at Teheran. The three leaders preferred to paper over the cracks rather than endanger the Grand Alliance, which all believed still necessary in order to defeat Germany and Japan. But the Teheran talks prefigured the decisions that would come, particularly at Yalta, although the devil was in the details, particularly for FDR, whose bureaucracy, already embarked on postwar planning, had little understanding of his thinking.

One of the papered-over cracks was the matter of France, which stood as a symbol for weakness in both Europe and in the colonial world. On the first day of the talks Stalin roundly condemned "the entire French ruling class" for being "rotten to the core" and for having "delivered over France to the Germans."[14] FDR agreed, saying anyone over forty should be kept out of the postwar French government. When Stalin suggested that the Allies should not "shed blood to restore Indochina" to France, FDR agreed and then implied that China, which had forsworn any "designs" on Indochina, should act as a trustee while Indochina prepared for independence, which would take "20 to 30 years." No sense in talking to Churchill about India, Roosevelt commented privately to Stalin, but perhaps reform from the bottom up, "somewhat on the Soviet line," was the best solution. That would mean "revolution," was the candid reply. The president made no reply but then seized on Stalin's comment that the French should not control any strategic points to insist that Dakar, on the bulge of West Africa, had to be "under the trusteeship of the United Nations."

Roosevelt's jargon left Stalin and Churchill confused, although FDR had mused years earlier about a Pan-American trusteeship over those Western Hemisphere territories belonging to Nazi-occupied nations.[15] The worry for the British and other colonial powers was the president's insistence on international accountability for the trusteeship scheme. What later became the United Nations Organization had not been agreed to, and he obviously did not mean the entire "united nations," which were allied against the Axis. More crucial, what did the president mean by "trustees" and "trusteeships"? Were those code words aimed at making spheres of influence palatable to Americans? FDR's comment that "Dakar in unsure hands was a direct threat to the Americas" left the impression that whatever the niceties of terminology, Dakar was something the United States wanted to control. Churchill gave vague assent to unilateral control of strategic points. Stalin, sensing a deal, thereafter treated American and British concerns about strategic territories with great seriousness. Charles Bohlen, on loan from the American Embassy in Moscow for translation duty in Teheran, pointedly observed, "No specific mention was made of bases which might be held by the Soviet Union," although Stalin indicated he would speak of Soviet "desires" at the appropriate time and did ask what might be done for the USSR in the Far East.[16]

The partitioning of Germany remained something that both Roosevelt and Stalin supported, though the Soviet leader's primary concern was with making Germany "impotent ever again to plunge the world into war." Churchill agreed that Prussia should be "detached" from the rest of Germany but backed away from much more than that. They could agree that the European Advisory Commission (EAC) had to deal with the details, but that led ineluctably to the question of postwar frontiers, and that brought the Polish question to the table.

Stalin's proposal, offered on the first day and never modified, was that Poland should have a western boundary on the Oder River and generally along the old Curzon Line in the east. Pounds of paper and gallons of ink have since been expended in arguments over just which Oder River line should apply and what adjustments were needed to the Curzon Line, which Churchill accurately but cantankerously insisted on calling the "Ribbentrop-Molotov Line." But the basic agreement was crystal clear. For the British

prime minister's part, "he would like to see Poland moved westward in the same manner as soldiers at drill execute the drill 'left
close' and illustrated his point with three matches representing the
Soviet Union, Poland and Germany." His instinctive solution to
the dangers of postwar confrontation was to establish clearly defined boundaries and spheres of influence. Churchill, whose sense
of history underpinned his policies, reckoned that such arrangements had worked in the nineteenth century, why not again? The
Great Powers of Europe would, he hoped, seek their own interests
and create a great peace. "I did not think we were very far apart
in principle," he told Stalin.[17] Ten months later, during his talks
in Moscow with Stalin, Churchill took the next logical step and
spelled out in clear, certain terms just who would get what.

Roosevelt had gone to bed by the time Churchill played with
his matches, but the president had no quarrel with the proposal.
He had even brought his own map showing the Curzon Line
boundary between the Soviet Union and Poland, a map that Stalin
marked up to show the boundaries he wanted. FDR recognized
that the "piddling" issues could cause emotional and political
problems at home and abroad, but Great Power cooperation had
to precede settlements on the details of boundaries and political
reconstruction. He had acceded to Soviet insistence that the Baltic
states were an integral part of the Soviet Union, repeating in a
serious jest to Stalin the substance of what he had said earlier to
the Polish ambassador: "Do you expect us and Britain to declare
war on Joe Stalin if they cross your previous frontier? Even if we
wanted to, Russia can still field an army twice our combined
strength, and we would just have no say in the matter at all," a
sentiment Churchill repeated to Eden a few weeks later.

Roosevelt was not assuming that the Red Army would liberate
and occupy Eastern Europe all the way to Germany; that eventu-
ality was, in December 1943, only a possibility. The reality for FDR
was that the Soviet Union would be the major player in the politics
of that region. The choice seemed clear: Try to work with that
dominant power or adopt Churchill's approach of setting up clear,
and exclusive, spheres of influence. But when FDR suggested that
some sort of plebiscite in the Baltic states would be "helpful to

him personally" and then expressed confidence that the people would vote to be part of the Soviet Union, Stalin seemed less confident and rejected any "international" role in the Baltic region. The president's attempt to separate security from ownership was either too subtle or too unthinkable for the Soviet leader.[18]

FDR's concern for appearances unpinned his supposed concern for " 'the Polish vote'—six to seven million Polish-Americans," he told Stalin. But that number was "evidently plucked from the air." There were less than half that number of Polish-Americans, many of whom were not voters.[19] FDR's hyperbole was perhaps a bit more calculated and less casual than it appeared, for it allowed him to escape public responsibility for the political fact that he, Churchill, and Stalin's Red Army together ensured that in the short run Poland's independence would depend on Moscow's self-restraint, not on Anglo-American guarantees.

There were ways to push the Russians to exercise that self-restraint. The Anglo-Americans had long assumed that the Soviet Union would be dependent on postwar aid for economic reconstruction. In January 1942 Churchill had written of "the United States and the British Empire" being "the most powerfully armed and economic *bloc* the world has ever seen, and that the Soviet Union will need our aid," although by late 1943 Britain had begun to take its own place in line for such postwar assistance. FDR presumed that the Soviet Union's need for postwar economic aid would give the United States continued leverage, although perhaps thinking of the remarkable Soviet industrial performance, he seems not to have placed as much faith in that mechanism as some others. At Averell Harriman's prodding, Roosevelt authorized discussions with the Russians about postwar aid, but despite initial, if cautious, expressions of interest from Moscow (Molotov later claimed to have seen through the American scheme), the president failed to pursue the tactic.[20]

Roosevelt's view was not as Eurocentric as that of the other two leaders. Stalin and Churchill focused, by necessity and history, on their nations' security in Europe. The British Empire gave Churchill a broader set of concerns, but by 1943 those concerns were more defensive than global. For the president, geography and the global economic interests of the United States—signified by its worldwide logistics strategies during the war—suggested a more expansive perspective. As *New York Times* columnist Arthur Krock put it, "economic freedom for all" constituted the American foreign policy for war prevention. " 'Political freedom' can be read whenever 'economic freedom' is used in an American State paper."[21]

Like Churchill, FDR read history, and both men concluded that practicality had to precede principle. Where they differed was in their assessment of what was practical. Colonial empires were, for FDR, impractical and doomed. But long-term "trusteeships" that put a developed nation in charge of preparing a less developed society for independence could work. Churchill reversed the equation, asserting "that British imperialism has spread and is spreading democracy more widely than any other system of government since the beginning of time." Roosevelt believed that tight, controlled spheres of influence that operated to the exclusion of others caused only tension and quarrels. For Churchill, such arrangements were a sensible way to prevent competition from leading to violence. Balancing power so that no single nation could dominate fitted Britain's experience and capabilities. American leaders, becoming accustomed to thinking in global terms, thought comfortably in terms of worldwide American influence. The United States would seek out the world, not the other way around. Thomas Paine was being stood on his head.[22]

That seemingly "imperial" vision was not, in Roosevelt's thinking, a military conception. He consistently warned that American military forces could not remain in Europe more than a year or two after the war, a threat made possible by his almost mechanical application of a combination of disarmament and the four policemen, who would cooperate and enforce law and order. Writing Churchill shortly after Teheran, Roosevelt pleaded: " 'Do please don't' ask me to keep any American forces in France. I just cannot do it! I would have to bring them all back home." But it was not just getting stuck in France that FDR feared. He went on to "denounce and protest the paternity of Belgium, France, and Italy"—

and, by implication, the rest of Europe. "You really ought to bring up and discipline your own children."[23]

But withdrawal from Europe, by the United States or its two allies, required facing Germany as threat, the central issue for the Big Three. Germany had, in one way or another, caused two world wars and untold suffering. The Germans had been "Prussianized," thought Roosevelt, and Churchill proposed that Prussia be separated from the rest of Germany. No one pointed out that Hitler was not a Prussian—the American notes for the entire discussion never mention him or the Nazis—but Stalin rejected the notion of great differences among Germans. Roosevelt quickly agreed and proposed three to five permanently separated German states, though he quipped that "Germany had been less dangerous to civilization when in 107 provinces." The British Foreign Office had earlier warned that to contain "80,000,000 aggressive Germans . . . we need Russian collaboration,"[24] but Churchill had begun to worry about the terms of that collaboration. He concurred with dismemberment, but he expressed a hope for "larger units" and wondered if Stalin planned for all Europe to be made up of small, weak states. They then referred the details to the EAC, although the moving matchsticks and a Soviet claim to the northern half of East Prussia (today's Kaliningrad province of Russia) predetermined some degree of dismemberment.

FDR never mentioned his preference for retaining economic unity in Germany. The "partition of Germany into three or more states, completely sovereign, but joined by a network of common services" was what he suggested to State Department planners, dismissing concerns that a "customs union" would "become a powerful instrument of re-unification." He likely had in mind the historically exaggerated success of the nineteenth-century German customs unions, the Zollverein, but whatever his reasoning, FDR's distinction between economic unity and political dismemberment suggested the one he was beginning to draw between closed and "open" spheres of influence, distinctions that fitted neatly with American thinking about the postwar world. By the time of the Teheran Conference war aims were changing along with wartime strategies. The Americans, propelled by World War II into more global thinking, assumed their political economy was the best solution for the world, and Roosevelt's thoughts about German economic unity fitted that assumption. In the summer of 1944 it would become reality at the Bretton Woods Conference on global monetary and financial policies.[25]

Throughout the Teheran Conference Roosevelt avoided getting into specifics on political issues, fearing that premature attention to detail could raise threats, both at home and abroad, to the international relationship he hoped to foster. He treated Churchill as a charter member of the board of directors and spoke directly at Stalin during the first Big Three session. Welcoming the "new members to the family circle," FDR spoke with bland optimism of friendship, frankness, and his confidence that "our three great nations" would cooperate closely to win the war and "for generations to come."[26]

The next afternoon, during a tête-à-tête with Stalin, the president sketched out his concept of the four policemen. When the Soviet leader questioned having China play a role in European affairs, FDR warned that the United States could not participate in an exclusively European committee that might try to force the dispatch of American troops to Europe, a comment that suggests Eden was correct when he surmised that the president was using the American public's "feeling for China" to "lead his people to accept international responsibilities." When Stalin pressed him about an American response to a request from the other policemen, FDR resorted to his prewar notion of sending only planes and ships from the United States to keep the peace in Europe. Then he slipped back another couple of years to 1937, suggesting that the "quarantine method" might be best. If FDR's recollection is to be trusted, he also tried to explain to Stalin how the Good Neighbor policy worked in the Western Hemisphere, suggesting that the Soviet Union would have an easier time since the Slavic nations were "nearer in blood" than were the United States and Latin America.

Stalin got the message and the next day agreed that any international organization should be worldwide, not regional, although

FDR remained uncertain of Stalin's conversion. But trying to work out the details could derail the concept, and the four policemen then nearly disappeared from the American record of the conference, except for a passing reference to the idea in another FDR-Stalin talk and a cryptic sketch by the president of his thoughts about a postwar international organization in which one of three circles was labeled "4 Police," the other two circles being an executive committee and "40 U.N." members (a general assembly).[27]

"We leave here friends in fact, in spirit, and in purpose," said Roosevelt at the closing dinner. Churchill used more relative terms when he cabled Attlee that "relations between Britain, United States and USSR have never been so cordial and intimate. All war plans are agreed and concerted." Politics was conspicuous by its absence from the prime minister's report. But he too left Teheran with renewed hope for a closer working relationship with Stalin. He suggested regular meetings between them and sent Stalin a number of brief, chatty messages that culminated in Churchill's getting the music score for the newly composed official Soviet anthem. When he promised the anthem would be played on the BBC after Soviet victories, Stalin bantered that he hoped Churchill "would set about learning the new tune and whistling it to members of the Conservative Party."[28]

Roosevelt and Churchill held an unnecessary meeting in Cairo following the historic conference in Teheran. Neither man felt good. Churchill had still not shaken the cold and cough he had brought with him to Teheran, and he ended up in Tunis (near ancient Carthage, which intrigued him) seriously ill with pneumonia and heart fibrillations, followed by a two-and-one-half-week convalescence in his favorite city, Marrakech. "If I die, don't worry," he said with black optimism to his daughter Sarah, "the war is won." A week after Roosevelt returned to the United States, he suffered an attack of what he invariably called the flu, this time diagnosed by his doctors as life-threatening hypertension and congestive heart failure. The attack was probably brought on by the strain of the long round-trip flights across Africa to Teheran, since flying invariably caused problems for the wheelchair-bound president's sinuses and respiratory system. According to his doctors, FDR never fully recovered his "usual vigor."[29]

Rest would have done both men a great deal more good than the second round of Cairo talks. All Churchill got out of a meeting with Turkish President Ismet Inönü was a cheek-to-cheek embrace—hardly a commitment to enter the war—prompting Eden to comment caustically that it was not much to gain after fifteen hours of argument. That evening Churchill puckishly told his daughter Sarah, who had accompanied him on the trip, that "the Turkish President kissed me. The truth is I'm irresistible. But don't tell Anthony, he's jealous."[30] Roosevelt overruled his military advisers and accepted British arguments that amphibious operations in the Pacific plus the requirements (primarily landing craft) for invasions of both western and southern France precluded any attack on Burma—despite the commitment to Chiang. The Americans set a schedule at both Cairo conferences that prevented Anglo-American discussions about the main military points, particularly shipping for the Italian campaign, prompting General Brooke to vent his anger in his diary, accusing the Americans of "some of the worst sharp practice. . . ." He exonerated Marshall but had marked Roosevelt's evasive tactics. The only positive note at the second set of Cairo talks came when Roosevelt casually told Churchill during a car ride out to Luxor to see the Pyramids that Eisenhower would get command of Overlord.[31]

One of Winston Churchill's most endearing, admirable, and irritating traits was his stubborn refusal to accept defeat. Never, never give way "in things great or small, large or petty," he admonished, and he often followed his own advice. He managed to portray the cancellation of the "Far East adventure" and appointment of a British commander for the Mediterranean theater as a triumph for his overall strategy.[32] Even as he lay ill in Tunis and then at Marrakech, he continued to pin his hopes on the Italian campaign to redeem Britain's fortunes in the Mediterranean. It was not an impossibility.

Military events elsewhere provided a small window of opportunity. Early in 1944 the Red Army broke the siege of Leningrad, having already moved across the prewar Soviet-Polish boundary.

The mere threat of an Anglo-American invasion of western France, so close to the German homeland, had accomplished just what the Soviets had expected from the second front. With vast amounts of ground to give in the East, Hitler cut off reinforcements to the Russian front in order to prepare for the cross-Channel attack. Such an invasion posed an enormous problem for Hitler, as he acknowledged, for it could threaten the Rhine-Ruhr region in 1944, whereas a successful Soviet offensive in that year could, thought the Führer, only hope to push the Germans out of the western Soviet Union.[33] The Red Army did not begin its rapid roll westward until shortly after the launching of Overlord, but during the first six months of 1944 Soviet campaigns to clear the Crimea, the western Ukraine, and the area between Leningrad and Estonia wore down German strength. In the Crimea alone only 27,000 of 150,000 Wehrmacht troops managed to evacuate the peninsula.

In the war against Japan the Americans had taken the offensive, but as with the Russians, the rapid rollback of the enemy's defense line—in this case Japanese-occupied islands—did not accelerate until mid-1944. MacArthur's forces in the Southwest Pacific had by then neutralized Japanese forces on New Guinea, while a steady bombing campaign made the vast Japanese naval and air bases at Rabaul on New Britain unusable. A similar campaign against their naval facilities at Truk atoll began in February. By then, in a series of small but bloody battles, the American Navy and Marines occupied the Gilbert and Marshall Islands, including the large Kwajalein atoll, in the Central Pacific. The next step would be to bypass the Caroline Islands and invade the Marianas, which lay within bombing range of the Japanese homeland.

The war in the European theater focused on the amassing of troops and equipment for the Normandy assault. In February 1944 British and American strategic bombing forces renewed daylight bombing raids, suspended in the autumn of 1943 to await better weather and fighter escorts with longer range. The six-day Operation Big Week "aimed" twenty thousand tons of bombs at German aircraft production facilities. It was followed by a steady bombing campaign that not only severely damaged German industry but, given the inaccuracy of "precision" bombing, embraced the same strategy used by Hermann Göring in 1941 over Britain: indiscriminate bombing designed to force the defenders to respond. The German Air Force did so and suffered heavy air combat losses, which, combined with slowed production, virtually eliminated it as a factor in the war. When Overlord came, Luftwaffe sorties over the Normandy beaches consisted of a handful of obedient or romantic pilots flying doomed missions.[34]

Militarily the first six months of 1944 were essentially a prelude to the Normandy invasion and the successes that were to come in the Pacific and on the Russian front. It was an ideal time to move some other theater of operations to the center of both public and strategic attention, precisely what Churchill hoped for.

Let us keep, he asked Roosevelt on the day after Christmas 1943, fifty-six LSTs for just two weeks beyond their scheduled withdrawal from the Mediterranean. To do so would allow an amphibious invasion that would outflank the German defense line centered on Cassino, south of Rome. Perhaps Churchill's doggedness and his melancholy reference to the "painful" cancellation of operations in the Aegean persuaded the president. Perhaps the public relations benefits of American troops taking Rome convinced FDR. Whatever the reason, Roosevelt (and General Marshall) agreed, though they insisted on the "tyranny" of Bolero and Overlord: Nothing could be allowed to interfere with those operations.[35]

With the cross-Channel campaign looming, only speedy success could rescue Churchill's hopes. But Operation Shingle, the mid-January invasion at Anzio, southwest of Rome, proved a dismal failure. The Anglo-Americans landed successfully but did not break out from the beachhead until May. What had been designed as a "cat claw" had become a "stranded whale." The main Allied campaign in Italy continued at a crawl. Dreams of liberating Rome in January 1944 crumbled along with the walls of the sixth-century Benedictine monastery overlooking the town of Cassino—some one hundred miles south of the capital—where the Germans held on and stopped the Allied advance for four months, despite massive air and artillery bombardment.

Rome was not liberated until June 4, and then only because

American General Mark Clark, with unerring political instincts, won the race to be the first to enter the ancient capital. Churchill had encouraged the Allied military commander in Italy, British General Harold Alexander, to enter the city at the same time as the Americans, but Alexander's strategy called for cutting off the retreating German army, and he arrived in Rome a day late. With Rome's liberation coming two days before Overlord, the publicity benefits for the Americans proved fleeting. FDR celebrated the victory in a radio address on the evening of June 5, even as Allied forces were heading across the English Channel toward Normandy. But the episode illustrated that defeating the Germans in Italy was a secondary issue. "It is clear," wrote Harold Macmillan in his diary that day, "that Washington and London are not as close as they were. The honeymoon stage between the President and the Prime Minister is over, and the normal difficulties and divergencies, inseparable from staid married life, are beginning to develop."[36]

Almost from the outset the Italian campaign had been a drain, not a drive, particularly once the capture of Sicily opened the sea-lanes through the Mediterranean. Stalin's warning during the Teheran Conference proved accurate: The Germans would keep "as many allied Divisions as possible in Italy where no decision could be reached. . . ." In a military sense the Italian theater was, in the phrase of historian David Reynolds, "a slogan not a strategy."[37]

But Churchill had not given up on his scheme of using the Italian campaign to establish Britain's "place" in the wartime and thus the postwar lineup. Hoping to gain more troops and shipping for that theater, he and his military chiefs began to argue vigorously that the invasion of southern France, Operation Anvil, would divert only a few German divisions. Overlord should be strengthened even more, the British proposed, but any forces and shipping that could then be spared from the Normandy operation should go toward breaking the stalemate in Italy. Certainly Anvil should not be expanded, whatever Stalin had suggested at Teheran. Eisenhower, still in Italy as of early February 1944, had begun to think as SCAEF, the supreme commander Allied Expeditionary Force (a pretentious designation that prompted his aide, Navy Commander Harry Butcher, to wisecrack about the big job of designing appropriate stationery to carry so "exalted" a title). Ike commented to his diary that if Italy required more troops, then "ANVIL is doomed. I hate this," he wrote, even if "the Italian fighting will be some compensation for a strong ANVIL."[38] It was an argument that was to simmer, and by summer it had begun to boil as the prime minister advanced his notion of attacks through Istria (Yugoslavia) toward the so-called Ljubljana gap. It became the most bitter of the Churchill-Roosevelt disputes. But it was always a political argument, even if phrased in military terms.

Another indication of the primacy, and ambiguity, of politics was the Declaration on Iran signed by the Big Three at Teheran. In the decade preceding the Second World War, the shah (king) and government of Iran (which Churchill insisted on calling Persia: "Foreign names were made for Englishmen, not Englishmen for foreign names," he wrote[39]) had sidled up to the Germans in order to offset attempts by both Britain and the Soviet Union to gain political and economic privileges. That provided London and Moscow with a ready-made reason to occupy Iran in August 1941, and within a month they had forced the shah to abdicate in favor of his son. American military forces came in shortly afterward to build, operate, and protect the lend-lease supply line running through Iran from the Persian Gulf to the Caucasus and thence north into Russia.

Ostensibly the Big Three Declaration on Iran committed the Great Powers to that nation's "independence, sovereignty and territorial integrity" and even included a reaffirmation of the Atlantic Charter. The declaration also promised "such economic assistance as may be possible." A few months after the Teheran meeting FDR wrote Churchill that "Iran certainly needs Trustees." With Britain already on the scene, that call for more than one "trustee" was a not-so-subtle suggestion that Britain needed a new partner. Iranian fears that neither the Soviets nor the British would leave the country had basis in history, but an Iranian request in late 1942 for American assistance with finances (again to offset British and Russian influence) proved a bit of a Trojan horse. By 1944 the head of the American mission in Teheran, Dr. Arthur Millspaugh, had gained control over the Iranian economy and had become a force in national politics. Secretary of State Hull was quite candid: "[O]ne facet of [U.S.] diplomacy consisted in supporting the efforts of American companies to obtain petroleum concessions there." Roosevelt assured Churchill that the United States was "not making sheep's eyes at your oil fields in Iraq or Iran," but events suggested otherwise.

By 1944 Roosevelt had endorsed Hull's plan for Anglo-American talks about fair (i.e., American) access to Middle Eastern petroleum. Churchill worried that arguments over oil could jeopardize Anglo-American cooperation, but the British Cabinet recognized what the Americans were about and tried to delay the talks. The prime minister, reacting to FDR's mention of the need for political reform in Iran, denied any "irrepressible conflict between imperialism and democracy," but the struggle was not over political systems. The Anglo-American agreement that eventually emerged in August 1944 used the niceties of diplomatic language to create the appearance of disinterested liberal economic reform, but it was reform on American terms. Oil would be developed and made available to "all peaceable countries at fair prices and on a nondiscriminatory basis." But special "collective security arrangements" could supersede such "fairness," and legally valid concessions would be respected. To put it crudely (pun intended), so long as Britain allowed the United States to have its "fair" share of oil, the two nations could share the Middle East's petroleum resources. Democracy and fulfillment of the Atlantic Charter principles would have to come later.[40]

(In 1979, thirty-five years after the Declaration on Iran, the young shah the British had placed on the Peacock Throne was deposed, and the flow of oil to the Anglo-Americans finally stopped. Democracy and the Atlantic Charter never arrived.)

But for the British and the Americans in spring 1944, everything seemed to be in a state of suspended animation as they waited for D-Day. The Teheran talks had settled on the cross-Channel invasion as the ("tyrannical") priority for Anglo-American military action against Germany. But the political dynamic depended on the degree of success for Overlord and the campaign that would then follow.

During the discussions aboard the USS *Iowa* prior to the Cairo/ Teheran conferences, Roosevelt remarked that "there would definitely be a race for Berlin. We may have to put the United States divisions into Berlin as soon as possible." Hopkins added that they should be prepared to send in an airborne division on two hours' notice. This was no minideclaration of "cold war" and confrontation with the Soviet Union. Roosevelt had commented a few months earlier at the Quebec Conference that he only wanted to get to Berlin just as quickly as the Russians, while the American chiefs of staff called for collaboration with the Soviets in the event that such plans (Rankin) were implemented.[41] Yet at the same time the premise of Rankin was that to ensure an appropriate degree of Anglo-American influence on the postwar settlement in Europe, British and American forces had to be on the Continent and participate actively in the defeat of Hitler's Germany. To put it simply, a seat at the peace table was earned, not awarded. The D-Day invasion was the means to defeat Hitler, but it was also the prerequisite to being a player in European politics.

"The destinies of two great empires," complained Churchill, ". . . seem to be tied up in some god-damned things called LSTs."[42] The shortage of those and other landing vessels forced a month's delay of Overlord from May to June and an even lengthier postponement of the invasion of southern France. Finally, just after midnight on June 6, 1944, the Normandy invasion began with 23,000 airborne troops landing by parachute and glider at the east and west flanks of what became the landing beaches. A fleet of some seven thousand vessels of every imaginable type either bombarded the coast or, at dawn, began landing more than 130,000 British, Canadian, and American troops on the five beaches designated Utah, Omaha, Gold, Juno, and Sword (names still used fifty years later on French maps of the coast), an area stretching from the Orne River on the east, westward to the beginning of the Cotentin Peninsula, just across the mouth of the Merderet River— a total of roughly one hundred kilometers (sixty miles).

Allied strategy reversed the German attacks on France in both the world wars by sliding up through Belgium and the Ardennes. The plan called for Anglo-American armies to move northeast through Normandy and Picardy and to shift east to liberate Paris and north along the French and Belgian coasts toward the Netherlands to secure port facilities and, as it turned out, to capture the launching sites of Hitler's *Vergeltungswaffen* (retaliation weapons). Those V-1 flying-bombs and V-2 rockets began to hit British cities a week after the Normandy invasion, ostensibly in retaliation for British bombing of German cities.[43] From Belgium, Allied armies were to head into Germany on a straight line for Berlin, although always on a broad front (according to Eisenhower's plans) to ensure the security of their flanks. The delayed invasion of southern France, Operation Anvil (renamed Dragoon), would put Allied and French troops ashore on the Riviera, from which they could move up the Rhône River valley and meet in the Rhine Valley with armies advancing across France from Normandy.

The Normandy invasion was the largest amphibious attack in history, a logistical tour de force. Men and equipment were landed on the beaches, at adjacent small ports, and later using the Mulberries (floating harbors) constructed once the beachheads were secure. One of the two much-publicized Mulberries, which the British convinced themselves were indispensable to Overlord, was destroyed by the wind and seas raised in a moderate storm (later called the Great Storm despite its having winds no higher than thirty-six miles per hour). The tonnage of supplies landed on Omaha and Utah beaches proved about the same as that scheduled for the lost Mulberry. Much more damaging to Allied plans was the German destruction of the port of Cherbourg, at the end of the Cotentin Peninsula. Within three weeks the Allies managed to land more than 850,000 men, nearly 150,000 vehicles, and some 570,000 tons of supplies, but deliveries remained behind schedule, prompting Eisenhower to tell Marshall that Churchill's proposal for "wandering overland via Trieste to Ljubljana" (the soft-underbelly strategy) made no sense. General Henry Wilson, the British commander in the Mediterranean, "should be directed to undertake Operation ANVIL at the earliest possible date," Ike wrote to Marshall.[44]

Battles on the Russian front dwarfed Overlord in sheer size and numbers, but the immense difficulties and unpredictability of a seaborne invasion made comparisons meaningless. Stalin's military adviser at the Teheran talks, the very political Marshal Voroshilov, seemed abysmally uninformed on the technical difficulties of amphibious warfare, although he may have feigned that ignorance so not to give the Allies any excuse to delay the landing. When he drew parallels between crossing the English Channel and the Red Army's advance across "several large rivers, the most recent of which was the Dnieper," General Marshall, with obvious irritation, retorted that "the failure of a river crossing is a reverse while the failure of a landing operation from the sea is a catastrophe." But whatever the old Bolshevik's lack of knowledge about tactics, his main concern was that the Allies had the "will to do it."

D-Day demonstrated that will. With the second front a reality, Stalin seemed more understanding of the dangers inherent in Overlord. "This is an enterprise unprecedented in military history as to scale, breadth of conception and masterly execution," he cabled Churchill. "As is known, Napoleon's plan for crossing the Channel failed disgracefully. Hitler the hysteric, who for two years boasted he would cross the Channel, did not venture even to make an attempt to carry out his threat." If imitation is the sincerest form of flattery, then Stalin paid the Anglo-Americans a compliment by forming some forty naval infantry brigades (amphibious assault forces) by 1945.[45]

Part of the Allied success came from a deception plan, Operation Bodyguard, much of which was made possible by British signals intelligence and the "turning" of German spies. Through a series of ruses and misinformation that ranged from the creation of a fictitious army group headed by General George Patton, to the "loss" of plans for an invasion at the Pas de Calais, to hints of an attack on Norway, the Germans were fooled into dispersing their forces and holding back reinforcements while they waited for the "main" invasion. Churchill had alluded to the deception operations at Teheran when he remarked that "truth deserves a bodyguard of lies."[46] Stalin not only agreed but offered Soviet assistance to the deception operation.

In the understated phrasing of historian Michael Howard, the Allied officers who went to the Soviet Union in January–February

1944 to negotiate cooperation on Bodyguard experienced "all the frustrations common to everyone who tried to negotiate with the Russians on any subject below the very highest level of command." A direct appeal to Stalin and Molotov broke the logjam, and constructive discussions followed. Inexplicably communications ceased for two weeks. Then, with equal suddenness and without explanation, the Soviets accepted all the Anglo-American proposals and, more important, in June did just what they promised to do: They conducted "menacing operations" in the Arctic and the Black Sea, applied political pressure on Bulgaria and Romania, and sent false information to the Germans through Soviet intelligence agents.[47] Whatever the peculiarities of making the arrangements, they were a striking example of effective cooperation between the Allies and the Soviet Union.

Six days after the invasion Churchill sailed to Normandy from Portsmouth, toured the beaches, and lunched with General Montgomery at his field headquarters some five miles inland. As the prime minister left the beaches aboard the British destroyer *Kelvin*, he persuaded the naval commander in the area to allow the ship to fire a salvo in the direction of the shore. The guns fired, and the vessel quickly fled seaward for safety lest the Germans retaliate unknowingly against the very symbol of resistance to them. A few days later the prime minister cabled Roosevelt with childish exuberance about having "had a jolly day on the beaches and inland."[48]

But the troops who landed had few "jolly" days. Logistics, air supremacy, sabotage, and deception could not win the field. That had to be done by soldiers on the ground and proved to be no easy task. The Allies quickly secured and consolidated their beachhead, though speed did not equate to ease. Had the Germans brought in heavy reinforcements to Omaha Beach, for example, they could have forced at least a partial, if temporary, withdrawal, for they had the high ground and controlled the flanks. Units lost their mobility as they exited the various beaches into the rugged hedgerows and ditches of Normandy's bocage country, which the German defenders used to great advantage. Six weeks after the invasion Allied forces had pushed forward only some twenty miles.

They had taken the entire Cotentin Peninsula, although the port of Cherbourg was not usable until mid-August. German counterattacks failed, but they did not withdraw until mid-August, just as Dragoon (Anvil) took place in time to prevent the Germans from sending reinforcements to northwestern France.

Symbolic victory came on the evening of August 24, when units of a Free French armored division arrived at the Place de l'Hôtel de Ville in Paris and formally liberated the city after the German commander, General Dietrich von Choltitz, had chosen to disobey Hitler's orders to defend it stone by stone. The landings in southern France centered on the posh resort of St-Tropez east of Marseilles and quickly turned to pursuit as Hitler withdrew his forces, although the Germans managed to evade most of the entrapments set by the Allies. By early September Allied and French forces moving north had joined with Patton's Third Army just south of the Vosges Mountains and Alsace. More important, the capture of Marseilles gave Eisenhower what he wanted and, as it turned out, what he needed, a port capable of handling vast amounts of supplies, supplies that could not be sent to his armies through northwestern Europe until the ports on the Scheldt estuary were finally taken, with assistance from Dutch patriots, in November 1944.[49]

Huge, bloody battles were to follow on the western front before Germany was defeated. Liberating the Netherlands proved brutal and bitter, as the Germans starved the Dutch and destroyed the countryside in order to delay the Allied advance. Attempts by Eisenhower to hasten the outcome met with failure. A joint airborne-land attack (Market-Garden) in September through central Holland toward Arnhem fell apart because of poor military coordination and faulty use of intelligence. In December 1944 a German counteroffensive through the Ardennes Forest in Belgium, aided by storm and snow that prevented Allied planes from flying, seemed for the moment to threaten the port of Antwerp, indispensable to Eisenhower's supply lines. But even there a German breakthrough would have only delayed the inevitable. Mobility allowed forces led by Generals Patton and Courtney Hodges to reinforce and relieve the embattled American troops, winning what came to be called the Battle of the Bulge by doubling the number of Allied soldiers in the area within just four days. Then, once the weather cleared, Allied aircraft shattered German supply lines.

But whatever the intensity of specific battles, once the Allies broke out from their beachheads at Normandy, the issue was never in doubt. *When* would victory come, not would it come, was the only question.

Overlord did not "win" the war or determine Hitler's fate, though it contributed mightily. Those things were accomplished by Britain's survival in 1940 and 1941, by the killing ground in Russia that stopped the Wehrmacht and then bled it dry, by the economic and production strength of the United States, by the accumulated weight of all the military offensives against what Hitler called *Festung Europa* (Fortress Europe), and by the Nazi leader's own inhumanity, which made compromise and negotiation unthinkable.

What the cross-Channel invasion did ensure was an Anglo-American presence on the Continent at war's end, a presence that would provide stability, order, and the opportunity to exercise Stalin's axiom and determine the course of political (and hence economic and social) reconstruction in Western Europe. At the same time the invasion of Western Europe also preserved the Grand Alliance, at least for the rest of the war. The implication that Overlord aimed at getting into Western and Central Europe before the Russians writes Cold War thinking into World War II, since the decision to invade at Normandy came well before the Red Army began to roll inexorably across Central Europe. But fear of the Soviet Union was there. Roosevelt and Churchill hedged their bets by drawing up the Rankin plans and by keeping the atomic bomb secret from everyone else. Yet even while the president admitted that "he didn't know what to do about Russia,"[50] he pursued goals that went against a get-tough approach toward the Soviet Union.

Any Anglo-American reconstruction of Europe and the world required much more than just a military occupation. The very destructiveness of war seems to present a tantalizing opening for grand reform of the entire international system. Woodrow Wilson had tried to seize the moment in 1919 but found the opportunities deceptive. In July 1944 the British and the Americans were ready to try again and, with Roosevelt's support and Churchill's disinterest, convened the United Nations Monetary and Financial Conference in Bretton Woods, New Hampshire.[51]

The talks aimed at avoiding the chaos of currency collapse and devaluation that had come with the Great Depression. The American plan was to set up a cooperative international monetary system, thus escaping national currency controls and bilateral exchange agreements that restricted currency exchanges and hampered the liberalizing of trade. A United Nations Bank for Reconstruction and Development would operate a "stabilization" fund that would dampen extreme swings in currency values. British economist John Maynard Keynes had earlier presented an innovative scheme that avoided the gold standard and emphasized lower tariffs and postwar loans, but the Americans, particularly Harry Dexter White of the Treasury Department, insisted on the more conservative approach. By using gold and the U.S. dollar as the medium for settlement of international debts, the Bretton Woods system recognized the existing economic and financial dominance of the United States, strength that made the U.S. dollar the international currency for the next twenty-five years.[52]

Roosevelt's opening remarks at the conference (read by Treasury Secretary Henry Morgenthau, Jr.) revealingly connected two basic American values—trade and liberty—just as he had back in 1941, when he included freedom from want as one of his Four Freedoms. "Commerce is the lifeblood of a free society," he told the delegates. "We must see to it that the arteries are not clogged again." The British might have wished for a delay regarding preferential trade within their empire, but they firmly supported the Bretton Woods system. Great Britain was, after all, the only other "liberal" nation left with any economic power.[53]

But not just economic liberals signed the agreement. The Soviet delegates rarely participated and seemed uninterested in, even bewildered by, the debates over technical monetary issues. Possibly they saw the Bretton Woods system as a way to borrow money and assets in order to build and rebuild after the war; possibly Stalin viewed it as a way to promote Great Power postwar cooperation. Certainly they demanded equal treatment when it came to issues that had the appearance of designating status in the postwar world. Soviet involvement in the agreements had to have at least the same dollar values as the amounts assigned to the British. Image, not substance, was the Soviet concern. When they decided to participate in the system, Assistant Secretary of State Dean Acheson sensed the importance of such signals from the Kremlin, calling Soviet agreement a "diplomatic victory" and of "great political significance." The British thought the Americans had grossly over-exaggerated the ability of the Soviet economy to play a role in international monetary stabilization, but that was beside the point. Soviet cooperativeness held out hope that Roosevelt's plans for the postwar world might work.

It was no accident that the apogee of Soviet-Western cooperation came in July 1944. The second front had finally become a reality. The Soviets launched a major offensive in support of Overlord and had promised to join the war against Japan. Now, at Bretton Woods, Stalin indicated a willingness to work with the Anglo-Americans on the economic reconstruction needed in the postwar world.[54] Practicality, not ideology, seemed to prevail. It was the most promising postwar scenario that ever appeared during the war.

The Soviets continued to exhibit interest in postwar cooperation when, from late August through early October 1944, they participated in the Anglo-American-Soviet conference convened to draft a charter for the postwar international organization. Although FDR had little faith that such an organization could be effective, his appearance at the conference demonstrated his conviction that such a structure would be useful to the Great Powers—his policemen. More important, Soviet and British commitment to an international organization would incline them toward cooperation and "open" areas of responsibility rather than toward regional autonomy and "closed" spheres of influence.

The conference had the task of putting flesh on the skeleton of an international organization promised in the Atlantic Charter and periodically thereafter. The venue—the lovely Dumbarton Oaks mansion in the Georgetown section of Washington, comfortable even in the heat of August and September—marked both America's commitment and its leverage. The president's scheme, as imperfectly understood by his representatives as it was imperfectly articulated by him, called for continuing the United Nations alliance against the Axis, declared back in January 1942, as the United Nations Organization (UNO). But the members had to accept the leadership of the Great Powers. FDR had marshaled domestic support for American participation in an international organization; now the trick was to get the rest of the world to go along. International disarmament of all but the policemen would lessen tensions, while the UNO would provide a forum for "smaller" nations to blow off steam, as FDR put it.[55]

As at Bretton Woods, the Big Three left the details to subordinates, although the conferees soon ran into disputes that only their leaders could decide. The veto (could it be used to prevent even discussion of an issue in which one of the Great Powers was involved?); the "X" issue (membership for additional Soviet republics, the British Commonwealth nations were already members of the Grand Alliance); and regionalism (should there be regional councils?) all were matters of national policy, particularly for FDR, who continually fretted about a resurgence of American "isolationism." Had the Big Three attended, those issues could have been resolved right then and there without letting them fester and create tensions. Instead solutions had to await the meeting at Yalta, although the broad commitment of the Big Three to cooperation allowed those solutions to come easily once they met.[56]

Even as the delegates from the Big Three meeting at Dumbarton Oaks were coming to fundamental agreement on the UNO, whatever their differences over technical issues, two of the Big Three got together at the Citadel in the charming city of Quebec. (Of course international meetings are rarely held in any place less than lovely or exotic—at least until the Bosnian peace conferences in Dayton, Ohio, in 1995). The Octagon Conference was the second meeting for Churchill and Roosevelt in that farthest west of all European cities, whatever its physical location in Canada.

The Quebec Conference of September 11–16, 1944, was as important for what was not discussed as for what was, and much of what was not said was determined by who was not at the meetings.

Canadian Prime Minister Mackenzie King, the ostensible host, was not there, having been firmly relegated to appearances at social occasions. America's nominal partner in postwar East Asia, China's Chiang Kai-shek, was nowhere to be seen—in person, proxy, or potentiality—nor were the leaders of any of the dozens of other United Nations, FDR's label for all those allied against the Axis powers. (Churchill and Roosevelt had worried that holding the first Quebec Conference in Canada would give the British Commonwealth and nations like Brazil and Chile a reason to demand seats; at least that was the excuse for excluding Mackenzie King from the formal talks at the first and, presumably, the second Quebec Conference.)[57]

Most conspicuous by his absence was the Soviet leader Joseph Stalin. That was not because Churchill and Roosevelt failed to try to arrange another Big Three meeting. Meeting aboard battleships off Invergordon, Scotland, was FDR's favorite proposal until Stalin demurred. At that point Harry Hopkins, once the president's closest adviser and still someone who could touch chords in Roosevelt's thinking, warned that the Russians and (he inferred) the American public might interpret a Churchill-Roosevelt meeting in England or Europe "as a political meeting with Russia out in the cold."[58]

There were of course a number of important issues that needed decisions in autumn 1944. Many were military questions that required military answers, but those questions and answers also had political implications that were accentuated by the approach of war's end. Octagon took place amid a general atmosphere of military optimism. The stated objective—the earliest possible unconditional surrender of Germany and Japan, to be accomplished "in conjunction with Russia and other Allies"—seemed within reach. Anglo-American operations following Overlord were going well, while the strategic bombing campaign continued to rain destruction on German cities, accompanied by an equally heavy downpour of claims that it alone could drive the Germans to their knees.[59]

On the Russian front the Red Army, facing a German force twice the size of that in the West, had swept into Poland, reaching the outskirts of Warsaw. Finland, Bulgaria, and Romania—enemies of the Russians more than they were Germany's allies—had surrendered, and the Soviets stood poised to move into Slovakia (which the Germans had established as an "independent" state). The war in Europe will end by Christmas, trumpeted the rumor mill, with support from intelligence estimates.[60]

The Pacific war generated similar, if more restrained, optimism. No one questioned that the fight against Japan could prove long and costly (the first atomic device was not exploded for another seven months). But the success of the U.S. Navy's island-hopping campaign, the invasion of the Philippines planned for October, and the repeated promise from Stalin that his forces would attack Japan after the German surrender added to the sense of impending victory.

Yet the major military questions could not be answered in straightforward terms of battlefield tactics and broad campaign strategies. Politics, which generated a less optimistic atmosphere, had begun to move as quickly as the military lines. Both the British and the ever-impatient General Patton predicted quick victory if they could launch a sharply focused single thrust into Germany. Eisenhower, concerned about supply problems and sensitive to Roosevelt's political agenda, insisted on his broad-front approach.[61] Buried, not too deeply, was the political issue of getting into Germany and Berlin before, or at least as quickly as, the Russians.

The August 1944 invasion of southern France, which Churchill angrily opposed, had precluded any significant enlargement of the Allied effort in Italy. Nevertheless, he continued to push for expanded operations in that theater, well aware that Italy was the last place that offered an opportunity for a British-led victory. The prime minister held on to the option of an amphibious attack on Istria (the peninsula at the head of the Adriatic, just south of Trieste), a proposal that U.S. Navy chief Admiral King supported—to everyone's surprise (King, crankily anti-British, perhaps hoped to keep them too busy to get involved in "his" navy's war in the Pacific). Wrapped up in Churchill's broad concern was his oft-stated desire that European (i.e., British) troops liberate the empire lest people in Singapore, India, and Burma conclude that after all, Japanese propaganda was correct: Asians could stand on their own two feet. Roosevelt quickly accepted Churchill's offer to put the British fleet at the disposal of the Americans once Hitler surrendered (prompting the droll comment that "at this point Admiral King was carried out"), but in private the president sardonically dismissed the British offer with the comment "All they want is Singapore back." Privately, Churchill confirmed FDR's suspicion, telling his chiefs of staff that a "major attack" on Singapore "is the Supreme British objective in the whole of the Indian and Far Eastern theatres. It is the only prize that will restore British prestige in this region. . . ."[62]

In proposing a move into Istria, Churchill again put postwar politics ahead of military victory. It would, he argued, put the Allies in position to move toward Vienna and counter "the dangerous spread of Russian influence in this area"—the prime Minister's famous and quixotic Ljubljana gap strategy, deprecated even by his own military chiefs.[63]

Actually, Churchill's proposals for military action in Southeast Europe aimed more at propping up British interests in Greece than at beating the Red Army to the prize. The night before the prime minister made his unappetizing allusion to an attack on the German "armpit" (toward Vienna from the Adriatic), he learned that the Russians had advanced more quickly into Bulgaria than expected. His reaction and that of his foreign secretary were concern not for Bulgaria but for British interests, with Eden proposing the immediate launching of Operation Manna, a landing in Greece. What mattered was not liberation but who did the liberating— Stalin's axiom. What Churchill feared was that the Russians would take the prize—Greece, along with Hungary, Yugoslavia, and even Vienna—before the German Siegfried Line in the West was broken. "However desirable militarily such a Russian incursion may be, its political effect upon Central and Southern Europe may be formidable in the last degree."[64]

All these issues had to be considered in an atmosphere of Anglo-American frustration over their inability to provide even a cosmetically satisfying package of aid to the Warsaw uprising that had begun on August 1. Stalin accurately characterized the motives of the Polish underground as an attempt "to seize power" rather than to aid in the war against Germany, although the Poles were hardly the "criminals" he called them. The underground, fearful of Soviet domination, hoped to liberate the city from the Germans before the Red Army arrived. When Hitler chose to retaliate in force, underground leaders condemned that same Red Army they feared for failing to come to Warsaw's rescue. (The leading American historian of the Red Army in World War II, retired U.S. Army Colonel David Glantz, concludes that "German resistance in the region was probably sufficient to halt any Soviet attack, at least until mid-September." Even then a Red Army offensive against Warsaw would have required a "major reorientation," would have been "costly, and victory would have gained the Soviets no strategic advantage.[65]) To Churchill's dismay, Roosevelt refused to participate in sending aircraft from the West to parachute supplies to the underground and thence to fly to nearby Soviet airfields because Stalin threatened to refuse to let such aircraft land. FDR viewed the plan as quixotic and feared such supply drops would accomplish nothing beyond pacifying domestic opinion, nor did he want to jeopardize ongoing negotiations for U.S. bombers to use Siberian air bases in connection with the bombing of Japan. As for Stalin, he told his subordinates that the growing number of landings in Soviet-occupied territory by Anglo-American aircraft indicated "unnecessary trustfulness and loss of vigilance which allowed hostile elements to use these landings to infiltrate Polish terrorists, saboteurs and agents of the Polish government in London."[66]

Only two major political issues surfaced and also produced decisions at Octagon: the postwar reconstruction of both Britain and Germany, issues that seem to have been joined at the hip. The controversial Morgenthau Plan of September 1944, with its call for returning Germany to its agricultural origins, came when Treasury Secretary Morgenthau learned of War Department plans for "the gradual rehabilitation of peacetime industry" and the quick restoration "of the German civil government . . . [so that] the machine works and works efficiently." The War Department held no brief for gentle treatment of the Germans, but it did hope to promote law, order, and efficiency, so as to avoid long-term political and economic responsibilities.

But both Morgenthau and Roosevelt believed that the German people, not just Nazis, had been "Prussianized" into a militaristic, warlike society. The president's angry response to Morgenthau's description of War Department proposals was to insist on being "tough with Germany and I mean the German people, not just the Nazis," metaphorically calling for castrating the Germans if they didn't stop breeding militarists.[67] Make Germany like Denmark, argued Morgenthau, "where the people, through small-scale farming, were in intimate association with the land and were peace-loving and without aggressive designs upon others." As with most New Dealers, both men accepted grand planning as the way to solve problems, and like the two Jeffersonian gentlemen farmers they pretended to be, they proposed cleansing the German character by starting them out again as farmers. Punishment for Nazis reflected the reaction of the president as well as Morgenthau and the Treasury Department to their growing awareness of the horrors of the Holocaust, but reform reflected the long-range humanism of the New Deal in particular and Americans in general.[68]

Secretary of State Hull and Foreign Secretary Eden shared a very different view. Each believed an economically sound and self-supporting Germany essential to the rehabilitation of Europe. Moreover, American and British prosperity depended heavily upon that recovery. And for Hull there was economic liberalism: "German economic self-sufficiency for war must be replaced by an economy which can be integrated into an *inter-dependent world economy*. . . ." Moreover, State Department officials had warned that the Soviet Union would become a threat to world peace, thus the need to reintegrate Germany into "the projected world order," lest Moscow "establish a Russian hegemony" in that country. Such recommendations led the United States in the direction of just what Stalin suspected, a new version of a cordon sanitaire directed against the Soviet Union.[69] Roosevelt, firmly committed to his policy of turning uncivilized Bolsheviks into civilized Russians, never seriously considered that approach, relying instead on using the war to create a relationship of trust and cooperation.

On September 15, 1944, Roosevelt and Churchill initialed a memorandum that called for the elimination of "the war-making industries in the Ruhr and in the Saar" and the conversion of "Germany into a country primarily agricultural and pastoral in its character."[70] Churchill was ambivalent. He did not yet share General Brooke's belief that Germany should be "gradually converted to an ally to meet the Russian threat of twenty-five years hence," though he was inclined to accept Brooke's characterization of Russia as "not entirely European."[71] When FDR mentioned the existence of groups in the United States and probably Britain who thought "evil could be eradicated from the German makeup and the nation could be rejuvenated by a kindly approach to them," Churchill assured him that no such sentiments would be tolerated in the U.K. But when Morgenthau laid out the specifics of his plan, the prime minister condemned it as "unnatural, unchristian and unnecessary," commenting that the scheme would chain them to a dead body. Only after Churchill's adviser Lord Cherwell conjured up visions of new markets for British production, and Morgenthau pointedly discussed postwar aid to Britain (so-called stage II lend-lease), did the prime minister change his mind. After all, a happy Roosevelt was more important than an unhappy Germany, and Britain desperately needed an extension of lend-lease into the postwar period. Moreover, an Anglo-American entente was fundamental to Churchill's long-term policies. Ever subject to extreme enthusiasms, he switched from contemptuous opposition to strong support, so much so that it was he who suggested the word "pastoral" to replace weaker language.

Despite opposition from his Cabinet, particularly from Eden, Churchill explained and supported the Morgenthau Plan when he met with Stalin in Moscow a month later. The Soviet leader concurred and, once again, endorsed the German dismemberment. The two agreed that Britain should get the markets previously dominated by Germany and that the defeated nation should not have a merchant fleet. Stalin's statements during these talks, as well as his comments to Charles de Gaulle in December 1944, again demonstrated his preference for a permanently partitioned Germany.[72]

Whatever Roosevelt's own doubts about the feasibility of making Germany an agricultural nation, the rest of Morgenthau's proposal seemed sound, particularly since FDR viewed the plan as a statement of general purpose rather than a precise policy directive. It fit in with previous Soviet statements, offered economic benefits to Britain, and promised the kind of broad reform of Germans and Germany that he believed necessary. It even offered a way out of having the American occupation zone in southern Germany—just east of the Rhine and Alsace—something FDR had opposed lest it turn into a lengthy entanglement in French domestic problems. Since deindustrialization would eliminate German war-making potential, American occupation troops could return home more quickly. Moreover, giving Britain the northwestern zone would leave it in charge of the difficult dismantling program in the most industrialized part of Germany.

German war crimes, particularly the systematic extermination of Europe's Jews, received little formal attention at the Quebec talks, even though compelling evidence of those horrors had mounted. But the Morgenthau Plan demonstrated that the steady stream of rumors and evidence concerning German atrocities had made an impression. The curt language of the proposal for "Punishment of Certain War Crimes" was the more effective for its cold lack of emotion: "Any person who is [convicted] of being responsible for (through the issuance of orders or otherwise), or having participated in, causing the death of any human being . . . because of his nationality, race, color, creed, or political conviction . . . shall be sentenced to death. . . . Upon conviction, the sentence shall be carried out immediately." Churchill and his government disliked the idea of lengthy war crimes trials that had no justification in international law but proposed immediate execution of major Nazi leaders. FDR agreed, but the matter was postponed until the Yalta Conference.[73] If the concentration and death camps were mentioned, they did not make the printed record of the talks.

But Churchill and Roosevelt knew what was happening. Early in July 1944, when Chaim Weizmann (head of the Jewish Agency for Palestine) asked for the bombing of rail lines leading into Auschwitz, where the Germans were gassing some twelve thousand

Jews a day, Churchill told Eden to "get anything out of the Air
Force you can." Those bombings never happened largely because
the Americans, who would have to do it, could never develop a
plan they thought would work (rail lines could quickly be restored,
something the Germans did routinely during the war). Perhaps
more important was the unwillingness to believe that the stories,
whatever the evidence, could be true in all their grisly detail. The
British and Americans would not comprehend the facts at an emotional level until the camps were liberated and the Allies came face-
to-face with the emaciated, near-dead inmates of a Dantean horror.

   That recognition process began a few weeks after Morgenthau
presented his plan in early September, when Allied armies came
upon the Breendonck prison in Belgium. Although the facility was
not one of the death camps where the Germans had begun their
gruesome murders of Polish Jews in March 1942 (Operation Rein-
hard), Breendonck contained shocking evidence of torture using
equipment reminiscent of medieval "interrogation" instruments.
That discovery added to the impact of Soviet revelations about
extermination camps found in eastern Poland.[74] Even so, Roosevelt's and Churchill's discussions about war crimes seem, at least
in the printed record, to have been firm but emotionally unen-
gaged. Europe's Jews received attention primarily as a political
problem for relations with the Arabs, particularly in the last year
of the war, when Churchill and Roosevelt had to face the compulsive desire of Jews to migrate from Europe to the psychological
safe haven of Palestine and a Jewish state.[75]

   The pastoralization of Germany eventually became a throwaway
line in history books, not a reality. But the rest of the Morgenthau
Plan—disarmament, denazification, dismemberment, and demili-
tarization—set Anglo-American policy toward Germany until the
hidden agenda that became the Cold War displaced compromise,
negotiations, and diplomacy. That change, which began shortly
after the Yalta Conference, found Nazi politicians, scientists, and
spies working for Washington, London, and Moscow; while the
German military—East and West—rebuilt and rearmed in the service of its respective superpower. There remained only limited dismemberment, accomplished by redrawing Germany's boundaries

to make major territorial commitments to the Soviet Union, Czechoslovakia, and Poland in the east and to France in the west and by the detachment of Austria from the Reich. Although the boundary details had been sketched out at Teheran, that limited dismemberment remains—fifty years after the war—one of two major Octagon legacies.

The other Octagon legacy came in surroundings strikingly different from the grandeur and history of Quebec City. After the formal conference adjourned, Churchill and Roosevelt rejoined on September 18 for two days in Hyde Park. In that comfortable, casual surrounding the two again agreed to perpetuate the Anglo-American monopoly over the Tube Alloys project, the atomic bomb. (Churchill had never told FDR of a British agreement, made with the French just after their surrender in 1940, to share atomic research, an agreement that was not kept.) But if trust and cooperation were the keys to Roosevelt's goals, why keep the atomic bomb secret from the USSR?[76] He knew the Russians knew about the bomb but did not tell them. Why not? (Perhaps comedians Abbott and Costello asked an equally important question: Did he know that they knew that he knew that they knew?)

Possibly Roosevelt wished to maintain the image of secrecy lest Stalin demand access. Perhaps the president was reluctant to brag about something that had not yet been tested and about which unsophisticated advisers remained skeptical. After all, in a world where the United States was jockeying with the USSR for position, false bravado could weaken his bargaining strength.

Another part of the answer may be that Roosevelt, like most nonscientists, did not comprehend the revolutionary potential of nuclear weapons. His key scientific adviser on atomic energy, James B. Conant, believed that FDR had "only fleeting interest in the atom, and that the program never got very far past the threshold of his consciousness." He "really had no idea of the enormous importance of our [atomic] secrets." A number of American military experts tended to see the bomb as nothing more than just a bigger bang. Roosevelt's old friend and chief of staff Admiral William Leahy later scoffed to Truman that "the bomb will never go off, and I speak as an expert in explosives." It appears that Stalin was similarly ignorant. He took a personal interest in Soviet atomic bomb research, but at the same time his scientists assured him that development of such a weapon would take ten to twenty years.[77]

Yet if the Americans were skeptical of the bomb's utility, why not share the secret with the Soviets and promote a sense of trust? Even if Stalin's appreciation of the bomb's potential was just as benighted as Roosevelt's may have been, Anglo-American refusal even to mention the project could only reinforce Soviet suspicions of Western designs since it fitted into a larger pattern of Anglo-American reluctance to share information, particularly regarding intelligence, technology, and specific military plans (just as excessively broad Soviet shopping lists requesting technical information raised suspicions among the British and Americans).[78]

Continued secrecy may have been just an opportunity lost, but if Stalin somehow grasped the real nature of the bomb, then Roosevelt's dream of a "family circle" was doomed from the start. That was the basis of an appeal to Roosevelt by Niels Bohr, the Danish physicist and atomic scientist, who pleaded with the president to disclose the atomic secret to the world lest it poison postwar relationships. But Bohr's proposal fell afoul of now discredited suspicions that he had leaked information to the Soviet Union.[79]

The easy answer is that the president was waiting for the right moment, when he could confront the Soviet Union with the new superweapon and gain effective political leverage. Was Roosevelt the first practitioner of atomic diplomacy? Do we have FDR, Cold Warrior? But how to reconcile that with his consistent and persistent policy of trusting the Soviets in the hope of convincing them that the United States could likewise be relied upon? The likely answer is that the atomic bomb might work, and might not, but Franklin Roosevelt was firmly rooted in the practical present. He knew that Stalin had intelligence on the atom bomb project, so there was no secret. To tell the Soviets and then refuse to share the information would not quiet any of Stalin's suspicions and could lead to an open argument. Why make a decision until the decision had to be made? And there were so many other decisions to be made about the postwar world.[80]

As for using the atomic weapon, that decision had to await the first successful test of a bomb, the Trinity explosion at Alamo-gordo, New Mexico, on July 16, 1945. From the beginning of the Manhattan/Tube Alloys Project, British and American leaders assumed that the weapon was legitimate and would be used. Within that framework Germany was the initial target. But by the time of the Quebec Conference in September 1944 Germany was expected to surrender before the bomb would be ready, so the target shifted. Churchill and Roosevelt agreed to use the bomb on Japan, but only after "mature consideration," a phrase that suggests they had some perception that it was not just a "bigger bang." Certainly both demonstrated the ability to think beyond the simplistic notion that weapons had no ethical or moral questions attached. Churchill understood well what the so-called strategic bombing of Germany meant for civilians. Roosevelt would, a few months later, veto the use of poison gas at the bloody battle for Iwo Jima, but not for the usual reason: that the vagaries of winds made gas as dangerous to the user as to the target. The American military argued that it would be very effective in the caves and tunnels and save thousands of American lives. FDR rejected its use because of the kind of weapon it was.[81] But the ethical-moral issues attached to using the atomic bomb never received "mature consideration" during the final months of Roosevelt's presidency. There was no reason to do so until the weapon was tested, and FDR never crossed bridges until he came to them. There is some evidence that he mused about dropping a demonstration bomb to convince the enemy to surrender, but at no time before Roosevelt's death did top-level American leaders seek to avoid the use of the A-bomb.[82]

Discussions at Quebec about fundamental issues of international politics were brief and inconclusive, but those questions hung cloudlike over the talks, driving home the reality of the sea change taking place. The USSR was now a Great Power, while the Anglo-American relationship, special as it was, did not allow creation of an entente aimed at containing (cordon sanitaire-ing) the Soviets. The wartime alliance and Roosevelt's policy of cooperation took precedence. Moreover, regardless of whether Churchill and Roosevelt were (pick, as with a Chinese menu, any one or combination of the following) wise, naive, realists, idealists, sick, opportunists, or realpolitikers, it is hard to escape the conclusion that in 1944 any such Anglo-American entente would have achieved little or nothing. There was, after all, a stalemate in Italy, and Operation Market-Garden (the Arnhem attack) was about to fail in the Netherlands, thus ensuring that dreams of a German surrender by Christmas were not to be. The war in the Pacific found the British already scrambling to find enough troops to attack Singapore and the Americans counting on Soviet intervention in Manchuria. To what advantage an earlier declaration of "cold war"? Perhaps the main result would have been the absorption of even more of Germany by the Red Army, the "liberation" of Denmark by the Soviets (a possibility the British actually prepared for), and a swing by the Russians toward the Low Countries. Would a swap of Antwerp for Prague, or Amsterdam for Vienna, have improved Anglo-American security or the chances for world peace?[83]

As a summit meeting the Quebec Conference was in fact unnecessary and perhaps counterproductive. Stalin was not the only absentee. The worlds of geopolitics and of ideals and ideas (revolutionary or not) required more than just Anglo-American discussions, as the UNO talks then going on at Dumbarton Oaks demonstrated. Not only were the Soviets absent, but the discussions failed to focus on other forces in the world that would have to be faced—from decolonization to nationalism. What Churchill and Roosevelt mostly did was to enjoy the beautiful city, the hospitality of its people, and the elegance of the Château Frontenac while mulling over the great issues of the Second World War. The decisions had to wait.

But not for long if Churchill had his way. The liberation of Europe was proceeding in a manner that called for a geopolitical understanding with Stalin. A week before the Normandy invasion the prime minister explained to FDR that the British had worked out an arrangement with the Russians regarding Romania and Greece. With the Germans beginning to withdraw from the southern Balkans, Churchill feared that the Communist-influenced EAM (National Liberation Front) and other Greek guerrilla forces that had resisted the Axis occupation would take control before the British could reinstall the monarchy or some equally anti-

Communist regime. The various partisan groups understandably opposed a monarch from a German family who refused to accept constitutional limitations on his authority and who had supported the prewar dictatorial regime of Ioannis Metaxas. Roosevelt considered the Greek king, George II, a "charming fellow, considering what an empty head," but the British were stuck with him. When they tried to replace the unpopular king with a regent, George balked, and the British needed the support of promonarchist elements in the Greek Army.[84] What Churchill wanted was a Soviet commitment not to aid EAM. In return Britain would acquiesce to Stalin's control of Romania. Unspoken, but surely understood, was that the British could intervene with force in Greece without protest from Moscow.

When Stalin asked if FDR had agreed to such an arrangement, the prime minister went to the president for his "blessing." Churchill denied any "wish to carve up the Balkans into spheres of influence," claiming the deal was just a temporary wartime measure, but the State Department would have no part of it and got FDR to reject the proposal. The State Department and the British Foreign Office then engaged in complicated diplomatic maneuvering while Churchill and Roosevelt cut a deal. The prime minister suggested limiting the arrangement to a three-month trial period, and the president, who, like everyone else, had consigned Romania to the Soviets, agreed. Both the British and the Soviets would exercise Stalin's axiom in Greece and Romania respectively, but Roosevelt had avoided a formal agreement for exclusive control that could carry over into the postwar era.[85]

By the time Churchill boarded the *Queen Mary* on September 20 for his return home from the Quebec Conference, he was ready to broaden such Anglo-Soviet arrangements, agreeing with Eden's conclusion that the Russian move into Romania and Bulgaria created problems, particularly in Yugoslavia, that required "conversation in Moscow." A Soviet military representative, Colonel Grigory Popov, had parachuted into Greece for talks in early August with EAM and ELAS (Hellenic People's Army of Liberation) leaders. It could hardly be a coincidence that a week later EAM became more cooperative, eventually agreeing to participate in a liberal government headed by George Papandreou. But the time had come, Churchill decided, to "ask the Russians plainly what their policy is."[86]

Five years earlier, when Churchill was first lord of the admiralty, he had viewed the Nazi-Soviet Pact as a legitimate expression of Soviet national interests, an agreement that "was clearly necessary for the safety of Russia against Nazi menace," even though he "wished that the Russian armies should be standing on their present line as the friends and Allies of Poland instead of as invaders." Moreover, Churchill observed, German designs on the Baltic states threatened "the historic life-interests of Russia." Despite his claim that he merely "put the best construction on their [the Russians'] conduct," Churchill had sent a clear message to Stalin. The Baltic states were in the Soviet sphere of influence.[87]

By mid-autumn 1944, as the Germans were crushing the Warsaw uprising, Churchill again found a spheres of influence arrangement more practical than confrontation, despite his intense dislike of bolshevism. In 1939 he had sought to limit German expansion by exploiting Nazi-Soviet rivalry. Now, in 1944, he sought to protect British interests in the Mediterranean and Central Europe; that necessitated limiting Soviet expansion. In each case he proposed diplomacy and compromise to accomplish what Britain could not achieve by arms.

Churchill had tried to arrange an immediate Big Three conference, but Roosevelt insisted that he could not attend until after the American presidential election in early November. The prime minister contemptuously dismissed further delay with the comment that the Red Army would not wait for the election results. He cabled Stalin and suggested a meeting in Moscow, with a tripartite conference, possibly in The Hague, to follow the presidential election. Stalin agreed to the Moscow meeting, though he firmly rebuffed any proposal for a Big Three meeting that would take him out of the Soviet Union.[88]

When Churchill told FDR of the meeting, the president accepted Admiral Leahy's draft reply that merely wished the prime minister "every success" and then went on to emphasize FDR's consistent theme: the importance of Big Three agreement, this time at the Dumbarton Oaks talks. But aides persuaded the president to send a different message that called for Averell Harriman, then the U.S. ambassador in Moscow, to act as "observer," though FDR warned that he "could not permit anyone to commit me in advance."

That off again, on again reaction did not signal some sort of shift in American policy. The president's cable to Churchill was not a proclamation of American globalism but a reaffirmation of Roosevelt's commitment to perpetuating Great Power cooperation. As Hopkins and Charles Bohlen warned, a casual expression of uninterest could prompt the conclusion that the United States was returning to "isolationism," leaving Britain and Russia to divide Europe between them, an unacceptable variation of the European regionalism Churchill had proposed earlier. Regional leadership was one thing—the United States jealously guarded its special relationship with Latin America, as Churchill sarcastically pointed out on numerous occasions—but exclusive spheres of interest were quite another. Lest Stalin misunderstand, Roosevelt warned him that the Moscow talks were merely "preliminary to a meeting of the three of us. . . ." But the Soviet leader remained persuaded that the Anglo-Americans were in combination, probably against him. He replied that he presumed Churchill and Roosevelt had reached agreement at Quebec and "was somewhat puzzled" by the president's admonition.[89] His puzzlement did not last long.

With Roosevelt not in Moscow to preach his own hybrid form of "open" spheres of influence, Churchill and Stalin got down to serious horse trading. The talks, code-named Tolstoy, were long (October 9–17, 1944), but the key discussions came early. Taking advantage of Harriman's absence from the first meeting (Roosevelt had agreed that Churchill should conduct some private discussions[90]), the prime minister offered his notorious "percentages" proposal—what he later called a "naughty document." The note, which he slid across the table to Stalin, seemed a callous return to an era when princes swapped chunks of territory like pieces on a chessboard. Ninety percent influence for the Soviets in Romania; the same for Britain in Greece. Seventy-five percent in Bulgaria went to Moscow, while Yugoslavia and Hungary were split fifty-fifty. Churchill warned that they should "express these things in diplomatic terms and not to use the phrase 'dividing into spheres,' because the Americans might be shocked" and suggested destroying the paper; Stalin "ticked" the proposal and told the prime minister to keep it. When Stalin agreed that "Britain must be the leading Mediterranean power," Churchill endorsed a request that the Soviet Union gain unrestricted access to the Mediterranean from the Black Sea, despite a long-standing British-sponsored international agreement that allowed Turkey to close the Dardanelles to warships. Both the British and the Soviets took the percentages formula seriously, with Eden and Molotov subsequently haggling over 5 percent here and 10 percent there.[91]

Like Roosevelt, Churchill could see no way to prevent the Russians from dominating Eastern Europe. Why not make the best of a bad situation and protect British prestige and interests in the Mediterranean and, at the same time, get the Soviet Union to agree to limit its expansion?

Churchill also tried to play Soviet power against that of the United States (just as Roosevelt's advisers had feared). Obviously having little faith in the United Nations Organization, the prime minister ignored FDR's request not to discuss the results of the Dumbarton Oaks talks and came out in favor of Great Power unanimity (the veto) in any postwar international organization. Without it, he feared, if "China asked Britain to give up Hong Kong, China and Britain would have to leave the room while Russia and the U.S.A. settled the question."[92]

Churchill found the combination of nationalism and Roosevelt's calls for Britain to grant independence to its empire as great a threat to British interests as was Soviet expansion into Eastern Europe. Britain's place in East Asia, specifically China, deeply concerned the prime minister. Seeking Stalin's support, or at least neutrality, in a region of intensifying nationalism, he outlined concessions he thought should go to the Soviet Union in the Far East. The deal between Stalin and Churchill was implied, not the sort of explicit arrangement they had made over Greece and Romania, but the approach was the same. The Soviet Union should have "effective rights at Port Arthur," said Churchill. Why worry about Soviet naval power in the Far East? he told his chiefs of staff; the Soviet fleet was "vastly inferior" and would be "hostages to the stronger Naval Powers." More important, "any claim by Russia for indemnity at the expense of China, would be favourable to our resolve about Hong Kong." The Hong Kong issue led Churchill quickly to instruct that no agreements be reached with the United States to oppose a "restoration of Russia's position in the Far East."

Four months later, at Yalta, Roosevelt worked out a Far Eastern settlement with Stalin that paralleled the quid pro quo Churchill had floated at Moscow, but FDR's reasons were a bit different. First and foremost, the Soviet Union's entry into what all expected to be a long and bloody war against Japan had always been framed to include something for Russia. Roosevelt had no doubt Stalin would live up to his promise so long as the United States and Great Britain lived up to theirs. Beyond that, FDR was, like Churchill, concerned about China, although it was the impending conflict between Mao and Chiang, not the decolonization of Hong Kong, that worried him. Persuading Stalin not to throw in with the Chinese Communists and thus give the Kuomintang a chance to consolidate its rule was Roosevelt's goal. The danger was that Chiang's chance would come at the expense of Chinese sovereignty and territory, running the risk of alienating the nationalism that Chiang had to harness in order to survive. But whatever the differences in motives between Roosevelt and Churchill, they both gave positive endorsement to the commitments made to Stalin in return for Soviet entry into the war against Japan.

Eight years after the Yalta Conference, at the height of Cold War tensions, Churchill distanced himself from the Far Eastern settlement at Yalta. Since the State Department had released the Far Eastern protocol to the public in February 1946, Churchill could only pretend that Britain had played no role in the arrangement, claiming the matter was, for Britain, "remote and secondary." We signed the agreement, but "neither I nor Eden took any part in making it," Churchill wrote. "In the United States there have been many reproaches about the concessions made to Soviet

Russia. The responsibility rests with their own representatives. To us the problem was remote and secondary." This was technically correct. Churchill had not helped draft the language adopted at Yalta. Why bother? He had cut his deal five months earlier.[93]

As the Moscow meeting drew to a close, Churchill wrote King George with unintended double meaning that "the political atmosphere is extremely cordial. Nothing like it has been seen before."[94] Little wonder that cordiality prevailed. Stalin's sway over Eastern Europe had been ratified, while his country's interests in the Far East were endorsed, though ratification would have to await the Americans. Churchill hoped that the accommodation would protect Britain's place in Europe and that the Russians would be satisfied. But the arrangement hardly qualified for the conclusion "nothing like it has been seen before." It was a division of territory and influence, a balancing of power that was reminiscent of medieval kings exchanging principalities, and repeated regularly since then—including in 1919 and in 1939. Britain was far from powerless, but it lacked the strength to confront the United States and the Soviet Union in Europe, East Asia, or the colonial world. Were the Tolstoy agreements and Far Eastern concessions a new appeasement, this time of the Soviet Union, or an attempt to find a practical accommodation to the insoluble problem of British inability to control events? How could Britain "sell out" Eastern Europe unless Eastern Europe was Britain's to sell?[95]

Churchill and Stalin had begun their talks by swapping crude Polish jokes and commiserating with each other about Polish intransigence. (Put two Poles in a room, and they would argue with each other, said Churchill; put one Pole in a room, and he would argue with himself out of boredom, retorted Stalin.) The gist of Churchill's quips was that he would not confront the Soviet Union over Poland—the position he had taken since 1942. The Poles would have to live with the Russian bear, he kept warning the London Polish government, and fundamentally on the bear's terms.

When Stanislaw Mikolajczyk, the leader of that Polish government, responded to an invitation from Churchill and Stalin to come to the Tolstoy talks, he found to his dismay that both Churchill and Roosevelt had endorsed the Curzon Line during the Teheran Conference. Churchill switched to the issue of the makeup of the government of liberated Poland, but Stalin rejected any separation of the issues of boundaries and governance. Any settlement of the Soviet-Polish frontier would be, he pointed out, only as good as the intentions of the Polish government in power. In July 1944 Stalin had granted a Soviet-sponsored Committee of National Liberation, in Lublin, the authority to administer the lands Moscow accepted as Polish—territory west of the Curzon Line. That Lublin committee had accepted the Soviet-Polish border demanded by the Russians and was well on the road to being the "friendly" Polish government that Stalin insisted upon.

At Moscow the Soviets insisted on the Curzon Line frontier; the London Poles insisted on Lwow and significant eastward adjustments to that line. The Soviets then insisted on doing business only with Poles who would accept the Curzon Line. Exit the London Poles.[96] Churchill's anger at those London Poles in the aftermath of the 1944 Tolstoy talks was conscience-salving romanticism carefully subordinated to immediate British interests. He did speak out, and speak out clearly, for something other than a Soviet-dominated puppet government in Poland, but those sentiments were never accompanied by consistent action—at least until after the Yalta Conference.

Although Churchill and Stalin saved their most sensitive conversations for the times Harriman was excluded, the American "observer," a confidant of the prime minister and a close friend of many of the Churchills (he and Randolph Churchill's wife, Pamela, had an affair while Harriman was in London), soon found out what was going on. When the ambassador accurately reported the spheres of influence arrangement that was developing for the Balkans, Roosevelt blandly replied that his concern was to take practical steps "to insure against the Balkans getting us into a future international war." Spheres of influence were neither endorsed nor rejected. Since Stalin's insistence on a "friendly" government in Poland meant that Poles in the West would be unhappy, FDR asked Churchill for a two-week delay in any announcement of an agreement, should one be reached. Roosevelt had no expectations of a change of heart on Stalin's part, but two weeks would take him past the presidential election. "I am delighted," he cabled Stalin, "to learn from your message and from reports by Ambassador Harriman of the success attained by you and Mr. Churchill. . . ." FDR reserved the right to disagree when the Big Three next met but gave no hint of concern about the results of the Churchill-Stalin talks.[97]

That presidential election turned out the way each of the Big Three hoped, even if Roosevelt's popular vote margin, 52.8 percent, was the lowest of his four presidential victories. FDR's opponent, Thomas Dewey, the governor of New York State, represented the internationalists in the Republican party, but neither Churchill nor Stalin wanted to deal with an unknown quantity. Stalin had predicted Roosevelt's defeat, perhaps believing Dewey's effort to tar the Democrats as sympathetic to communism would strike a chord with American voters. (Stalin also predicted a Conservative party victory in Britain; so much for his credentials as a pundit.) For a while FDR adopted a Rose Garden strategy: trying to appear "presidential" and above politics in the midst of war. But when that strategy fell flat, he launched a vigorous campaign that focused on the achievements of the New Deal, mocked his opponent, and regularly referred to military victories. His government had, he boasted, managed "to carry out major offensive operations in both Europe and the Philippines—thirteen thousand miles apart from each other." His public appearances at outdoor rallies buried persistent rumors of ill health. To Churchill's relief (and Stalin's, according to the prime minister), FDR triumphed. The prime minister, apparently still piqued that Roosevelt had never acknowledged the congratulatory message sent after the 1940 election, dispatched the same text. FDR sent his thanks, lamely claiming that he had certainly not forgotten Churchill's earlier cable.[98]

But Roosevelt's reelection did not clarify the mixed signals that came out of the Tolstoy meetings. Churchill had suggested dividing up Central and Eastern Europe into numerically calculated spheres of influence. What should Stalin conclude but that Churchill and Roosevelt (given Harriman's presence) were backing away a bit from their commitment to an interactive, cooperative postwar working relationship, choosing instead an old-fashioned delineation of what belonged to whom? As Harriman ruefully concluded, the argument over Poland and the percentages arrangement negotiated at Tolstoy made the "job of getting the Soviet Government to play a decent role in international affairs . . . more difficult than we had hoped."[99]

Perhaps Roosevelt's four policemen, Churchill's spheres of influence, and Stalin's axiom all could be made to work together to create a workable and effective postwar system. Principles and ideals might be a bit worse for the wear, but conflict between the Great Powers would be even worse. But it was much more than just reconciling three different yet related systems of Great Power control. Hitler not only had upset the balance of politics in Europe but had unleashed a virulent nationalism, as the crisis (for Britain) in Greece illustrated. During the Tolstoy talks Stalin caught the threat to Great Power control when he responded to another of Churchill's proposals for federations in Eastern Europe: ". . . after this war all States would be very nationalistic. . . . The feeling to live independently would be the strongest. Later, economic feelings would prevail, but in the first period they would be purely nationalistic and therefore groupings would be unwelcome. The fact that Hitler's regime had developed nationalism could be seen in the example of Yugoslavia where Croats, Montenegrins, Slovenes, &c. all wanted something of their own. It was a symptom."[100] Perhaps Stalin was mostly concerned with countering any thoughts of establishing a new cordon sanitaire, but lurking in the background was the ghostly image of Czar Alexander and his fellow monarchs bemoaning the virulent epidemic set loose by Napoleon.

The "Holy Alliance"—for the moment

CHAPTER 9

The "Holy Alliance"
December 1944–War's End

*Unfortunately, this must all be done under the cloak of a holy
alliance between England, Russia and America.*

—GENERAL ALAN BROOKE, July 27, 1944

The nationalism that was to play a major role in destroying Big
Three collaboration after the war took various forms. Nationalism
frequently incorporated social reform as part of its appeal, often
making it seem revolutionary to the Anglo-Americans. In Greece
republicanism and the "left"[1] expropriated nationalism. But in
France nationalism coalesced in the person of Charles de Gaulle,
who, with single-minded intensity, rekindled French pride and self-
respect after the debacle of 1940. In the colonial world, particularly
South and Southeast Asia, Japanese and American propaganda reinforced long-repressed desires for independence. In China, while
the civil war between Chiang and Mao remained in suspended animation, both protagonists worked to don the mantle of Chinese
nationalism. In Eastern Europe Polish self-determination became
for many in the West the litmus test of Soviet intentions. Even in
Italy, where British-sponsored and American-sponsored politicians
vied for power, the maneuvering took on the cloak of republicanism and self-determination. Republicanism, pride, independence,

self-determination—all different, but all forms of nationalism that challenged Great Power cooperation. Power at the service of ideology, and vice versa, came to dominate the Soviet-Western relationship after World War II, but nationalism, in all its varied guises, played an even greater role in preventing the extension of wartime cooperation into the postwar world.

The British had encouraged the European states occupied by the Axis to establish governments-in-exile, usually in London. They were recognized by the United Nations as the legitimate governments and proved useful for propaganda purposes as well as legal fictions that allowed the Allies to make use of the overseas properties and resources of occupied states. Only a few managed to maintain credibility at home by becoming symbols of resistance to the Axis. Republican governments did a bit better than monarchies. De Gaulle came to personify independent France in the minds of his countrymen, while Eduard Beneš of Czechoslovakia, who had resigned in protest after the 1938 Munich Pact, continued as a symbol of opposition and was reelected president in 1945.

Some monarchies came out relatively unscathed. Constitutional monarchs in Norway and Luxembourg returned to their thrones. But in Belgium, demonstrations by the resistance—composed mainly of workers and Flemish nationalists—were aimed at forcing leaders just returned from exile to make social and political concessions. Although the protests quickly ended when the Germans launched their Ardennes Forest offensive and the resistance joined the fight, the king had to abdicate in favor of his son.[2] The Dutch, overwhelmingly middle class, had less interest in social and political reform, and Queen Wilhelmina was restored with little trouble, although nationalists in the Dutch East Indies (subsequently Indonesia) seized the opportunity to begin a successful revolution. (Also in Asia, Sergio Osmeña, president of the American Commonwealth of the Philippines, was restored to office by the United States.)

But other governments-in-exile, forced to view the scene from afar, forfeited popular support. The peoples of occupied Europe were much more impressed with and sympathetic to local resistance forces that harassed and even fought the unwanted invaders.[3] Popular heroes and heroines came out of the mountains of Yugoslavia and Greece, not fancy town houses in London. Moreover, most governments-in-exile were led by kings, aristocrats, and large landowners. Local resistance forces not only fought the Germans and Italians, and sometimes the Japanese, but also recognized the opportunity to take control by combining nationalism and a program of social and economic change—"revolution," in the rhetoric of exiled leaders. The elitist Polish government in London had to rely—unsuccessfully as it turned out—on the underground Home Army to return it to power. The king of Yugoslavia lost what little popular support he had enjoyed and never regained power (also true for the Italian king, although he was never "in exile"). George II, king of the Hellenes, had spent the war in Egypt. That, his German background, his stubborn defense of royal prerogatives, and his association with the prewar Metaxas dictatorship in Greece all guaranteed his unpopularity.

The Greek situation, which greatly worried the British, came to a head in December 1944. On October 4, with the Germans withdrawing, British Army units landed in the south. They arrived in Athens ten days later. By then guerrilla forces, primarily but not exclusively those of the EAM, had established control over much of the countryside. But Athens, the political and psychological soul of Greece, was the prize that would determine the future, and Winston Churchill was determined that Britain should control events in Athens.

A popular nationalist coalition that included the "left," even one as liberal as might have been achieved under Papandreou, might reject British political guidance and strike out on too independent a course. The British, desperate for native Greek support, created a "national guard" out of two Royal Greek Army units that had fought in Italy, plus security battalions organized earlier by the Germans. ELAS and other guerrilla groups, which viewed the new force as made up of either traitors or fools, refused to turn in their arms lest they lose all leverage and be eliminated from the government. Churchill, questioned in the House of Commons about the suppression of democracy in Greece, argued that those to whom Britain had given guns to fight the Nazis had not, "by fee simple," gained "the right 'to govern vast complex communities such as Belgium or Holland—it may be Holland next—or Greece.' " The point was clear: Political reconstruction in Greece (or anywhere else, for that matter) was for the Great Powers to control.

Claiming EAM/ELAS would try to seize power, the British rushed forces into Athens to "restore order" and install the royal government. On December 3 the confrontation came to a head when police fired on a crowd of thousands of pro-EAM demonstrators in the center of the city, killing between ten and twenty-one and wounding more than one hundred. The agents provocateurs may have been members of the Greek Communist party, members of some British agency, or perhaps just honest policemen frightened for their lives. Whatever the spark, by the next day ELAS and the British were locked in warfare. Churchill quickly took charge and, without consulting his Cabinet, gave orders to maintain his Greek government in power, using British military force as necessary. For the next two months a brutal civil war, with British military forces playing a crucial role, ripped Greece apart.[4]

Stalin said not a word, nor did he aid either EAM/ELAS or the Greek Communists, while American and British politicians and press condemned Churchill for intervening in the internal affairs of an ally. Secretary of State Edward R. Stettinius (who had replaced the ailing Cordell Hull), annoyed by British opposition to American-sponsored politicians in the new Italian government, called for "the Italians to work out their problems of government along democratic lines without influence from outside." He followed that by stating that "this policy would apply to an even more pronounced degree with regard to governments of the United Nations in their liberated territories"—a remark that the American press correctly interpreted as directed at British actions in Greece. Angered, Churchill had his diplomats ask the State Department to say something in support of British policy in Greece, but Stettinius did not back away from his call for self-determination in that country. A debate and vote of confidence in the House of Commons that followed were far more bitter and serious than Churchill let on.[5]

Even though Roosevelt had approved the dispatch of British

forces for the very purpose of preventing a coup by EAM/ELAS, he warned that he could not endorse the prime minister's actions, blaming American public opinion. But in Roosevelt's system Greece was Britain's responsibility. FDR came down solidly, if privately, on Churchill's side by recommending a regency in place of George II and "the disarmament and dissolution of all the armed groups now in the country, . . . leaving your troops to preserve law and order alone until Greek national forces can be reconstituted on a non-partisan basis and adequately equipped."[6]

It is difficult to explain why Churchill was so obsessed with events in Greece. Whatever his dedication to "constitutional" liberties and a British-style rule of law, his percentages agreement with Stalin conceded that those values would not prevail in the Baltic states, Romania, and Bulgaria. Why then his all-out commitment in Greece? Perhaps it was a geopolitical view generated by the events of two world wars, each of which found Greece a linchpin in the control of the eastern Mediterranean. Perhaps Churchill's image of Greece as the "cradle of democracy" inspired a romantic desire to protect that society from bolshevism. Perhaps Churchill was right when he equated an EAM triumph with a Communist takeover. A massacre "would have ensued," he told Roosevelt, "followed by a ruthless terror in the name of a purge. I am sure you would not like us to abandon this thankless task now and withdraw our troops and let things crash."[7] But those reasons were window dressing. Churchill got tough over Greece because he concluded that Britain's Great Power status had to be tested, and Greece was where it could pass that test. Stalin had agreed that Greece should be a British sphere of influence, and British military power seemed sufficient for the situation. Even without Soviet aid, the Greek Communists (the label Churchill applied to all those opposed to a "British solution") posed a challenge to what the prime minister wanted. If Britain could not control events in a small part of the world, how could it play the role of Great Power? Greece was important more as an expression of Britain's place in the world than as a place where freedom had to be defended. Rightly or not, Churchill concluded that the "cradle of democracy" needed help from Anglo-Saxon warriors.

The Greek nationalists, whether disguised as monarchists, reformers, or the "left," were not the only "small" government (recognized or not) to reject Great Power dictates. De Gaulle and the French Committee of National Liberation (FCNL) did the same and with much more success. De Gaulle consistently presented himself as the only alternative to communism in France and effectively prevented Communists (or any other rival) from gaining positions of importance in his regime, but during much of the war that argument failed to sway either Churchill or Roosevelt (though it persuaded many in the Foreign Office and the State Department). The prime minister, who liked to picture himself as a stubborn adherent to principle, grudgingly admired de Gaulle's refusal to back down even in the face of unanimous Anglo-American demands. The Foreign Office argued that Britain needed a strong France as an ally, but de Gaulle's arrogance and Roosevelt's opposition made the British leader reluctant to recognize the FCNL as a legitimate government. The Frenchman recalled Churchill's telling him and British officials present that "each time we must choose between Europe and open sea, we shall always choose the open sea. Each time I must choose between you and Roosevelt, I shall always choose Roosevelt."[8]

The president found the Frenchman's "Jeanne d'Arc complex" exasperating, but at the same time Roosevelt continued to believe that France would fall into civil war. The revolving door governments in Paris during the 1930s and the abrupt collapse of French military resistance to Hitler in 1940 caused FDR to question if France should remain as a single nation-state, prompting his proposal to create a new state called Wallonia—a many-humped camel made up of French speakers in Belgium, Luxembourg, and possibly the Ruhr, northern France, and Alsace-Lorraine.[9]

When de Gaulle visited Washington a month after the Normandy invasion (FDR said he was willing to meet with de Gaulle but would not "invite" the Frenchman), Roosevelt described how his four policemen would operate in the postwar world. "A permanent system of intervention" necessitating military bases throughout the world was de Gaulle's characterization. The president's easy assumption that such bases would be in French colonies while France was not one of the policemen colored de Gaulle's reaction, but his portrait of FDR was perceptive: "It was by light touches that he sketched his notions, and so skillfully that it was difficult to contradict this artist, this seducer, in any categorical way." De Gaulle warned that balancing Soviet power would require a strong Western Europe and thus a strong France, and a strong France required that it retain its colonies. FDR did not rise to the bait, instead reminding de Gaulle of how French weakness had opened the door to Hitler.[10]

But by summer 1944 de Gaulle seemed the only alternative to disorder and, even worse, revolution. Those fears prompted Eisenhower to make a show of military support for the French general after he had received an enthusiastic welcome when he entered Paris. With de Gaulle in place and no reasonable alternative to choose from the French resistance (carefully orchestrated by the general), Roosevelt and Churchill had little choice but to extend formal recognition to the FCNL as the government of France, although both men had to be pushed and cajoled by their advisers finally to relent. But FDR still believed France was Britain's "baby and will take a lot of nursing in order to bring it to the point of walking alone." Formal recognition came in late October 1944, but the president remained unconvinced. Two months later, during the Christmas holidays, he offered his grandson Curtis Roosevelt a large "toy submarine, a mechanical marvel made by the workers in the Bizerte (Tunisia) arsenal" that actually worked. When Eleanor Roosevelt reminded him that it had been a present from a head of state, Charles de Gaulle, FDR disdainfully commented that the Frenchman was not a head of state but merely the head of some French committee or another.[11]

When de Gaulle asserted that a strong France required its colonial empire (he claimed the same for Britain and even the Italians), the general went to the heart of a growing dilemma for Roosevelt and his postwar scheme. Nationalism was not just a European passion. The fifty-year Sino-Japanese confrontation had begun in the late nineteenth century, when Chinese nationalism challenged foreign domination. With the Europeans distracted by war during the twentieth century, Japanese imperialism posed the most aggressive threat to China's independence. Even with the split in China's nationalist movement between the Communists, led by Mao, and the Kuomintang, led by Chiang, those two bitter enemies constructed a "peace of the castle" during World War II, ostensibly so each could concentrate on fighting the foreigners, the Japanese. Actually both focused their efforts on preparing for the civil war they knew would come. Mao worked to convince China's millions of peasants that his movement would give them a better life, and within the limits of his army's capabilities, he fought the Japanese effectively. Chiang, robbed of middle-class economic and political support when Japan occupied most of China's major cities, had to rely on provincial warlords whose interests were all too often based on privilege, profit, and power at the expense of the peasantry. American and British assessments of China's politics were often misguided, but they all agreed that nationalism could not be ignored. Late in 1944 Roosevelt, recognizing that the United States would not have enough military forces in China to control events at war's end, dispatched the so-called Dixie Mission to talk to Mao in what proved an unsuccessful effort to shoehorn the Chinese Communists and Nationalists into some sort of coalition.[12]

But China was only part of the challenge raised by Asian nationalism. Roosevelt had steadily pursued his campaign against European colonial empires throughout the war. Churchill bragged that he had quieted the president on that issue by being tough, but that was meaningless bravado. In countless ways FDR kept the pressure on Churchill and the leaders of other European colonial powers to begin the process of decolonization. Roosevelt pushed one of his favorites, Dutch Queen Wilhelmina ("Minnie" he called her, with militant casualness), to begin the process of granting self-government to the Netherlands East Indies. But she would have none of it. She told FDR that Java could, perhaps, become independent in something between fifteen and fifty years, but anything for the backward areas was " 'sheer speculation.' " Roosevelt did not push the issue, leading the Dutch to believe that he agreed to a restoration of their control.[13]

But the Dutch confused politeness with agreement. Roosevelt

was convinced that the pressure of nationalism in the European empires was a most serious threat to postwar peace. Yet he believed that the Europeans had time—perhaps as long as twenty-five or thirty years—to prepare for colonial independence, so long as they made public commitments to self-determination and established some sort of schedule for devolution. He more than once offered the British a history lesson based on the American experience with the Articles of Confederation after the American Revolution. Churchill mocked the analogy but missed the point (as have so many historians). Decolonization was inevitable, Roosevelt believed. "India is not yet ready for home government," he told the Pacific War Council. "That takes time. The training of thousands of persons over a number of years is necessary for good government." That, he explained, the United States had learned through trial and error during the era of the Articles of Confederation.[14]

The United States, with its own colonies, certainly practiced a "combination of populism and arrogance" about European empires, even if it had scheduled independence for the Philippines as soon as the war ended (something FDR constantly threw up to Churchill). But eliminating empires fitted American commitments to open the world, including empires, to commercial access—"free markets," in the political jargon of the 1990s. "Roosevelt did not confine his dislike of colonialism to the British Empire alone," wrote Eden, "for it was a principle with him, not the less cherished for its possible advantages."

American policy did not create the desire for self-determination. General de Gaulle gave the United States too much credit (or blame) when he claimed it had forced the Dutch "to renounce their sovereignty over Java." Independence for India, Indonesia, and most of the colonial world came primarily from the demands of the native peoples, not because of anything done or said by the United States. By the end of the Second World War the Asian colonies were neither Europe's to lose nor America's to win—or to destabilize. Nationalism could not be denied, though it could be delayed.[15]

Churchill remained adamant in his defense of empire, arguing that "the British alone had managed to combine Empire and Liberty." In December 1944 he instructed Eden that " 'Hands off the British Empire' is our maxim, and it must not be weakened or smirched to please sob-stuff merchants at home or foreigners of any hue." Holding on to the empire was part of why Britain had gone to war. Hitler had challenged British interests in Europe, but Japan was a direct rival for empire in Asia. Moreover, Japan's conquests had given Indian nationalists an opportunity to use the war as leverage for independence. Churchill's contempt for the Indians, heightened by what he viewed as treasonous demands that Britain "quit India" as the price of support for the war, only strengthened his resolve. India was the very symbol of the empire, and he would not negotiate that symbol away. A number of other British leaders had begun to rethink the question of empire, but Churchill and Eden invariably blocked American efforts to conduct direct Great Power discussions about colonialism.[16]

With the instincts of a politician, Roosevelt had focused his attack against colonialism on two very visible examples: British India and French Indochina. Churchill and the British government had rejected FDR's prompting about India ("pitiless publicity" was how the president described his own tactic), although the ruthless suppression of Indian nationalists, which had required more than fifty battalions in addition to police forces, had the effect Roosevelt expected: heightened and angry nationalism.

That left Indochina, which as early as May 1942 the president had held up as an example of colonial mismanagement. Exploitation and indifference had, he told the Pacific War Council, left the natives unprepared for self-government and in need of major reform. He and Stalin had agreed at Teheran that the colony should not be returned to French rule, and FDR made sure that Churchill learned of the conversation.[17]

But the prime minister and his government would have no part of a piecemeal attack on colonial empires. If France could be kept out of Indochina, then India, Burma, and other parts of the British Empire were next. Moreover, the Foreign Office argued strenuously, Britain needed a strong and cooperative France in order to have a secure position in Europe, and General de Gaulle's minimum conditions for cooperation began with retention of the

French Empire. Churchill counseled against any discussions with Roosevelt about Indochina until after the presidential election of November 1944, but the British military had already in the summer of 1944 begun to integrate FCNL military and political personnel into its Southeast Asian Command (SEAC), headed by Admiral Louis "Dickie" Mountbatten. The president refused to recognize the French presence and rejected proposals to provide transport or supplies for the French in Indochina. But he could not force them out without British cooperation.[18]

Had empire been the only thing at stake, Roosevelt could have put near-irresistible pressure on the British to block the French in Indochina and to make specific commitments to the Indian nationalists, commitments that would have set a powerful precedent for other independence movements. But FDR's first prerequisite for avoiding another world war was Great Power cooperation, his four policemen. Britain was to be a policeman. Without the British playing that role, the system the president envisaged could not work. He had managed to use the Bretton Woods and Dumbarton Oaks agreements to keep cooperation as an option, but alienating the British over empire in Southeast Asia—particularly with Churchill openly emotional on the issue—might push them toward the narrow regionalism that FDR feared would only re-create the tensions that had led to two world wars.

Had China been ready and able to play the role of Great Power, Roosevelt would have had more options. But the colonial issue was coming to a head in South and Southeast Asia, where the weakest of the four policemen was supposed to be "responsible." Not only was China about to plunge into civil war, but Roosevelt's designated policeman, Chiang Kai-shek, seemed all too inclined to expand into Southeast Asia at the expense of Britain and France. Self-determination in Eastern Europe had to be postponed in order to bring the Soviet Union into the "family circle." Now expediency seemed to require a similar compromise in Southeast Asia.

Nor was military intervention by the United States in Indochina an option in 1945, despite the successful invasion of the Philippines in October 1944 and the destruction at Leyte Gulf of a Japanese battle fleet that had no aircraft cover. The president may have toyed with the idea of an invasion of Tonkin (northern Indochina), but if so, that diversion away from the enemy's homeland never received serious consideration. The campaign in the Philippines and the navy's successful leapfrogging across the central Pacific eliminated any consideration of a costly invasion of Formosa (Taiwan) and pushed the navy toward plans for invading Iwo Jima and Okinawa (though those two campaigns turned out to be far bloodier than anyone expected). As for China, the problem, thought Roosevelt, having no faith in the willingness of either Chiang or Mao to play a "responsible" role, was that "three generations of education and training would be required before China could be a serious [political] factor." With no American military force in East or Southeast Asia, and with China needing "tutelage" before it could play the role of responsible policeman, Roosevelt's only option was to have the Europeans reclaim their empires.[19]

Roosevelt was, in his own way, as stubborn as Churchill. For the president, decolonization had always been a process, not an immediate act. His patience and belief in the superiority of American institutions brought him to conclude that most colonies would need long periods of benevolent guidance (what he called trusteeships) before they could govern themselves. He agreed, for example, with State Department arguments that Korea might require a forty-year training period because the thirty-five-year Japanese occupation had politically "emasculated" Koreans and left them without experience in self-government.[20] That kind of paternalism did not take into account the intensity of nationalism, but FDR's willingness to wait for the internal development of what Americans call democracy distinguishes Roosevelt's foreign policy from the experiments in nation building of his Cold War successors.

It led Roosevelt to a tactic. He had long proposed that preparation for self-government be done under the supervision of international "trustees." He could modify that to allow the Europeans back into their Asian empires but only as trustees, whose actions would be monitored by an international organization, the United Nations. FDR backed away from any strenuous confrontation with Britain, or with France by proxy, lest that jeopardize his plans for Great Power cooperation, but he consistently argued for the colonial masters to become colonial trustees, accountable to an international community in which the United States would be a dominant figure. What Roosevelt feared, and with good historical reasons, was that if the colonial powers were left to decide when their colonies were "ready" for self-government, they would act the way "Minnie" had spoken: The Europeans would drag their feet, set one ethnic group against another, and do whatever they could to spin a web of control around their colonies before granting even the facade of self-determination.[21]

But FDR never backed away from believing that a smooth, nonviolent transition from empire to independence for Europe's colonies was a key to creating a peaceful world, even if he could not prevent the Europeans from reclaiming their Asian empires. He spoke patronizingly of the Asians—"The Indochinese were people of small stature," he told Stalin, "and were not warlike"—but that silly statement did not mean he abandoned them to colonialism. When the British secretary of state for colonies, Oliver Stanley, visited Washington in mid-January, Roosevelt restated his conviction that European empires would disappear. Indochina would not be returned to France, he said, but would be "administered by a group of nations selected by the United Nations." The movement toward self-determination was irresistible, thought FDR, whether in Burma, the Netherlands East Indies, or even British Gambia and French Morocco. The United States would support that movement.[22]

Asian nationalism, East European nationalism: two movements in the same symphony. Stalin had good reason to fear that the people of Eastern Europe "all wanted something of their own."[23] The Red Army may often have been greeted as liberators, but that welcome faded quickly as Soviet political commissars moved in—sometimes because they were Communists but always because they were agents of a "foreign" government in Moscow. The largest and best organized nationalist insurgency was in the Ukraine, where some hundred thousand armed insurgents challenged Russian control until 1947. (Historian Gerhard Weinberg has plausibly speculated that Stalin insisted that the Czechoslovak government-in-exile cede Ruthenia, or Carpatho-Ukraine, to ensure that the only large group of Ukrainians left outside the Soviet Union come under his—i.e., Russian—authority.)[24]

In Yugoslavia, a nation-state concocted in haste after the First World War, the inability of that creation and its Serbian monarchy to generate strong nationalism had allowed bitter ethnic/religious/cultural rivalries—among Serbs, Croats, Orthodox Catholics, Roman Catholics, Muslims, and Albanians, to mention only the major protagonists—to divide the society. But as was the case in so much of occupied Europe, intense popular opposition to the Italo-German occupation stimulated that missing nationalism and gave the most effective guerrilla force legitimacy. In Yugoslavia that force was the partisans led by the head of the Communist party, Tito (Josip Broz). The mutual maneuverings and betrayals by Tito and his major domestic challenger, monarchist Draža Mihailović, resulted in perhaps the bloodiest of Europe's wartime civil wars. But Yugoslavia was also the scene of Europe's most effective resistance outside the Soviet Union. By the time of the Teheran Conference Tito had convinced the British that supporting his partisans was the best way to kill Germans and divert Axis resources—and to gain a postwar friend.[25]

But it was Poland that came to represent the desire of Eastern Europeans for self-determination, just as Indochina and India did for Asians. Moreover, as Harry Hopkins told Stalin, shortly after Roosevelt's death, Poland became "a symbol of our ability to work out problems with the Soviet Union."[26] Polish nationalism could be neither denied nor quieted, and that clashed with Great Power control. Just before Churchill went to Moscow for the Tolstoy talks in October 1944, he told the House of Commons that he could not "conceive that it is not possible to make a good solution whereby Russia gets the security she is entitled to have, . . . and, at the same time, the Polish nation have restored to them that national sovereignty and independence, for which they have never ceased to strive." But in almost the next breath he set the stage for the percentages agreements. Sounding like FDR, the prime minister stated that the "future of the whole world and certainly the future of Europe, perhaps for several generations, depends on the cordial, trustful and comprehending association of the British

Empire, the United States and Soviet Russia, and no pains must be spared and no patience grudged which are necessary to bring that supreme hope to fruition."[27]

In mid-December, with the Greek crisis still current news, Churchill implied to the House of Commons that the United States supported territorial concessions by Poland to Russia. The American press and Congress heatedly questioned if Roosevelt had abandoned the Atlantic Charter. They had a point. FDR led reporters to assume he had not agreed to such concessions, but he never mentioned the message he had sent to Stalin a few days before about Poland's boundaries. While the United States preferred "that territorial questions await the general postwar settlement," he told the Soviet leader, it "recognizes that a settlement before that time is in the interest of the common war effort" and that "mutual agreement between the parties" would be perfectly acceptable. In other words, the agreements sketched out at Teheran were still in place.[28]

Stalin's recognition on December 31 of the Lublin committee as the legitimate Polish government merely stated the obvious. Roosevelt had asked the Soviet leader to postpone choosing between the London Poles and the Lublin group, but Stalin showed no concern for appearances. Churchill and Roosevelt continued to propose gestures that would make the situation palatable to their publics: Allow some non-Communists from the London Poles into the Soviet-sponsored government; let observers into the country; promise elections. But even had the Soviets complied, such cosmetic gestures would not have changed the situation.[29]

Poland had provided the occasion of war for Britain, but the war in Europe had been fought to defeat Hitler's Germany and then win the peace, not to achieve the aims of Polish nationalists. From 1941 to 1943 defeating Hitler required the Red Army. At the same time the search for a postwar peace, which both Roosevelt and Churchill defined as a cooperative postwar relationship among the Great Powers, required the participation of the Soviet Union. Soviet domination over Eastern Europe was not the simple and inevitable result of the Red Army's military victories; Stalin gained predominance there because Hitler had to be defeated and because

Churchill and Roosevelt chose to adopt positive measures for postwar peace rather than confront the Soviet Union, a necessary ally that was only a potential enemy. By the time the Soviets liberated and occupied Eastern Europe in 1944 and 1945, the region had already been consigned to the Soviet orbit. Roosevelt and Churchill were increasingly uneasy about the crude, brutal style of Soviet rule, but Stalin's axiom prevailed, as it prevailed in Western Europe as well.

But all these tensions and contradictions would be worked out, thought Roosevelt and Churchill, when they sat down with "Uncle Joe" at their meeting scheduled for February 1945 in the Crimean town of Yalta. The Black Sea resort, strikingly situated at the foot of steep mountains that shelter it from the biting winds sweeping across the steppes, is favored by a strangely temperate climate; palm trees can survive! The czars frequently established court there in the nineteenth and early twentieth centuries, setting off a spree of palace and villa building as Russian aristocrats tried to live up to expectations and outdo their neighbors. (For a few decades after the Bolshevik Revolution many of the palaces and villas served as sanitoriums for the ill, particularly for tubercular patients. The Soviet government exuberantly claimed that forty thousand citizens could make use of them at one time. Soviet government officials, the new "nobility," eventually appropriated the best of the buildings on the ground that exhausted government leaders needed them as rest homes.)

Because of the difficulty of travel from palace to palace through the steep hills of Yalta, the Livadiya (New) Palace, where Roosevelt stayed, served as conference headquarters. There was ample meeting space in the fifty-room Italian Renaissance edifice, built for Czar Nicholas II in 1911 to take advantage of a sweeping view of the Black Sea and the coast. But the rooms for all but the highest-level members of the American delegation were cramped, and there was an "acute shortage of bathrooms," in Stettinius's words. Only the president had a private facility, giving high-level diplomats and military brass more of a shared experience than they might have wished.

The conference provided the bizarre scene of Joseph Stalin, head of a revolutionary people's socialist government, comfortably ensconced in the impressive Koreiz Palace (officially only a "villa"). That contradiction perhaps explains why the palace was not routinely open to visitors, Soviet or foreign, even as late as 1992, a policy perhaps begun by Soviet bureaucrats embarrassed that the leader of a "people's" government would stay in so ostentatious a place. Some six miles from the Livadiya Palace, Koreiz had been built in 1850 and belonged at one time to Prince Yusupov, supposedly the assassin of Rasputin.[30]

Churchill's quarters were ten miles from Livadiya, in the Vorontsov "villa." Although the prime minister thought the Livadiya Palace "even more splendid" than his accommodations, he should have felt comfortable in a hundred-year-old mock-Scottish castle with Moorish archway and decorations, the perfect combination of Churchill's two favorite places, Britain and Marrakech. Most of the British were put up in small rooms designed for servants, and they too suffered from a shortage of bathrooms—only two in the entire villa. Churchill had called Yalta only "good for typhus and deadly lice" (he had stopped there briefly in October 1944 after leaving Moscow), and part of that dire prediction proved true. When he complained about bedbugs, an extermination squad (for bugs) from the USS *Catoctin*, moored eighty miles away at Sevastopol because, said the Soviets, of mines in the waters around Yalta, took care of the problem, as it had done at Livadiya before FDR arrived. Bedbugs were not the only bugs. Casual remarks by the British about no goldfish in a large tank and the lack of lemon peel for cocktails quickly brought live goldfish and a small lemon tree planted in the hall. But bugs, bedbugs, and bathrooms were the least of the problems.[31]

The run-up to the Yalta Conference included the usual Churchill-Roosevelt games. FDR evaded a serious meeting with Churchill despite the prime minister's insistence that they needed to work things out together before they met Stalin. "I do not see any other way of realizing our hopes about world organization in five or six days. Even the Almighty took seven," Churchill complained. But FDR made their meeting in Malta little more than a brief tourist stop en route to their final destination, more than thirteen hundred miles and a world away from the British colony in the Mediterranean.[32]

At the beginning of 1945 had the Anglo-Americans sought to redirect the thrust of the postwar settlement that had already emerged, they had very little military leverage. The Trinity test of the atomic bomb was five months away, a lifetime in the midst of frantic postwar peacemaking. As the conference opened, the Red Army stood on the Oder River, a mere 40 miles from Berlin, having rolled some 250 miles westward in only three weeks. Soviet forces had liberated almost all of Poland, and the Anglo-Americans assumed the final assault on Berlin was only a few days or weeks away. Meanwhile, Eisenhower's armies were still recovering from the disruption caused by the German offensive in the Ardennes (the Battle of the Bulge). Nervous American diplomats, unaware that the Red Army needed time to consolidate its positions and let its supply system catch up, advised Roosevelt to endorse the occupation zone boundaries for Germany worked out by the European Advisory Commission before Stalin could claim that no agreement existed and moved his forces into the western part of Germany.[33]

Nor did the war against Japan give the Anglo-Americans any psychological advantage. MacArthur and the American Army were still fighting their way through the Philippines and would not liberate Manila until early March. (That came before Berlin fell—just as Stalin predicted to Roosevelt, who claimed to have made shipboard bets on that timetable during his transatlantic voyage aboard the cruiser USS *Quincy*.[34]) The British offensive in Burma would not begin for a few weeks, while U.S. naval operations in the Pacific were suspended until the invasion on February 19 of Iwo Jima, southeast of Japan. And all American planners agreed that Soviet participation in the Pacific war was essential to the invasion of the Japanese home islands if casualties were to be kept at an acceptable level.

The Yalta Conference acquired a distorted image in postwar European and American popular culture that exaggerated its importance, treating it apart from the wartime events that set the stage for the meeting. Fifty years after the Big Three met in the Crimea, a supermodel, appearing in a motion picture depicting her vacuous, if remunerative, occupation, specified the place of the conference in historical memory. Searching for a stark contrast between what she did and what was truly important, she quipped: "I mean, the worst thing that can happen to me is I break a heel and fall down. This is not Yalta, right?"[35]

Mistakenly thinking that history repeats itself, Roosevelt always assumed that the peace settlement would come at a great conference following the end of the war, just as had happened in Paris in 1919, even if the Great Powers were to make the decisions. But by 1945 the arrangements and structure of the postwar peace that were to follow the Second World War had already been determined. To start with, Stalin's axiom—"whoever occupies a territory imposes on it his own social system"—had been followed in Europe by each of the Big Three. The Red Army's occupation of Eastern Europe and the Anglo-American military liberation of Western and Southern Europe came before the Yalta talks. The application of Stalin's axiom was more liberal in countries like Italy and Belgium than in Poland and Hungary, but those outcomes could not be changed at Yalta.

Roosevelt and Churchill tried during and after the Crimea talks to get Stalin to make concessions in Eastern Europe that would improve appearances rather than substance, an approach they had taken since autumn 1944. The Soviet leader, either hostile toward or unbelieving about their domestic political concerns, conceded a few words and phrases but not an inch of control. A vague promise to allow "all democratic and anti-Nazi parties" to participate in "free and unfettered elections" guaranteed nothing for the London Poles since those elections would be supervised by Soviet officials. A tripartite commission for Poland turned out to be just like the one in Italy, only this time the Anglo-Americans were excluded. Stalin was nothing if not a fast learner. Little wonder, then, that Roosevelt and Churchill admitted that implementation of the Yalta accords depended on Stalin's goodwill, for it did.[36]

The Teheran Conference in December 1943 had sketched out the European political picture that emerged. The three leaders agreed to principles for Soviet-Polish-German postwar boundaries as well as for the treatment of Germany. Those general agreements received definition during 1944, particularly through the Morgenthau Plan and the work of the European Advisory Commission, which drew up recommendations for occupation boundaries and policies. Churchill and Roosevelt accepted some of those recommendations, rejected others, and allowed still others to apply by failing to act. But either way, by 1945 the Big Three had set the parameters for much of the German settlement—from presumably temporary occupation zones to the frontiers between the Germans and other European states. By the time the Yalta Conference took place, the only two significant decisions left to make about Germany concerned its economic future: reparations versus reconstruction and reintegration into the European economy and whether Germany would remain a unitary state or be dismembered (beyond the territory already awarded to Poland, the Soviet Union, France, and others).

Although most of the discussions at Yalta about Germany's future took place among the three foreign ministers—Molotov, Eden, and Stettinius—the attitudes of the Big Three set the context. Unconditional surrender, agreed upon from the outset, remained tripartite policy. They all agreed that nazism had to be extirpated and that Germany must never again threaten the peace of Europe. But each had a different take on how best to accomplish that. Stalin's solution was a weak Germany, unable to threaten the Soviet Union. Roosevelt's was a reformed Germany, uninterested in threatening peace. Churchill seemed to see nazism as a veneer imposed by a powerful few. Fearful of the changing power relationships in Europe, he argued against any permanent partitioning of Germany and toyed with the idea of Germany's again acting as Prussia had in the eighteenth and nineteenth centuries: as a British-financed barrier to any powerful rival, this time against Soviet expansion.

Stalin remained quietly adamant that Germany must never be able to threaten Russia, but faced with the enormous task of rebuilding a devastated nation, he talked most about reparations, proposing a ten-year reparations-in-kind program and extensive removals of German industrial plants. Churchill considered the plan unreasonable and impractical. Roosevelt, uncertain about what policy to pursue, avoided specifics. Remembering the American experience following World War I, he rejected any notion that the United States should or would provide aid to assist the Germans in meeting reparations demands or to prevent the collapse of the German economy. He never brought up the issue of postwar reconstruction aid to the Soviet Union—despite, or perhaps because of, Harriman's arguments that the promise of loans could be used to pry concessions out of Stalin. Then, in typically contradictory Roosevelt fashion, he endorsed large short-term reparations from Germany, with half of an estimated twenty billion dollars' worth going to the Soviet Union. But even that agreement was vaguely labeled a "basis for discussion" by a "reparation commission."[37] The tough decisions on German dismemberment and its economy were postponed.

When, in late 1943, Stalin had agreed to enter the war against Japan, both Churchill and Roosevelt understood there would be a quid pro quo that, in Churchill's later words, provided for the " 'restoration' of Russia's position in the Far East." At the Tolstoy talks in October 1944, Churchill and Stalin spelled out the Eastern European settlement in clear terms, even if the two had no appreciation for FDR's careful distinction between "closed" and "open" spheres of influence. That arrangement taken care of, the British prime minister closed the deal by suggesting concessions in the Far East that mirrored what Roosevelt and Stalin agreed to at Yalta.[38]

Thus the Yalta agreement on the Far East, vilified later for "giving away" so much of China to Stalin, did little more than spell out what had been agreed to earlier. Territory and privilege Russia claimed it had lost in 1905 after the Russo-Japanese War were returned: the southern part of Sakhalin Island, the Kurile Islands, and control of railroads in Manchuria. The Big Three confirmed the status of Outer Mongolia, which had been a Soviet-sponsored "people's republic" since the 1920s. Stalin was guaranteed use of two ports, Dairen (Dalian) and Port Arthur (now Lushun), on the Liaotung Peninsula, just west of Korea. (Roosevelt understood the desire for naval bases, although he wanted both ports internationalized, which Stalin rejected in the case of Port Arthur.) All this was to be done with Chiang Kai-shek's approval, but getting that approval was Roosevelt's job.

The arrangement was imprecise but clear. The Soviet Union's position in the Far East was defined in much the same way Churchill had sought to define and limit the Soviet Union's position in Central Europe: clear boundaries and spheres of influence. The United States would have the job of helping China play its role as a Great Power, and Stalin would not interfere. And just as Roosevelt had acquiesced to the Tolstoy bargains, so Churchill approved the Far Eastern settlement.

It may be that Roosevelt sought to eliminate British influence from northern China. He suggested privately to Stalin that they exclude Britain from the occupation of Korea. But that latter proposal was more likely aimed at preventing Britain from being a "trustee" responsible for tutoring Korea (or any other nation) to be independent. Stalin, careful to follow his arrangements with Churchill, warned that "the Prime Minister might 'kill us' " and suggested consulting him.[39]

The subject of Korea never came up again at Yalta, but since the Soviets had already approved the trusteeship principle and wanted it included in the Charter of the United Nations Organization, the president brought up the general concept of international trusteeships over colonial territories. Predictably Churchill exploded in protest: 'I absolutely disagree. . . . After we have done our best to fight in this war and have done no crime to anyone I will have no suggestion that the British Empire is to be put into the dock and examined by everybody to see whether it is up to their standard.'[40] FDR had Stettinius explain to the prime minister that the whole system was "voluntary" except for the defeated Axis nations. But Roosevelt's notion of "voluntary" was different from Churchill's. Even before the president got back to the United States he had renewed his unstinting campaign of "pitiless publicity," damning French colonial rule in Indochina to reporters in an "off the record" press conference on board the USS *Quincy*. But, he told them, when it came to trusteeships, "Stalin liked the idea. China liked the idea. The British don't like it. It might bust up their empire, because if the Indo-Chinese were to work together and eventually get their independence, the Burmese might do the same thing to the King of England. . . ." But there was a bit of bluster in those comments, for he quickly added that "it would only make the British mad. Better to keep quiet just now." Britain was a Great Power, and the Great Powers had to get along.[41]

Roosevelt's agreement to Stalin's territorial proposals in the Far East was political since Soviet intervention was a foregone conclusion so long as the Americans lived up to their promises. General Marshall and his aides at Yalta assumed the Soviets would keep their promise to enter the Pacific war.[42] An amicable arrangement with Stalin gave Roosevelt another opportunity to move toward his postwar vision of a cooperative, civilized Soviet Union. More important, it offered a chance to foster a China that would accept American leadership, which required that Mao not emerge the winner if he were Soviet-sponsored.

The only "new" agreement at Yalta was the Declaration on Liberated Europe, and it proved the most disillusioning agreement of all. Signed by the Big Three, it called for free elections. Yet it was not new, only a restatement of the Atlantic Charter principle: "the right of all people to choose the form of government under which they will live." But the persistent Soviet demand for a "friendly" government in Warsaw demonstrated that none of the anti-Soviet Poles in London would be acceptable in a new Polish government, elected or not, while British actions in Greece and American policy in Italy demonstrated that Stalin's axiom still governed. The declaration was put together with a minimum of time and bargaining, suggesting that all three leaders understood full well what it meant—or did not mean. "It was the best I could do," Roosevelt told one adviser.[43]

The State Department recognized the danger, real and political, of allowing the Soviets free rein in Eastern Europe. During the Malta talks between Stettinius and Eden, the American had mentioned a proposal for an Emergency High Commission to monitor the implementation of what became the Declaration on Liberated Europe, though he admitted that FDR had doubts about the idea. The proposal never went anywhere. Eden, unenthusiastic (he made no mention of the proposal in his memoirs), feared the commission might undercut the authority of the various foreign ministers and then pointed to the fatal weakness. "The Russians," he said laconically, "would find this particularly difficult." Indeed. Presidential adviser James F. Byrnes (brought to Yalta because of his "knowledge of our domestic situation") disliked setting up an independent authority, and FDR, who had been edgy about the broad mandate given the EAC, quickly dismissed the notion. The president never spoke of how the Soviets would react, saying only that he disliked a " 'big' organ[ization]" and preferred meetings of the foreign ministers. But implicit in that comment was his unwillingness to confront Stalin about the political reconstruction of Eastern Europe. The Soviets had to feel secure before liberal democracy could grow; trying to reverse that process could destroy Great Power "harmony" (the conferees' favorite word).[44]

Moreover, the president had consistently opposed formal regional structures in Europe despite Churchill's repeated proposals. Such formal structures could hinder the broad Great Power cooperation Roosevelt believed indispensable to a peaceful world. Just as the persistence of colonial empires prompted him to turn to the UNO to serve as the international trustee, so the political reconstruction of Eastern Europe prompted him to place greater reliance on the United Nations Organization, or at least on the Security Council, where the Great Powers would be represented. There the policemen could conduct an ongoing "summit" meeting, providing the combination of formal and informal discussions that were part of FDR's leadership style.

All that made agreement on the structure of the United Nations come more easily. Roosevelt wanted to take advantage of the strong internationalist sentiment that had developed in the United States and bind Congress to the UNO (Woodrow Wilson's troubles with the League of Nations seemed always in the minds of the Americans). The disputes over the veto and membership left over from the Dumbarton Oaks Conference preoccupied the Americans, particularly Stettinius, more than the British, but those were technical rather than real issues. With the growing importance of the UNO in Roosevelt's scheme of things, compromises (usually favoring the Soviet position) were quickly reached.[45]

Like the United Nations Organization, the Declaration on Liberated Europe perhaps met some inner need of Roosevelt's "for high moral purpose and a statement of American liberal political ideals," particularly given his temporizing on those principles in order to preserve Great Power harmony. Perhaps domestic public opinion in the United States lay behind his endorsement of the declaration. But how could he, or Churchill, have any realistic expectation that those ideals would immediately be implemented anywhere in Europe, particularly in those areas occupied by the Soviet Union? Roosevelt certainly did not believe they could work in postwar France. Even Churchill pulled back from those provisions in the declaration that called for the Allies to "establish machinery," lest that provide a lever for interference in the British Empire or places like Greece. Instead he and Eden changed the wording to a toothless call for the allies to "consult together." Roosevelt may have sincerely wanted to secure for Poland "democratic guarantees through the promise of elections." But as with much of his thinking about postwar policy, liberal goals could be met only in the long term. Winston Churchill once called the Atlantic Charter "not a law, but a star."[46] He and Roosevelt could have said the same for the Declaration on Liberated Europe and most of the Yalta agreements.

The collapse of colonial empires was not a product of Yalta. Neither was the division of Europe or the Soviet-American settlement in the Far East, even if some details were worked out. Neither were the Bretton Woods agreements, which recognized the existing reality of American economic power. Neither was the United Nations Organization, a structure that became more important than Roosevelt ever imagined. In most ways Yalta was a fulfillment of what had already been worked out, no more important than a supermodel's "broken heel."

But the Yalta "myth" became, like the Versailles Treaty and World War I, a misleading symbol of what might have been or, rather, what critics wished had been. Winston Churchill and Franklin Roosevelt came back from Yalta whistling in the dark, trumpeting optimistic predictions that it heralded a new era. "Poor Neville Chamberlain believed he could trust Hitler. He was wrong," said Churchill. "But I don't think I'm wrong about Stalin." The president reported to Congress that "the agreements ought to spell the end of the system of unilateral action, the exclusive alliances, the spheres of influence, the balances of power, and all the other expedients that have been tried for centuries—and have always failed" and expressed confidence that "Congress and the American people will accept the results of this Conference as the beginnings of a permanent structure of peace."[47]

Shortly after the Yalta meeting came another Gilbert and Sullivan–like moment, always appropriate when grand high poobahs meet. It might have been an operetta entitled *Roosevelt and the Three Kings of the Orient.* When the president left Yalta, he toured the battlefield of Balaclava, near Sevastopol, the scene of the Crimean War episode battle made famous by Alfred Lord Tennyson's poem "The Charge of the Light Brigade." He then flew to Egypt where he reboarded the *Quincy,* moored in Great Bitter Lake at the south end of the Suez Canal. Egypt's King Farouk was the first to climb aboard, and after a friendly chat, it was the Oriental king who got the gift: a twin-engine transport plane. On the second day Ethiopia's Emperor Haile Selassie paid a call, chatted greedily about the redistribution of Italy's African empire, and received his gift: four army vehicles.

On the third day Saudi Arabia's monarch, Ibn Saud, arrived with scimitar-waving bodyguards, an astrologer, a food taster, an entourage of more than forty—and a flock of some eighty sheep, in case he got hungry! "A great whale of a man," Roosevelt later told reporters, "sitting there in a Quinze chair . . . upon a great pile of Turkish carpets." FDR had teasingly warned his daughter, Anna, who had traveled with him to Yalta, to stay out of sight lest she be "confiscated" by the king. But better he had warned the Jews in the American party to hide—or, preferably, stand next to him. Saud asked what present he might get, perhaps hoping it would be a supply of the new wonder drug penicillin, in which the king had indicated an inordinate personal interest. FDR, in a feeble attempt to create a good-old-boys atmosphere, reverted to the worst kind of WASP country club humor, suggesting he might offer six million Jews from the United States. Responding with equally bad taste, Saud gave a lengthy and angry diatribe about how bringing more Jews into Palestine would bring war to the region. The king got his present, an airplane. Roosevelt got an uncomfortable education: The next day he predicted a serious confrontation over Palestine. The experience should have been a lesson for Roosevelt that Great Power "eldering" would not always work.[48]

Act Two of the operatic farce came because Churchill, like de Gaulle, feared that FDR would seduce previously compliant monarchs if he "jingled the marvels of independence" before them. Informed of Roosevelt's plans to meet the three kings, the prime minister immediately set up similar meetings, adding the Syrian president for good measure (that must have distressed de Gaulle who already suspected that the British were scheming to prevent the reestablishment of French control over Syria). Churchill made out better in the gift department than Roosevelt, giving Ibn Saud a car and receiving jewels worth twice the price of the motorcar (he turned most of them over to the British government to be sold to pay for the automobile). The prime minister also won a small victory, saying that while the king's religion required that he abstain from alcohol and tobacco, "my religion prescribed as an absolute sacred rite smoking cigars and drinking alcohol before, after, and if need be during, all meals and the intervals between them." Churchill reported Ibn Saud's "complete surrender."[49]

But important as the Middle East was to become, Churchill's and Roosevelt's focus was elsewhere. Throughout the war Roosevelt had warned Churchill and Stalin that American forces would be out of Europe within a few years after Germany's surrender. By war's end the overwhelming majority of Americans called themselves internationalists, but FDR remained concerned that opinion could swing back the other way. When he drafted his speech reporting on the Yalta Conference, avoiding any chance of disillusioning the public was more important than providing a realistic picture of the pluses and minuses.[50] He dared not try to explain that they had to travel some distance to get from old-style power politics to a new internationalism and that the change required compromises and patience. Americans had demanded instant reform after the First World War and then pouted when things did not go as they had hoped. Roosevelt did not want that to happen again.

Churchill faced a different political problem at home. During the Yalta talks the prime minister pointed out that despite his "constantly being 'beaten up' as a reactionary," he was the only one of the Big Three who could be thrown out of office at any time by a vote of his people. This time Stalin played "Lord Root of the Matter," remarking that the prime minister must be worried about the British elections that would come at war's end. The comment hit the mark. The Americans had also detected Churchill's concern about politics at home. When he opposed an early meeting on the United Nations Organization, Hopkins slid a memo to Roosevelt saying that the prime minister's real reasons were hidden. FDR scrawled back: "All this is rot!" Then he crossed out "rot" and substituted "local politics." Hopkins agreed, jotting back, "I am quite sure now that he is thinking about the next election in Britain."[51]

The problem was growing discontent over the settlement with Stalin in Eastern Europe. Churchill's old confidant Lord Beaverbrook confirmed that a few weeks later when he wrote Hopkins that "over Poland the opposition is strong. It is led by a powerful Tory group who are the erstwhile champions of Munich. These followers of Chamberlain make the undercover case that Churchill beat them up in 1938 for selling the Czechs down the river, and now has done to the Poles at Yalta exactly what Chamberlain did to the Czechs at Munich."[52]

A measure in the House of Commons deploring the Yalta agreements on Poland as violations of the Atlantic Charter and of existing treaties failed by a vote of 396 to 25, but as Churchill told the president, there was "a good deal of uneasiness in both parties that we are letting the Poles down." Churchill may have told Harold Nicolson of being "amused . . . that the warmongers of the Munich period have now become appeasers, while the appeasers have become the warmongers," but as Nicolson observed, it was awkward to defend the Polish settlement on grounds of principle while promising Polish soldiers unwilling to go home that they could settle in Britain.[53]

One British MP neatly captured the problem of false, or at least premature, expectations when he told the House: "I believe the real difficulty in which my hon. Friends find themselves is not so much Poland at all. I believe it is in the apparent conflict between documents like the Atlantic Charter and the facts of the European situation. . . . You do not move suddenly from a world in which there are international rivalries into a world where there is international cooperation."[54] That was the warning that Roosevelt failed to give Congress and the American public.

Stalin's performance following Yalta fell far short of the "responsible" behavior expected of one of the world's policemen, and Churchill had no more prepared his public for the gap between ideals and reality than did Roosevelt his. The Soviets took control in Romania, Hungary, and Bulgaria with speed and brutality—an impression strengthened by the growing controversy over Stalin's demands for forcible repatriation of German-held Soviet prisoners of war. Many of those POWs, often from the Baltic states and the Ukraine, refused to return to a homeland now dominated by a "foreign" power, the Soviet Union.[55]

But Poland remained the litmus test. Molotov, who handled the "diplomacy" of the situation, had refused to allow the London Poles any role in the new government, leaving no alternative but the Lublin committee. Since Soviet control over all those areas had long been agreed to by the British, as well as the Americans, style rather than substance was the only cause for concern. Yet a mere two weeks after Yalta Churchill shifted from support of those agreements to arguing that he had been deceived by Stalin. With an election coming up the prime minister found an immediate reason to back away from agreements he could not change but did not like. He could now take the position that Eden and a number of Foreign Office officials (as well as Labour leaders) had begun to advocate: that compromise with Stalin only increased the Russian's appetite, an obvious variation on the critique of appeasing Hitler in the 1930s. The time had come to confront the Soviet Union.

But Churchill had to be careful to protect the benefits for Britain gained by his arrangements with Stalin. He warned Eden on March 5 not to let Foreign Office officials challenge Soviet actions in Romania lest they end up "compromising our position in Poland and jarring Russian acquiescence in our long fight in Athens." A week later he reminded the foreign secretary that Britain had, "for considerations well known to you [i.e., Greece], accepted in a special degree the predominance of Russia in this theatre [Romania]."[56]

If Britain could not stand up to the Soviets, that left only the United States to do the job. On March 8, Churchill asked Roosevelt to do just that. The prime minister explained that he could not protest Russian actions in the southern Balkans lest the Soviets get involved in Greece, but he asked the president to make clear his and Churchill's discontent about events in Romania. Although the prime minister held out hope for Poland, he gave a bleak summary of where things stood in that country. It was the "test case," he argued, for what was meant by "Democracy, Sovereignty, Independence, Representative Government and free and unfettered elections."

Those were trenchant, stirring words that resonated deeply in British and American self-perceptions, although they rang a bit hollow in the aftermath of India, Greece, and Iran or the neocolonialism that developed during the Cold War. More important, they came at the end of a four-year process wherein Stalin had been assured that he could do as he liked in his area of responsibility (or sphere of influence, depending on whether Roosevelt or Churchill was doing the assuring). In the midst of the message to FDR, Churchill referred briefly but revealingly to his political situation: "I must let you know that the government majorities here bear no relation to the strong under current of opinion among all parties and classes and in our own hearts against a Soviet domination of Poland." It was a bit late.[57]

For the next two months Churchill repeatedly pushed the president to challenge Stalin, but FDR's responses were consistent: Let us not be hasty; give the Yalta accords a chance to work. "I cannot agree that we are confronted with a breakdown of the Yalta agreements until we have made the effort to overcome the obstacles," said Roosevelt in a message drafted in the State Department. He, and those drafting his messages, repeated that practical advice over and over, for the only other choice seemed confrontation and the collapse of any hope for postwar cooperation.[58]

Nor could Churchill persuade FDR to enter the "race" for Berlin, even if the president had himself raised that possibility more than a year earlier. Roosevelt's refusal to order a dash for the German capital followed the recommendations of his military advisers who disliked the very idea of a president's interfering with the field commander. Moreover, American generals argued that there was little military advantage in attacking Berlin since the Red Army was in position to launch an offensive. Eisenhower, with Marshall's strong support, insisted on pursuing the military objective, the German Army. Rumors of a last-ditch stand by fanatical Nazis holed up in an strong redoubt somewhere in southern Germany made Ike even more cautious.

But Churchill's argument was openly political, not military. "The Russian armies will no doubt overrun all Austria and enter Vienna," he cabled Roosevelt. "If they also take Berlin, will not their impression that they have been the overwhelming contributor to our common victory . . . lead them into a mood that will raise grave and formidable difficulties in the future? I therefore consider from a political standpoint that we should march as far east into Germany as possible. . . ." This was not the time to debate whether or not the Red Army had in fact "earned" the right to take Berlin.

FDR was not prepared to confront Stalin. The president's response ignored completely the "political standpoint" raised by Churchill and endorsed Eisenhower's plan for the Anglo-American armies to move into central Germany.[59] In addition, why move into eastern Germany, including an attack on Berlin, when the zonal boundaries drawn up by the EAC had assigned that area to the Soviet Union while establishing a quadripartite regime in occupied Berlin? (France was now included—at Britain's insistence—as an occupying power.) One of Ike's key commanders, General Omar Bradley, combined the political and military arguments, wondering whether casualties as high as one hundred thousand were not "a pretty stiff price to pay for a prestige objective, especially when we've got to fall back and let the other fellow take over."[60]

Churchill later pretended to blame the decision on Roosevelt's deteriorating health. "We can now see the deadly hiatus which existed between the fading of President Roosevelt's strength and the growth of President Truman's grip of the vast world problem. In this melancholy void one President could not act and the other could not know."[61]

Roosevelt and Churchill both had returned from Yalta feeling, as the prime minister put it, "tired all through." But the president never recovered his strength. After staying at Hyde Park in hopes of regaining his energies, Roosevelt went on March 30 to "the little White House" in Warm Springs, Georgia, where he always went when he felt ill. During the six weeks between his return to the United States after Yalta and his death on April 12 he drafted fewer of his messages to Churchill than usual, although the ones proposed were always forwarded for his approval to Warm Springs, where, according to Daisy Suckley, he worked (too long and hard, as far as she was concerned) almost every day on "those everlasting piles that are replenished as soon as removed!"[62]

But FDR's health was not why American policy remained constant. He did not have to make significant changes to the draft messages provided him by aides in the White House. The advisers who had been with Roosevelt at Yalta—Hopkins, Byrnes, Admiral Leahy—had returned home believing the president's approach had been successful. Even Harriman in Moscow had not lost faith in Roosevelt's dream of Soviet cooperation, although he was cautious, telling FDR that if the United States was "definite and firm," the Soviets will "make substantial concessions." Avoiding tension and confrontation with the Soviets was the tactic. Within the context of the dispute over the makeup of the "new" Polish government, and with the Soviets preparing for an assault on the German capital, a "race" for Berlin in spring 1945 would have had the wrong effect. Perhaps if the Arnhem operation had worked, or if the German counterattack in the Ardennes had not delayed the Anglo-Americans, things would have been different. But in April 1945 it was too late—if it had ever mattered.

The one incident that prompted Roosevelt to depart from his usual conciliatory and optimistic style with Stalin turned out to be a brief, if nasty, contretemps. It came after the commander of German SS (*Schutzstaffeln*) forces in northern Italy indicated, in February 1945, that he could arrange the surrender of all German troops in the region. Underlying that offer were German hints that they wanted to surrender to the Anglo-Americans and join an alliance against the Soviet Union (following earlier insinuations that without such an alliance the Germans might move back and let the Soviets move into Central Europe). The Office of Strategic Services (the major wartime U.S. intelligence agency) mission in Switzerland, headed by Allen Dulles, eagerly seized an opportunity for a flashy success that would help it in its struggle for resources and survival within the Washington bureaucracy. British and American officials agreed to hold what were designated "preliminary" talks in Bern and informed the Soviets, but at the insistence of the Americans, particularly Dulles, Russian representatives were excluded lest the Germans back out. Roosevelt agreed with that decision after Stimson argued that the Bern talks were "strictly military" and would not get "into political affairs. . . ." Harriman promised the Russians they would be brought into any formal discussions, but Molotov, fearing that the actual deal would be made at Bern, protested that there was no "misunderstanding—it is something worse."

In this case the tit-for-tat exchange of messages between Roosevelt and Stalin is revealing. The president told the Soviet leader that the Bern talks were the actions of commanders in the field and without political implications, but Stalin would have none of it. German armies in northern Italy were neither encircled nor endangered, he argued, so the discussions "must have some other, more far-reaching aims affecting the destiny of Germany." When FDR insisted that no "negotiations for surrender have been entered into," Stalin derisively suggested that Roosevelt was, apparently, "not fully informed." Egged on by Churchill and prompted by General Marshall, who drafted the response, Roosevelt responded angrily to that not-so-diplomatic accusation of "lying" by expressing "astonishment" at the "vile misrepresentations" Stalin had received (a barely veiled retort equivalent to "liar, liar, pants on fire"). Shrewdly Roosevelt (and Marshall) closed with an appeal to the president's personal integrity and the suggestion that if the German commander's purpose was to sow dissension amid the Grand Alliance, then "your message proves that he has had some success." Stalin suggested that having all three Allies represented at all surrender negotiations would avoid "mutual suspicions," pointed out that the Germans seemed to resist the Soviet advance with greater vigor than in western Germany, and then backed off, assuring FDR that his integrity had never been in question. At that point Roosevelt replied that "the Bern incident seems to have faded into the past without having achieved any useful purpose," as was true, since the hints of a German surrender came to naught.[63]

Perhaps FDR was "not fully informed," but his subordinates were, including Stimson. That said, there is no question that Roosevelt had no plan or thought of creating any sort of anti-Soviet coalition or of backing away from demanding unconditional surrender from the Germans. But as Stalin perceptively asked, why would a German army not threatened by defeat choose to surrender? A few, like Allen Dulles and John McCloy, were convinced that there was an "other Germany" that could and should be worked with, but a Nazi SS commander hardly qualified as one of the "other" Germans. Dulles was, perhaps, motivated by a desire to do just what his SS contact suggested: Include Germany in a coalition against the USSR or at least not insist on unconditional surrender.[64] Trivial as the episode turned out to be, it reflected the growing distrust between the Anglo-Americans and their Soviet allies.

Not all the roiling of the waters came from Soviet behavior. Even as Roosevelt struggled with the international political structure, he and his aides continued to promote American liberal economic values. Pressure from Washington for the decolonization of European empires was in part political—Roosevelt believed that they posed a threat to world peace—and in part a matter of security, inasmuch as Roosevelt and his military chiefs wanted to move European outposts farther away from the Western Hemisphere and to extend American military strength. Economic motives also came into play; closed spheres ran counter to traditional American convictions that restrictions on trade were unfair, unwise, and even vaguely immoral.[65] With the president's support, American negotiators tried throughout the war to use lend-lease as a lever to eliminate special trading arrangements between Britain and its Commonwealth. Even in the midst of the Yalta Conference Roosevelt prodded Churchill to open serious official talks on the matter. The prime minister responded with a vague statement about the usefulness of current informal talks and suggested that the entire question be postponed.[66]

Roosevelt had told Churchill in February 1942 that the United States had no intention of asking Britain "to trade the principle of imperial preference as a consideration for lend-lease," but the reality was that lend-lease and British economic concessions were linked. In autumn 1944, for example, the Americans demanded access to commercial air routes within the British Empire—an issue of principle, the liberalization of world trade. As the president put it to the prime minister, "We are doing our best to meet your lend-lease needs. We will face Congress on that subject in a few weeks and it will not be in a generous mood if it and the people feel that the United Kingdom has not agreed to a beneficial air agreement." Churchill could only respond with sarcasm and an appeal to the American sense of fair play. The British never signed that civil aviation agreement, and the United States eventually resorted to bilateral negotiations. What this illustrates is that during the war the Americans developed specific strategies designed to put their assumptions into practice, and FDR supported those strategies.

Concern over congressional opposition prompted Roosevelt to evade any commitment to continuing lend-lease to Britain in the postwar era, but British refusals to endorse American-style liberal economics gave Congress ammunition and added to his reluctance. Most American leaders, and particularly FDR, expressed little concern about Soviet opposition to the "liberalization" of international trade, particularly after the Soviet decision go along with the Bretton Woods accords. The Americans deeply feared the growth in Europe of socialism—the "left"—but expected Great Britain to pose the most immediate major obstacles to liberalized trade. That, and Britain's long-standing role as a major commercial empire, prompted Roosevelt and his cohorts to concentrate on bringing the British around to the American point of view.[67]

The Pacific war, fought where colonial empires were at issue, complicated the European question—more for Roosevelt than Churchill. British concerns were defensive: Hold on to India, "liberate" Singapore and Malaya, keep Hong Kong, and insulate Britain's Asian empire from any sort of international accountability. Over time Stalin's crude behavior in Poland and Eastern Europe could only have helped Churchill's campaign to persuade Roosevelt that British colonialism was far preferable to Soviet domination, as happened in the decade following the Second World War, when the United States "gave priority to anti-communism over anti-colonialism."[68]

But FDR had to focus on winning a war against Japan that could, according to military estimates in the spring of 1945, last up to two more years—with tens of thousands of American casualties. This assumed that Britain and, more significantly, the Soviet Union would participate actively in the fight. Even if FDR had not had a postwar vision of perpetuating the Grand Alliance, he could not risk alienating the Soviets in Europe lest Stalin renege on his commitments to join the war in the Pacific.

The atomic bomb would become the ultimate "complication," and Roosevelt may have sensed that. When Stettinius spoke to FDR and General Marshall about the bomb, presumably asking if it should be mentioned to Stalin, the general opposed raising the issue. FDR must have agreed, for the subject was not broached during the talks. The Manhattan Project leaders did not expect to have a test explosion until August (the test came on July 16) but the president continued to refuse to discuss the bomb with Stalin, even though the Americans understood that the Soviets knew about the project. From the outset Roosevelt, and most of his advisers, were reluctant to share the atomic secret, even with the British, who had provided early assistance with the project. Byrnes claims that he had been thinking of the political implications of the bomb months before the Yalta talks; certainly Stimson had as well. But who knows about FDR? The last recorded comments he made about atomic research came in his final meeting with Churchill, a luncheon aboard the *Quincy* in Great Bitter Lake, just after Roosevelt met with his three kings. The prime minister described a proposal for continued British work, presumably on both a bomb and atomic energy. The president offered no objections, commented that the commercial value of atomic energy seemed less likely than they had thought, then said "the first important trials" would be in September 1945.[69]

The massiveness of the Soviets' invasion of Manchuria in August 1945 suggests that they could very well have entered the war months earlier if "alliance" had been what Stalin had had in mind. But like the Anglo-Americans and the second front, the Soviet leader saw no reason to sacrifice his men and resources when the Americans were willing to do the brunt of the fighting, even though the Soviets were prepared for their invasion of Manchuria well in advance of the actual attack. Stalin could have been conducting "atomic diplomacy" even without a bomb. His growing knowledge of the details of the Manhattan Project may have prompted him to step up plans for an attack on Japan just in case the new weapon could end the war quickly. At any rate, enter the war quickly is precisely what he did after the dropping of the Hiroshima bomb.

Despite his knowledge of the Manhattan project, Stalin did not give his atomic program unlimited support until after the Americans had dropped that bomb on Hiroshima. Given his apparent ignorance of the bomb's potential, Anglo-American secrecy about the Manhattan Project did not undermine, in a fatal way, Roosevelt's efforts to perpetuate Great Power cooperation. Along with British Spitfires, the (much-overpraised) Norden bombsight, and the Ultra/Magic code-breaking successes, the atomic secret was just another example of the West's war-long refusal to share military technology, even if some Soviet requests related clearly to postwar rather than wartime use. (Nor did the Soviets fully share their intelligence with their allies.) Keeping the Manhattan Project secret from Stalin only reinforced Soviet suspicions that the anti-

Bolshevik crusade would be renewed at war's end and that they had best look to their own security. "The question of Poland is not only a question of honor but also a question of security," Stalin told Churchill and Roosevelt. "Throughout history, Poland has been the corridor through which the enemy has passed into Russia."[70]

But in spring 1945 the bomb was not the overriding factor. As the USS *Quincy* steamed east through the Mediterranean from Cairo, word came of the American invasion on February 19 of the small island of Iwo Jima, 650 miles southeast of Tokyo and desired as an air base for the strategic bombing campaign against Japan.[71] Despite massive American bombing and shelling (which had only made the Japanese defenders dig in deeper into the volcanic rock), the campaign took five weeks instead of two, with more than twenty-three thousand American casualties.

Even as that battle ended, the bloody and frightening invasion of Okinawa followed. Officially one of the "home islands" of Japan, Okinawa was defended by major forces as well as by kamikaze pilots willing to crash their planes into the enemy's ships. The operation, which began on April 1, involved more than five hundred thousand American troops and twelve hundred warships; only the Normandy invasion was bigger. Just seventy-four hundred of some seventy-seven thousand Japanese regular troops survived; casualty figures of twenty thousand Okinawan militia are less certain. The Americans suffered nearly fifty thousand casualties. The battle did not end until late May and early June, two months after FDR's death.

But the Pacific war always played a secondary role in the Churchill-Roosevelt relationship, whatever their arguments over colonial empire in Asia. It was the Americans' war, a theater they jealously guarded, using Admiral King as the point man. Churchill wanted to insert British forces into the final stages of the campaign, but King and the rest of the Americans held him at arm's length. They wanted the Russians to tie down Japan's Kwantung (Quangdong) Army in Manchuria, but the invasion and subsequent occupation of Japan belonged to the United States.[72]

By the time Franklin Roosevelt died on April 12, 1945, the war in Europe was virtually over. Thirteen days later Soviet and American army forces met at Torgau on the Elbe River, nearly a hundred miles south of Berlin and deep inside the occupation zone assigned the Soviet Union. (The Americans withdrew as called for by the EAC zonal boundary agreements, as they would have from Prague or Vienna or any other territory occupied in a "race" against the Red Army.) Hitler cheated justice five days later by committing suicide, and on May 8, the German military commanders who had succeeded him surrendered—unconditionally.

Franklin Roosevelt's death followed a massive cerebral hemorrhage. Stalin seemed "deeply distressed" and revealed his own insecurity when he suggested to the State Department that an autopsy be performed to see if the president had been poisoned. Churchill quickly cabled both Harry Hopkins and Eleanor Roosevelt his condolences. To the president's wife he wrote of having lost "a dear and cherished friendship which was forged in the fire of war." To Hopkins he wrote: "I feel a very painful personal loss, quite apart from the ties of public action which bound us so closely together. I had a true affection for Franklin." The prime minister's speech before the House of Commons five days later focused on the good years of their personal alliance—before the Americans and the Russians came to dominate the war, when war was "exciting" for Churchill. By the time of Roosevelt's death the Churchill-Roosevelt relationship had become routine—more than a facade, but less than the personal, near friendship that it had been. That too was much more than a matter of FDR's declining health.

Anglo-American wartime closeness, the "special relationship" during World War II, had always been made up of two parts. One part was the traditional ties of language, culture, and the permanently intertwined history that comes from the colonial relationship. The other part of the equation was the special threat posed to Britain by Hitler's Germany, a threat that prompted Churchill to turn to the Americans, and Roosevelt to respond. Churchill gambled Britain's survival and his career on that response, and as he told the Commons after FDR's death, "There was never a moment's doubt, as the quarrel opened, upon which side his sympathies lay."[73] But with the end of the war in Europe the "special relationship" became half as strong.

Churchill's first message to the new president, Harry Truman, suggested just how "public" the Roosevelt-Churchill relationship had become: "I hope that I may be privileged to renew with you the intimate comradeship in the great cause we all serve that I enjoyed through these terrible years with him."[74] It is doubtful that the new "comradeship" Churchill proposed could ever become "intimate" without being forged in another war, but either way, events intervened.

Postscript

Henry Kissinger, writing as a self-confessed realist, has used the Far Eastern settlement after World War II to disparage the apparent contradictions in FDR's actions: "Roosevelt had granted Stalin a sphere of influence in northern China to encourage him to participate in a world order that would make spheres of influence irrelevant."[75] Kissinger, apparently unaware that Churchill had outlined the Far Eastern settlement before the president agreed to Stalin's requests, understood that Roosevelt hoped to persuade the Soviets to take part in a new world order, but concluded that the president knew full well it would have spheres of influence. Why else his four policemen?

But the nature of Roosevelt's spheres of influence was different from what Stalin established in Eastern Europe (though not in Manchuria and North Korea, where direct Soviet military intervention was not a factor during the postwar era). Nor were Roosevelt's ideas what Churchill had in mind for Britain's colonial and neocolonial empires.

Roosevelt's awkward, imprecise, poorly articulated distinction between "closed" or "exclusive" spheres of influence and what might be called "open" spheres was the bridge he tried to construct between the structure proposed by Churchill and Stalin and the one suggested twenty-five years earlier by Woodrow Wilson. FDR tried to make Wilsonian idealism practical. "Open spheres" would permit the flow of culture, trade, and the establishment of what he called "free ports of information." He seems casually to have assumed that such openness would, in the fullness of time, expand American-style political and economic liberalism since those concepts worked. He had seen Wilson's experiment collapse under the weight of nationalism and political insecurity. Why bother to re-create that system if it would only fail?

Adolf Berle caught part of Roosevelt's distinctions when, in September 1944, he wrote: "A Soviet 'sphere of influence' in these areas [Eastern Europe] operated in somewhat the same fashion as we have operated the good neighbor policy in Mexico and the Caribbean area would be no threat to anyone." But Berle also recommended that the United States practice "prompt and careful elimination of political responsibility," particularly in Eastern Europe, where it had no leverage, allowing Americans to take the moral high ground by remaining aloof from situations they did not like (reminiscent of what George Kennan was to recommend in his "long telegram"). That position of aloof superiority was not at all what Roosevelt thought would work. Cooperation did not mean lecturing one's partners but working with them. Roosevelt's policemen would succeed or fail together.[76]

Churchill, eager to create a long-term Anglo-American entente, allowed himself to support Roosevelt's scheme, although the prime minister never understood "open" spheres, nor did he embrace full cooperation with the Bolsheviks. But his options were more limited. Britain had never been able to protect its interests by exercising the kind of raw power that the Americans and the Soviets had developed by the end of the Second World War. Churchill tried to position his nation as best he could, but his choices were uncomfortable.

Joining a coalition to defeat Hitler was the only rational choice in the early war years. Hitler triumphant, or even in power, was unacceptable. But lining up with the Soviets was almost as politically and morally unpleasant. Nor had Stalin given any indication that he would meet Britain halfway. A "swap" of little Greece for all of Eastern Europe was hardly even. Soviet ideology made that state an unlikely ally in Britain's struggle to hold on to its empire, colonial and neocolonial, in the face of pressures for national self-determination and social reform. That left the Americans, who posed no ideological challenge but, in Churchill's mind, might act, as Kennan later described, like a great prehistoric monster, slow to realize his interests are threatened but once aroused laying "about him with such blind determination that he not only destroys his adversary but largely wrecks his native habitat."[77] The problem was that the Americans, at least under Roosevelt's leadership, saw their goals and even their interests threatened by Britain and its empire, as much as by the Soviet Union and its ideology.

For both Roosevelt and Churchill, security and ideology combined to pose serious difficulties. In mid-1943 Eden's private secretary, John Harvey, perceptively observed:

> America is an old-fashioned country itself, fearful of political and economic change, and its bankers, business men and politicians side naturally with the Right and Right Centre in Europe. Yet, under the stimulus of Russia and of a strong Leftward wind in England, Europe is moving Leftwards. The "comfortable" capitalist regimes of pre-war are doomed. Unless it is to be communist, it must at least be Beveridge [social welfare]. The bitterness against the Pétains and Quislings has not penetrated to America.[78]

But he misgauged the Americans. A State Department briefing paper prepared for the Yalta Conference warned that the postwar governments in Europe "must be sufficiently to the left to satisfy the prevailing mood in Europe and to ally Soviet suspicions. Conversely, they should be sufficiently representative of the center and *petit bourgeois* elements of the population so that they would not be regarded as mere preludes to a Communist dictatorship."[79] It was good advice—be all things to all men—but it was hardly practical. What FDR did, and with Churchill's support at Yalta, was play for time. Create a structure that would do more than just avoid war between the Great Powers, but allow those policemen to learn to work together and thus to trust one another.

The day before Roosevelt died, the same day that he closed the Bern episode with Stalin, he personally drafted a short message to

Churchill. "I would minimize the general Soviet problem as much as possible because most of these problems, in one form or another, seem to arise every day and most of them straighten out as in the case of the Bern meeting.

"We must be firm, however, and our course thus far is correct."[80]

It was classic FDR. Don't be distracted by side issues. Soviet cooperation was far more important than small insults. The enemy of progress is the search for perfection. Roosevelt did not move to challenge the Soviet Union before his death, nor is there any evidence that he would have done so, without provocation, had he lived. He did not so much deny the contradictions in the world he had helped create as refuse to accept them as inevitably destructive.

In late 1942 Roosevelt had sent his friend Thomas Lamont some observations on Soviet-American relations. Back in autumn 1933 Roosevelt had told the Soviet ambassador in the United States, Maksim Litvinov, during arguments over terms of American recognition of the Soviet regime: "Your people and my people are as far apart as the poles." Litvinov replied: "In 1920 we were as far apart as you say. . . . In these thirteen years we have risen in the scale to, let us say, a position of twenty. You Americans . . . have gone to a position of eighty . . . in the next twenty years we will go to forty and you will come down to sixty. I do not believe the rapprochement will get closer than that." Roosevelt then told Lamont, "Perhaps Litvinov's thoughts of nine years ago are coming true." Sometime in 1943 he spoke to Harriman about "his hopes for a gradual blurring of differences between the two systems" and to Sumner Welles about how the USSR had moved toward "a modified form of state socialism" and the United States toward "true political and social justice." The two would never reach the middle ground, he judged, but they could perhaps get to a 60–40 relationship. That "convergence" thesis, as Harriman put it, was fundamental to Roosevelt's postwar vision.[81] What happened in the spring of 1945 was that Churchill, never persuaded that Bolshevik revolutionaries could ever become defenders of the status quo, lost confidence in Roosevelt's grand strategy. At the same time and afterward Stalin lived up to all of Churchill's dire predictions, and then some.

Speculating about what would have happened had Roosevelt lived is silly. He died. Churchill did not have that historical advantage of dying at the moment of victory, though he made up for it by writing his memoirs. Three months after Roosevelt's death Churchill was turned out of office as the British public focused its attention on the less "exciting" issues of postwar reconstruction and social reform and chose the Labour party to lead it. Three weeks later the Japanese surrendered.

But the structure that Churchill and Roosevelt helped create, even if it was not what either had in mind, what historians have come to call the Yalta system, lasted for nearly fifty years—until the early 1990s, when the Soviet Empire crumbled. During that time the old colonial empires collapsed only to be replaced by less formal ones, nationalism changed the maps time and again, and the Great Powers—the Anglo-Americans and the Soviets—confronted each other. But they never went to war directly, and Europe, the cockpit of war for the first half of the twentieth century, avoided that horror. In one sense Yalta firmed up a settlement that, like the Congress of Vienna, created an era of peace—or, more precisely, an era without war.

Yet that ignores the ceaseless near wars and wars by proxy that took place in what Americans and Europeans casually dismissed as the "third world." In Korea, Vietnam, and Afghanistan, the Soviet Union and the West fought each other. In Germany, Hungary, Poland, Cuba, and even in the tiny Caribbean island of Grenada, they challenged each other in ways that brought the world to the brink of war. At the same time the third world nations fought the "foreigners" who tried to control their politics, their economies, and their beliefs. Yesterday's reform is always today's problem, which Roosevelt tried to confront and Churchill tried to ignore.

Former Soviet Foreign Minister Eduard Shevardnadze, writing his memoirs in the early 1990s, argues that "even though we had lived 45 years without a war, a war was actually going on—precisely because of the order established in Europe after 1945."[82] All he had to do was stretch that analysis to include the entire world.

But that Cold War perspective distorts history. Caught up in the celebratory atmosphere of the 1990s, Britons and Americans have focused on all that went wrong with the results of the Second World War, forgetting that few, if any, of those "mistakes" could have been made if Hitler's Germany and militaristic Japan had won or even survived the war intact. Winning the Second World War was the prerequisite to all the failures, and all the successes, that followed. Had Churchill and Roosevelt chosen to fight the war solely for postwar advantage against Russia, communism, and the left, they could not have won the struggle. But almost always, when faced with crucial choices about victory versus postwar political advantage, Roosevelt, Churchill, or both made the decision to keep the Grand Alliance together and to defeat the Axis. They could not solve all the political, social, and economic problems of the world, but they could lead their nations to victory and prevent a far worse set of problems.

And they did.

Lifestyles of the rich and famous

Appendix:
On Health and the History of the
Second World War[1]

Popular history has it not only that Roosevelt "gave away" Eastern Europe and too much of the Far East to Stalin at Yalta but that the President did so because he was a frail, sick, dying man.[2] It did seem as if a generation was leaving the scene. Pa Watson, Roosevelt's military aide who served primarily as gatekeeper and crony, died aboard the *Quincy* heading home from Yalta. Harry Hopkins, chronically ill to begin with, had a petty quarrel with Watson just before his death; then Hopkins's own health forced him to leave the ship and fly home. (That greatly annoyed FDR, who had counted on Hopkins to help draft a speech to Congress and the public about the Yalta Conference. Sadly Roosevelt died before his most loyal friend ever saw him again.)[3]

Churchill lived on for twenty years after the Second World War, serving another term as prime minister and dying at the ripe old age of ninety-one. His physical condition during the war never became an issue, despite a 1966 memoir by his physician (Charles Wilson, later Lord Moran) that suggested that Churchill's health played a significant role in his decision making. Churchill's aides and family quickly rallied around his memory and roundly dismissed the charges, condemning Moran for violating the patient-doctor privacy. Yet Churchill was often much sicker than FDR, suffering angina pectoris during his visit to Washington in Decem-

ber 1941 and nearly dying of pneumonia after the Teheran Conference, necessitating a long convalescence at Marrakech. In late
December 1944, just before the Yalta Conference, John Colville
feared that Churchill was "hopelessly tired and at seventy his powers of recuperation may not be very good." After the prime minister had returned from Yalta, he told Harold Nicolson "that he
felt 'tired all through.' "[4]

But considered policy, not health, determined Churchill's decisions. At the 1944 Tolstoy Conference in Moscow and again at
Yalta, the prime minister accepted Soviet predominance in Eastern
Europe and Northeast Asia, his later pretense of British opposition
and helplessness to the contrary notwithstanding. He made the
agreements because he believed they were in Britain's best interests, not because he was ill. As for his drinking, whatever the effect
of his prodigious consumption of alcohol, it was a lifetime habit,
not a temporary response to the pressure and tension of wartime
leadership. There is no evidence, factual or anecdotal, to indicate
that Churchill's drinking affected his policies during the war any
more than it affected his policies before the war.

Many of Roosevelt's health problems were either caused by his
paralysis or accentuated by that condition. His anemia stemmed
from bleeding hemorrhoids, made chronic by his inability to walk
or stand. His confinement to a wheelchair made him susceptible
to upper respiratory problems and continual chest and sinus congestion (all exacerbated by cigarette smoking), hence his liking for
the "sinus treatments" he received from his personal doctor and
crony, Rear Admiral Ross McIntire.

But there was more to FDR's poor health than the aftereffects
of polio. He had high blood pressure, so high in autumn 1944 as
to constitute what his doctor, heart specialist Howard Bruenn,
called "a bona fide medical emergency" that could cause brain and
other organ damage, although Bruenn did not conclude that such
damage had occurred. In 1943 Roosevelt's increasingly high blood
pressure prompted his doctors to put him on digitalis (which can
bring on a gray pallor and loss of appetite) and to insist on significant loss of weight. In December of that year, immediately after
the Teheran Conference, he had a serious attack of what he called

the "grippe," but what was actually congestive heart failure aggravated by hypertension. As Bruenn confided in his notes, "After this he failed to regain his usual vigor and subsequently had several episodes of what appeared to be upper respiratory infections. There had been occasional bouts of abdominal distress and distention, accompanied by profuse perspiration."[5]

More troubling, insufficient blood supply to the brain—a result of his high blood pressure, congestive heart disease, lung congestion, and anemia—caused occasional periods of forgetfulness, a condition called secondary metabolic encephalopathy. There can be little doubt that he was having such an episode at the Yalta Conference when those much-printed photographs of a slack-jawed, gape-mouthed FDR were taken. Roosevelt was unquestionably ill at Yalta, exhausted by the physical and mental stress of wartime leadership and the cumulative debilitating effects of his paralysis. Following the conference he repeatedly complained of tiring quickly, and once he went to recuperate in Warm Springs, Georgia, on March 30, he never regained his strength.[6]

But, as with Churchill, illness and tiredness did not determine his policies. Whether or not Roosevelt knew how ill he was is likewise a red herring. Nothing he did at Yalta, or immediately afterward, altered the approach he had taken throughout the war, an approach toward a postwar settlement that, by the time of the Yalta talks, had been outlined in some detail. His assessment of Stalin may have been overoptimistic and mistaken, but that was a conscious and consistent position, not a matter of health.[7]

ENDNOTES

Chapter 1: The Players

1. "Pink and cuddly," is from Robbins, "Reporting Churchill," 10; Bryant, *Turn of the Tide,* 263.
2. General V. Freyberg: recollection (September 3, 1940), in Gilbert, ed., *The Churchill War Papers,* II, 781. See p. 707 for John Colville's description of Churchill, during an air raid, "wearing his flowery dressing-gown and a tin hat."
3. Quoted in Gilbert, *Churchill: A Life,* 69.
4. Henry Pelling, "Churchill and the Labour Movement," in Blake and Louis, eds., *Churchill,* 128. But the differences were deeper than that implies.
5. Rose,*Churchill,* 277.
6. Robert Blake, in his essay "How Churchill Became Prime Minister," asserts that a Conservative party election in May 1940 to choose a new head of the party and presumably Chamberlain's successor would undoubtedly have chosen Foreign Secretary Lord Halifax, not Churchill: Blake and Louis, eds., *Churchill,* 264.
7. Ward, *A First-Class Temperament,* 93n.
8. Ibid., xiii.
9. The characterization is from Morgan, *FDR,* 261–62. For his foreign policy articles, see F. D. Roosevelt, "Our Foreign Policy: A Democratic View," and "Shall We Trust Japan?"
10. The quotation and remarks about the three losers is from Weinberg, *A World At Arms,* 119; the Norwegian fiasco is placed in context in Chapter 3. Churchill's comment is from his memoirs as quoted by Rose, *Churchill,* 318. For Chamberlain's resignation and Churchill's selection, see Blake, "How Churchill Became Prime Minister," Blake and Louis, eds., *Churchill,* 257–73.
11. Burns, *The Lion and the Fox* repeatedly cites such public opinion polls; see, for example, 399–400. For some examples of seemingly contradictory poll results, see Kimball, *The Most Unsordid Act,* 57–58.
12. Quoted in Burns, *Lion and the Fox,* 449.
13. Quoted in Leutze, *Bargaining for Supremacy,* 219. FDR's early predictions are in Reynolds, *Anglo-American Alliance,* 67. His hope that Hitler would be assassinated or overthrown was expressed as early as January 1939: Cole, *Roosevelt and the Isolationists,* 305.
14. This is the argument of historians like Arthur Schlesinger, Jr., Robert Dallek, and Thomas A. Bailey, all seeming to agree with Burns's claim that "Roosevelt was less a great creative leader than a skillful manipulator and a brilliant interpreter": Burns, *Lion and the Fox,* 400–04. Reynolds in *The Creation of the Anglo-American Alliance* finds that until autumn 1941 Roosevelt continued to hope the United States could avoid all-out war.
15. Manfred Landecker, *The President and Public Opinion* (Washington: Public Affairs Press, 1968), 123, n.7.
16. This thesis is buttressed by the evidence in Schneider, *Should Amer-*

ica Go to War?, although, like most, he argues that public pressure "forced" Roosevelt to move slowly. Taft's position is described in Shogan, *Hard Bargain*, 110.

17. Rose, *Churchill*, 331; D. J. Wenden "Churchill, Radio, and Cinema," in Blake and Louis, eds., *Churchill*, 215–39, examines Churchill's image-building efforts.

18. Paul Fussell's *Wartime*, which attacks the romanticizing of the Second World War, received strong criticism. For an example of Anglo-American tension as headline news, see *The New York Times*, July 11, 1984, 1.

19. See Hitchens, *Blood, Class, and Nostalgia*, esp. 180–86; Sullivan, "Winstoned! America's Churchill Addiction," *New Republic*. For Churchill leading the United States into the Cold War, see Harbutt, *The Iron Curtain*.

20. Lash describes the relationship in the subtitle of his book *Roosevelt and Churchill, 1939–1941: The Partnership That Saved the West*. The popular view of Churchill can be most easily found in the pages of the Churchill Society publication *Finest Hour*. As for scholars, the wartime volumes of Gilbert's official biography *Winston S. Churchill* follow closely the picture drawn by Churchill in his own history, *The Second World War* (cited as WSC). Recent examples of Churchill as hero and savior are Jablonsky, *Churchill: The Great Game and Total War*, and Lukacs, *The Duel*. A summary of the literature is Boyle, "The Special Relationship." Among the more important assessments of the "special relationship" are the essays in Louis and Bull, eds., *The "Special Relationship"*; Reynolds, "A 'Special Relationship' "; Dobson, "Special in Relationship to What?"; Thorne, *Allies of a Kind*; Charmley, *Churchill's Grand Alliance*.

21. Sainsbury, *Churchill and Roosevelt at War*, xi; Sherwood, *Roosevelt and Hopkins*, 364; de Gaulle, *War Memoirs*, 574.

22. Eden is quoted in Reynolds, *Anglo-American Alliance*, 266. The Tom Sawyer image is that of Gelb, *Anglo-American Relations, 1945–1949*, 47. Taylor, *English History, 1914–1945*, 577. See also Rose, "Churchill and Zionism" and Kimball, "Wheel Within a Wheel," both in Blake and Louis, eds., *Churchill*.

23. The warning is that of Edmonds, *The Big Three*, 18. See the working papers published by the Cold War International History Project at the Woodrow Wilson Center in Washington, D.C., for examples of the latest new evidence from Soviet sources. Transliteration from Chinese to English is done throughout this book in the Wade-Giles system, as was the case during the Second World War.

24. This was the suggestion of Soviet diplomat Ivan Maisky in "Maisky's Note" dated January 11, 1944, as quoted in Pechatnov, "The Big Three After World War II."

25. These conferences were: Atlantic (August 1941), 1st Washington (December 1941–January 1942), second Washington (June 1942), Casablanca (January 1943), third Washington (May 1943), first Quebec (August–September 1943), first Cairo (November 1943), Teheran (November–December 1943), second Cairo (December 1943), second Quebec (September 1944), Malta (February 1945), Yalta (February 1945), Great Bitter Lake, Egypt (February 1945).

26. The Churchill-Stalin meetings were both in Moscow, in August 1942 and October 1944.

27. Rex Applegate, who had been a bodyguard for FDR, recalled "sit-

ting in earshot when Roosevelt and Churchill met at Shangri-la—you should have heard them cuss each other out!" Found, with thanks to Lloyd Gardner, in Wills, *The Second Civil War*, 63. Churchill, convalescing in Marrakech, said of Roosevelt: "I love that man." *Moran Diaries*, 243.

28. Churchill's Victorianism is discussed in Kimball, *The Juggler*, 66–67, and seen as an asset by Jablonsky in *Churchill: The Great Game and Total War*.

On FDR's fears of Churchill's drinking habits, see Beschloss, *Kennedy and Roosevelt*, 200. When Roosevelt and Canadian Prime Minister Mackenzie King met in April 1940, they spent much of the time gossiping about Churchill's drinking: J. L. Granatstein, *Canada's War*, 117. When Churchill became prime minister, Roosevelt commented he "supposed Churchill was the best man that England had, even if he was drunk half of his time": Reynolds and Dimbleby, *An Ocean Apart*, 136. Wendell Willkie, asked by Roosevelt in 1941 if Churchill was a drunk, replied that he had as much to drink as Churchill did when they met, "and no one has ever called me a drunk." See Kimball, *The Juggler*, 225–26, n.6. The Roosevelt martini is described with distaste by Bohlen, *Witness to History*, 143. See Sherwood, *Roosevelt and Hopkins*, 115, for some other "vile" concoctions, and Ward, ed., *Closest Companion*, 163, for a story of Churchill spitting out a mouthful of what FDR's cousin, Polly Delano, made with different kinds of rum and called a Tom Collins.

29. *Moran Diaries*, entry for February 5, 1945, 240. See also Morgan, *FDR*, 759. Averell Harriman claimed that Roosevelt saw Churchill as "pretty much a nineteenth century colonialist": Harriman and Abel, *Special Envoy*, 191. Sherwood describes Churchill's White House quarters: *Roosevelt and Hopkins*, 203. For the concerns of New Dealers see, for example, the diaries of Henry Morgenthau, Jr., at the Franklin D. Roosevelt Library (Hyde Park, New York [FDRL]), or the diaries of Assistant Secretary of State Adolf Berle, *Navigating the Rapids*. See also Harbutt, *The Iron Curtain*, esp. 15–19. FDR's "wonderful old Tory" comment is from Gunther, *Roosevelt in Retrospect*, 16. Goodwin, *No Ordinary Time*, 312, quotes Mrs. Roosevelt's letter to Anna; Freidel, *Franklin D. Roosevelt*, quotes Eleanor Roosevelt's quip about FDR in the nineteenth century; Harvey, *War Diaries*, 228 (March 11, 1943).

30. Churchill later denied delivering such a line, but there are three different sources for the basic story: Sherwood, *Roosevelt and Hopkins*, 442–43; Ward, ed., *Closest Companion*, 384–85; and citations in Gilbert, *Road to Victory*, 28.

31. Dalton Diary, July 21, 1941; Cadogan Diaries, July 17, 1941; Cadogan Diaries, July 21, 1941, 393; Duff Cooper to Churchill, July 22, 1941, PREM 3/224/2, 69–70.

32. For example, despite a number of written pleas from me and other historians, a number of PREM 3 files for late 1941 on British relations with Japan remain closed. The dubious accusations of Rusbridger and Nave, *Betrayal at Pearl Harbor*, would likely be laid to rest if those and other relevant but still-closed British files were opened for research.

33. A recent study of Churchill's problems with domestic politics during the war is Jefferys, *The Churchill Coalition*.

34. Kennedy's retrospective memoir (a dubious source) is quoted in Beschloss, *Kennedy and Roosevelt*, 200, 230. See also Sherwood, *Roosevelt and Hopkins*, Wilson, *The First Summit*, 80–81; Harry Hopkins to Felix

Frankfurter, December 14, 1948, Frankfurter papers, box 102, folder 2112. For Churchill's revised recollection of their meeting, see WSC, I, 440.

Elliott Roosevelt, the president's son, and Joseph Lash, who edited FDR's letters, thought Winston S. Churchill and FDR met in Washington on July 26, 1917, at a luncheon. But as the staff at the Franklin D. Roosevelt Library in Hyde Park has determined, the Winston Churchill who had a meeting with Woodrow Wilson was an American painter: FDR to Eleanor (she at Campobello Island), July 26, 1917, Elliott Roosevelt, ed., *F. D. R. His Personal Letters*, 354.

35. Kimball, *Churchill & Roosevelt*, I, 23. The *Marlborough* volume was inscribed: "With earnest best wishes for the success of the greatest crusade of modern times." Churchill's ambivalence about the New Deal was balanced by his praise for the repeal of Prohibition.

36. Begbie, *The Mirrors of Downing Street*, 104.

37. For an instructive lesson in reading the perspectives of historians, see the discussions of Roosevelt's maneuverings in 1940 by Burns, *Lion and the Fox*, 408–18, 422–30; and Shogan, *Hard Bargain*, 95–116. Each offers fundamentally the same evidence, but one exculpates while the other condemns.

38. WSC, II, ix. Churchill's talent and efforts are discussed in Robert Rhodes James, "Churchill the Parliamentarian, Orator, and Statesman," in Blake and Louis, eds., *Churchill*, 503–17. Murrow is quoted in Reynolds, "1940," in *Churchill*, 254.

39. Dean Acheson, "The Supreme Artist," 36–40.

40. Quoted in Kimball, *Most Unsordid Act*, 154; and Morgan, *FDR*, 686.

41. Colville in Wheeler-Bennett, *Action This Day*, 60. The list of such memoirs grows daily, but Colville, *The Fringes of Power* is typical. This picture of fondness is challenged by Churchill's crony and intelligence adviser Major Desmond Morton, who claimed that "his junior staff, with few, if any, exceptions, disliked him to the point of detestation. He treated them like 'flunkeys,' without any apparent interest in them or humanity." Quoted in Thorne, *Allies of a Kind*, 117n. Colville claims that Morton's usefulness dropped off during the war and that Churchill used him less and less. Colville closes bitingly: "because he had been over-ambitious he died a sad and embittered man": *The Fringes of Power*, 760. See also Gilbert, *In Search of Churchill* for additional examples of praise from those who worked for Churchill.

42. Suckley diary, March 31, 1945, Ward, ed., *Closest Companion*, 403.

43. Goodwin, *No Ordinary Time*, 350, 459, 480.

44. Interview with Edward Foley, general counsel, U.S. Treasury Department 1939–1942 (Washington, November 3, 1966). See also the puzzled, hurt comments made by Morgenthau during various Treasury Department meetings about his discussions with Roosevelt. Those talks are in the Henry Morgenthau, Jr., diaries, Franklin D. Roosevelt Library, Hyde Park, NY (hereafter FDRL), particularly in the presidential diaries. General George Marshall commented: "I always felt that he treated Mr. Morgenthau rather roughly, and I always thought it was for my benefit because they were close friends and neighbors": Bland, ed., *Marshall Interviews*, 515. Two examples of embittered ex-Roosevelt aides are Raymond Moley and James Farley. For Harriman's remarks, see interview with Herbert Feis, November 10, 1953, Harriman papers, box 872, Feis Interviews; and Harriman recollections, November 16, 1953, Harriman papers (LC), Feis files.

45. Kimball, *Churchill & Roosevelt*, II, C-330. Hinsley, "Churchill and the Use of Special Intelligence," in Blake and Louis, eds., *Churchill*, 407–26; WSC, V, 662; Jacob in Wheeler-Bennett, *Action This Day*, 186–89. The phone call to Bletchley Park story was told by Sir Harry Hinsley, who received the call.

46. Quoted in Heinrichs, *The Threshold of War*, 140; and Presidential Diary, August 4, 1941 (Morgenthau papers, FDRL).

47. Kimball, *Churchill & Roosevelt*, I (R–198), October 24, 1942.

48. Churchill's personal physician, Lord Moran (Dr. Charles Wilson), discusses his patient's mental health in his Diaries, 179–80 et al. Daisy Suckley, in a letter to Roosevelt of September 16, 1935, refers to his being depressed, but it was not the kind of melancholy that visited Churchill. The summer of 1935 was politically difficult and stressful for FDR, and he responded with unusual testiness: Ward, *Closest Companion*, 32.

49. Martin, *Downing Street*, 43.

50. Ward, *A First-Class Temperament*, 629.

51. One of the rare examples is "The President at Home," an account by a British officer, Lieutenant Miles, of a weekend with President and Mrs. Roosevelt, Hyde Park, October 31–November 2, 1943, PRO, FO 371/38516/122037 (courtesy of Verne Newton).

52. Ward, *A First-Class Temperament*, 725.

53. On Hopkins's health, see Sherwood, *Roosevelt and Hopkins*, 92–93, 118–22, and McJimsey, *Harry Hopkins*; Hull's conditions are detailed in Gellman, *Secret Affairs*, 30, 359–60. On Stalin's health, see Edmonds, *The Big Three*, 32.

54. FDR to Suckley, January 20, 1943 (at Casablanca), Ward, *Closest Companion*, 199. Reports of FDR's elevated blood pressure are in ibid.

55. The December 1941 problem is from Moran, *Churchill*, 17ff. Churchill's temperature is mentioned in Martin, *Downing Street*, 158, and Churchill to Roosevelt, August 31, 1944 (C-773), Kimball, *Churchill & Roosevelt*, III, 302.

56. Edmonds, *The Big Three* summarizes Churchill's health problems on 363–68.

57. The most plausible description of Churchill's steady drinking is Jacob, in Wheeler-Bennett, *Action This Day*, 182–83. The other stories are in James, *Anthony Eden*, 262n.; Gilbert, *Finest Hour*, 336, n.1; Sherwood, *Roosevelt and Hopkins*, 241; Dilks, ed., *Cadogan Diaries*, 707. Arthur Bryant, *The Turn of the Tide*, 566; Bryant, *Triumph in the West*, 187. Eden's report is in Eden, *The Reckoning*, 494 (emphasis added). The Cherwell estimate is quoted in Wilson, *The First Summit*, 53–54. The C. P. Snow remark is from personal correspondence. All the references to Churchill's drinking in Gilbert, *In Search of Churchill* take the weak "mouthwash" position.

58. Kimball, "Dieckhoff and America," 230–32. A persuasive study of British overestimates of German strength is Kimche, *The Unfought Battle*. Churchill's separation of external and internal matters is discussed in Rose, *Churchill*.

59. Roosevelt is quoted in Divine, *Roosevelt and World War II*, 53. For a recent claim that American isolation was a factual reality in the nineteenth century, see Rossini, "Isolationism and Internationalism in Perspective," pp. 11–23.

60. Rock, *Chamberlain and Roosevelt*, 32. "Military isolationism" is the phrase of Barnett, "Anglo-American Strategy in Europe," 178.

61. The latest assessment is Parker, *Chamberlain and Appeasement*.
62. Rock, *Chamberlain and Roosevelt*, 85–86 and passim. For British-Soviet relations in this period see Parker, *Chamberlain and Appeasement*, 222–45.
63. The transcript of the meeting is "Conference with the Senate Military Affairs Committee, Executive Offices of the White House, January 31, 1939, 12:45 P.M.," President's Personal File 1-P, FDRL.
64. Butow, "The F. D. R. Tapes," 8–24; *Presidential Press Conferences*, No. 523 [115], February 3, 1939; No. 525 [140, 141], February 17, 1939; Cole, *Roosevelt and the Isolationists*, 306, 307.
65. Conference with the Senate Military Affairs Committee, January 31, 1939, PPF 1-P (FDRL), 16, 17, 18. The use of "Axis" to describe the coalition is taken from the 1936 Italo-German agreement known as the Rome-Berlin Axis, after Hitler and Mussolini called their nations' relationship "the axis on which the rest of the world would turn."
66. The Dieckhoff quotes are from reports to the Foreign Office in *Documents on German Foreign Policy*, No. 440, 689–90 and No. 391, 605. For discussions of these issues that both agree and differ, see MacDonald, *The United States, Britain and Appeasement*; Rock, *Chamberlain and Roosevelt*; Hearden, *Roosevelt Confronts Hitler*; Ovendale, *"Appeasement" and the English Speaking World*; Cohen, *Empire Without Tears*.
67. A recent summary by a Russian historian is Rzheshevsky, "The Soviet-German Pact of August 23, 1939," 13–32.
68. Stalin's "gamble" is persuasively described by Miner in "Stalin's 'Minimum Conditions,' " in Sevost'ianov and Kimball, eds., *Soviet-U.S. Relations*, 72–87, and Miner, *Between Churchill and Stalin*.
69. On the Soviet delay in occupying eastern Poland, see Weinberg, *A World At Arms*, 55–56. Kennedy is quoted in Dallek, *Roosevelt and American Foreign Policy*, 198.
70. This curious British interpretation was advanced casually by A. J. P. Taylor, more seriously by Maurice Cowling, and repetitively by John Charmley.
71. Roosevelt to Churchill, letter of September 11, 1939, Kimball, *Churchill & Roosevelt*, I, R-1x. Roosevelt misspelled Marlborough, but Churchill diplomatically did not correct the error.
72. Ibid., I, 3; II, C-386; I, R-194. Gray's Inn is one of London's old and honored legal associations.
73. The phrase of Alex Danchev, "Great Britain: The Indirect Strategy," in Reynolds, Kimball, Chubarian, eds., *Allies at War*, 2.
74. WSC, IV, 603.
75. "Nazi" is the acronym for Hitler's political organization, the *Nationalsozialistiche deutsche Arbeitpartei*, founded in 1919. Whatever reformist ideas it pretended to advocate, however it tried to picture itself as an alternative between communism and exploitative capitalism, the party was merely a vehicle for Hitler's virulent racialism and personal power.

Chapter 2: "If Britain Is to Survive"

1. Beschloss, *Kennedy and Roosevelt*, 200.
2. Kennan, *Memoirs*, 161.
3. Generally on FDR and his ambassadors, see Dallek, *Roosevelt and Foreign Policy*. Lothian's impressions of FDR are quoted in Rock, *Chamberlain and Roosevelt*, 212n. Ambassador MacVeagh, in December 1943, had supported a British proposal for a regent to replace the Greek king. FDR disliked the British plan and warned MacVeagh not to associate himself with it: Iatrides, ed., *Ambassador MacVeagh Reports*, 406–08. Donovan's role is well described in Smith, *The Shadow Warriors*; "cookie pushers" is from Bohlen, *Witness to History*, 135; "professional priesthood" is the phrasing of Arthur Schlesinger, Jr., *New York Times*, op-ed page, August 25, 1988.
4. Rock, *Chamberlain and Roosevelt*, esp. 28–33, 111; Lash, *Roosevelt and Churchill*, 24–28; Reynolds, *Anglo-American Alliance*, 16–25; Watt, *How War Came*.
5. Reynolds, *Anglo-American Alliance*, 85–87; Charmley, *Churchill's Grand Alliance*, 3–4.
6. Churchill to Chamberlain, October 4, 1939, Chamberlain papers, NC July 7, 1964; Reynolds, *Anglo-American Alliance*, 87; Lash, *Roosevelt and Churchill*, 23.
7. Reynolds, *Anglo-American Alliance*, 87.
8. Ibid., 87–88.
9. Schrader "Diary," October 1939, 4–12, Navy Historical Center; Churchill-Roosevelt/telephone-1, October 5, 1939, in Kimball, *Churchill & Roosevelt*, I, 25. Gilbert concludes that Roosevelt initiated the phone call, although that is not absolutely clear: *Finest Hour*, 54–55, and Lord Fraser, "Churchill and the Navy," 80–81. During this telephone call (there is no record of others at this time) Churchill apparently promised to write FDR. A month later he apologized for not having done so, explaining that the two cables he had sent "gave all my news": Kimball, *Churchill & Roosevelt*, I, C-2x.
10. The FDR quotes are from Sherwood, *Roosevelt and Hopkins*, 125; Divine, *The Illusion of Neutrality*, 296. "Feeding" is in Leutze, *Bargaining for Supremacy*, 46.
11. Quotes from Divine, *Illusion of Neutrality*, 289; Rosenman, *Working with Roosevelt*, 191. See also *Presidential Press Conferences*, 14:135 (September 5, 1939) and 14:149 (September 8, 1939).
12. Freda Kirchwey, quoted in Divine, *Illusion of Neutrality*, 312.
13. Kimball, *Churchill & Roosevelt*, I, C-1x (October 5, 1939); C-2x (October 16, 1939).
14. Kimball, *Churchill & Roosevelt*, C-3x (December 25, 1939). Churchill sent FDR a full description of the *Graf Spee* incident, aware that like himself, FDR enjoyed naval stories.
15. Kimball, *Churchill & Roosevelt*, C-5x, C-6x, C-7x, R-2x, R-3x. In R-2x (February 1, 1940), Roosevelt referred to "our conversations," which suggest he and Churchill spoke occasionally on the telephone.
16. Woodward, *British Foreign Policy*, I, 160–61.
17. Kimball, *Churchill & Roosevelt*, I, C-5x, C-6x; Churchill's memo, quoted in Gilbert, *Finest Hour*, 117.
18. Kimball, *Churchill & Roosevelt*, I, R-2x (February 1, 1940).

19. *Presidential Press Conferences*, 15:139 (February 9, 1940); for Hitler as "nut" and "wild man" see Conf. with Senate Military Affairs Committee, January 31, 1939, PPF 1-P (FDRL), 4–5, 7–8.

20. Freidel, *Roosevelt*, 329; Gilbert, *Finest Hour*, 191–92.

21. This is the argument of Reynolds, *Anglo-American Alliance*, 69–72. In a different sort of "Wilsonianism," the State Department warned Welles to keep in mind that "history has shown the danger" of "indicating that we are collaborating with the British for common peace terms." State Department to Welles, February 29, 1940, Welles papers, FDRL, box 155, "memoranda, Jan–Feb 1940." The Welles papers were opened at the FDR Library too late for full use in this study, but my cursory examination suggests that those papers do not provide any unequivocal explanation of Roosevelt's intentions.

22. The British record of Welles's talks with them is most revealing. See Woodward, *British Foreign Policy*, I, 164–72. For the day-by-day details of the Welles mission, see Gellman, *Secret Affairs*, 166–202. Gellman dismisses the chance that the mission was a serious effort to arrange a peace settlement.

23. Quoted in Gilbert, *Churchill: A Life*, 635.

24. WSC, I, 581.

25. Ibid., 657.

26. Charmley, *Churchill: The End of Glory* happily chronicles the faulty Norwegian plans and Churchill's narrow escape, 380–92.

27. *Presidential Press Conferences*, 15:239–242 (April 9, 1940); 15:265–66 (April 18, 1940).

28. Churchill's designation as prime minister is discussed above, Chapter 1.

29. Gilbert, ed., *Churchill War Papers*, II, Randolph Churchill recollection (May 18, 1940), 70–71.

30. Kimball, *Churchill & Roosevelt*, I, C-9x (May 15, 1940) (emphasis added); on a commitment to France, see ibid., C-14x, C-15x, R-6x, C-16x, R-7x, C-17x, C-18x.

31. Kimball, *Most Unsordid Act*, 54; Kimball, *Churchill & Roosevelt*, I, R-4x (May 16, 1940).

32. Kimball, *Churchill & Roosevelt*, I, C-10x, C-11x, C-17x; Reynolds, *Anglo-American Alliance*, 115–20; Leutze, *Bargaining for Supremacy*, 73–80; Shogan, *Hard Bargain*, 193–202.

33. Kimball and Bartlett, "Roosevelt and Prewar Commitments to Churchill," 291–311. Bearse and Read, *Conspirator* adds detail and context but draws the same conclusions. Magic intercepts indicate that late in 1941 Japanese agents believed anti-interventionist leaders Charles Lindbergh and Robert McCormick planned to use the Kent documents in a scheme to impeach Roosevelt: Morgan, *FDR*, 583.

34. On Hitler's pause, see Irving, *Göring*, 289–90.

35. WSC, II, 118. Ellipses are omitted from the speech to enhance readability; Spears, quoted in Charmley, *The End of Glory*, 411–12. Some have claimed that this speech was recorded for radio broadcast by an actor impersonating Churchill; the evidence, which does not bear out the tale, is sifted in Wenden, "Churchill, Radio, and Cinema," in Blake and Louis, eds., *Churchill*, 236–39. The "home ground" comment, a reference from soccer, is quoted in Jacob, in Wheeler-Bennett; *Action This Day*, 175.

36. Roosevelt, *FDR/PPA*, 1940, 259–64.

37. Sulzberger, *American Heritage Picture History of World War II*, 95. Hitler appeared to be dancing his jig in the second film in Frank Capra's *Why*

We Fight series of motion pictures made for the U.S. Army. The photograph was actually of Hitler at his headquarters in Belgium, edited to suggest Compiègne. For the broad story of British efforts to influence American public opinion, see Cull, *Selling War.*

38. On the Ultra intercepts, see Smith, *The Ultra-Magic Deals.*

39. Kimball, *Most Unsordid Act*, 54–56; Cantril, ed., *Public Opinion*, 82, item 14.

40. Kimball, *Churchill & Roosevelt*, I, C-16x, C-17x, C-18x June 14, 15, 1940). Churchill to Lothian, June 28, 1940, and Churchill interview with Edgar Ansel Mowrer, July 17, 1940, both in Gilbert, ed., *Churchill War Papers*, II, 436, 533. Brendan Bracken, an adviser to Churchill, called Mowrer's write-up of the interview "awful" and persuaded Mowrer not to print it: ibid., 534–35.

41. Kimball, *Churchill & Roosevelt*, I, C-19x (July 9, 1940); Oursler, "Secret Treason," 52–68.

42. Reynolds, "Churchill the Appeaser? Between Hitler, Roosevelt and Stalin in World War Two," in Dockrill and McKercher, eds. *Diplomacy and World Power*, 201–02; Colville, *Fringes of Power*, July 24, 1940, 200.

43. Reynolds, *Anglo-American Alliance*, 115, 116.

44. For two differing pictures of what led to Roosevelt's nomination for a third term, see Burns, *Lion and the Fox* and Shogan, *Hard Bargain.*

45. Hurstfield, *America and the French Nation*, 53, 162; Reynolds, *Anglo-American Alliance*, 119.

46. Kimball, *Churchill & Roosevelt*, I, C-18x (June 15, 1940).

47. The formal documents of the deal, which were immediately made public, are in Kimball, *Churchill & Roosevelt*, I, C-25x, R-10x, C-26x.

48. Reynolds, *Anglo-American Alliance*, 65.

49. Pollock, "Roosevelt, the Ogdensburg Agreement, and the British Fleet," 203–19; Shogan, *Hard Bargain*, 207.

50. Quoted, in Davis and Lindley, *How War Came*, 86.

51. Quoted in Shogan, *Hard Bargain*, 222.

52. Tully, *F. D. R.: My Boss*, 244.

53. Shogan, *Hard Bargain*, 233.

54. Ibid., 11.

55. Churchill is quoted in Reynolds, *Anglo-American Alliance*, 169. For a penetrating portrait of Hull, see Gellman, *Secret Affairs.*

Chapter 3: "A Year of Indecision"

1. Lee, *Goering*, 91. Ultra and detection of German radio beams used to guide air attacks gave the British some warning of raids. But it took only six minutes for German bombers to cross from France to England, so such advance warning left little time to prepare. See Hinsley, *British Intelligence*, I, Chapter 10 and Appendix 9. "Blitz" is derived from the German word *Blitzkrieg* (lightning war). Churchill quotes himself in WSC, II, 340.

2. Churchill was later accused of sacrificing Coventry in order to keep the secrets of British intelligence (ULTRA and radio beam detection) from the Germans. That appears to be a canard; see Hinsley, *British Intelligence*, I, appendix 9.

3. Gilbert, *Finest Hour*, 963.

4. Kimball, *Churchill & Roosevelt*, I, R-9x (August 19, 1940).
5. Ibid., I, R-11x/A; R-11x/B.
6. Hurstfield, *America and the French*, 20–21.
7. Leutze, *Bargaining for Supremacy*, 162.
8. Roosevelt's comment was made to Lothian; Gilbert, *Finest Hour*, 805.
9. WSC, II, 530.
10. *Presidential Press Conferences*, 16 [255], October 4, 1940.
11. Dallek, *Roosevelt and Foreign Policy*, 250; Kimball, *Most Unsordid Act*, 77–78.
12. Kimball, *Churchill & Roosevelt*, I, C-37x; III, C-816, C-817, R-646.
13. Colville, *Fringes of Power*, November 1, 1940, 283; Reynolds, *Anglo-American Alliance*, 148–50.
14. Hinsley, *British Intelligence*, I, 481–83.
15. Reynolds, "Lord Lothian and Anglo-American Relations," 48–49; Churchill, *The Birth of Britain*, 474.
16. Sherwood, *Roosevelt and Hopkins*, 222.
17. Kimball, *Most Unsordid Act*, 107.
18. Kimball, *Churchill & Roosevelt*, I, 87-111 (C-43x and various drafts).
19. Kimball, *Most Unsordid Act*, 116–17.
20. *Presidential Press Conferences*, 16 [350–56] December 17, 1940.
21. Sherwood, *Roosevelt and Hopkins*, 226–27; Rosenman, *Working with Roosevelt*, 260–61; Kimball, *Most Unsordid Act*, 128–30. The obvious lack of democracy in the Soviet Union raised concerns that the phrase might prevent extending aid if the rumored German attack took place, but that was too esoteric to consider in December 1940.
22. See Doenecke, *In Danger Undaunted*, 16–18.
23. Kimball, " '1776': Lend-Lease Gets a Number," 260–67; Kimball, *Most Unsordid Act*, 206–07, 216–18.
24. WSC, II, 569.
25. Kimball, *Churchill & Roosevelt*, I, C-9x (May 15, 1940).
26. Leutze, *Bargaining for Supremacy*, Chapters 14–15; memo from Marshall to General [Leonard] Gerow, January 17, 1941, in Larry Bland, ed., *The Papers of George Catlett Marshall*, II, 391–92. There is some confusion about the "C" in the abbreviation ABC. Did it mean "Canadian" or "conversations"? American records show the former; British records, the latter. Either way the Canadians did not participate.
27. Andrew, *For the President's Eyes Only*, 107; Smith, *The Ultra-Magic Deals*, 43–63. The British did not pass the Ultra secret to the Americans until 1942, and even then only in bits and pieces.
28. PREM 4/17/1/86–94 (PRO).
29. Kimball, *Churchill & Roosevelt*, I, 119–24.
30. Sherwood, *Roosevelt and Hopkins*, 4–5, 236. Churchill had earlier introduced Sir Walter Citrine to Roosevelt using the clause "He has the root of the matter in him"; Kimball, *Churchill & Roosevelt*, I, C-42x (November 1940). Hopkins's central heating promise is from Martin, *Downing Street*, 39.
31. Marquis Childs quoted in Sherwood, *Roosevelt and Hopkins*, 203.
32. Ibid., 13; WSC, III, 24; Pogue, *Organizer of Victory*, 434.
33. Oliver Lyttelton quoted in Gilbert, *Finest Hour*, 986. Sherwood heard a rumor of this story but discounted it; *Roosevelt and Hopkins*, 242.
34. Halifax to Sir John Simon, March 21, 1941, Halifax papers. For the

exchanges about Lloyd George and Halifax, see Kimball, *Churchill & Roosevelt*, I, C-46x, R-18x, C-48x.
35. Quoted in Beschloss, *Kennedy and Roosevelt*, 229.
36. Kimball, *Churchill & Roosevelt*, I, 140.
37. Ibid., I, C-52x, C-66x.
38. Colville, *The Fringes of Power*, 443 (September 28, 1941). SIGINT (signals intelligence) is obtained from intercepting and deciphering radio communications.
39. Quoted in MacDonald, *The Lost Battle*, 254. The British lost nine warships while two battleships, a carrier, three other warships were temporarily put out of action. More than eighteen hundred crew members were killed: ibid., 297.
40. Churchill and Roosevelt were extremely worried about rumors that the French battleship *Dunkerque* would be transferred to the Germans: Kimball, *Churchill & Roosevelt*, I, C-74x, C-75x, R-32x, R-33x, R-35x, C-78x.
41. WSC, III, 122–23; Churchill's first use of the term to FDR was on March 19, 1941: Kimball, *Churchill & Roosevelt*, I, C-69x.
42. Kimball, *Churchill & Roosevelt*, I, 192–98.
43. Ibid., I, R-36x (April 11, 1941); R-38x (May 1, 1941); Sherwood, *Roosevelt and Hopkins*, 310; Henrikson, "The Map as an 'Idea,'" 19–53.
44. Kimball, *Churchill & Roosevelt*, I, C-81x, C-82x.
45. Churchill to Eden, May 2, 1941, PREM 3/469/350; Kimball, *Churchill & Roosevelt*, I, R-38x (May 1, 1941); C-84x (May 3, 1941); R-39x (May 10, 1941).
46. Kimball, *Churchill & Roosevelt*, I, 207–08.

Chapter 4: "History Has Recorded Who Fired the First Shot"

1. The degree of Soviet unpreparedness remains open to debate. Immediately before the invasion Soviet forces were not alerted or ready for an immediate response, apparently to avoid providing Hitler with any pretext for war. A collection of intelligence documents available to Stalin suggests that he believed the Germans would use their military buildup to leverage more raw materials from the Soviet Union, thus prompting him to think he could buy more time to prepare: Federal'naia sluzhba bezopastnosti Rossii, *Sekrety Gitlera na stole u Stalina* (courtesy of Steven Miner). See also Kimball, *The Juggler*, 23–24, esp. n.7; Oleg Rzheshevsky, "The Soviet Union: The Direct Strategy," in *Allies at War*, 30–37. Churchill's ambiguity is quoted in Gardner, *Spheres of Influence*, 86; and CAB 120/691 (PRO), as quoted in Smith, *Sharing Secrets with Stalin*, 12.
2. Kimball, *Churchill & Roosevelt*, I, C-100x (June 14, 1941); WSC, III, 369.
3. Quoted by Rzheshevsky, "The Soviet Union," in *Allies at War*, 31, and in Weinberg, *A World at Arms*, 266. Statistics from Weinberg and the *Oxford Companion*. The military strategy and tactics of the Soviet-German war are treated in Glantz and House, *When Titans Clashed*.
4. Kimball, *The Juggler*, 24–28; Gilbert, *Finest Hour*, 1119. Truman's remark is from *The New York Times*, June 24, 1941, 7, quoted in LaFeber, *America, Russia, and the Cold War*, 6. For a perceptive look at American

wartime attitudes toward Stalin and the Soviet Union, see Alexander, " 'Uncle Joe,' " 30–42 (in Russian).

5. Sherwood, *Roosevelt and Hopkins*, 308–22; Kimball, *The Juggler*, 30–32.

6. Cadogan diary (microfilm), July 17, 1941; Dalton diary, July 21, 1941; *Cadogan Diaries*, July 21, 1941, 393.

7. Colville, *Fringes of Power*, 404 (June 21, 1941); Walter Citrine to Duff Cooper, July 7, 1941, Citrine papers. Citrine, a Trades Union Congress and Labour party leader, had supported Churchill's calls for rearmament before the war, opposed the radical wing of the Labour party, and condemned the Communists. He was obviously Churchill's kind of Labour leader. "Bowing down in the House of Rimmon" is a biblical reference to someone who conforms to an immoral requirement or custom (II Kings 5:18).

8. Gorodetsky, *Stafford Cripps' Mission to Moscow*, 198; Beaumont, *Comrades in arms*; Langer, "The Harriman-Beaverbrook Mission," in Laquer, ed., *The Second World War*, 300–19; Gilbert, *Finest Hour*, 1142–43.

9. *Stalin-Churchill Correspondence*, no. 4, 12–14; no. 6, 16.

10. Stalin's admission is in Military Report by H. L. Ismay, October 6, 1941, Great Britain, Cabinet Office, Cabinet papers (CAB) 120/36, enclosure II to the report of the Moscow Conference, September 29, October 1, 1941) (PRO). The Soviet ambassador in London, Ivan Maisky, spoke similarly, although he suggested there was, for the political leaders, "an overriding responsibility": Gorodetsky, *Cripps' Mission*, 196–98.

11. Sherwood, *Roosevelt and Hopkins*, 320.

12. Kimball, *The Juggler*, 32–36; the military recommendation came on September 11, 1941, only a month after Hopkins had returned from Moscow; Sherwood, *Roosevelt and Hopkins*, 417; Wilson, *The First Summit*, 77.

13. Sherwood, *Roosevelt and Hopkins*, 321–22, 308, 315; Gorodetsky, *Cripps' Mission*, 200.

14. Lash, *Roosevelt and Churchill*, 369.

15. Stalin's démarche, which began *before* Barbarossa and continued immediately afterward, is summarized succinctly in Gardner, *Spheres of Influence*, 79–89. See Feis, *Churchill, Roosevelt, Stalin*, 657–60, for a summary of the history of the Curzon Line.

16. Kimball, *Churchill & Roosevelt*, I, R-40x, C-87x. The persistence of Stalin's suspicions is in Andrew, "Anglo-American-Soviet Intelligence Relations," Lane and Temperley, eds., *Rise and Fall of the Grand Alliance*, 127. Perhaps if and when the British government releases the one remaining War Office file on Hess still closed, we will be able to sort out the truth, although the chain of speculation and accusation is now so twisted that final answers are unlikely; see Costello, *Ten Days to Destiny* and Kilzer, *Churchill's Deception*, which offer the various conspiracy theories, though both require a leap of faith. Hess's disclosures about Barbarossa are on p. 447 of Costello's book. Gilbert's treatment of the Hess affair in *Finest Hour*, 1087–88, is so scanty as to raise suspicions that relevant files were removed from the Churchill papers. British government refusals to open the files have prompted suspicions that prominent persons, perhaps even the royal family, were involved.

17. Kimball, *Churchill & Roosevelt*, I, R-50x (July 14, 1941). FDR wrote in this message of British deals concerning areas of the old Austro-Hungarian Empire, not Soviet territorial proposals, but he knew about Stalin's maneuvers.

18. Eden, *The Reckoning*, 316.

19. Kimball, *Churchill & Roosevelt*, I, C-50x (July 14, 1941). A classic presentation of Wilsonian arguments is Adolf Berle to Roosevelt, "Post-War Commitments," July 9, 1941, Map Room papers, FDRL.

20. In 1943 Hull used Krock to force Roosevelt to push Sumner Welles out of the State Department: Gellman, *Secret Affairs*, 316, 320. A year later Hull leaked information to Krock that helped undermine Roosevelt's endorsement of the Morgenthau Plan for Germany.

21. Roosevelt rarely spoke directly of Wilsonian failures, but the inferences were clear; see *The Juggler*, 187, 271–72. *Churchill & Roosevelt*, I, R-50x (July 14, 1941); Sherwood, *Roosevelt and Hopkins*, 311.

22. Zubok, "Cooperation or 'Go Alone,' " 24.

23. For full details on the background to the Atlantic Conference (codenamed Riviera) and the conference itself, see Wilson, *The First Summit*.

24. Poet Arthur Hugh Clough as quoted by Churchill in a radio address of April 27, 1941; James, ed., *Churchill: His Complete Speeches*, 6378–84. For Roosevelt's message, see Kimball, *Churchill & Roosevelt*, I, R-23x.

25. Quoted in Gilbert, *Finest Hour*, 1165. The Gray's Inn meeting is discussed above, p. 15. The impressions of Churchill and Roosevelt are from Wilson, *The First Summit*, 97–100. Churchill also designated Attlee the deputy prime minister, an unofficial title.

26. Sherwood, *Roosevelt and Hopkins*, 311.

27. Hinsley, *British Intelligence*, II, Chapter 19; Andrew, *For the President's Eyes Only*, 135–36. The significance of that intelligence coup was proved when the Germans made extensive changes in their cipher system in February 1942, "blinding" British code breakers for ten months. During that time German U-boats nearly cut the Atlantic supply lines.

28. The well-chosen words of Wilson, *The First Summit*, 127.

29. Ibid., 192, concludes that the *Daily Herald* (London) christened the declaration the Atlantic Charter.

30. Theodore A. Wilson, "The First Summit: FDR and the Riddle of Personal Diplomacy," in Brinkley and Facey-Crowther, eds., *The Atlantic Charter*, summarizes the drafting of the charter and provides more detail in *The First Summit*. The British draft was written at Churchill's instruction by Alexander Cadogan during the Atlantic Conference: *Cadogan Diaries*, 398.

31. Report to Congress, August 21, 1941, Roosevelt, *FDR/PPA*, 10: 334. The Four Freedoms speech and its antecedents are discussed in Burns, *Soldier of Freedom*, 33–35.

32. The charter began with the declaration that neither the United States nor Britain sought additional territory, a disavowal of the kinds of secret treaties that had stimulated the territorial scramble following the First World War. But while that injunction against self-aggrandizement aimed at quieting the American anti-interventionists, it also fell under the broad rubric of self-determination. The Atlantic Charter is printed in *Foreign Relations of the United States* (FRUS), 1941, I, 367–69. Attlee's comments are from the London *Daily Herald*, August 16, 1941, quoted in Louis, *Imperialism at Bay*, 125.

33. Harrod, *Keynes*, 512.

34. WSC, III, 437.

35. Kimball, *Churchill & Roosevelt*, I, R-80x, C-165x (not sent); Wilson,

"The Road to Bretton Woods," 46; Meade diary, file 1/1, 52 (September 22, 1943).

36. For the Anglo-American negotiations on the lend-lease master agreement, see Kimball, *The Juggler*, 43–61; Colville, *The Fringes of Power*, 433 (August 30, 1941).

37. Minute by Cadogan, May 6, 1943, FO 371: 35311 (U 2062), quoted in Louis, *Imperialism at Bay*, 123, n.5.

38. Quoted in Reynolds, "The Atlantic 'Flop': British Foreign Policy and the Churchill-Roosevelt Meeting of August 1941," in Brinkley and Facey-Crowther, eds., *Atlantic Charter*, 136.

39. CAB 65/19, WM 84(41), August 19, 1941 (italics added). Three months later Churchill repeated that claim in a message to South African Prime Minister Jan Smuts: "He [Roosevelt] went on to say to me 'I shall never declare war; I shall make war. If I were to ask Congress to declare war they might argue about it for three months' ": Churchill to Smuts, November 9, 1941, FO 954/4A/100670, 340 (Dom/41/24), PRO. But Churchill made no mention of such a promise from Roosevelt in a cable to Smuts sent only a month after the Atlantic Conference, referring only to American naval actions that they had agreed upon; Churchill to Smuts, September 14, 1941, ibid., 333. See also Reynolds, *Anglo-American Alliance*, 202, n.38, and 213–20, n.116.

40. Sherwood, *Roosevelt and Hopkins*, 365, 355.

41. *Cadogan Diaries*, 396 (August 6, 1941); Wilson, "First Summit" in Brinkley and Facey-Crowther, eds., *Atlantic Charter*, 18; Gilbert, *Finest Hour*, 1176–77. The letter to Randolph Churchill was sent on August 29, 1941.

42. Cole, *Roosevelt and the Isolationists*, 438, 439.

43. Ibid., 441.

44. The conclusion of Wilson, "The First Summit," in Brinkley and Facey-Crowther, eds., *The Atlantic Charter*, 21. The vote for war in 1917 was 82–6 in the Senate, 373–50 in the House.

45. Quoted in Paterson et al., *American Foreign Relations*, II, 219; Heinrichs, *Threshold of War*, 195.

46. Quoted in Hurstfield, *America and the French*, 74.

47. Churchill offered Singapore to the Americans in his first message as prime minister to FDR: Kimball, *Churchill & Roosevelt*, I, C-9x.

48. That is the theme offered by Gellman, *Secret Affairs*, though he does not discuss Hull's exclusion from the Atlantic Conference.

49. Kimball, *Churchill & Roosevelt*, I, R-53x (August 18, 1941).

50. See Barnhart, *Japan Prepares for Total War*.

51. Wilson, *The First Summit*, 206–11, summarizes the evolution of the statement but argues the changes were crucial.

52. The literature on this is becoming extensive. The best known study is Dower, *War Without Mercy*. For a short course see the essays in Iriye and Cohen, eds., *American, Chinese, and Japanese Perspective on Wartime Asia, 1931–1949*. For a brief, perceptive summary of the misunderstandings see Larrabee, *Commander in Chief*, 85–91.

53. Stalin to Churchill, September 3, 1941, *Stalin-Churchill Correspondence*, no. 10.

54. Quoted in Larrabee, *Commander in Chief*, 240. It was the only meeting between FDR and Stevenson.

55. Herring, *Aid to Russia*, 14–17; Kimball, *Churchill & Roosevelt*, I,

239; Gilbert, *Finest Hour*, 1178; Kimball, *The Juggler*, 37–41; Langer, "The Harriman-Beaverbrook Mission," in Laquer, ed., *The Second World War, Marshall Interviews*, 514. Harriman's adventures with the Bolsheviks are described in Abramson, *Spanning the Century*, 139–63.

56. See Kimball, *Churchill & Roosevelt*, I, C-124x, C-125x; Dallek, *Roosevelt and American Foreign Policy*, 291; Bratzel and Rout, "FDR and the Secret Map," 167–73; Andrew, *For the President's Eyes Only*, 102–03; Andrew, "Anglo-American-Soviet Intelligence Relations," in Lane and Temperley, eds., *Rise and Fall of the Grand Alliance*, 112–14.

57. Gilbert, *Finest Hour*, 1180; Kimball, *Churchill & Roosevelt*, I, 268–74.

58. Kimball, *Churchill & Roosevelt*, I, R-62x; C-136x. Maud was the code name assigned by the British to their atomic research program.

Chapter 5: "It Is Fun to Be in the Same Decade with You"

1. This discussion among FDR and his Cabinet is quoted in Dallek, *Roosevelt and American Foreign Policy*, 307. Hull is quoted by Burns, *Soldier of Freedom*, 157. Utley, *Going to War with Japan*, 170–73, suggests that the White plan could have broken the stalemate, as did George Kennan thirty years later; Larrabee, *Commander in Chief*, 85. On the Japanese modus vivendi, see Barnhart, *Japan and the World*, 137–39; Costello, *The Pacific War*, 116–20.

2. Thorne, *Allies of a Kind*, 8; Day, *The Great Betrayal*, 245. Thorne mentions and Day discusses in more detail the effects of the "White Australia Policy," a perspective ignored by some scholars of racism during World War II.

3. The stubborn refusal of British authorities to open certain fifty-five-year-old PREM 3 records related to Japan for November 1941 fuels all sorts of speculation on Churchill's actions and motives. I first requested access to those files in 1973 and, along with others, have repeated the request to no avail. See, for example, Costello, *The Pacific War*, 627–37. The wildest accusations, that Churchill knew the details of the impending Japanese attack and withheld them from Roosevelt so as to ensure American entry into the war, are offered in Rusbridger and Nave, *Betrayal at Pearl Harbor*.

4. Spector, *Eagle Against the Sun*, 99.

5. The modus vivendi and the American counterproposal are summarized in a message from Roosevelt to Churchill: Kimball, *Churchill & Roosevelt*, I, R-69x (November 24, 1941). The "thin diet" message is C-133x.

6. A cogent discussion of the details of all this is in Reynolds, *Anglo-American Alliance*, 240–50. See also Gilbert, *Finest Hour*, 1263–64; Utley, *Going to War with Japan*, 154–75.

7. Utley, *Going to War with Japan*, p. 180. Thanks to Lieutenant Colonel Conrad Crane of the U.S. Military Academy for providing a copy of that program. The Italian battleships sunk at Taranto in November 1940 by British aircraft were hit by torpedoes, not bombs, although the message of air power should have been as clear to the Americans as it was to the Japanese, who studied it carefully while planning for their attack on Pearl Harbor.

8. See the delightful essay by Gaddis Smith, "Roosevelt, the Sea, and International Security," in Brinkley and Facey-Crowther, eds., *The Atlantic Charter*, 33–43.

9. For succinct summaries of this debate, see Andrew, *For the President's Eyes Only*, 103–22; Spector, *Eagle Against the Sun*, 93–100; Morgan, *FDR*, 619–22. Marshall is quoted in Stoler, *Marshall*, 74.

10. WSC, III, 608.

11. Kimball, *Churchill & Roosevelt*, I, C/R telephone-2 (December 7, 1941); C-138x (December 9, 1941); Gilbert, *Finest Hour*, 1268; Gilbert, *Road to Victory*, 4–5.

12. Kimball, *Churchill & Roosevelt*, I, R-71x, R-73x drafts A and B, R-73x (December 10, 1941). A literate and penetrating presentation of Anglo-American suspicion amid alliance is Danchev, *Very Special Relationship*.

13. WSC, III, 609.

14. Hitler as quoted in Burns, *Soldier of Freedom*, 173–74. The "Master Race" comment is that of DeWitt C. Poole summarizing the response of various Nazi officials he interrogated after the war when he asked them why Hitler declared war on the United States: "Light on Nazi Foreign Policy," 147.

15. Larrabee, *Commander in Chief*, 83, claims that Germany declared war "obligingly . . . but also puzzlingly." Hitler's question is in Conference between Hitler and Raeder, December 12, 1941, *Führer Conferences on Matters Dealing with the German Navy*, II, 79. See also Kittredge, "A Military Danger," 731–40. Overy, *Why the Allies Won*, 323. For Hitler's assessment of Japan's naval strength, see Weinberg, *A World at Arms*, 262.

16. The apt phrase of Freidel, *Roosevelt* 408; Sherwood, *Roosevelt and Hopkins*, 441.

17. Kimball, *Churchill & Roosevelt*, I, C-141x.

18. *Oxford Companion*, 711.

19. Spector, *Eagle Against the Sun*, 103.

20. Reynolds, *Anglo-American Alliance*, 249; Andrew, *For the President's Eyes Only*, 121–22; Dower, *War Without Mercy*, 100–02, 105.

21. Churchill's four papers, plus a summary he wrote partway through the conference, are in Kimball, *Churchill & Roosevelt*, I, C-145x, C-153x; Stoler, *The Politics of the Second Front*, 22.

22. Memo by Orme Sargent (deputy undersecretary), February 5, 1942, and minute by Alexander Cadogan (permanent undersecretary), February 7, 1942, in Ross, ed., *The Foreign Office and the Kremlin*, 87–89.

23. Gilbert, *Road to Victory*, 24–25. For a summary of these home front issues, see O'Neill, *A Democracy at War*. On Bundles for Britain, see Kimball, *Churchill & Roosevelt*, I, C-102/1 (June 14, 1942).

24. On West African plans, see Stoler, *Second Front*, 56; WSC, III, 551–52; Gilbert, *Road to Victory*, 24. The comment to Attlee, who was in Washington for an International Labor Office Conference, is in Sainsbury, *The North African Landings*, 34.

25. Kimball, *Churchill & Roosevelt*, I, C-122x (October 20, 1941); *FRUS, Washington Conference, 1941*.

26. Barnett, "Anglo-American Strategy in Europe," 175. For an example of Churchill-Roosevelt cooperation, see Kimball, *Churchill & Roosevelt*, I, C-158x. Churchill's suggestion in February that he and the president number their exchanges consecutively (Churchill beginning at 25, FDR at 100)

was more than an attempt to keep track of things; it constituted recognition of their growing closeness: ibid., C-25.

27. Quoted in Gilbert, *Road to Victory*, 4; Bryant, *Turn of the Tide*, 282.

28. Harvey, *War Diaries*, 31 (August 31, 1941); ibid., 49 (October 6, 1941).

29. The summary of and quotes from Churchill's comments and speech are from Gilbert, *Road to Victory*, 27–30.

30. Hitchens, *Blood, Class, and Nostalgia*, 180–86, and Sullivan, "Winstoned! America's Churchill Addiction," 16–18. Even as this is written, in October 1995, British Air is using a full-page photo of Churchill in its current newspaper advertising campaign.

31. Gilbert, *Road to Victory*, 28; Sherwood, *Roosevelt and Hopkins*, 442–43, states that Churchill insisted he would have had a towel wrapped around himself and would never have claimed he had nothing to conceal. Daisy Suckley repeated a version that FDR told frequently in which he wheeled himself into the room to find Churchill naked but went ahead and threw out the name he had conceived for a new League of Nations. "United Nations!" exclaimed Roosevelt. "Good!" responded Churchill: Ward, ed., *Closest Companion*, 384–85. Roosevelt's stories invariably improved with the telling, so I am inclined to accept Gilbert's version because it is based on a letter to him from Churchill's secretary, who was there.

32. Dower, *War Without Mercy*, 12; Kimball, *Churchill & Roosevelt*, I, C-27 (February 11, 1941); the quote is from Spector, *Eagle Against the Sun*, 118. See ibid., 106–19, 134–39, for full details on the Philippine campaign in 1941–42. The Bataan Death March did not become public knowledge until 1944. To be fair to MacArthur, the president had instructed, on February 9, that forces in the Philippines fight on "as long as there remains any possibility of resistance": Quoted in Larrabee, *Commander in Chief*.

33. Kimball, *Churchill & Roosevelt*, I, C-141x, R-74x; Day, *The Great Betrayal*, 234–60.

34. Churchill had worked to limit spending on improving Singapore's defenses; see Robert O'Neill, "Churchill, Japan, and British Security in the Pacific: 1904–1942," and John Keegan, "Churchill's Strategy," both in Blake and Louis, eds., *Churchill*. The Churchill quote is from WSC, IV, 92.

35. Quoted in Spector, *Eagle Against the Sun*, 118. On the psychological aspects of Bataan and Corregidor, see 138–39, 396–98. The OWI quote is from Koppes and Black, *Hollywood Goes to War*, 258. As they describe, OWI exercised effective wartime censorship and context control over American motion pictures.

36. Churchill to Ismay, June 24, 1944, quoted in Gilbert, *Road to Victory*, 834. *FRUS, Quebec, 1944*, 314, meeting of September 13, 1944. See also Gilbert, *Road to Victory*, 959, 963–66.

37. Kimball, *Churchill & Roosevelt*, I, R-115; C-46. On the Pacific War Council, see ibid., R-78x, C-58, and Kimball, "Roosevelt and the Southwest Pacific," 103–26. On Australian nationalism, see Day, *The Great Betrayal*, with the Curtin statement discussed on p. 227.

38. For differing arguments about Japanese strategy, see Spector, *Eagle Against the Sun*, 83–84.

39. *Stalin-Roosevelt Correspondence*, no. 10 (December 17, 1941), 18.

40. The Soviet Embassy would inform Pa Watson of a Stalin to Roose-

velt message. Watson would go to the Soviet Embassy for the message and hand-deliver it to FDR: Gromyko, *Memories*, 39–40.

41. Miner, *Between Churchill and Stalin*, 192; Roosevelt to Stalin, December 16, 1941, *Stalin-Roosevelt Correspondence*, 17–18; Harvey, *War Diaries* (December 16, 1941), 75. Molotov advised Stalin against joining any such war council, but Stalin did not always take Molotov's advice: Filitov, "The Soviet Union and the Grand Alliance," 97–101.

42. Quoted in Edmonds, *The Big Three*, 263–65; and Soviet documents of the meeting in Rzheshevsky, ed., *War and Diplomacy*. Stalin's call for German dismemberment is in ibid., Doc. 4 (December 16, 1941), 17–18; and Harvey, *War Diaries* (December 16, 1941), 74. Stalin refused to join the war against Japan but did offer to discuss the issue further in "a few months": Rzheshevsky, ed., *War and Diplomacy*, Doc. 13 (December 20, 1941), 57–58.

43. Quoted in Gilbert, *Road to Victory*, 16–17; Gardner, *Spheres of Influence*, 112–16; Miner, *Between Churchill and Stalin*, 186–201; Kimball, "The Atlantic Charter: With All Deliberate Speed," in Brinkley and Facey-Crowther, eds., *The Atlantic Charter*, 100–02. See also Gardner, "A Tale of Three Cities," 104–20, and Sainsbury, *The Turning Point*, 80–85.

44. Memo to the War Cabinet, "Policy Towards Russia," January 31, 1942, Great Britain, Foreign Office (FO) files, 954/25A/100731, PRO. Beaverbrook was British minister of supply at the time.

45. Kimball, *Churchill & Roosevelt*, I, C-40 (March 7, 1942); Gardner, *Spheres of Influence*, 133–34, detects Churchill still inclined toward a territorial agreement with the Russians as of August 18.

46. WSC, IV, 209.

47. Churchill used those words when, talking to the American ambassador to China in March 1945, the prime minister defended British control over Hong Kong: Louis, *Imperialism at Bay*, 548.

48. *FRUS, Teheran*, 486. Rosenman, *Working with Roosevelt*, 316–17; Ward, ed., *Closest Companion*, 384–85; Sherwood, *Roosevelt and Hopkins*, 453.

49. For a detailed discussion of Roosevelt and colonialism, see Pollock and Kimball, " 'In Search of Monsters to Destroy,' " in Kimball, *The Juggler*, 127–57.

50. Kimball, *Churchill & Roosevelt*, I, C-34 (March 4, 1942).

51. Quoted in Kimball, *The Juggler*, 134.

52. The "First Minister" statement is from a luncheon speech quoted in Gilbert, *Road to Victory*, 254. Churchill's string of "cuss words" is from the Henry L. Stimson diaries, April 22, 1942, quoted in Kimball, *Churchill & Roosevelt*, I, 447; see also ibid., R-132 and C-68, draft A (not sent).

53. David Reynolds, "Legacies: Allies, Enemies, and Posterity," in Reynolds et al., eds., *Allies at War*, 420; Kimball, *Churchill & Roosevelt*, I, R-78x (January 30, 1942).

54. Kimball, *Churchill & Roosevelt*, I, C-40 (March 7, 1942); Eden to Churchill, March 23, 1942, FO 954/25 (SU/42/30), is a survey of military strategy that recommends that 1942 be a year of maximum effort so as to prevent a German victory in Russia, necessitating, perhaps, an "attempt to seize and to hold some part of the enemy's long and exposed coast-line."

55. Reported by Flying Officer R. I. G. Boothby (RAF) to Eden, April 16, 1942, FO 954/25, 97–100 (SU/42/56).

56. Rzheshevsky, ed., *War and Diplomacy*, Doc. 72 (May 30, 1942), 185–86; Phillips, "Mission to America," 269; Eden, *The Reckoning*, 375–77; Gardner, *Spheres of Influence*, 122–33; Gardner, *Architects of Illusion*, 33–35. The Litvinov-Roosevelt conversation is mentioned by FDR in a message to Churchill, but no American record has been located: Kimball, *Churchill & Roosevelt*, I, R-123/1 (March 18, 1942). Eleanor Roosevelt's warning to Churchill is quoted in Goodwin, *No Ordinary Time*, 311.

57. Stoler, *Marshall*, 94; Weigley, *Eisenhower's Lieutenants*, 2–7; Matloff, *Strategic Planning*, 5.

58. Kimball, *Churchill & Roosevelt*, I, R-129 (April 1, 1942); R-131/1.

59. Quoted in Stoler, *Second Front*, 35.

60. Pogue, *Ordeal and Hope*, 319–20; WSC, IV, 324; Kimball, *Churchill & Roosevelt*, I, C-68, C-70.

61. WSC, IV, 332–37; Stoler, *Second Front*, 44; Rzheshevsky, ed., *War and Diplomacy*, Doc. 71 (May 29, 1942), 179–80, and Doc. 72 (May 30, 1942), 185–86; Filitov, "The Soviet Union and the Grand Alliance," 98.

62. See all the documents in Rzheshevsky, ed., *War and Diplomacy*, 163–261, but especially Doc. 71 (May 29, 1942), 179–80; Doc. 72 (May 30, 1942), 185–87; Doc. 81 (June 1, 1942); Doc. 83 (June 2, 1942), 204–06; Doc. 100 (June 7, 1942), 227–28; and editor's commentary on p. 221 (my comment in brackets is based on Doc. 94 [June 4, 1942], 219). Edmonds, *The Big Three*, 286–87; *FRUS*, 1942, III, 594; Chuev and Resis, eds., *Molotov Remembers*, 45–46; Stoler, *Second Front*, 46.

63. Kimball, *Churchill & Roosevelt*, I, R-152 (May 31, 1942). As often happened, Roosevelt mixed up the code words, this time writing Bolero when he meant Sledgehammer. Straightening it all out eventually took a set of Churchill-Roosevelt exchanges during early July: Kimball, *Churchill & Roosevelt*, I, C-106, R-163.

64. Quoted in Edmonds, *The Big Three*, 287; WSC, IV, 332; Chuev and Resis, eds., *Molotov Remembers*, 45–46; Stoler, *Second Front*, 44–46. Churchill informed Molotov, who stopped in London on his way back to Moscow from the United States, that "only a partial operation is possible in 1942": Rzheshevsky, ed., *War and Diplomacy*, Doc. 130 (June 11, 1942), 308.

65. Harriman, *Special Envoy*, 134; *Stalin-Roosevelt Correspondence*, Nos. 17 and 18; Kimball, *Churchill & Roosevelt*, I, R-123/1 (March 18, 1942).

66. The quotation from Miner, *Between Churchill and Stalin*, 201. The same argument is made repeatedly by Charmley, *Churchill's Grand Alliance*.

67. Kimball, *Churchill & Roosevelt*, I, C-89, May 27, 1942.

68. Eden's report to the Cabinet, January 1, 1942, quoted in Gardner, *Spheres of Influence*, 115.

69. Berle, *Navigating the Rapids*, April 30, 1942, 412.

70. The details on travel and other arrangements for the various Churchill-Roosevelt conferences are taken from the relevant volume of *FRUS* and Gilbert, *Road to Victory*. On Tube Alloys, see WSC, IV, 377–81. A good brief summary of Anglo-American relations and the atomic bomb is Edmonds, *The Big Three*, 395–406.

71. Hinsley, *British Intelligence*, II, 94–99.

72. *Oxford Companion*, 713.

73. Spector, *Eagle Against the Sun*, 143–46.

74. The "flip over" expression was Churchill's: Kimball, *Churchill & Roosevelt*, I, C-62 (April 1, 1942).

75. Stimson diary, June 17, 1942, quoted in *FRUS, Washington Conference, 1941–1942*, 421; Kimball, *Churchill & Roosevelt*, III, C-914 (March 17, 1945).

76. Danchev, *Very Special Relationship*, 66–68; Stoler, *Second Front*, 52–57. Roosevelt's memo to Marshall is quoted in Edmonds, *The Big Three*, 295. The Japanese report is in Japanese minister, Madrid, to Foreign Minister, Tokyo, no. 845 of August 4, 1942, "TO" intelligence (LONDON, July 28), HW1/818, XC13030, PRO. This is a Magic decryption of Japanese radio traffic sent from Madrid.

77. Sherwood, *Roosevelt and Hopkins*, 588–615; Stoler, *Second Front*, 3–63, with the Stimson quote on p. 110. Passchendale was the bloodiest and most futile British campaign of the First World War. The "suction pump" analogy is quoted from Pogue, *Organizer of Victory*, 22. Stimson to Roosevelt, June 19, 1942, *FRUS, Washington Conference, 1941–1942*, 458.

78. Roosevelt to Harriman, June 20, 1942, quoted in Abramson, *Spanning the Century*, 330.

79. Marshall quoted in Stoler, *Second Front*, 58; Roosevelt quoted in Danchev, *Very Special Relationship*, 67.

Chapter 6: "The End of the Beginning"

1. Stoler, *Second Front*, 57–58. The verse is in Bryant, *Turn of the Tide*, 473–74.

2. Kimball, *Churchill & Roosevelt*, I, R-145 (May 2, 1942), R-166 (July 15, 1942). The Arctic convoys sailed to Murmansk and, ice conditions permitting, Archangelsk and Molotovsk on the White Sea. The Germans had been operating in Norwegian waters the battleships *Tirpitz, Lützow*, and *Scharnhorst*, along with a number of cruisers.

3. Keegan, *The Second World War*, 228.

4. Churchill to Stalin, no. 56 (July 18, 1942); Stalin to Churchill, no. 57 (July 23, 1942), *Stalin-Churchill Correspondence*; Woodward, *British Foreign Policy*, II, 263, 264–65.

5. WSC, IV, 475; Kimball, *Churchill & Roosevelt*, I, C-126A; Gilbert, *Road to Victory*, 155; Harriman, *Special Envoy*, 160.

6. Edmonds, *The Big Three*, 300–04, summarizes the evidence. General A. P. Wavell wrote the verses during the return trip to London. They are reprinted in Bryant, *Turn of the Tide*, 473–74.

7. Quoted in Andrew Roberts, "Many Finest Hours for Churchill Fans," *Wall Street Journal*, August 25, 1995, citing Gilbert, *Churchill War Papers*, II.

8. WSC, IV, 472–502; Gilbert, *Road to Victory*, 173–208; Stoler, *Second Front*, 60–63; Kimball, *Churchill & Roosevelt*, I, C-134 (August 18, 1942).

9. Kitchen, *British Policy Towards the Soviet Union*, 142–43. There seems no basis for implying that Churchill, in 1942 or thereafter, supported Jupiter in order to preempt Norway from being "liberated" by the Red Army, possibly incorporating that country into the Soviet sphere. Alarmists raised the issue in 1944, but Eden dismissed such fears: Woodward, *British Foreign Policy*, III, 130. The alarmist argument is resuscitated in Gaullist fashion by Kersaudy, "Churchill and de Gaulle," 133.

10. Stoler, *Second Front*, 62; the deletion of the expletive is from *Moran Diaries*, 78. The "essay contest" quote is from Funk, *The Politics of Torch*, 100. The debate can be followed in Kimball, *Churchill & Roosevelt*, I, starting with C-134 (August 18, 1942) and ending with R-185 and C-145 on September 5–6. Message R-180 contains FDR's request for an invasion before the election. Marshall and King communicated to Roosevelt their objections to Jupiter and the peripheral strategy by drafting a message to Churchill: R-186/3 (not sent). Harriman, *Special Envoy*, 172.

11. COS(42)345(0)(Final), "American-British Strategy," 30 October 1942, PREM 3/499/6, PRO, (quoted in Danchev, "Great Britain: The Indirect Strategy," in Reynolds et al., eds.), *Allies at War*, 4.

12. *Stalin-Roosevelt Correspondence*, no. 42 (October 7, 1942); *Stalin-Churchill Correspondence*, no. 75 (October 3, 1942). "Changed for the worse" was the translation of the message to Churchill. On convoys, see *Stalin-Churchill Correspondence*, no. 77 (October 9, 1942), no. 78 (October 13, 1942). Churchill records Molotov's demand, WSC, IV, 581; Gilbert, *Road to Victory*, 243.

13. Gilbert, *Road to Victory*, 236; Kimball, *Churchill & Roosevelt*, I, R-189, R-192, C-157 through C-160, C-172. Churchill's comment about Velvet is in C-159. See then Kimball, *Churchill & Roosevelt*, II, C-220, R-227, C-225, R-229, R-237; Lukas, *Eagles East*, 139–63.

14. Kimball, *Churchill & Roosevelt*, I, R-202 (October 27, 1942).

15. JCS 85 series with supporting JCS minutes, "Strategic Policy of the United Nations on the Collapse of Russia," August–September 1942, CCS 381 (6-1-42), RG 218, NARA; Mark Stoler, "The Soviet Union and the Second Front in American Strategic Planning, 1941–1942," delivered at the 1st Joint Symposium on the United States and the USSR in the Second World War (Moscow, October 1986); published under that title in abridged form in Sevost'ianov & Kimball, eds., *Soviet-U.S. Relations, 1933–1942*, 88–103.

16. A most colorful description of the crises over convoys to Russia and of the Malta siege is in WSC, IV, 255–76, 290–312, 505–07. The Churchill phrase is on p. 507. Roosevelt had earlier acceded to Churchill's plea and dispatched the carrier *Wasp* to help deliver fighter aircraft for the island's air defense: Kimball, *Churchill & Roosevelt*, I, R-130, R-140 (April 1942).

17. Quoted in *Oxford Companion*, 1271.

18. WSC, IV, 419, 431. In hindsight, the so-called First Battle of Alamein ended any real threat from Rommel to Egypt and the Suez Canal, but that could not be known in summer 1942; Barnett, *The Desert Generals*, 502.

19. Sherwood, *Roosevelt and Hopkins*, 626; WSC, IV, 511; Villa, *Unauthorized Action*.

20. Gilbert, *Auschwitz and the Allies*; Gilbert, *Road to Victory*, 245.

21. The Air Force did not become a separate branch of the U.S. military until after the Second World War.

22. The compelling description is that of Spector, *Eagle Against the Sun*, 197; FDR's instructions are quoted on p. 209.

23. Quoted in Spector, *Eagle Against the Sun*, 214.

24. Quotations and statistics from Theodore A. Wilson, "The United States: Leviathan," in Reynolds et al., eds., *Allies at War*, 173–96; *Oxford Companion*, 1235 and elsewhere. For criticism of America's economic mobilization, see O'Neill, *A Democracy at War*.

25. The story of Red Army offensive failures is only just beginning to

emerge from previously closed Soviet archives: Glantz and House, *When Titans Clashed*, 175 (n.26).

26. Halifax to FO, December 5, 1942, FO 371: 31515 (U1644/27/370), courtesy of Lloyd Gardner.

27. Kimball, *Churchill & Roosevelt*, II, C-504 (November 13, 1943).

28. Kersaudy, "Churchill and de Gaulle," 127.

29. St. Louis *Post-Dispatch*, December 26, 1941, quoted in Hurstfield, *America and the French*, 131. An excellent summary of the St. Pierre-Miquelon affair is in ibid., 120–38.

30. Kimball, *Churchill & Roosevelt*, I, C-157x. Although St. Pierre and Miquelon were settled by sailors from Brittany, the islands had been awarded to the British in the Peace of Utrecht in 1714. For the next hundred years they were swapped back and forth between Britain and France and finally reverted to France in 1814 with the provision they be unfortified. The standard work is Anglin, *The St. Pierre and Miquelon Affaire*.

31. Kimball, *Churchill & Roosevelt*, I, C-44 and ff., and C-84 and ff.; WSC, IV, 222–37.

32. Kimball, *Churchill & Roosevelt*, I, C-169 (October 21, 1942); C-144 (September 5, 1942). Roosevelt did not take up either suggestion: R-197.

33. Harriman recollections (Feis files), *Torch*, November 12, 1953, Harriman papers (LC); Kimball, *Churchill & Roosevelt*, I, C-180/1 (October 31, 1942). For examples of the Americanization of Torch, see C-180 and R-208. Churchill repeatedly used phrases he liked, and "loyal lieutenant" was one of them.

34. Hinsley, *British Intelligence*, II, 416–25; Behrendt, *Rommel's Intelligence in the Desert Campaign*; Winterbotham, *The Ultra Secret*, 119–21.

35. WSC, IV, 602; Barnett, *The Desert Generals*, 267–313.

36. WSC, IV, 618; Howard, *British Intelligence*, vol. V: *Strategic Deception*, 60–62.

37. Quoted in Burns, *Soldier of Freedom*, 291.

38. Edmonds, *The Big Three*, 303; Hurstfield, *America and the French*, 164; Robertson, *The Ship with Two Captains*; Kimball, *Churchill & Roosevelt*, I, C-182 (November 3, 1942).

39. Hurstfield, *America and the French*, 163.

40. Kimball, *Churchill & Roosevelt*, II, C-205 and C-206 (November 22, 1942). Some of the details of the deal remain shrouded in mystery, but Funk, *The Politics of Torch*, has re-created the story.

41. Sherwood, *Roosevelt and Hopkins*, 645.

42. Quoted in Hurstfield, *America and the French*, 167–68.

43. Gilbert, *Road to Victory*, 277–78; James, ed., *Churchill Speeches*, VI, 6718–30; Kimball, *Churchill & Roosevelt*, II, C-193 (November 17, 1942).

44. Kimball, *Churchill & Roosevelt*, II, 3–4.

45. Ibid., II, R-211/1 (November 16, 1942). See also R-213 and R-214 (November 17, 1942).

46. Specifically, the evening of August 25, 1944: de Gaulle, *War Memoirs*, 650.

47. Joint U.S. Intelligence Committee Daily Summary no. 353, November 28, 1942, MR 71, FDRL. "The War This Week," OSS no. 60, November 26–December 3, 1942, PSF 154, FDRL. Michela (Moscow) to MILID, January 18, 1943, MR 300, Box 100, FDRL. London Embassy to MILID,

February 2, 1943, reporting data from the British mission in the USSR, MR 300, Box 100, FDRL. For Operation Uranus, see Glantz, *Soviet Military Deception*, 108–19. American intelligence grossly underestimated the size of the force encircled by the Red Army in Stalingrad, claiming as late as January 18, 1943, that only 70,000 German troops were there, but estimates then rose to a more accurate 350,000 Germans by the time Hitler admitted the Stalingrad defeat. For statistics, see Weinberg, *A World at Arms*, 453–54. Thirty thousand German troops were flown out of the city. "Entombed in the ruins" is the phrase of Keegan, *The Second World War*, 234. On cooperation with the Germans by various Soviet nationalities, see Mikhail N. Narinsky, "The Soviet Union: The Great Patriotic War?" in Reynolds et al., eds., *Allies at War*, 275.

48. "The War This Week," OSS No. 64, December 24–31, 1942, PSF 154, FDRL, 26–29. For a full discussion of the American appreciation of Stalingrad, see Kimball, "Stalingrad," 89–114.

49. "Weekly Strategy Resume," 23 January 1943, ABC 334.3 Policy Committee (August 1, 1942), 3, Records of the Joint Chiefs of Staff (JCS), RG 218, National Archives and Records Administration (NARA); see also Stoler, *Second Front*, 87.

50. See, for example, a memo by Orme Sargent (deputy undersecretary in the British Foreign Office), February 5, 1942, in Ross, ed., *The Foreign Office and the Kremlin*, 127–30. Roosevelt appears to have been aware of Soviet problems; see the minutes of the 7th Pacific War Council Meeting (Washington), May 13, 1942, MR, Box 168, "Pacific War Council," FDRL.

51. On Eleanor Roosevelt's trip, see Kimball, *Churchill & Roosevelt*, I, C-175, C-181; Goodwin, *No Ordinary Time*, 382.

52. James, ed., *Churchill Speeches*, VI, 6693.

53. Kimball, *Churchill & Roosevelt*, II, C-241, R-244.

54. Ibid., I, R-210, R-211. Stoler, *Second Front*, 64, refers to the "strategic paradox." Marshall's prediction of pushing the Axis into the Mediterranean in "two or three weeks" is in Sherwood, *Roosevelt and Hopkins*, 658.

55. *Stalin-Churchill Correspondence*, no. 88 (November 24, 1942); Kimball, *Churchill & Roosevelt*, II, C-216 (December 2, 1942).

56. Kimball, *Churchill & Roosevelt*, I, C-91 (May 28, 1942). Churchill's history as quoted in David Reynolds, "Churchill and Allied Grand Strategy in Europe," 1–2.

57. Kimball, *Churchill & Roosevelt*, II, C-194 (November 17, 1942), C-195 (November 18, 1942); WSC, IV, 651; Bryant, *Turn of the Tide*, 529–31.

58. Kimball, *Churchill & Roosevelt*, II, C-211 (November 24, 1942).

59. Eisenhower, *Crusade in Europe*, 113–24, describes the problems.

60. Gilbert, *Road to Victory*, 285.

61. Kimball, *Churchill & Roosevelt*, I, R-224.

62. Ibid., II, R-222, C-214, R-224, C-219, R-234/1, R-242; *FRUS, Casablanca, 1943*, 488–505.

63. Here is where I would agree with John Charmley's narrowly conceived argument that Churchill overromanticized the Anglo-American relationship; see Charmley, *Churchill: The End of Glory* and *Churchill's Grand Alliance*. The plans for an apartment in England designed for use by the crippled president are in the Map Room papers, FDRL. In this instance FDR

told Churchill that a visit to Britain was impossible "for political reasons": Kimball, *Churchill & Roosevelt*, II, R-234/1.

64. Sherwood, *Roosevelt and Hopkins*, 665.

65. Kimball, *Churchill & Roosevelt*, II, R-252, C-253; Harriman, *Special Envoy*, 180.

66. Ward, ed., *Closest Companion*, (January 20, 1943), 1 199; *FRUS, Casablanca*, 524–25, 532–33.

67. Ward, ed., *Closest Companion* (November 27, 1942), 187.

68. On Stalin's active role in military operations, see Erickson, *The Road to Berlin*, and *The Road to Stalingrad*; Volkogonov, *Stalin*; Shtemenko, *The Soviet General Staff at War*. See also Kimball, "Stalingrad," *Journal of Military History*. Churchill thought Stalin cared only about the second front; see, for example, Churchill to Roosevelt, Kimball, *Churchill & Roosevelt*, II, C-224 (December 7, 1942); Kimball, *The Juggler*, Chapter 4. On Stalin's reluctance to fly, see Volkogonov, *Stalin*, 488.

69. For examples of British interest in the Aegean, see two memos by the British chiefs of staff, one dated January 3, 1943, the other of January 18, 1943, in *FRUS, Casablanca*, 749–51, 768. See also Howard, *Grand Strategy, August 1942–September 1943*; and Kimball, *The Juggler*, 63–81.

70. Combined chiefs of staff minutes, January 21, 1943, *FRUS, Casablanca Conference*, 668–72; Hinsley, *British Intelligence*, II, 753–56; Levine, *The Strategic Bombing of Germany*, 51, 83.

71. For Roosevelt's early interest in an attack on Sicily, see Kimball, *Churchill & Roosevelt*, I, R-210 (November 11, 1942); Churchill is quoted from his message to the deputy prime minister and War Cabinet, STRATAGEM no. 56, January 17, 1943, PREM 3/420/3/64–65; *FRUS, Casablanca*, 584–85. The planning command for the invasion of France was designated COSSAC—chief of staff to the (as yet unnamed) supreme Allied commander. For Marshall's reaction to Casablanca, see Bland, ed., *Marshall Interviews*, 613; Stoler, *Marshall*, 101–02.

72. *FRUS, Casablanca*, 746–47, 781–82.

73. Churchill's disclaimer is in Sherwood, *Roosevelt and Hopkins*, 696. Gilbert, *Road to Victory*, 300, 309; WSC, IV, 684–91; Pogue, *Organizer of Victory*, 32–35; O'Connor, *Diplomacy for Victory*, 50–53.

74. See Kimball, "Aus der Sicht Washingtons," 57–78. For intelligence reports see, for example, MID 904 memorandums on "German Soldier and Civilian Morale," Henry Morgenthau, Jr. papers, Morgenthau accretion, Box 3, FDRL.

75. Weinberg, *A World at Arms*, 754.

76. Macmillan, *War Diaries: Politics and War in the Mediterranean*, 9–10.

77. *FRUS, Casablanca*, 506; Churchill quoted in Gilbert, *Road to Victory*, 313.

78. Sherwood, *Roosevelt and Hopkins*, 696.

79. Reynolds, "Churchill the Appeaser?," 210–19; Smith, *Churchill's German Army*.

80. Kersaudy, "Churchill and de Gaulle," 127–28, has Churchill mirroring FDR's attitude. On Churchill and Alan Brooke, see Michael Carver, "Churchill and the Defence Chiefs," in Blake and Louis, eds., *Churchill*, 366–68. Roosevelt's dislike of MacArthur is legendary.

81. See the very fine study by Hurstfield, *America and the French*, which argues that Roosevelt believed France was and should be a second-rate power,

something de Gaulle obviously sensed. The same point, greatly exaggerated into an American conspiracy, is made by Verrier, *Assassination in Algiers*.

82. Kimball, *Churchill & Roosevelt*, II, R-256 (February 5, 1943); Hurstfield, *America and the French*, 185; Funk, "The 'Anfa Memorandum,' " 246–54.

83. Churchill was the only British representative at the dinner: WSC, IV. Nor is the dinner mentioned in the official biography, Gilbert, *Road to Victory*.

84. Sherwood, *Roosevelt and Hopkins*, 685, 689–90; Elliott Roosevelt, *As He Saw It*, 109–12.

85. Roosevelt to Suckley, January 13, 1943, Ward, ed., *Closest Companion*, 197; *Presidential Press Conferences*, no. 933 [30–35] (February 5, 1944), 23.

86. De Gaulle, *War Memoirs*, 923.

87. Amery, *The Empire at Bay* (February 19, 1943), 873–74.

88. Churchill quoted in Gilbert, *Road to Victory*, 343, and paraphrased in Amery, *The Empire at Bay* (February 7, 1943), 872, minutes of the twenty-eighth Pacific War Council meeting, February 17, 1943, MR-FDRL; Churchill's "in the dock" remark came during the Yalta Conference, *FRUS, Yalta*, 856. Churchill's attitude toward Indians is well surveyed in Sarvepalli Gopal, "Churchill and India," in Blake and Louis, eds., *Churchill*, 457–71; on the Advisory Council, see p. 461. The Eden visit is discussed below, Chapter 8.

89. Kenneth Pendar, who was the host, describes the scene in *Adventure in Diplomacy* (New York: Dodd, Mead, 1945), 149. Averell Harriman described Pendar as effeminate; interview with Herbert Feis, November 16, 1953, Harriman papers, box 872, Feis Interviews (LC). Kimball, *Churchill & Roosevelt*, II, 618–19; R-262/1; C-259-A1 ("Morning Thoughts"). Gilbert, *Road to Victory*, 310–11. Taylor (Flower) Villa is described in *FRUS, Casablanca Conference*, 535.

Chapter 7: "I Am Not a Wilsonian Idealist"

1. Howard, *Grand Strategy*, 327; Kimball, *Churchill & Roosevelt*, II, C-260 (February 3, 1943). The Soviet definition of the second front was an attack that would, in addition to German forces already in Western Europe, divert forty divisions from the Russian front; above, Chapter 6.

2. Erickson, "Stalin, Soviet Strategy and the Grand Alliance," 146.

3. Glantz and House, *When Titans Clashed*, 147.

4. Thorne, *Allies of a Kind*, 139.

5. Churchill, *The World Crisis*, IV, 256, 259; Eleanor Roosevelt to FDR, August 21, 1944, PSF: GB: WSC, FDRL. Kimball, *Churchill & Roosevelt*, I, R-123/1; II, R-297, R-418. See also *FRUS, Tehran*, 194ff. The "broker" image is that of both Averell Harriman and Joseph Davies. See Harriman to Roosevelt, July 5, 1943, PSF-Harriman, FDRL, and MacLean, "Joseph E. Davies" and her book, *Joseph E. Davies*, 95–113.

6. Eden, *The Reckoning*, 434–35. For a detailed treatment of the visit, see Warren F. Kimball, "Anglo-American War Aims, 1941–1943," 1–21.

7. Kimball, *Churchill & Roosevelt*, II, R-262/1 (March 17, 1943).

8. See Notter, *Postwar Foreign Policy Preparation* (hereafter PFPP) and

the archives of that planning process, "Postwar Foreign Policy Preparation," available at the National Archives (Washington, D.C.) and on microform with a printed finding aid, a set of which is in the Rutgers University Library (New Brunswick, N.J.): *Post World War II Foreign Policy Planning* [Notter files]. Sumner Welles usually chaired the meetings until Hull took over during Eden's visit.

9. FDR actually used the phrase "ganged up" in a message to Churchill just before the Teheran Conference: Kimball, *Churchill & Roosevelt*, II, R-418 (November 11, 1943); Sherwood, *Roosevelt and Hopkins*, 707–08.

10. Quoted in Harper, *American Visions of Europe*, 113.

11. For the Molotov-Roosevelt conversations of May–June 1942 and Stalin's comments, see Rzheshevsky, ed., *War and Diplomacy*, Docs. 68, 77, 82; and *FRUS, 1942*, III, 573–74; Woodward, *British Foreign Policy*, V, 32. President and Mrs. Roosevelt are paraphrased in "Unfinished Notes" (August 1941), Belle Willard Roosevelt papers, LC (courtesy of Theodore Wilson). Belle Roosevelt was the wife of Kermit Roosevelt, one of former President Theodore Roosevelt's sons. His comment about "too many nations to satisfy" was made to Molotov in spring 1942, and quoted in Schild, *Bretton Woods and Dumbarton Oaks*, 23. A clear reference to his disarmament enforcement idea came in discussions with King Peter of Yugoslavia: June 24, 1942, *FRUS, Washington Conferences, 1941–1942*, 444–45, and Iatrides, ed., *MacVeagh Reports*, 396–97.

For additional references to the policemen idea, see Wilson, *The First Summit*, 198–99; Harvey, *War Diaries*, 32; Sherwin, *A World Destroyed*, 88; Kimball, *The Juggler*, 85; Australia, *Documents on Australian Foreign Policy, 1937–1949*, VII, no. 13. A convenient summary, reflecting unsympathetic British reactions to Roosevelt's postwar plan, is in Woodward, *British Foreign Policy*, V, Chapters 61–62.

12. Halifax to the Foreign Office, March 28, 1943, FO 371/35366, U 1430/G, PRO, reporting on the Eden-Roosevelt conversations. Berle, *Navigating the Rapids*, 357. Roosevelt's reference to the Good Neighbor policy came in a magazine article that the White House carefully edited: Davis, "Roosevelt's World Blueprint," 110. White House approval is in the Roosevelt papers, Official File (OF) 4287. See also Kimball, *The Juggler*, 107–25; Divine, *Second Chance*.

13. Notter files (microform), 548–1, summary dated March 18, 1943, of a White House meeting on February 22, 1943.

14. Eden, *The Reckoning*, 437; Sherwood, *Roosevelt & Hopkins*, 716; Woodward, *British Foreign Policy*, V, 36. For additional discussions of China, see *FRUS, 1943*, III, 36–38; Eden, *The Reckoning*, 440.

15. Roosevelt's remark was to Myron Taylor and is quoted in Hilderbrand, *Dumbarton Oaks*, 16. Hilderbrand provides a cogent summary postwar planning through 1943 on pp. 5–25.

16. Eden to Halifax, January 22, 1942, FO 954/29xc/100818, PRO; Woodward, *British Foreign Policy*, V, 9–10; *FRUS, 1943*, III, 13; Sherwood, *Roosevelt & Hopkins*, 708–09.

17. Roosevelt's meetings were usually with selected members of the Subcommittee on Political Problems—primarily Hull or Welles, Leo Pasvolsky, Norman Davis, Myron Taylor, and Isaiah Bowman: Notter, *PFPP*, 92–93, 96–97; and the Notter files (microform), file 548–1 (a summary of contacts with the president).

18. *FRUS, 1943*, III, p. 39.
19. Charmley, *Churchill*, 460–61. This is not to single out Charmley; he is only the latest such accuser in what is a very long line.
20. That is not of course the interpretation of historians like D. C. Watt, whose title I have borrowed: *Succeeding John Bull*.
21. Memorandum of July 7, 1943, Woodward, *British Foreign Policy*, V, p. 51.
22. "Postwar Planning," broadcast March 21, 1943, in James, ed., *Churchill Speeches*, VII, 6758. The cordon sanitaire was a system of alliances created by the French with the small states of Central Europe that aimed at quarantining bolshevism and offsetting Soviet influence.
23. Churchill minute to Eden, October 21, 1942, M.742/2 [T8/8/11], Churchill Archives, Churchill College; WSC, IV, 561–62. Gilbert, *Road to Victory*, 239–40, substitutes Russia for Prussia and thus erroneously quotes Churchill calling for "keeping Russia disarmed." That mistake apparently led Gilbert to assume that Churchill excluded Russia from the United States (Council) of Europe, which does not appear to be Churchill's intent, although his phrase "former Great Powers" could be so interpreted. Foreign Office thinking at this time is presented in Woodward, *British Foreign Policy*, V, 1–21.
24. WSC, IV, 562.
25. Kimball, *Churchill & Roosevelt*, II, C-269, R-262/1; *Moran Diaries*, 95–99.
26. Kimball, *Churchill & Roosevelt*, II, R-262/1, R-262/2, C-274, C-276, R-267, R-272. A photograph of a short snorter bill appears on II, p. 171. Memo for Harriman's Personal and Secret Files, September 4, 1942 (with attachments), Harriman papers (LC), box 162. The short snorter craze is described delightfully by Steinbeck, "The Short Snorter War Menace," in the collection of columns he wrote as a war correspondent *Once There Was a War*, 133–39.
27. Djilas quoting Stalin, cited in Schild, *Bretton Woods and Dumbarton Oaks*, 175; Volkogonov, *Stalin*, 489; Churchill quoted in Callahan, *Churchill: Retreat from Empire*, 185. Churchill wrote similarly to Eden in January 1942: WSC, III, 696. On Sicily, see Kimball, *Churchill & Roosevelt*, II, C-282, R-271.
28. Kimball, *Churchill & Roosevelt*, C-274-A (March 25, 1943); *Stalin-Churchill Correspondence*, no. 129 (March 15, 1943).
29. The Soviet Union admitted guilt for the Katyn massacre in 1990, and two years later the Russian government gave the Poles documentary evidence. Additional mass graves were identified at that time. The precise number executed remains uncertain, but recently published Soviet records state that 14,736 "former" Polish officers, and another 11,000 "members of various counterrevolutionary, spy, and diversionist organizations, former landowners," etc., were killed. Stalin also ordered the deportation to Kazakhstan of between 75,000 and 100,000 family members of those executed: See Beria to Stalin of March 5, 1940, Politburo protocol, of March 5, 1940, Beria order to the NKVD, March 7, 1940—all in *Organy gosudarsetvennoi*, 153–61, 165–71 (courtesy of Steven Miner). See also *Oxford Companion*, 645–46; Kimball, *Churchill & Roosevelt*, II, C-284, C-285, C-289, C-290, C-412/2 (August 13, 1943), R-274/1 (not sent), and various exchanges during April 1943 in *Stalin-Roosevelt Correspondence* and *Stalin-Churchill Correspondence*.

30. WSC, V, 397. The sad story of Polish-Soviet relations is summarized in most wartime histories, although the story needs a full study. The best available are Ciechanowski, *The Warsaw Rising of 1944* and, more recently, Prazmowska, "Poland Between East and West," 86–96; and Prazmowska, "Churchill and Poland," 110–23. For Grand Alliance diplomacy over Poland, see Sainsbury, *Churchill and Roosevelt at War*, 91–108, and Gardner, *Spheres of Influence*.

31. Suckley diary, August 26, 1943, Ward, ed., *Closest Companion*, 231. In autumn 1943, when Admiral William Standley returned from Moscow after being replaced as ambassador by Averell Harriman, Roosevelt asked whether Stalin would "make a separate peace." Standley said Stalin would fight on to Berlin, although he would reevaluate if the second front was not established. Standley, *Admiral Ambassador to Russia*, 498; Leahy, *I Was There*, 187.

32. Mastny, *Russia's Road to the Cold War*, 79–84; Fleischhauer, *Die Chance des Sonderfriedens;* an example of American worries is JCS 283-283/1, "Current British Policy and Strategy in Relationship to That of the United States," May 3, 1943, CCS 381 (4-24-43), Sec. 3. See Kimball, "Stalingrad," and MacLean, *Joseph Davies*, 115–16, for additional citations.

33. Hinsley, *British Intelligence*, III, pt. 1, 44.

34. Matloff, *Strategic Planning, 1943–1944*, 225–27; Kolko, *The Politics of War*, 28–30, 315–17; *FRUS, Tehran*, 253–56; *FRUS, 1943*, III, 17, 22, 26; Sherwood, *Roosevelt & Hopkins*, 714–15; Notter files (microform), file 548-1; Eden to Churchill, March 16, 1943, FO 371/35365/1316 (PRO). The Bullitt proposal is discussed in Kimball, "Anglo-American War Aims," 1–21.

35. Gilbert, *Road to Victory*, 398.

36. Stimson Diary, May 27, 1943 (courtesy of Mark Stoler).

37. The documents of the Trident (third Washington) Conference of May 12–25 are in *FRUS, Conferences at Washington and Quebec, 1943*. See also Gilbert, *Road to Victory*, 399–419.

38. Churchill to Hopkins, February 27, 1943, Hopkins papers, A-Bomb folder, FDRL; Sherwood, *Roosevelt and Hopkins*, 703–04; Eden, *The Reckoning*, 657; Kimball, *Churchill & Roosevelt*, II, C-354 (July 9, 1943); *FRUS, Conference at Washington and Quebec, 1943*, 221, 630–53.

39. Sherwin, *A World Destroyed*, 82–89; Holloway, *Stalin and the Bomb*, 82.

40. *Stalin-Roosevelt Correspondence*, no. 92 (June 11, 1943). He sent the same message to Churchill. We are beginning to get small glimpses of Soviet archival evidence of the kind of information Stalin's diplomats and intelligence agents provided him. See, for example, Rzheshevsky, ed., *War and Diplomacy* and *Sekrety Gitlera* (Hitler's Secrets on Stalin's Desk). Other recent disclosures from Soviet wartime files strongly suggest that their military intelligence section (GRU) had some kind of access to British diplomatic correspondence.

41. Kimball, *Churchill & Roosevelt*, II, R-280, R-289/B, C-309, C-328, R-297; Sherwood, *Roosevelt and Hopkins*, 733–34; Harriman to Roosevelt, July 5, 1943, PSF:GB:1943, FDRL; MacLean, *Joseph Davies*, 95–115. Hopkins's comment is from Elliot Roosevelt, *As He Saw It*, 151.

42. Kimball, *Churchill & Roosevelt*, II, C-R/telephone-4 (July 29, 1943), 356–57.

43. Ibid., II, R-331 (June 30, 1943), R-334 (July 30, 1940), C-394 (July 31, 1943).

44. O. A. Rzheshevsky, "The Soviet Union: The Direct Strategy," in Reynolds et al., eds., *Allies at War*, 44–46. The statistics are from the *Oxford Companion*, 658–60. Glantz and House, *When Titans Clashed*, 165, offers somewhat different numbers, but the overall picture is the same.

45. *Stalin-Churchill Correspondence*, no. 165 (June 24, 1943); Churchill to Clark Kerr (Moscow), 29 June 1943, quoted in Gilbert, *Road to Victory*, 437.

46. *Stalin-Roosevelt Correspondence*, no. 97 (June 24, 1943); Harvey, *War Diaries*, 276 (July 16, 1943).

47. Churchill to Eisenhower quoted in Reynolds, "Churchill and Allied Grand Strategy," (p. 6 in mss.); Churchill to Stimson and FDR's conclusion from minutes of a meeting between President and Chiefs of Staff, August 10, 1943, MR Box 29, FDRL; Gilbert, *Road to Victory*, 445; Brooke diary quoted in ibid., 448.

48. The "governing principle" is in *FRUS, Conference at Washington and Quebec, 1943*, 1123. The general summary is from ibid., 849–967.

49. *Stalin-Churchill Correspondence*, no. 170 (August 9, 1943); Kimball, *Churchill & Roosevelt*, II, C-412/4 (August 15, 1943).

50. *FRUS, Conference at Washington and Quebec, 1943*, 1117–19. Edmonds provides a devastating picture of American lying and deception to the British about this agreement; see his *The Big Three*, 401–02, and *Setting the Mould*, 52–53; Holloway, "The Atomic Bomb and the End of the Wartime Alliance," 207–10; Holloway, *Stalin and the Bomb*, 82–83; Hershberg, *Conant*, 217; Sherwin, *A World Destroyed*, 82–89.

51. For additional personal details of the Churchills' visit, see Ward, ed., *Closest Companion*, 228–37. Churchill's Harvard speech is in James, ed., *Churchill Speeches*, VII, 6823–27. On Clementine Churchill's feelings toward Roosevelt, see Lash, *Eleanor and Franklin*, 660–61, 663–64; Soames, *Clementine Churchill*, 448.

52. Hinsley, *British Intelligence*, II, pt. 1, 4–5, 14–15. Enigma/Ultra did not reveal Hitler's decision to adopt defensive positions south of Rome until October 2. As German lines of communication became shorter and restricted to the European continent, they relied more on landlines (telephone/telegraph lines). That made Ultra, which was intercepted radio messages, somewhat less reliable as an indicator of German intentions, particularly German Army operations.

53. Quoted in *Oxford Companion*, 574; Bryant, *Triumph in the West*, 28–34.

54. The back-and-forth arguments over control in Italy can be followed in remarkable detail in the exchanges between the president and the prime minister: Kimball, *Churchill & Roosevelt*, II, 351–488. A readable brief summary is Edmonds, *The Big Three*, 325–39. For Roosevelt's relationship with his senior military officers, see Kimball, " 'Dr. New Deal,' " 87–105. Churchill's repeated insistence on political rather than military control of occupation policy is found throughout his correspondence with FDR.

55. Macmillan, *War Diaries*, 200, 352–53, 388, 584.

56. Winant to FDR and Hull, July 26, 1943, *FRUS, 1943*, II, 335. Kolko, *Politics of War*, 43–63.

57. Kimball, *Churchill & Roosevelt*, II, C-545 (January 16, 1944); WSC, V, 393–94.

58. One unlikely example of such simplification is Ehrman, *Grand Strat-*

egy, August 1943–September 1944, 75–88. Ehrman also asserts that the "revolutionary" unconditional surrender policy helped keep the Turks out of the war because they, and the British, "favoured the traditional type of negotiated peace, which would diminish Germany's influence before Russia's influence could become unduly exalted." That may have been true, but how different it reads when one adds the two words implied, so the first part reads "negotiated peace *with Hitler*": ibid., 90.

59. Fifty years later some of those edifices on Rhodes still stand as a metaphor for the Italian Empire—dilapidated and crumbling, but still evoking a romantic, pastel image of benevolent dominance. The ornate resort for the elite at Thermes Kalitheas, a few miles from the main city of Rhodes, is a perfect example.

60. Gilbert, *Road to Victory*, 503. Alexander was deputy commander in chief to Eisenhower, the C in C of what was still called the North African Theater of Operations. Kimball, *Churchill & Roosevelt*, II, C-438 (October 7, 1943).

61. Bland, ed., *Marshall Interviews*, 415. The dependence of the Americans on landing craft and landing ships in the Pacific war has some irony. The British and Americans copied Japanese designs developed in the 1930s for a flat-bottomed boat with a bow door that could drop in shallow water and serve as an off-loading ramp.

62. Kimball, *Churchill & Roosevelt*, II, R-379, R-381; Bland, ed., *Marshall Interviews*, 13.

63. Eisenhower quoted in Ambrose, *The Supreme Commander*, 286; Brooke diary (October 8, 1943) quoted in Bryant, *Triumph in the West*, 51.

64. Kimball, *Churchill & Roosevelt*, II, C-449 (October 10, 1943); Gilbert, *Road to Victory*, 555.

65. Holland, *The Aegean Mission* offers a devastating critique of the campaign and of Churchill's role in it. But see WSC, V, 218ff., and Parish, *Aegean Adventures 1940–1943*, which offer a ringing, if implausible, defense of the prime minister's "dream." German air power made both evacuation and a successful defense of Leros impossible. British forces finally surrendered on 16 November.

66. Kimball, *Churchill & Roosevelt*, II, C-549 (19 January 1944).

67. Roosevelt to Grace Tully, October 16, 1943, PSF:GB:WSC, FDRL.

68. The distasteful story of petty jealousy and intrigue surrounding Welles is related in detail in Gellman, *Secret Affairs*.

69. Schild, *Bretton Woods and Dumbarton Oaks*, 26.

70. All these proposals and the entire Moscow Conference are very well described in Keith Sainsbury's very excellent *The Turning Point*, 53–109. The spheres of influence quotation is from ibid., 97. See also Woodward, *British Foreign Policy*, II, 581–99, and the carefully tailored account in Harriman, *Special Envoy*, 234–50.

71. Harriman, *Special Envoy*, 236, 245; *FRUS, 1943*, I, 590; Polish nationalism is characterized by Edmonds, *The Big Three*, 382.

72. The declaration is reprinted in Sainsbury, *The Turning Point*, 315. Eden concern about detail is in Eden, *The Reckoning*, 482.

73. Sainsbury, *The Turning Point*, 90–92; Hull, *Memoirs*, II, 1299–1300.

74. Eisenberg, *Drawing the Line*, 23; Sainsbury, *The Turning Point*, 85–86.

75. Erickson, "Stalin, Soviet Strategy and the Grand Alliance," 150–51, speculates, without evidence, on changes in Stalin's motives for calling for the second front. On other issues, see Sainsbury, *The Turning Point*, 53–109, with the Turkish issue found on 97–99.

76. Kimball, *Churchill & Roosevelt*, II, C-484 (November 2, 1943); Glantz, "Soviet Military Strategy *vis à vis* Japan," 24–25.

77. Hull, *Memoirs*, II, 1313.

78. Ibid., 1315–16.

79. These and subsequent details about arrangements for the talks at Cairo and Teheran are taken from *FRUS, Tehran*, unless otherwise noted. Stalin's only flight outside the USSR during the war was to Teheran: Volkogonov, *Stalin*, 497.

80. Gilbert, *Road to Victory*, 548–49; Kimball, *Churchill & Roosevelt*, II, C-598/1 (November 25, 1943); C-512 (December 19, 1943); minutes of meeting between President and Chiefs of Staff, August 10, 1943, MR Box 29 (FDRL). The "laurels" quote is that of General Brooke in Rey nolds, "Churchill and Allied Grand Strategy," 8. Eisenhower commanded in the Mediterranean, but when he took over the AEF, British General Maitland Wilson became supreme commander in the Mediterranean. The single supreme commander idea would also protect Roosevelt against accusations he wanted to "demote" Marshall to a theater commander and move him out of Washington so the president could put a pro–New Deal general in charge: Hopkins to Churchill, September 26, 1943, MR, FDRL; Sherwood, *Roosevelt and Hopkins*, 762–64; Parrish, *Roosevelt and Marshall*, 363–69.

81. Charmley, *Churchill's Grand Alliance*, 74.

82. The story of Roosevelt's evasions and the various preparations for the Cairo and Teheran talks can be followed in Kimball, *Churchill & Roosevelt*, II, starting with R-374 (October 4, 1943), and in *FRUS, Tehran*, 3–107, 293–300.

83. Lash, *Roosevelt and Churchill*, 38; Freidel, *Roosevelt*, 10, 109.

84. Thorne, *Allies of a Kind*, 3–13, 326, 374, 489–91. For recent rethinking on Japan and Asian nationalism, see the essays in Gerhard Krebs and Christian Oberländer, eds., *1945 in Europe and Asia: Reconsidering the End of World War II and the Change of the World Order* (Munich: Iudicium, 1996), particularly the paper by Nemoto Kei.

85. Thorne, *Allies of a Kind*, 325–26; Campbell and Herring, eds., *Stettinius Diaries*, 39–40 (March 17, 1944); Elliott Roosevelt, *As He Saw It*, 142, 152–66; Bryant, *Triumph in the West*, 79. FDR to Chiang, June 30, 1943; Hopkins papers, Box 331, FDRL; FDR to Chiang, October 27, 1943, *FRUS, 1943*, 154; Stimson diaries, November 4, 1943, reel 8, 16, Yale University Library (courtesy of Nancy Wehlau). See also Hess, *The United States' Emergence as a Southeast Asian Power*, 85–86; Iriye, *Power and Culture*, 49–95; Louis, *Imperialism at Bay*, 157. An excellent summary of American policy toward China during the war is Schaller, *The U.S. Crusade in China*. The Cairo Declaration is printed in *FRUS, Tehran*, 448–49.

86. Ehrman, *Grand Strategy*, 167; Gilbert, *Road to Victory*, 561, 566; Thorne, *Allies of a Kind*, 294.

87. Gilbert, *Road to Victory*, 568.

88. For Ismay's concern, see Gilbert, *Road to Victory*, 569. Harriman describes his role *Special Envoy*, 263–65, although that description is at var-

iance with Harriman to Jerome Merin, August 3, 1966, Harriman papers, Box 874 (LC). The Soviet spy's report is from Dm. Medvedev, *Silnye Du-khom*, 328–29. *Stalin-Churchill Correspondence*, no. 210 (November 23, 1943); WSC, V, 343–44, 346–47. Harriman later claimed that Churchill "was much relieved" since the quarters available in the British Embassy were inadequate; *FRUS, Tehran*, 463, n.11.

89. Kimball, *Churchill & Roosevelt*, II, R-418 (November 11, 1943).

90. Churchill later denied, with vehemence, that he had tried to prevent Overlord: WSC, V, 344.

91. Ward, ed., *Closest Companion* (July 19, 1943); 227. Daisy Suckley wrote that FDR "wants to talk, man to man, with Stalin, & try to establish a constructive relationship. He says that the meeting may result in a complete stalemate, or that Stalin may refuse to work along with the United Nations, or, as he hopes, that Stalin will be willing to work *with* the U.N."

92. *FRUS, Tehran*, 496.

Chapter 8: "A New Heaven and a New Earth"

1. The details are in *FRUS, Tehran Conference*, 279–80; Sherwood, *Roosevelt and Hopkins*, 768–70; and Burns, *Soldier of Freedom*, 402. Not surprisingly, Admiral Leahy downplayed the danger in his memoir, *I Was There*, 196.

2. "Unfinished Notes," (August 1941), Belle Willard Roosevelt papers, LC.

3. Eleanor Roosevelt quoted in "The President at Home," an account by Lieutenant Miles of a weekend with President and Mrs. Roosevelt, Hyde Park, New York, October 31–November 2, 1943, PRO, FO 371/38516/ 122037 (courtesy of Verne Newton).

4. "The President at Home," FO 371/38516/122037, PRO. The sentiments were attributed to Eleanor Roosevelt, but they reflected FDR's thinking as well. The intelligence analyst's comment is in "Weekly Strategy Résumé," January 23, 1943, ABC 334.3 Policy Committee (August 1, 1942), 3, records of the Joint Chiefs of Staff (JCS), RG 218, NARA, Washington, D.C.

D-Day was a redundant term (*D*=day) used to designate the opening day of a military operation. With the invasion of western France on June 6, 1944, and the accompanying publicity, the term passed into popular usage as meaning just the Normandy invasion.

5. *FRUS, Tehran Conference*, 469; Alexander, " 'Uncle Joe' "; Schild, *Bretton Woods and Dumbarton Oaks*, 44. Stalin specifically praised American aircraft production of eight to ten thousand planes per month.

6. Quoted by Colville in *Action This Day*, 96; and Colville, *Fringes of Power*, 564. Churchill's complaints are reported in Harriman, *Special Envoy*, 265.

7. Stalin's linking of the second front and the Pacific war is from Gromyko, *Memories*, 90. Those memoirs are hardly trustworthy, but this comment seems most plausible.

8. Quotations from *FRUS, Tehran Conference*, 489, 491, 494.

9. Gilbert, *Road to Victory*, 578–80, 583–84; *FRUS, Tehran Confer-*

ence, 535. The quoted exchange is on p. 579. Stalin's anger is described in Berezhkov, *History in the Making*, 281–82. Stalin's threat to leave is not in the American or British records and may not have been translated, but his "irritation" was evident.

10. *FRUS, Tehran Conference*, 481; George Earle to Admiral [Wilson] Brown, September 3, 1944, MR 163, FDRL. For a compendium of examples of Churchill's disinterest in formal postwar planning, see Charmley, *Churchill*, 456–58, 525–29, 537–38; Charmley, *Churchill's Grand Alliance*, 58; and above, pp. 207–08. On the American assumption of Britain's wealth see Kimball, *The Juggler*, 43–61, and Herring, "The United States and British Bankruptcy," 260–80.

11. Minutes of meeting between president and chiefs of staff, August 10, 1943, MR Box 29, FDRL: Elliott Roosevelt, *As He Saw It*, 184.

12. *FRUS, Teheran Conference*, 333, 515–28; Bryant, *Triumph in the West*, 82.

13. Gilbert, *Road to Victory*, 586; *FRUS, Tehran Conference*, 583. The "teasing" of Churchill by Stalin is mentioned in all the sources; see particularly Harriman, *Special Envoy*, 273–74; Gilbert, *Road to Victory*, 580–81, and *FRUS, Tehran Conference*, 553–55.

14. *FRUS, Tehran Conference*, 509.

15. Kimball and Pollock, "In Search of Monsters to Destroy," in Kimball, *The Juggler*. Roosevelt also claimed that his 1936 arrangement with the British to postpone the issue of sovereignty over Canton Island was an early example of his trusteeship idea: *Stettinius Diaries* (March 17, 1944), 38–39.

16. *FRUS, Tehran Conference*, 483–86, 532, 554, 567–71, 846; Kimball, *The Juggler*, 142–44; Sherwood, *Roosevelt and Hopkins*, 790, quotes Stalin on future "desires." The remark by FDR about reform has been interpreted as everything from an endorsement of communism to proof of his naiveté. It is neither. He and Stalin had just been talking about the inadequacy of the French "ruling classes," and the president was merely emphasizing that reform would not be implemented by an Anglo-Indian elite.

17. WSC, V, 395–97; *FRUS, Tehran Conference*, 512, 599. Actually, Stalin had adjusted the Curzon Line in Poland's favor, giving up the area around Bialystok and eliminating two bulges awarded to Russia (populated largely by Ukrainians) in southern Galicia. But he insisted that the largely Polish city of Lwow, surrounded by "an overwhelmingly Ukrainian region," remain in the Soviet Union: ibid., 601. Stalin's firm preference for dismemberment of Germany is one of the few instances in which the British and American records are not seconded by the published Soviet record, USSR, *The Tehran, Yalta and Potsdam Conferences*, a distortion by omission made positive by Gromyko in his dubious memoir when he claimed that Stalin had opposed dismemberment of Germany during the Teheran talks: *Memories*, 80–81.

18. *FRUS, Tehran Conference*, 594–95; the president's map of Poland is reprinted in facing p. 601. FDR is quoted in Dallek, *Roosevelt and Foreign Policy*, 436–37. For a similar statement to Francis Cardinal Spellman, see Eubank, *Summit at Teheran*, 361. Churchill to Eden (January 7, 1944) quoted in Gilbert, *Road to Victory*, 641.

19. Arthur Schlesinger, Jr., "Roosevelt's Diplomacy at Yalta," 145; *FRUS, Tehran Conference*, 594.

20. WSC, III, 696. This initiative is covered in Gardner, *Spheres of Influence*, 148–49, 170–81, 223–25.

21. Quoted in Schild, *Bretton Woods and Dumbarton Oaks*, 107.
22. Kimball, *Churchill & Roosevelt*, III, C-678/1 (May 21, 1944). During the American Revolution, Thomas Paine argued that access to America's foreign trade was so important to foreign nations that the United States did not need political alliances to protect itself.
23. Ibid., II, R-483/1 (February 29, 1944). See also Kimball, *The Juggler*, 98–99.
24. Sir William Strang, May 29, 1943, quoted in Ross, ed., *Foreign Office and the Kremlin*, 129–30.
25. *FRUS, Tehran Conference*, 600–04; memorandum of conversation with Roosevelt and State Department officials, October 5, 1943, *FRUS, 1943*, I, 542. The literature about American thinking about the extension of its political economy can be approached through Blum, *From the Morgenthau Diaries*, III, 228–78; Maier, "The Politics of Productivity," 607–33; Gramer, "Reconstructing Germany, 1938–1949"; Eisenberg, *Drawing the Line*, 14–120 (about Germany); and Kimball, "U.S. Economic Strategy in World War II," 139–57. Bretton Woods is discussed below.
26. *FRUS, Tehran Conference*, 487.
27. Ibid., 530–32, 595–96, 622; Kimball, *The Juggler*, 110; Eden, *The Reckoning*, 437.
28. Gilbert, *Road to Victory*, 593, 650; *Stalin-Churchill Correspondence*, 179–85.
29. Gilbert, *Road to Victory*, 604–12; quotation on 606. Kimball, *The Juggler*, 205–06, 238; Kimball, *Churchill & Roosevelt*, II, C-511; R-430.
30. Eden, *The Reckoning*, 497.
31. Bryant, *Triumph in the West*, 104 (December 3, 1943); Churchill, V, 418.
32. Churchill painted the triumphal picture for Harold Macmillan; Macmillan, *War Diaries* (December 7, 1943), 321.
33. Ambrose, *D-Day*, 28–29.
34. Overy, *The Air War*, 73–81.
35. Kimball, *Churchill & Roosevelt*, II, C-521; R-427.
36. WSC, V, 488 (Anzio), 606–10 (Rome); Burns, *Soldier of Freedom*, 438–40, 476; Kimball, *Churchill & Roosevelt*, III, C-692/1 (not sent/June 5, 1944); Macmillan, *War Diaries* (June 5, 1944), 455.
37. *FRUS, Tehran Conference*, 490; Barnett, "Anglo-American Strategy in Europe," 182; Reynolds, "Churchill and Allied Grand Strategy in Europe."
38. Eisenhower, *Crusade in Europe*, 211; memo for diary (February 7, 1944), *Eisenhower Papers*, III, no. 1712 (ellipses omitted). The Churchill-Roosevelt debate was long and acrimonious. For some examples, see Kimball, *Churchill & Roosevelt*, II, C-536; C-570; R-461; C-581; R-481; Chiefs of staff (U.S.) to Joint Staff Mission, COS(W) 1168, February 23, 1944, MR (FDRL).
39. Churchill claimed to prefer "Persia" to "Iran" lest there be confusion with "Iraq," though one suspects that he simply preferred the old names for both countries, Mesopotamia and Persia, for their romantic historical connotations. "I do not consider that names that have been familiar for generations in England should be altered to study the whims of foreigners living in those parts," he wrote in a minute of April 23, 1945: WSC, III, 479–80; VI, 752–53.

40. Hull quoted in Sainsbury, *The Turning Point*, 258. Kimball, *Churchill & Roosevelt*, II, C-591; III, R-483/2 (February 29, 1944) and encl. Hurley to Roosevelt (December 23, 1943); R-485, C-678/1, R-554. Hull's irritation with the British (and with Harold Ickes, the secretary of the interior) over oil comes through clearly in his *Memoirs*, II, 1511–27. *FRUS, Tehran Conference*, 646–47, 841–42. Iranian nationalists continued throughout the war to challenge attempts by the Great Powers to obtain oil concessions; Kimball, *Churchill & Roosevelt*, III, C-890 (January 15, 1945).

41. *FRUS, Teheran*, 253–56; Kimball, *Swords or Ploughshares?*, 14.

42. Quoted in Weigley, *Eisenhower's Lieutenants*, 42.

43. By autumn 1944 the Germans were launching V weapons from the Netherlands aimed at Antwerp, a key port in what was then liberated Belgium. The Allied offensive bypassed North Holland, and V weapons were launched from sites there until late March 1945. The V-1 flying bomb had a pulse-jet engine. V-2 rockets began hitting Britain in early September.

44. Weigley, *Eisenhower's Lieutenants*, 102–09; WSC, VI, 12; Eisenhower to Marshall (June 20, 1944), *Eisenhower Papers*, III, 1938–39.

45. *FRUS, Tehran Conference*, 526–28; *Stalin-Churchill Correspondence*, no. 279 (June 11, 1944); *Oxford Companion*, 33.

46. *FRUS, Tehran Conference*, 578.

47. Howard, *Strategic Deception*, 110–12. For a most readable overview of Anglo-American deception operations, particularly those surrounding D-Day, see Howard, "Reflections on Strategic Deception."

48. Kimball, *Churchill & Roosevelt*, III, C-703 (June 14, 1944); Gilbert, *Road to Victory*, 805–08.

49. For details, see Herman Amersfoort, "Warfare in the Netherlands, Fall 1944: Old and New"; John A. English, "Cinderella Campaign: The Genesis and Conduct of First Canadian Army Operations to Open Scheldt Estuary, 1944"; Jeffery Williams, "The Capture of Walcheren Island, 1944," all in Brower, ed., *World War Two in Europe* (in press).

50. Notter files (microform), file 548-1 (1943).

51. Churchill's lack of interest in the Bretton Woods conference is testified to by the absence of any mention of the meeting in his memoirs or in the detailed official biography by Gilbert, *Road to Victory*.

52. Schild, *Bretton Woods and Dumbarton Oaks*, 130–31.

53. Quoted in Burns, *Soldier of Freedom*, 514.

54. Schild, *Bretton Woods and Dumbarton Oaks*, 103, 112–22; Acheson is quoted on p. 122.

55. By the time of the Teheran Conference government papers had begun to refer to a postwar international organization as the organization of the United Nations, and even FDR jotted a note to the effect that "40 U.N. [United Nations]" would constitute some sort of "large organization" that "would meet periodically at different places, discuss and make recommendations to a smaller body." *FRUS, Tehran Conference*, 530, 622.

56. Hilderbrand, *Dumbarton Oaks*, and Schild, *Bretton Woods and Dumbarton Oaks* provide the details of the talks. The Big Three representatives met August 21–September 28. Then the Chinese replaced the Soviets until the conference ended on October 7, 1944.

57. Kimball, *Churchill & Roosevelt*, C-377 (July 23, 1943); R-323 (July 24, 1943).

58. Hopkins to Roosevelt, July 26, 1944, *FRUS, Quebec, 1944*, 12.

59. That objective was reconfirmed in that language during Octagon: *FRUS, Quebec, 1944,* 469–70: Crane, *Bombs, Cities, and Civilians* is a critical assessment of the limits of the strategic bombing campaign, but see also Levine, *The Strategic Bombing of Germany.*

60. For examples of intelligence overoptimism about the end of the war, see Feis, *Churchill, Roosevelt, Stalin,* 396.

61. On Ike's agreement with FDR's politics, see Eisenhower, *Eisenhower at War.*

62. Churchill to COS, September 12, 1944, quoted in Gilbert, *Road to Victory,* 955. See also ibid., 959, 963–66. *FRUS, Quebec, 1944,* 314, meeting of September 13, 1944; Pogue, *Organizer of Victory,* 453; *FRUS, Quebec, 1944,* 350.

63. Churchill as paraphrased in *FRUS, Quebec, 1944,* 314 (meeting of September 13, 1944). The thrust toward Vienna was dismissed as impractical at the time by his military and later by historians; see Barker, "The Ljubljana Gap Strategy," 57–85, and Edmonds, *The Big Three* 378.

64. Gilbert, *Road to Victory,* 942; Churchill's concern about Greece is evident in a cable to FDR sent a few days after the Normandy invasion; Kimball, *Churchill & Roosevelt,* II, C-700 (June 11, 1944).

65. Glantz and House, *When Titans Clashed,* 213–14.

66. Gilbert, *Road to Victory,* 925. The dispute over aid to Warsaw hardly broke Anglo-American unity, whatever the suggestion in ibid., 927. See also Prazmowska, "Churchill and Poland" and Kimball, "Churchill, Roosevelt and Postwar Europe." The Soviets finally did allow one such relief flight to drop supplies, most of which landed in German-held territory. On Stalin's fears, see Volkogonov, *Stalin,* 491.

67. FDR unknowingly echoed Churchill's talk in September 1940 of "castrating the lot" after he viewed the destruction from the blitz in the Wandsworth section of London: Gilbert, *Finest Hour,* 800. Shortly afterward, during a discussion about German use of parachute mines, which killed and maimed indiscriminately, Churchill proposed one-for-one retaliation and remarked, "When we've abolished Germany, we'll establish Poland—and make the Poles a permanent thing in Europe": Gilbert, *Finest Hour,* 801.

68. *FRUS, Quebec, 1944,* 466–67; Morgenthau, memo of a Conference at Red Rice, Andover, England, August 15, 1944, Harry Dexter White papers, Box 7; Morgenthau, memo for the president, August 25, 1944, Presidential diaries, Morgenthau papers, FDRL. See also Kimball, *Swords or Ploughshares?*

69. Memo of the Executive Committee on Foreign Economic Policy, August 14, 1944, *FRUS, 1944,* 285. See Morgenthau, memo to the president, "Suggested Post-Surrender Program for Germany," September 5, 1944, *FRUS, Quebec, 1944,* 101–06. The committee went on to recommend that in order to create "an effective democracy in Germany," there had to be "a tolerable standard of living," "a minimum of bitterness against the peace terms," and "harmony of policy between the British and American Governments on the one hand and the Soviet Government on the other": "The Political Reorganization of Germany," Recommendation of the Interdivisional Country Committee, September 23, 1943, in *PFPP,* 558–59. See also Kuklick, *American Policy and the Division of Germany.*

70. *FRUS, Quebec, 1944,* 466–67.

71. Brooke, diary entry for July 27, 1944, quoted in Bryant, *Triumph*

in the West, 242. For Churchill's later attempts to set up Germany as a barrier to the USSR, see Smith, *Churchill's German Army*.

72. Gilbert, *Road to Victory*, 961; Moran, *Churchill*, 190–95; *FRUS, Quebec, 1944*, 326, 390; Morgenthau memo of conversation with Roosevelt, August 19, 1944, Presidential Diaries, 1386–88, Morgenthau papers, FDRL; Kimball, *Swords or Ploughshares?*, 38–41; PREM 3/192/1, PRO; records of the meetings at the Kremlin, Moscow, October 9–17, 1944 (Tolstoy), PREM 3/434/2, PRO. British Cabinet and Foreign Office reactions included, among other arguments, the suspicion that the Americans were trying to avoid a domestic political fight over postwar aid to Britain by providing new markets for Britain; see minutes on Halifax to the Foreign Office, September 14, 1944, no. 4941, FO 371/39080/4010, paper C12073/G18, PRO.

73. *FRUS, Quebec, 1944*, 91–93, 106, 297, 467, 489–90. In December 1942 Rabbi Stephen Wise, head of the American Jewish Congress, gave Roosevelt a report describing the Nazi plan for the extermination of Europe's Jews: Burns, *Soldier of Freedom*, 395.

74. Eisenhower, *Eisenhower at War*, 522–23.

75. Gilbert, *Road to Victory*, 846–47; Kimball, *Churchill & Roosevelt*, III, C-920, R-725 (March 22, 1945); for Churchill-Roosevelt discussions about the political problems between Jews and Arabs, see the index entries, ibid. Generally see Gilbert, *Auschwitz and the Allies*, esp. 255–56, 299–312, and Newton, ed., *FDR and the Holocaust*, on the decisions not to bomb the Auschwitz death camp.

76. Hershberg, *Conant*, 217. On the Anglo-French arrangement, see Costigliola, *France and the United States*, 37.

77. Hershberg, *Conant*, 207; Truman, *Year of Decisions*, 11; Sherwin, *A World Destroyed*, 125 n.; Holloway, "The Atomic Bomb and the End of the Wartime Alliance"; Holloway, *Stalin and the Bomb*, 85–86, 90, 102–03, 115; Bernstein, "Understanding the Atomic Bomb and the Japanese Surrender," 227–73. But also see Alperovitz, *The Decision to Use the Atomic Bomb*.

78. The Soviets were not members of the Combined Chiefs of Staff Committee; attempts in April 1943 to exchange technical information failed in face of opposition from both British and U.S. military leaders, the Americans disingenuously claiming the Russians might turn over secrets to Japan; and in March 1943 FDR rejected an exchange of missions between the American OSS and the Soviet intelligence agency, NKVD, apparently on advice from Leahy and FBI Director J. Edgar Hoover: Kitchen, *British Soviet Policy*, 145–47; Harriman, *Special Envoy*, 291–95. But see Smith, *Sharing Secrets with Stalin* and "Anglo-Soviet Intelligence Cooperation and Roads to the Cold War," 50–64. The Russians sometimes made requests for information on military technology that went way beyond their wartime needs or capabilities. See, for example, memo to Admiral Brown from W. C. Mott, March 17, 1943, MR 300, Box 100, FDRL, outlining a shopping list that Harry Hopkins adamantly opposed fulfilling.

79. *FRUS, Quebec Conference, 1944*, 492 n. There is an indication that at Yalta Roosevelt considered telling Stalin about the A-bomb, but that was only because of talk of telling the French, and the president believed that the secret would quickly leak out from Paris; see Gilbert, *Road to Victory*, 1265. Neither Stalin nor the French were told. Edmonds, *Setting the Mould*, 52–53; Sherwin, *A World Destroyed*, 63, 85–86, 96, 100–02, 104. The decision not to share atomic secrets with the Soviets was paralleled by a refusal to use

lend-lease to provide the Russians with the four-engine bombers needed to deliver an atomic bomb; see Gardner, "The Atomic Temptation," 179. Burns, *Soldier of Freedom*, 456–57.

80. Harper, *American Visions of Europe*, 108–12, offers a very useful summary of these questions.

81. Rhodes, *The Making of the Atomic Bomb*, 594.

82. Aide-Mémoire initialed by Roosevelt and Churchill, September 19, 1944, *FRUS, Quebec Conference, 1944*, 492–93; Bernstein, "The Author Replies," 214–21. The evidence on FDR's caution is summarized in Alperovitz, *The Decision to Use the Atomic Bomb*, 661–62.

83. Fears that the Red Army would in fact liberate Denmark worried Churchill, and prompted Allied military planners to draw up plans to land paratroopers in Denmark. See Kaarsted, "Churchill and the Small States of Europe—The Danish Case"; Gilbert, *Road to Victory*, 1299ff.

84. Elliott Roosevelt, *As He Saw It*, 150. Roosevelt met with King George in Egypt at least twice during the two Cairo Conferences. The Greek Army had been evacuated to Egypt in 1941.

85. Kimball, *Churchill & Roosevelt*, III, C-687, R-557, C-700, R-560. The diplomatic dance, complicated by Roosevelt's failure to keep the State Department informed, is described in Gardner, *Spheres of Influence*, 186–92.

86. Gilbert, *Road to Victory*, 972–73. For details on the Greek crisis, see Wittner, *American Intervention in Greece, 1943–1949*.

87. James, ed., *Churchill Speeches*, 6, 6161; and WSC, I, 448–49; Resis, "Spheres of Influence in Soviet Wartime Diplomacy," 422–24, 431–36.

88. WSC, VI, 215; Woodward, *British Foreign Policy*, III, 148; Moran, *Churchill*, 204–05; Harriman, *Special Envoy*, 349–53; *Stalin-Churchill Correspondence*, no. 326, 328; Kimball, *Churchill & Roosevelt*, III, C-789.

89. Kimball, *Churchill & Roosevelt*, III, R-626-draft A (not sent), R-626 (October 4, 1944); Gardner, *Spheres of Influence*, 196–98; for a discussion of American myopia about its relationship with Latin America, see Kimball, *The Juggler*, 107–25.

90. The code name Tolstoy remained secret until the British opened their Second World War documents in 1972. Churchill mistakenly listed Harriman as present at the "percentages" meeting: WSC, VI, 226; Harriman, *Special Envoy*, 356.

91. The British minutes of the Tolstoy talks are in PREM 3/434, PRO. The "naughty document" remark is in FO 800-303/7505, 4, PRO, and other "unofficial" notes are in adjacent files. For fuller summaries of the talks, see Gilbert, *Road to Victory*, Chapters 53 and 54; and Kimball, *The Juggler*, 159–68.

92. Schild, *Bretton Woods and Dumbarton Oaks*, 175.

93. Churchill minute to Eden and the COS Committee, October 23, 1944, M.1024/4, Churchill papers; Gilbert, *Road to Victory*, 1038–39; WSC, VI, 389–90; *FRUS, Yalta Conference*, 984. Churchill makes no mention of this quid pro quo in his war memoirs, though he discusses Stalin's commitment to join the war against Japan: WSC, VI, 236–37. I have found no evidence of Churchill-Roosevelt agreement (or disagreement) prior to the Yalta talks regarding Far Eastern concessions to the USSR.

94. WSC, VI, 238–39.

95. Reynolds, "Churchill the Appeaser?" argues for practical accommodation. Charmley, *Churchill: The End of Glory* and *Churchill's Grand Al-*

liance argues for appeasement made necessary by earlier compromises. Nadeau, *Stalin, Churchill, and Roosevelt Divide Europe*; Aga-Rossi, "Roosevelt's European Policy and the Origins of the Cold War," 65–85; and Raack, *Stalin's Drive to the West, 1938–1945* all offer, with some emotion, the curious interpretation that Churchill (as well as FDR) sold out Eastern Europe to the Soviet Union but without demonstrating that the area was Britain's (and America's) to "sell."

96. PREM 3/434/7, PRO; Gardner, *Spheres of Influence*, 196–206; Kimball, "Churchill, Roosevelt and Postwar Europe," 135–49; Kimball, *Churchill & Roosevelt*, III, C-801 (October 22, 1944).

97. Abramson, *Spanning the Century*, 311–16, 385–87; Harriman to Roosevelt, October 10, 1944; Roosevelt to Harriman, October 11, 1944, *FRUS, 1944*, IV, 1006, 1009; Kimball, *Churchill & Roosevelt*, III, R-632; Roosevelt to Stalin repeated in R-635 (October 24, 1944).

98. Burns, *Soldier of Freedom*, 521–30; Filitov, "The Soviet Union and the Grand Alliance," 100; Kimball, *Churchill & Roosevelt*, III, C-816, C-817, R-646; WSC, VI, 229–30.

99. Harriman to Hopkins quoted in Gardner, *Spheres of Influence*, 206; *Stalin-Roosevelt Correspondence*, no. 237.

100. Minutes of the Tolstoy Conference quoted in Gilbert, *Road to Victory*, 1026.

Chapter 9: The "Holy Alliance"

1. The "left" is an inclusive term that defies precise definition. It always encompassed the extreme—communism—and thus was a powerful political pejorative that often blurred significant distinctions, often driving moderates and extremists together. For example, many in the United States, including a few members of Roosevelt's Cabinet, viewed the British Labour party as part of the left, yet party leaders like Attlee and Ernest Bevin were adamant anti-Communists. In Greece the British used the term to describe any element opposed to a restoration of the monarchy or some sort of British-sponsored regency.

2. Kolko, *The Politics of War*, 96–98.

3. Also loosely called the underground, partisans, and guerrillas, though there were sometimes careful distinctions as, for example, in the Soviet Union, where partisan actions were coordinated from Moscow while guerrillas operated on their own.

4. See Churchill, *Triumph and Tragedy*, 288–89; Wittner, *American Intervention in Greece*.

5. *FRUS, 1944*, III, 1162; *Stettinius Diaries*, 191–92 (December 6, 1944).

6. The story can be followed in the exchanges between Roosevelt and Churchill; Kimball, *Churchill & Roosevelt*, III, C-648, C-845, C-849/1, C-850/1, R-673, C-851, C-852, C-855, C-858, C-859, C-860, C-864, C-865.

7. Kimball, *Churchill & Roosevelt*, III, enclosure to C-850/1 (Churchill to Hopkins letter, December 11, 1944).

8. De Gaulle, *War Memoirs*, 557.

9. Kimball, *Churchill & Roosevelt*, II, R-423. Kolko, *The Politics of*

War, 64–96; Hurstfield, *America and the French*, 207–24. Wallonia is from Eden, *The Reckoning*, 432–33; Sherwood, *Roosevelt and Hopkins*, 711; Eden to Churchill, March 16, 1943, FO 371/35365/1316, PRO.

10. De Gaulle, *War Memoirs*, 574–75.

11. Costigliola, *France and the United States*, 31–36. FDR used the "baby" metaphor earlier that year: Kimball, *Churchill & Roosevelt*, II, R-457 (February 7, 1944). The anecdote is told by Curtis Roosevelt. The description of the toy is that of de Gaulle, *War Memoirs*, 576.

12. De Gaulle, *War Memoirs*, 522; Thorne, *Allies at War*, 435–46.

13. Kersten, "Wilhelmina and Franklin D. Roosevelt," 85–96.

14. Minutes, seventeenth Pacific War Council meeting, August 12, 1942, MR, FDRL; Kimball, *Churchill & Roosevelt*, I, R-116, R-132, C-68, draft A (not sent); *FRUS, 1945*, I, 210; Louis, *Imperialism at Bay*, 492, and Chapters 30 and 32. For full details on Roosevelt's thinking about colonialism, see Fred Pollock and Warren F. Kimball, " 'In Search of Monsters to Destroy': Roosevelt and Colonialism," in Kimball, *The Juggler*, 127–57. FDR's reference to the Articles of Confederation may well have come from a 1939 best-selling book, *Union Now* (New York: Harper, 1939), by Clarence Streit, who called for a world federation dominated by the Anglo-Saxons and referred to the League of Nations as a learning experience, just as the Articles of Confederation had been for the United States. Now, Streit concluded, the time had come to write a Constitution for the world, as the United States had done for itself in the 1780s (courtesy of Douglas Brinkley).

15. Eden, *The Reckoning*, 593; de Gaulle, *War Memoirs*, 530. Watt, "American Anti-Colonialist Policies," 93–125, condemns American hypocrisy. Charmley, *Churchill's Grand Alliance*, agrees but is more concerned with condemning the prime minister for supposedly subordinating British interests to an alliance with the Americans. Vitalis, "The 'New Deal' in Egypt," 211–39, offers Egypt as an exception in which American anticolonialism provided Egyptian commercial leaders an opportunity to throw off British economic control.

16. Churchill to Eden, December 31, 1944, FO 371/50807, PRO; Randolph Churchill quoted by Colville in Wheeler-Bennett, ed., *Action This Day*, 74; Kimball, *The Juggler*, 140–41; Louis, *Imperialism at Bay* and Thorne, *Allies of a Kind* both discuss growing British awareness that decolonization was necessary.

17. *FRUS, Tehran Conference*, 485–86; eighth PWC meeting, May 23, 1942, MR, FDRL; Moran, *Churchill*, 144–45; Kimball, *The Juggler*, 144–46.

18. Tønnesson, *The Vietnamese Revolution of 1945*, 34–72; Kimball, *The Juggler*, 147–48.

19. Spector, *Eagle Against the Sun*, 494; Tøonnesson, *The Vietnamese Revolution*, 167–69, 274; *FRUS, Yalta Conference*, 544–45.

20. Weathersby, "Soviet Aims in Korea," 6, n.16.

21. Louis, *Imperialism at Bay*, 436–40. The American military pushed hard for the United States to imitate the very nation they were fighting in the Pacific and to acquire a series of islands that seemed essential to American military security (if it was to fight World War II once again). Roosevelt agreed on the need for overseas bases but insisted that those territories maintain sovereignty rather than be incorporated into the United States. A few days before he died he set up a meeting just with delegates headed for the United Nations Conference in San Francisco to reinforce his insistence on interna-

tional trusteeships for the colonial world, including the Pacific islands: Kimball, *The Juggler*, 155.

22. *FRUS, Yalta Conference*, 770. Not all historians agree. The debate is very well summarized in Tønnesson, *The Vietnamese Revolution*, 13–19.

23. Minutes of the Tolstoy Conference, quoted in Gilbert, *Road to Victory*, 1026.

24. Weinberg, *A World at Arms*, 787–88.

25. Woodward, *British Foreign Policy*, III, 278–382. Micronationalism took over in the former Yugoslavia during the 1990s.

26. Quoted in Edmonds, *Setting the Mould*, 47–48. See also Leffler, *A Preponderance of Power*, 25–54 (chapter titled "Ambivalence, Disorganization, and the East European Litmus Test, 1945").

27. Gilbert, *Road to Victory*, 978.

28. *Presidential Press Conferences*, 24:260–64 (December 19, 1944); Kimball, *Churchill & Roosevelt*, III, R-675 (December 16, 1944), which forwards without comment the president's cable to Stalin.

29. Kimball, *Churchill & Roosevelt*, III, R-684 (December 30, 1944).

30. FDR later told reporters that the Rasputin story "was apparently all blown up." *Presidential Press Conferences*, 25:49 (February 19, 1945). Only royalty could call their edifices "palaces."

31. The descriptions are from Clemens, *Yalta*, 111–17, and my personal impressions gained during the fifth Symposium on the Soviet, British, and American Experience in World War II, Yalta, the Crimea, April 24–28, 1992. Churchill's comment is from *FRUS, Yalta*, 460.

32. Kimball, *Churchill & Roosevelt*, III, C-884 (January 10, 1945). See the preceding messages for Churchill's pleas for a preliminary meeting and FDR's refusal to have a lengthy meeting at Malta. Anglo-American staff talks began in Malta on January 30, 1945, but Roosevelt did not arrive until February 2, the last day of the discussions. The Yalta (Crimea/Argonaut) Conference was held February 4–11. The basic text for the Malta and Yalta talks is the American record found in *FRUS, Yalta Conference*.

33. See, for example, *FRUS, Yalta Conference*, 133, 498.

34. Ibid., 570, 608. Predictably MacArthur prematurely claimed victory a month earlier. The Japanese decision to contest Manila resulted in terrible devastation and brutality. "Of all Allied cities, only Warsaw suffered greater damage during the war than Manila," writes historian Ronald Spector, *Eagle Against the Sun*, 524. The citizens of Minsk might argue the ranking, but the point remains.

35. Carla Bruni in a line from *Catwalk*, quoted in *The New York Times*, February 16, 1996 (courtesy of L. Calvin Gardner).

36. See Kimball, *The Juggler*, 159–83.

37. Gardner, *Spheres of Influence*, 223–27; *FRUS, Yalta Conference*, 620–22, 970–71, 978–79, 982–83.

38. See above, pp. 286–88.

39. Clemens, *Yalta*, 244–52; *FRUS, Yalta Conference*, 770; Soviet troops entered Korea before Japan surrendered. The United States agreed to dividing occupation duties (thus dividing the country), although Truman thought about trying to exclude the Russians: Stueck, *The Road to Confrontation*, 21; Cumings, *The Origins of the Korean War*, I.

40. Byrnes, *Speaking Frankly*, X. Even the understated official conference record caught Churchill's anger and outrage:

The Prime Minister interrupted with great vigor to say that he did not agree with one single word of this report on trusteeships. He said that he had not been consulted nor had he heard of this subject up to now. He said that under no circumstances would he ever consent to forty or fifty nations thrusting interfering fingers into the life's existence of the British Empire. As long as he was minister, he would never yield one scrap of their heritage. . . .

The less inflammatory State Department phrasing is in *FRUS, Yalta*, 844.

41. Roosevelt, *Presidential Press Conferences*, 25:70–73 (February 23, 1945); Gardner, *Approaching Vietnam*, 51–52.

42. Pogue, *Organizer of Victory*, 533–34. Marshall was concerned about making sure that the Soviets attacked at the right time.

43. Roosevelt to Berle quoted in Burns, *Soldier of Freedom*, 580.

44. *FRUS, Yalta Conference*, 502–03, 566, 570 (the Eden comment is from "agreed minutes"); Gardner, *Architects of Illusion*, 51–52; Byrnes, *Speaking Frankly*, 21. Woodward, *British Foreign Policy*, V, 267–69, says Eden was "much attracted by the proposal." I think not.

45. The interpretation is mine; the evidence is summarized in Hilderbrand, *Dumbarton Oaks* and Schild, *Bretton Woods and Dumbarton Oaks*.

46. Declaration on Liberated Europe, *FRUS, Yalta Conference*, 977–78. Clemens, "Yalta: Conference of Victory and Peace," 28, 34–35; *FRUS, Yalta Conference*, 899, 919. Churchill's comment is in his *The Second World War*, VI, 393.

47. Dalton, *Diary*, 836 n.; Athan Theoharis, *The Yalta Myths* (Columbia: University of Missouri Press, 1970); Kimball, "The Mythical Yalta Myth."

48. The best telling of the encounter with the three kings is Freidel, *Roosevelt*, 593–95; see also Burns, *Soldier of Freedom*, 578–79. The comments to reporters are from *Presidential Press Conferences*, 25:50–52 (February 19, 1945).

49. Gilbert, *Road to Victory*, 1225–27; the "jingling" of independence is de Gaulle's phrase; above, p. 193.

50. White, "The Nature of World Power in American History," 196–97; Dallek, *Roosevelt and American Foreign Policy*, 519–22.

51. Sherwood, *Roosevelt and Hopkins*, 852, 862–64; *FRUS, Yalta Conference*, 590, 729.

52. Harry L. Hopkins, personal letters, FDRL, microfilm roll 20, Beaverbrook to Hopkins, March 1, 1945.

53. Kimball, *Churchill & Roosevelt*, III, C-901 (February 28, 1945); Nicolson, *The War Years, 1939–1945*, 436–37.

54. Captain Peter Thorneycroft, MP, speaking to the British House of Commons, February 28, 1945, quoted in Thompson, *Winston Churchill's World View*, 11–12.

55. Kimball, *Churchill & Roosevelt*, III, R-710/1 (March 3, 1944).

56. Quoted in Carlton, *Anthony Eden*, 254, 255. On Stalin's search for non-Lublin representatives in the Polish government, see Antony Polonsky, "Stalin and the Poles 1941–7," 453–92.

57. Kimball, *Churchill & Roosevelt*, III, C-905 (March 8, 1945).

58. See the exchanges from March 8, 1945, and after in Kimball, *Chur-*

chill & Roosevelt, III. This entire episode is examined in detail in Kimball, *The Juggler,* 159–83.

59. Kimball, *Churchill & Roosevelt,* III, C-931 (April 1, 1945); R-734 (April 4, 1945).

60. Bradley quoted in Ambrose, *Eisenhower and Berlin,* 89; Eisenhower, *Eisenhower at War,* 725–33.

61. WSC, VI, 455.

62. Nicolson, *The War Years,* 437; Ward, ed., *Closest Companion,* 400, 401ff.

63. For the point and counterpoint, see *FRUS, 1945,* III, 722ff, quotation on 727; *Stalin-Roosevelt Correspondence,* nos. 281ff.; Kimball, *Churchill & Roosevelt,* III, 585–630. For details, see Smith and Agarossi, *Operation Sunrise,* passim; see p. 62ff, on German hints, and pp. 88–89, for Stimson's discussion with Roosevelt.

64. Allen Dulles, *The Secret Surrender* (New York: Harper and Row, 1966); Smith and Agarossi, *Operation Sunrise,* 186.

65. See Gardner, *Economic Aspects of New Deal Diplomacy,* passim., but especially 261–91; Reynolds, *Creation of the Anglo-American Alliance,* 251–92; Louis, *Imperialism at Bay,* esp. 226–28, 538; Kimball, *The Juggler,* Chapters 7 and 9.

66. See Woods, *A Changing of the Guard,* and Kimball, "U.S. Economic Strategy in World War II"; Kimball, *Churchill & Roosevelt,* III, R-707/1 (February 10, 1945) and C-899/3 (February 13, 1945).

67. Kimball, *Churchill & Roosevelt,* I, R-105 (February 11, 1942); III, R-655/1, C-836; Dobson, *Peaceful Air Warfare;* Herring, "The United States and British Bankruptcy"; Pollard, "Economic Security and the Origins of the Cold War," 271–72.

68. See Wm. Roger Louis and Ronald Robinson, "The Imperialism of Decolonization," *Journal of Imperial and Commonwealth History,* 22:3 (September 1994), 462–511.

69. Gilbert, *Road to Victory,* 1222–23.

70. *Stettinius Diaries,* 238 (February 4, 1945); *FRUS, Yalta Conference,* 383–84; Glantz, "Soviet Military Strategy *vis-à-vis* Japan." The question of the timing of the Soviet attack in Manchuria was raised during the fifth Symposium of Soviet-American-British historians of the Second World War, Yalta, Crimea, Ukraine, April 23–27, 1992. Following an ambiguous discussion, the Russian military historians present vigorously denied that the Soviet invasion schedule was advanced after Hiroshima. The belief in implacable Western hatred of the Bolsheviks is the most recurrent theme in Molotov's recollections: Chuev and Resis, eds., *Molotov Remembers.*

71. Sherwood, *Roosevelt and Hopkins,* 873.

72. Had the Americans not dropped the atomic bomb, the Soviets planned to invade northern Japan: Slavinsky, "The Soviet Occupation of the Kurile Islands," 95–114.

73. Bishop, *FDR's Last Year,* 892; *FRUS, 1945,* V, 826–29; WSC, VI, 474.

74. Churchill to Truman, April 13, 1945, in Kimball, *Churchill & Roosevelt,* III, 632.

75. Kissinger, *Diplomacy,* 416.

76. Report to the State Department Policy Committee in Berle, *Navigating the Rapids,* 460–68.

77. Kennan, *American Diplomacy, 1900–1950,* 59.

78. *Harvey Diaries,* 267 (June 14, 1943); William Beveridge, a British economist and Liberal member of Parliament, proposed expanded government action to insure full employment and the creation of a social security system for Britons.

79. Gardner, *Spheres of Influence,* 222, quoting from a State Department briefing paper prepared for the Yalta Conference.

80. Kimball, *Churchill & Roosevelt,* III, R-742 (April 11, 1945).

81. FDR to Thomas W. Lamont, November 12, 1942, in Elliot Roosevelt, ed., *FDR: His Personal Letters, 1928–1945,* 1365–66; Harriman, *Special Envoy,* 169–70; Welles, *Where are We Heading?,* 31–32.

82. Quoted in Vyacheslav Dashichev, "On the Road to German Reunification," 171.

Appendix

1. See also the remarks in Chapters 1 and 9.

2. *The Churchills,* telecast on the Public Broadcasting System (WNET), February 21, 1996, facilely dismisses Roosevelt's performance at Yalta as that of a dying man.

3. Sherwood, *Roosevelt and Hopkins,* 873–74.

4. Moran's *Diaries* was published in 1966, the year after Churchill's death. Two years later John Wheeler-Bennett edited a collection of reminiscences by various of Churchill's aides that, in its Introduction, stated that Moran's book had "impelled" the authors to respond: *Action This Day,* 10. Churchill's complaint is from Nicolson, *The War Years,* 437.

5. Bruenn, "Clinical Notes," 579–91.

6. See the entries in Margaret Suckley's diary beginning with March 5, 1945, in Ward, ed., *Closest Companion,* 398ff.

7. Bruenn, "Clinical Notes," 579–91, and Bert E. Park, *The Impact of Illness on World Leaders* (Philadelphia: University of Pennsylvania Press, 1986) remain the only reliable studies of FDR's health. The evidence is assessed in Kimball, *The Juggler,* 14–15, 205–06. On Churchill's health, see *Moran Diaries;* Colville, *The Fringes of Power,* 537; Gilbert, *Road to Victory,* passim, with Churchill's angina attack mentioned on 30–32. The evidence on Churchill's health is summarized in Rose, *Churchill,* 348–50. Churchill and Roosevelt frequently mentioned their health; for example, Kimball, *Churchill & Roosevelt,* II, R-420 (December 17, 1943); R-430 (December 30, 1943); C-529 (January 1, 1944), and passim.

ACKNOWLEDGMENTS

Writers accumulate vast debts of gratitude, particularly for a book that was part of a career-long project. The only chore in thanking colleagues is keeping track of those who helped. Inevitably I will have forgotten someone, and for that I apologize.

The pleasure is acknowledging the remarkable willingness, even eagerness of other historians to help. Charles C. Alexander, distinguished professor of history at Ohio University, read the entire manuscript and saved me from countless errors of logic, argumentation, fact, syntax, grammar, and style, not to mention my barbarous misuses of commas, semicolons, and dashes. He is a Renaissance scholar in the best sense of the word, and his eclectic wisdom and common sense have long been indispensable to me.

Mark A. Stoler, professor of history at the University of Vermont, is the country's leading historian of the relationship between high politics and military strategy during the Second World War. He read the entire manuscript and made extensive and invaluable comments and suggestions.

Lloyd Gardner, the Charles and Mary Beard professor of history at Rutgers University, has helped me in more ways than I can count. We talk history over the phone, at dinners, at pub sessions with graduate students, and (with the indulgence of our spouses) when we get together socially. We disagree, argue, debate, and concur, but without those discussions this book would be much less than what it is. I am in his debt.

Dr. David Reynolds of Cambridge University (Christ's College) likewise provided a sounding board for my work and answered an endless stream of questions. I only wish he were nearby so that I could bounce ideas off him on a regular basis. Nonetheless, I value his advice and comments—and his friendship.

A number of historians helped with specific questions, and for that I thank Anders Stephanson of Columbia University, Ted Wilson of Kansas University, Alex Danchev of Keele University, Steven Miner of Ohio University, Fred Pollock of Rutgers University, Douglas Brinkley of the University of New Orleans, Arthur Funk of the University of Florida, Colonel Charles Brower of the U.S. Military Academy, Colonel David Glantz, Christopher Andrew of Cambridge University (Corpus Christi College), and a number of historians at the Institute for Universal History in Moscow, Russia—particularly G. N. Sevost'ianov, A. O. Chubarian, O. A. Rzheshevsky, V. V. Pozniakov, M. N. Narinsky, and L. V. Pozdeeva.

My thanks to Rutgers University, specifically the steady support of Norman Samuels and David Hosford, the Newark provost and dean of the Newark Faculty of Arts and Science respectively, as well as that of my friends and colleagues Jan Lewis and Norma Basch, the chairs of the History Department while this book was gestating and being born.

The director and staff at the Franklin D. Roosevelt Library continue to provide the kind of cheerful and professional support that makes research a pleasure, and I am grateful to the Franklin and Eleanor Roosevelt Institute as well as the Roosevelt Study Center in Middelburg, the Netherlands, for providing me a number of venues at which to test my ideas.

As before, the fellows of Corpus Christi College (Cambridge) provided intellectual and physical sustenence during my research trips to the Churchill Archive. I am happy for their friendship.

I am grateful to the following publishers of the books, articles, and reviews I have written for allowing me to quote and closely paraphrase myself, even if I have sometimes failed to get their express permission: Princeton University Press, St. Martin's Press, Johns Hopkins University Press, Macmillan, Oxford University Press, Brassey, University Press of Kansas, J. P. Lippincott, Scholarly Resources, *Diplomatic History*, *Journal of American-East Asian Studies*, *Journal of Military History*, *Times Literary Supplement*, *Journal of Economic History*, *Political Science Quarterly*, and *Reviews in American History*. My apologies, and thanks, to any I missed.

I owe a debt of gratitude to Gerry McCauley who never lost faith, and helped here and abroad, guiding me through the thickets of the real world.

Like all who use government documents, I am grateful to those sensible lawmakers in the nations that have established national and international criteria allowing scholars to quote from the records.

As for Jackie, she knows.

Somerset, New Jersey
September 1, 1996

BIBLIOGRAPHY

Dear, I.C.B., gen. ed. *The Oxford Companion to the Second World War*. Oxford/New York: Oxford University Press, 1995. Statistical and factual data are from the *Oxford Companion* unless otherwise indicated.

SOURCES: Published Documents

Australia. Department of Foreign Affairs and Trade. *Documents on Australian Foreign Policy, 1937–1949*. Vol. VII. Canberra: Australian Government Publishing Service, 1988.

Bland, Larry I., ed. *The Papers of George Catlett Marshall*, vol. 3, *"The Right Man for the Job": December 7, 1941–May 31, 1943*. Baltimore and London: Johns Hopkins University Press, 1991.

———— et al., eds. *George C. Marshall Interviews and Reminiscences for Forrest C. Pogue*, rev. ed. Lexington, Ky.: George C. Marshall Research Foundation, 1991.

Cantril, Hadley, ed. *Public Opinion, 1935–1946*. Princeton: Princeton University Press, 1951.

Chandler, Alfred D., et al., eds. *The Papers of Dwight David Eisenhower: The War Years*. 5 vols. Baltimore: Johns Hopkins University Press, 1970.

Churchill, Winston S. *The Irrepressible Churchill*, comp. Kay Halle. New York and Oxford: Facts on File Publications, 1985.

Doenecke, Justus D. *In Danger Undaunted: The Anti-Interventionist Movement of 1940–1941*. Stanford: Hoover Institution Press, 1990.

Federal'naia sluzhba bezopastnosti Rossii; sluzhba vneshnei razvedki Rossii; Moskovskoe gorodskoe ob'edinenie arkhivov. *Sekrety Gitlera na stole u Stalina: Razvedka i kontrrazvedka o podgotove germanskoe agressii protiv SSSR Mart-Iiun' 1941g.; Dokumenty iz Tsentral'nogo arhkiva FSB Rossii* (Hitler's Secrets on Stalin's Desk: Intelligence and Counterintelligence about Preparations for German Aggression Against the USSR, March–June 1941: Documents from the Central Archive of the FSR of Russia). Moscow: Mosgoarchiv, 1995 (*Hitler's Secrets on Stalin's Desk*).

Germany. *Documents on German Foreign Policy: 1918–1945*. Series D, vol. I. Washington: U.S. Government Printing Office, 1949.

————. *Führer Conferences on Matters Dealing with the German Navy*. Translated and mimeographed by the Office of Naval Intelligence. 7 vols. Washington: ONI, 1947.

Gilbert, Martin, ed. *The Churchill War Papers*, vol. II, *Never Surrender, May 1940–December 1940*. New York: Norton, 1995.

James, Robert Rhodes, ed. *Churchill: His Complete Speeches, 1897–1963*. Vols. VI, VII. New York: Chelsea House, 1974 (*Churchill Speeches*).

Kimball, Warren F., ed. *Churchill & Roosevelt: The Complete Correspondence*. 3 vols. Princeton: Princeton University Press, 1984.

Pickersgill, J. W., and D. F. Forster, eds. *The Mackenzie King Record*, vol. II, *1944–1945*. Toronto: University of Toronto Press, 1968.

Roosevelt, Elliott, ed. *F. D. R.: His Personal Letters, 1905–1928*. New York: Duell, Sloan and Pearce, 1948.

Roosevelt, Franklin D. *Complete Presidential Press Conferences of Franklin D. Roosevelt.* 25 vols. New York: De Capo Press, 1972 (*Presidential Press Conferences*).

————. *The Public Papers and Address of Franklin D. Roosevelt*, comp. Samuel I. Rosenman. 13 vols. London: Macmillan, 1938–50. (*FDR/PPA*).

Ross, Graham, ed. *The Foreign Office and the Kremlin: British Documents on Anglo-Soviet Relations, 1941–1945*. Cambridge: Cambridge University Press, 1984.

Russian Federation, Federal Service of Counterespionage. *Organy gosudarstvennoi bezopastnosti SSSR v velikoi otechestvennoi voine: Sbornik dokumentov.* Tom 1; Nakanune: Kniga pervaia, 1995 (Noiabr' 1938g.–Dekabr' 1940g).

Rzheshevsky, Oleg, ed. *War and Diplomacy: The Making of the Grand Alliance: Documents from Stalin's Archives.* Amsterdam: Harwood Academic Publ./Overseas Publishers Assoc., 1996.

U.S. Department of State. *Foreign Relations of the United States.* Washington: U.S. Government Printing Office, 1862– (*FRUS*).

———— [Harley A. Notter]. *Postwar Foreign Policy Preparation, 1939–1945.* Washington: U.S. Government Printing Office, 1950 (PFPP).

————. *Post World War II Foreign Policy Planning: State Department Records of Harley A. Notter* (microform). Bethesda, Md.: 1987 (Notter files).

————. *Post World War II Foreign Policy Planning: State Department Records of Harley A. Notter* [guide to the microfiche collection]. 2 vols. Bethesda, Md.: 1987).

USSR. Ministry of Foreign Affairs. *Correspondence Between the Chair of the Council of Ministers of the U.S.S.R. and the Presidents of the U.S.A. and the Prime Ministers of Great Britain during the Great Patriotic War of 1941–1945.* New York: Capricorn Books, 1965 (*Stalin-Churchill Correspondence* or *Stalin-Roosevelt Correspondence*).

————. *The Tehran, Yalta and Potsdam Conferences: Documents.* Moscow: Progress, Publishers, 1969.

Archival Documents

Cadogan, Alexander. Diaries. Churchill College, Cambridge.

Chamberlain, Neville. Papers. University of Birmingham Library.

Churchill, Winston S. Papers. Churchill College, Cambridge.

Citrine, Walter. Papers. British Library of Political and Economic Science/ London School of Economics (LSE).

Dalton, Hugh. Diary. British Library of Political and Economic Science/ London School of Economics.

Frankfurter, Felix. Papers. Library of Congress (LC). Washington, D.C.

Great Britain, Cabinet Office. Cabinet papers (CAB). Public Record Office (PRO). Kew, England.

———, Foreign Office (FO). Files. Public Record Office (PRO). Kew, England.

———, Prime Minister's Office. Premier 3 and 4 files (PREM 3 or PREM 4). Public Record Office (PRO). Kew, England.

Halifax, Lord. Papers (microfilm). Winston S. Churchill Library, Churchill College, Cambridge.

Harriman, W. Averell. Papers. Library of Congress. Washington, D.C.

Meade, James. Diary. British Library of Political and Economic Science, London School of Economics.

Morgenthau, Henry, Jr. Diaries. Franklin D. Roosevelt Library, Hyde Park, N.Y. (FDRL)

Roosevelt, Franklin D. Papers. Franklin D. Roosevelt Library, Hyde Park, N.Y. (FDRL). File abbreviations: OF (Official File); PPF (President's Personal File); PSF (President's Secretary's File); MR (Map Room files).

Schrader, Captain Albert E., USN. "Diary." Navy Historical Center, Washington, D.C.

U.S. National Archives and Records Administration (NARA), record group 218.

Welles, Sumner. Papers. Franklin D. Roosevelt Library, Hyde Park, N.Y.

White, Harry Dexter. Papers. Princeton University Library, Princeton, New Jersey.

Published Diaries and Memoirs

Amery, Leo. *The Empire at Bay: The Leo Amery Diaries, 1929–1945*, ed. John Barnes and David Nicholson. London: Hutchinson, 1988.

Berezhkov, Valentin. *History in the Making: Memoirs of World War II Diplomacy*. Moscow: Progress, 1983.

Berle, Adolf. *Navigating the Rapids, 1918–1971: From the Papers of Adolf A. Berle*, ed. Beatrice Bishop Berle and Travis Beal Jacobs. New York: Harcourt Brace Jovanovich, 1973.

Bohlen, Charles E. *Witness to History, 1929–1969*. New York: Norton, 1973.

Byrnes, James F. *Speaking Frankly*. New York: Harper & Bros., 1947.

Campbell, Thomas, and George C. Herring, eds. *The Diaries of Edward R. Stettinius, Jr.* New York: New Viewpoints, 1975.

Chuev, Felix, and Albert Resis, eds. *Molotov Remembers*. Chicago: Ivan Dee, 1993.

Churchill, Winston S. *The Second World War.* 6 vols. Boston: Houghton Mifflin, 1948–53 (WSC).

Colville, John. *The Fringes of Power: 10 Downing Street Diaries, 1939–55.* New York: Norton, 1985.

de Gaulle, Charles. *The Complete War Memoirs of Charles de Gaulle.* New York: Simon and Schuster, 1972.

Dilks, David, ed. *The Diaries of Sir Alexander Cadogan.* New York: Putnam, 1972.

Eden, Anthony [Earl of Avon]. *Memoirs of Anthony Eden*, vol. 2, *The Reckoning*. Boston: Houghton Mifflin, 1965.

Eisenhower, Dwight D. *Crusade in Europe*. Garden City, N.Y.: Doubleday, 1948.

Gromyko, Andrei. *Memories*, tran. Harold Shukman, London: Hutchinson, 1989.

Harriman, W. Averell, and Elie Abel. *Special Envoy to Churchill and Stalin, 1941–1946*. New York; Random House, 1975.

Harvey, Oliver, ed. *The War Diaries of Oliver Harvey*, ed. John Harvey. London: Collins, 1978.

Hull, Cordell. *The Memoirs of Cordell Hull*. 2 vols. New York: Macmillan, 1948.

Iatrides, John, ed. *Ambassador MacVeagh Reports: Greece, 1933–1947*. Princeton: Princeton University Press, 1980.

Kennan, George. *Memoirs, 1925–1950*. Boston: Little, Brown, 1967.

Leahy, William D. *I Was There*. New York: Whittlesey House, 1950.

Macmillan, Harold. *War Diaries: Politics and War in the Mediterranean, January 1943–May 1945*. New York: St. Martin's, 1984.

Martin, Sir John. *Downing Street: The War Years*. London: Bloomsbury, 1991.

Moran, Lord [Charles Wilson]. *Churchill Taken from the Diaries of Lord Moran*. Boston: Houghton Mifflin, 1966 (*Moran Diaries*).

Nicolson, Nigel, ed. *Harold Nicolson: Diaries and Letters, vol. II, The War Years, 1939–1945*. New York: Atheneum, 1967.

Pimlott, Ben, ed. *The Second World War Diary of Hugh Dalton, 1940–45*. London: Jonathan Cape, 1986.

Roosevelt, Elliott. *As He Saw It*. New York: Duell, Sloan and Pearce, 1946.

Rosenman, Samuel I. *Working with Roosevelt*. New York: Da Capo, 1972.

Truman, Harry S. *Memoirs*, vol. I, *Year of Decisions*. Garden City, N.Y.: Doubleday, 1955.

Tully, Grace. *F. D. R.: My Boss*. New York: Charles Scribner's Sons, 1949.

Ward, Geoffrey C., ed. *Closest Companion: The Unknown Story of the Intimate Friendship Between Franklin Roosevelt and Margaret Suckley*. Boston and New York: Houghton Mifflin, 1995.

Welles, Sumner. *Where Are We Heading?* London: Hamish Hamilton, 1951.

SECONDARY WORKS: Books

Abramson, Rudy. *Spanning the Century: The Life of W. Averell Harriman, 1891–1986*. New York: William Morrow, 1992.

Alperovitz, Gar. *The Decision to Use the Atomic Bomb*. New York: Knopf, 1995.

Ambrose, Stephen E. *D-Day, June 6, 1944: The Climactic Battle of World War II*. New York: Simon & Schuster, 1994.

———. *Eisenhower and Berlin, 1945: The Decision to Halt at the Elbe.* New York: Norton, 1967.

———. *The Supreme Commander: The War Years of General Dwight D. Eisenhower.* Garden City: Doubleday, 1970.

Andrew, Christopher. *For the President's Eyes Only.* New York: HarperCollins, 1995.

Anglin, Douglas G. *The St. Pierre and Miquelon Affaire of 1941.* Toronto: University of Toronto Press, 1966.

Bailey, Thomas. *A Diplomatic History of the American People,* 10th ed. Englewood Cliffs, N.J.: Prentice-Hall, 1980.

Barnett, Correlli. *The Desert Generals,* rev. ed. Bloomington: Indiana University Press, 1982.

Barnhart, Michael A. *Japan and the World Since 1868.* London: Edward Arnold, 1995.

———. *Japan Prepares for Total War: The Search for Economic Security, 1919–1941.* Ithaca: Cornell University Press, 1987.

Bearse, Ray, and Anthony Read. *Conspirator: The Untold Story of Tyler Kent.* New York: Doubleday, 1991.

Beaumont, Joan. *Comrades in Arms: British Aid to Russia 1941–45.* London: David Poynter, 1980.

Begbie, Harold. *The Mirrors of Downing Street: Some Political Reflections by a Gentleman with a Duster.* Freeport, N.Y.: Books for Libraries, 1970. First published 1923.

Behrendt, Hans-Otto. *Rommel's Intelligence in the Desert Campaign.* London: William Kimber, 1985.

Bennett, Edward M. *Franklin D. Roosevelt and the Search for Victory.* Wilmington, Del.: Scholarly Resources, 1990.

Beschloss, Michael. *Kennedy and Roosevelt: The Uneasy Alliance.* New York: Norton, 1980.

Bishop, Jim. *FDR's Last Year.* New York: Pocket Books, 1975.

Blake, Robert and Wm. Roger Louis, eds. *Churchill.* Oxford: Oxford University Press, 1993.

Blum, John Morton. *From the Morgenthau Diaries.* 3 vols. Boston: Houghton Mifflin, 1959–67.

Brinkley, Douglas, and David R. Facey-Crowther, eds. *The Atlantic Charter.* New York: St. Martin's, 1994.

Bryant, Arthur. *The Turn of the Tide, 1939–1943.* London/Glasgow: Grafton Books, 1986.

———. *Triumph in the West, 1943–1946.* London/Glasgow: Grafton Books, 1986.

Burns, James MacGregor. *Roosevelt: The Lion and the Fox, 1882–1940.* New York: Harcourt Brace Jovanovich-Harvest ed., 1956.

———. *Roosevelt: Soldier of Freedom.* New York: Harvest/HBJ Book, 1970.

Callahan, Raymond A. *Churchill: Retreat from Empire.* Wilmington, Del. Scholarly Resources, 1984.

Carlton, David. *Anthony Eden: A Biography.* London: Allen Lane, 1981.

Charmley, John. *Churchill: The End of Glory.* London: Hodder & Stoughton, 1993.

——.*Churchill's Grand Alliance.* London: Hodder & Stoughton, 1995.

Churchill, Winston S. *The Birth of Britain.* New York: Dodd Mead, 1956.

——. *The World Crisis.* New York: Charles Scribner's Sons, 1929.

Ciechanowski, Jan M. *The Warsaw Rising of 1944.* Cambridge: Cambridge University Press, 1974.

Clemens, Diane. *Yalta.* New York: Oxford University, Press, 1970.

Clifford, J. Garry, and Samuel R. Spencer, Jr. *The First Peacetime Draft.* Lawrence: University Press of Kansas, 1986.

Cohen, Warren I. *Empire Without Tears.* Philadelphia: Temple University Press, 1987.

Cole, Wayne S. *Roosevelt and the Isolationists.* Lincoln and London: University of Nebraska Press, 1983.

Costello, John. *Ten Days to Destiny.* New York: William Morrow, 1991.

——. *The Pacific War.* New York: Rawson, Wade, 1981.

Costigliola, Frank. *France and the United States.* New York: Twayne, 1992.

Crane, Conrad C. *Bombs, Cities, and Civilians: American Airpower Strategy in World War II.* Lawrence: University Press of Kansas, 1993.

Cull, Nicholas John. *Selling War: The British Propaganda Campaign against American "Neutrality" in World War II.* New York: Oxford University Press, 1995.

Cumings, Bruce. *The Origins of the Korean War.* Vol. I; Princeton: Princeton University Press, 1981.

Dallek, Robert. *Franklin D. Roosevelt and American Foreign Policy, 1932–1945.* New York: Oxford University Press, 1979.

Danchev, Alex. *Very Special Relationship: Field Marshal Sir John Dill and the Anglo-American Alliance, 1941–44.* London: Brassey's, 1986.

Davis, Forrest, and Ernest K. Lindley. *How War Came.* New York: Simon and Schuster, 1942.

Day, David. *The Great Betrayal: Britain, Australia and the Onset of the Pacific War, 1939–1942.* North Ryde, New South Wales, and London: Angus & Robertson, 1988.

——. *Reluctant Nation: Australia and the Allied Defeat of Japan, 1942–45.* Oxford, Melbourne, et al.: Oxford University Press, 1992.

Divine, Robert A. *The Illusion of Neutrality.* Chicago: University of Chicago Press, 1962.

——. *Roosevelt and World War II.* Baltimore: Johns Hopkins University Press 1969; Penguin ed.; 1970.

——. *Second Chance: The Triumph of Internationalism in America During World War II.* New York: Atheneum, 1967.

Dobson, Alan P. *Peaceful Air Warfare: The United States, Britain, and the Politics of International Aviation.* Oxford: Clarendon Press, 1991.

——. *US Wartime Aid to Britain, 1940–1946.* London: Croon Helm, 1986.

Dower, John. *War Without Mercy: Race and Power in the Pacific War.* New York: Pantheon, 1986.

Edmonds, Robin. *Setting the Mould.* New York and London: Norton, 1986.

———. *The Big Three: Churchill, Roosevelt & Stalin in Peace and War.* London: Hamish Hamilton, 1991.

Ehrman, John. *Grand Strategy, August 1943–September 1944.* London: HMSO, 1956. British Official History of the Second World War.

Eisenberg, Carolyn W. *Drawing the Line: The American Decision to Divide Germany, 1944–1949.* Cambridge and New York: Cambridge University Press, in press.

Eisenhower, David. *Eisenhower at War, 1943–1945.* New York: Random House, 1986.

Erickson, John. *The Road to Berlin.* Boulder, Colo.: Westview Press, 1983.

———. *The Road to Stalingrad.* New York: Harper & Row, 1975.

Eubank, Keith. *Summit at Teheran.* New York: William Morrow, 1985.

Feis, Herbert. *Churchill, Roosevelt, Stalin.* Princeton: Princeton University Press, 1957.

Fleischhauer, Ingeborg. *Die Chance des Sonderfriedens.* Berlin: Siedler, 1986.

Freidel, Frank. *Franklin D. Roosevelt: A Rendezvous with Destiny.* Boston: Little, Brown, 1990.

Funk, Arthur L. *The Politics of Torch.* Lawrence: University Press of Kansas, 1974.

Fussell, Paul. *Wartime.* New York: Oxford University Press, 1989.

Gardner, Lloyd C. *Approaching Vietnam: From World War II Through Dienbienphu.* New York: Norton, 1988.

———. *Architects of Illusion.* Chicago: Quadrangle, 1972.

———. *Economic Aspects of New Deal Diplomacy,* Madison: University of Wisconsin Press, 1964.

———. *Spheres of Influence: The Great Powers Partition Europe, from Munich to Yalta.* Chicago: Ivan Dee, 1993.

Gelb, Leslie. *Anglo-American Relations, 1945–1949.* Harvard Dissertations in American History and Political Science. New York and London: Garland, 1988.

Gellman, Irwin F. *Secret Affairs: Franklin Roosevelt, Cordell Hull, and Sumner Welles.* Baltimore and London: Johns Hopkins University Press, 1995.

Gilbert, Martin. *Auschwitz and the Allies.* New York: Holt, Rinehart, and Winston, 1981.

———. *Churchill: A Life.* London: Heinemann, 1991.

———. *In Search of Churchill.* New York: Wiley, 1994.

———. *Winston S. Churchill,* vol. VI, *Finest Hour,* and vol. VII, *Road to Victory.* Boston: Houghton Mifflin, 1983, 1986.

Glantz, David. *Soviet Military Deception in the Second World War.* London: Cass, 1989.

———, and Jonathan M. House. *When Titans Clashed: How the Red Army Stopped Hitler.* Lawrence: University Press of Kansas, 1995.

Goodwin, Doris Kearns. *No Ordinary Time: Franklin and Eleanor Roosevelt: The Home Front in World War II.* New York: Simon & Schuster, 1994.

Gorodetsky, Gabriel. *Stafford Cripps' Mission to Moscow, 1940–1942.* Cambridge: Cambridge University Press, 1984.

Granatstein, J. L. *Canada's War.* Toronto: Oxford University Press, 1975.

Gunther, John. *Roosevelt in Retrospect.* New York: Harper, 1950

Harbutt, Fraser J. *The Iron Curtain: Churchill, America, and the Origins of the Cold War.* New York: Oxford University Press, 1986.

Harper, John Lamberton. *American Visions of Europe: Franklin D. Roosevelt, George F. Kennan, and Dean C. Acheson.* Cambridge and New York: Cambridge University Press, 1994.

Harrod, Roy F. *The Life of John Maynard Keynes.* New York: Harcourt, Brace & Co., 1951.

Hearden, Patrick. *Roosevelt Confronts Hitler.* De Kalb: Northern Illinois University Press, 1987.

Heinrichs, Waldo. *The Threshold of War: Franklin Roosevelt and American Entry into World War II.* New York and Oxford: Oxford University Press, 1988.

Herring, George C. *Aid to Russia, 1941–1946.* New York: Columbia University Press, 1973.

Hershberg, James. *James B. Conant.* New York: Knopf, 1993.

Hess, Gary. *The United States' Emergence as a Southeast Asian Power, 1940–1950.* New York: Columbia University Press, 1987.

Hilderbrand, Robert C. *Dumbarton Oaks: The Origins of the United Nations and the Search for Postwar Security.* Chapel Hill and London: University of North Carolina Press, 1990.

Hinsley, F. W. et al. *British Intelligence in the Second World War.* Vols. 1–3. London and New York: HMSO and Cambridge University Press, 1979–90 (*British Intelligence*).

Hitchens, Christopher. *Blood, Class, and Nostalgia: Anglo-American Ironies.* New York: Farrar, Straus & Giroux, 1990.

Holland, Jeffrey. *The Aegean Mission: Allied Operations in the Dodecanese, 1943.* Westport, Conn.: Greenwood Press, 1988.

Holloway, David. *Stalin and the Bomb: The Soviet Union and Atomic Energy, 1939–1956.* New Haven and London: Yale University Press, 1994.

Howard, Michael. *British Intelligence in the Second World War,* vol. V, *Strategic Deception.* New York: Cambridge University Press, 1990.

———. *Grand Strategy, August 1942–September 1943.* London: HMSO, 1970. British Official History of the Second World War.

Hurstfield, Julian G. *America and the French Nation, 1939–1945.* Chapel Hill and London: University of North Carolina Press, 1986.

Iriye, Akira. *Power and Culture: The Japanese-American War, 1941–1945.* Cambridge: Harvard University Press, 1981.

———, and Warren I. Cohen, eds. *Americans, Chinese, and Japanese Perspectives on Wartime Asia, 1931–1949.* Wilmington, Del.: Scholarly Resources, 1990.

Irving, David. *Göring: A Biography.* New York: William Morrow, 1989.

Jablonsky, David. *Churchill: The Great Game and Total War.* London: Frank Cass, 1991.

James, Robert Rhodes. *Anthony Eden.* London: Weidenfeld and Nicolson, 1986.

Jefferys, Kevin. *The Churchill Coalition and Wartime Politics, 1940–1945.* Manchester and New York: Manchester University Press, 1991.

Keegan, John. *The Second World War.* New York: Penguin Books, 1990.

Kennan, George F. *American Diplomacy, 1900–1950.* New York: Mentor Books, 1959.

Kilzer, Louis C. *Churchill's Deception.* New York: Simon & Schuster, 1994.

Kimball, Warren F. *Swords or Ploughshares? The Morgenthau Plan for Defeated Nazi Germany, 1943–1945.* Philadelphia: Lippincott, 1976.

———. *The Juggler: Franklin Roosevelt as Wartime Statesman.* Princeton: Princeton University Press, 1991.

———. *The Most Unsordid Act: Lend-Lease, 1939–1941.* Baltimore: Johns Hopkins University Press, 1969.

Kimche, Jon. *The Unfought Battle.* New York: Stein and Day, 1968.

Kissinger, Henry. *Diplomacy.* New York: Simon & Schuster, 1994.

Kitchen, Martin. *British Policy Towards the Soviet Union during the Second World War.* New York: St. Martin's, 1986.

Kolko, Gabriel. *The Politics of War.* New York: Vintage, 1968.

Koppes, Clayton R., and Gregory D. Black. *Hollywood Goes to War.* New York: Free Press, 1987.

Krebs, Gerhard, and Christian Oberländer, eds. *1945 in Europe and Asia: Reconsidering the End of World War II and the Change of the World Order.* Munich: Iudicium, 1996.

Kuklick, Bruce. *American Policy and the Division of Germany: The Clash with Russia over Reparations.* Ithaca: Cornell University Press, 1972.

LaFeber, Walter. *America, Russia, and the Cold War,* 5th ed. New York: Knopf, 1985.

Larrabee, Eric. *Commander in Chief: Franklin Delano Roosevelt, His Lieutenants and Their War.* New York: Harper & Row, 1987.

Lash, Joseph P. *Eleanor and Franklin.* New York: Norton, 1971.

———. *Roosevelt and Churchill, 1939–1941: The Partnership That Saved the West.* New York: W. W. Norton, 1976.

Lee, Asher. *Goering: Air Leader.* London: Duckworth, 1972.

Leffler, Melvyn P. *A Preponderance of Power.* Stanford: Stanford University Press, 1992.

Leutze, James R. *Bargaining for Supremacy: Anglo-American Naval Collaboration, 1937–1941.* Chapel Hill: University of North Carolina Press, 1977.

Levine, Alan J. *The Strategic Bombing of Germany, 1940–1945.* Westport, Conn., and London: Praeger, 1992.

Louis, Wm. Roger. *Imperialism at Bay: The United States and the Decolonization of the British Empire, 1941–1945.* New York: Oxford University Press, 1978.

———, and Hedley Bull, eds. *The "Special Relationship."* Oxford: Clarendon Press, 1986.

Lukacs, John. *The Duel: Hitler vs. Churchill: 10 May–31 July 1940.* London: Bodley Head, 1990.

Lukas, Richard C. *Eagles East: The Army Air Forces and the Soviet Union, 1941–1945.* Tallahassee: Florida State University Press, 1970.

MacDonald, Callum A. *The Lost Battle: Crete 1941.* New York: Free Press, 1993.

———. *The United States, Britain and Appeasement, 1936–1939.* London: Macmillan, 1981.

MacLean, Elizabeth Kimball. *Joseph E. Davies: Envoy to the Soviets.* Westport, Conn., and London: Praeger, 1992.

Mastny, Vojtech. *Russia's Road to the Cold War.* New York: Columbia University Press, 1979.

Matloff, Maurice. *Strategic Planning for Coalition Warfare, 1943–1944.* Washington: Office of the Chief of Military History, 1959.

McJimsey, George. *Harry Hopkins.* Cambridge: Harvard University Press, 1987.

Medvedev, Dm. *Silnye Dukhom.* Moscow: Soviet Writer, 1957.

Miner, Steven M. *Between Churchill and Stalin.* Chapel Hill and London: University of North Carolina Press, 1988.

Morgan, Ted. *FDR: A Biography.* London: Collins, Grafton Books, 1986.

Nadeau, Remi. *Stalin, Churchill, and Roosevelt Divide Europe.* Westport, Conn.: Greenwood Press, 1990.

Newton, Verne W., ed. *FDR and the Holocaust.* New York: St. Martin's, 1996.

O'Connor, Raymond G. *Diplomacy for Victory: FDR and Unconditional Surrender.* New York: Norton, 1971.

O'Neill, William L. *A Democracy at War.* New York: Free Press, 1993.

Ovendale, Ritchie. *"Appeasement" and the English Speaking World.* Cardiff: University of Wales Press, 1975.

Overy, Richard J. *The Air War, 1939–1945.* London: Papermac, 1980.

———. *Why the Allies Won.* New York and London: Norton, 1995.

Parish, Michael W. *Aegean Adventures 1940–1943 and the End of Churchill's Dream.* Sussex, U.K.: The Book Guild, 1993.

Park, Bert E. *The Impact of Illness on World Leaders.* Philadelphia: University of Pennsylvania Press, 1986.

Parker, R. A. C. *Chamberlain and Appeasement: British Policy and the Coming of the Second World War.* New York: St. Martin's, 1993.

Parrish, Thomas. *Roosevelt and Marshall.* New York: William Morrow, 1989.

Paterson, Thomas, Clifford, J. Garry, and Kenneth Hagan. *American Foreign Relations.* Vol. II. 4th ed. Lexington, Mass.: D. C. Heath, 1995.

Pogue, Forrest C. *George C. Marshall: Organizer of Victory.* New York: Viking, 1973.

Raack, R. C. *Stalin's Drive to the West, 1938–1945.* Stanford: Stanford University Press, 1995.

Reynolds, D., W. F. Kimball, and A. O. Chubarian, eds. *Allies at War: The Soviet, American, and British Experience, 1939–1945.* New York: St. Martin's, 1994.

Reynolds, David. *The Creation of the Anglo-American Alliance, 1937–1941.* Chapel Hill: University of North Carolina Press, 1982.

————, and Dimbleby, David. *An Ocean Apart: The Relationship Between Britain and America in the Twentieth Century.* New York: Random House, 1988.

Rhodes, Richard. *The Making of the Atomic Bomb.* London and New York: Penguin, 1986.

Robertson, Terence. *The Ship with Two Captains.* New York: Dutton, 1950.

Rock, William R. *Chamberlain and Roosevelt: British Foreign Policy and the United States, 1937–1940.* Columbus: Ohio State University Press, 1988.

Rose, Norman. *Churchill: The Unruly Giant.* New York: Free Press, 1995.

Rusbridger, James, and Eric Nave. *Betrayal at Pearl Harbor: How Churchill Lured Roosevelt into World War II.* New York: Summit, 1991.

Sainsbury, Keith. *Churchill and Roosevelt at War.* New York: New York University Press, 1994.

————. *The North African Landings, 1942.* Newark: University of Delaware Press, 1976.

————. *The Turning Point.* Oxford and New York: Oxford University Press, 1986.

Saiu, Liliana. *The Great Powers and Rumania, 1944–1946: A Study of the Early Cold War Era.* Boulder, Colo.: East European Monographs [No. 335], 1992.

Schaller, Michael. *The U.S. Crusade in China, 1938–1945.* New York: Columbia University Press, 1979.

Schild, Georg. *Bretton Woods and Dumbarton Oaks: American Economic and Political Postwar Planning in the Summer of 1944.* New York: St. Martin's, 1995.

Schneider, James C. *Should America Go to War? The Debate over Foreign Policy in Chicago, 1939–1941.* Chapel Hill: University of North Carolina Press, 1989.

Sherwin, Martin. *A World Destroyed: The Atomic Bomb and the Grand Alliance.* New York: Knopf, 1975.

Sherwood, Robert. *Roosevelt and Hopkins,* rev. ed. New York: Grosset and Dunlap, Universal Library, 1950.

Shogan, Robert. *Hard Bargain: How FDR Twisted Churchill's Arm, Evaded the Law, and Changed the Role of the American Presidency.* New York: Scribner, 1995.

Shtemenko, S. M. *The Soviet General Staff at War, 1941–1945.* 2 vols. Moscow: Progress, 1985–86.

Smith, Arthur. *Churchill's German Army.* Beverly Hills and London: Sage, 1977.

Smith, Bradley F. *The Shadow Warriors.* New York: Basic Books, 1983.

————. *Sharing Secrets with Stalin: How the Allies Traded Intelligence, 1941–1945.* Lawrence: University Press of Kansas, 1996.

————. *The Ultra-Magic Deals and the Most Secret Relationship, 1940–1946.* Novato, Calif.: Presidio, 1993.

Smith, Bradley F. and Elena Agarossi. *Operation Sunrise: The Secret Surrender.* New York: Basic Books, 1979.

Soames, Mary. *Clementine Churchill.* Boston: Houghton Mifflin, 1979.

Spector, Ronald H. *Eagle Against the Sun: The American War with Japan.* London: Penguin Books, 1987.

Standley, William H. *Admiral Ambassador to Russia.* Chicago: Regnery, 1955.

Stoler, Mark A. *George C. Marshall: Soldier-Statesman of the American Century.* Boston: Twayne, 1989.

————. *The Politics of the Second Front.* Westport, Conn.: Greenwood, 1977.

Stueck, William W. *The Road to Confrontation.* Chapel Hill: University of North Carolina Press, 1981.

Sulzberger, C. L. *American Heritage Picture History of World War II.* New York: Simon & Schuster, 1968.

Taylor, A. J. P. *English History, 1914–1945* New York: Oxford University Press, 1965.

Thompson, Kenneth W. *Winston Churchill's World View: Statesmanship and Power.* Baton Rouge and London: Louisiana State University Press, 1983.

Thorne, Christopher. *Allies of a Kind.* New York: Oxford University Press, 1978.

Tønnesson, Stein. *The Vietnamese Revolution of 1945: Roosevelt, Ho Chi Minh and de Gaulle in a World at War.* London: Sage/PRIO monographs, 1991.

Utley, Jonathan G. *Going to War with Japan, 1937–1941.* Knoxville: University of Tennessee Press, 1985.

Verrier, Anthony. *Assassination in Algiers: Churchill, Roosevelt, de Gaulle, and the Murder of Admiral Darlan.* London: Macmillan, 1990.

Villa, Brian L. *Unauthorized Action: Mountbatten and the Dieppe Raid.* Toronto: Oxford University Press, 1989.

Volkogonov, Dmitri. *Stalin: Triumph and Tragedy,* trans. Harold Shukman. New York: Grove Weidenfeld, 1991.

Ward, Geoffrey C. *A First-Class Temperament.* New York: Harper & Row, 1989.

Watt, Donald Cameron. *How War Came.* New York: Pantheon, 1989.

————. *Succeeding John Bull: America in Britain's Place, 1900–1975.* Cambridge: Cambridge University Press, 1984.

Weigley, Russell F. *Eisenhower's Lieutenants.* Bloomington: Indiana University Press, 1981.

Weinberg, Gerhard. *A World at Arms.* Cambridge and New York: Cambridge University Press, 1994.

Wheeler-Bennett, John, ed. *Action This Day.* London: Macmillan, 1968.

Wills, Garry. *The Second Civil War.* New York: New American Library, 1968.

Wilson, Theodore A. *The First Summit: Roosevelt & Churchill at Placentia Bay, 1941,* rev. ed. Lawrence: University Press of Kansas, 1991.

Winterbotham, F. W. *The Ultra Secret.* New York: Dell, 1975.

Wittner, Lawrence. *American Intervention in Greece, 1943–1949.* New York: Columbia University Press, 1982.

Woods, Randall B. *A Changing of the Guard: Multilateralism and Internationalism in Anglo-American Relations, 1941–1946.* Chapel Hill: University of North Carolina Press, 1989.

Woodward, Llewellyn. *British Foreign Policy in the Second World War.* 5 vols.; London: HMSO, 1970–76. (*British Foreign Policy*)

Articles

Acheson, Dean. "The Supreme Artist," in *Churchill: By His Contemporaries. An Observer Appreciation.* London: Hodder and Stoughton, 1965.

Adams, David. "The Concept of Parallel Action: FDR's Internationalism in a Decade of Isolationism," in *From Theodore Roosevelt to FDR: Internationalism and Isolationism in American Foreign Policy.* Daniela Rossini, editor. Staffordshire: Keele University Press/Ryburn, 1995.

Aga-Rossi, Elena. "Roosevelt's European Policy and the Origins of the Cold War: A Reevaluation." *Telos* 96 (Summer 1993): 65–85.

Alexander, Charles. " 'Uncle Joe': Images of Stalin at the Apex of the Grand Alliance," in *Annual Studies of America: 1989.* N. N. Bolkhovitinov, editor. Moscow: Nauk, 1990, 30–42. (In Russian)

Andrew, Christopher. "Anglo-American-Soviet Intelligence Relations," in *The Rise and Fall of the Grand Alliance, 1941–1945.* Ann Lane and Howard Temperley, editors. London & New York: Macmillan/St. Martin's, 1995.

Barker, Thomas M. "The Ljubljana Gap Strategy: Alternative to Anvil/Dragoon or Fantasy?" *The Journal of Military History* 56 (January 1992): 57–85.

Barnett, Correlli. "Anglo-American Strategy in Europe," in *The Rise and Fall of the Grand Alliance, 1941–1945.* Ann Lane and Howard Temperley, editors. London & New York: Macmillan/St. Martin's, 1995.

Berlin, Isaiah. *Mr. Churchill in 1940.* London: John Murray, n.d. (First published in 1949 in *The Atlantic Monthly* and *The Cornhill Magazine* as "Mr Churchill and F. D. R.").

Bernstein, Barton J. "The author replies," in "Correspondence." *International Security* 16, no. 3 (Winter 1991/92): 214–21.

———. "Understanding the Atomic Bomb and the Japanese Surrender." *Diplomatic History* 19, no. 2 (Spring 1995): 227–73.

Boyle, Peter. "The Special Relationship: An Alliance of Convenience?" *Journal of American Studies* 22 (December 1988): 457–65.

Bratzel, James F. and Leslie B. Rout. "FDR and the Secret Map." *The Wilson Quarterly* 9 (1 January 1985): 167–73.

Bruenn, Howard G. "Clinical Notes on the Illness and Death of President Franklin D. Roosevelt." *Annals of Internal Medicine* 72 (1970): 579–91.

Butow, R. J. C. "The F. D. R. Tapes." *American Heritage* 33, no. 2 (1982): 8–24.

Clemens, Diane. "Yalta: Conference of Victory and Peace," in *Yalta: Un Mito Che Resiste.* Paolo Brundu Olla, editor. Rome: Edizioni dell'Ateneo, n.d. (1987).

Dashichev, Vyacheslav. "On the Road to German Reunification: The View From Moscow," in *Soviet Foreign Policy, 1917–91: A Retrospective.* Gabriel Gorodetsky, editor. London: Frank Cass, 1994.

Davis, Forrest. "Roosevelt's World Blueprint." *Saturday Evening Post*, 115 (April 10, 1943).

Dobson, Alan. "Special in Relationship to What? Anglo-American Relations in the Second World War," in *Britain and the Threat to the Stability in Europe, 1918–1945*. Peter Catterall and C. J. Morris, editors. London: Leicester University Press, 1993.

Embick, Stanley D. "The Joint Strategic Survey Committee, and the Military View of American National Policy during the Second World War." *Diplomatic History* 6 (Summer 1982): 303–21.

Erickson, John. "Stalin, Soviet Strategy and the Grand Alliance," in *Rise and Fall of the Grand Alliance*. Ann Lane and Howard Temperley, editors. London & New York: Macmillan/St. Martin's, 1995.

Filitov, Aleksei. "The Soviet Union and the Grand Alliance: The Internal Dimension of Foreign Policy," in *Soviet Foreign Policy, 1917–91: A Retrospective*. Gabriel Gorodetsky, editor. London: Frank Cass, 1994.

Fraser, Lord of North Cape, "Churchill and the Navy," in *Winston Spencer Churchill: Servant of Crown and Commonwealth*. James Marchant, editor. London: Cassell, 1954.

Funk, Arthur L. "The 'Anfa Memorandum': An Incident of the Casablanca Conference." *Journal of Modern History* 26 (September 1954): 246–54.

Gardner, Lloyd C. "The Atomic Temptation, 1945–1954" in *Redefining the Past*. L. C. Gardner, editor. Corvallis: Oregon State University Press, 1986.

————. "A Tale of Three Cities: Tripartite Diplomacy and the Second Front, 1941–1942," in *Soviet-U.S. Relations, 1933–1942*. G. Sevost'ianov and W. F. Kimball, editors. Moscow: Progress Publishers, 1989.

Graebner, Norman. "Hoover, Roosevelt and the Japanese," in *Pearl Harbor As History*. Dorothy Borg and Shumpei Okamoto, editors. New York: Columbia University Press, 1973.

Harrison, Richard. "A Neutralization Scheme for the Pacific: Roosevelt and Anglo-American Cooperation, 1934–1937." *Pacific Historical Review* 57 (February 1988): 47–72.

Henrikson, Alan K. "The Map as an 'Idea': The Role of Cartographic Imagery During the Second World War." *The American Cartographer* 2 (1975): 19–53.

Herring, George C. "The United States and British Bankruptcy, 1944–1945: Responsibilities Deferred." *Political Science Quarterly* 86 (June 1971): 260–80.

Holloway, David. "The Atomic Bomb and the End of the Wartime Alliance," in *Rise and Fall of the Grand Alliance*. Ann Lane and Howard Temperley, editors. London & New York: Macmillan/St. Martin's, 1995.

Howard, Michael. "Reflections on Strategic Deception," in *Adventures with Britannia*. Wm. Roger Louis, editor. Austin: Univ. of Texas Press, 1995.

Johnson, Paul. "The Myth of American Isolationism: Reinterpreting the Past." *Foreign Affairs* 74, no. 3 (May/June 1995): 159–64.

Kaarsted, Tage. "Churchill and the Small States of Europe—The Danish Case," in *World War Two in Europe: The Final Year*. Charles Brower, editor. New York: St. Martin's Press, in press.

Kersaudy, François. "Churchill and de Gaulle," in *Winston Churchill: Studies in Statesmanship.* R. A. C. Parker, editor. London & Washington: Brassey's, 1995.

Kersten, Albert E. "Wilhelmina and Franklin D. Roosevelt: A Wartime Relationship," in *FDR and His Contemporaries: Foreign Perceptions of an American President.* Cornelis A. van Minnen and John F. Sears, editors. New York: St. Martin's, 1992.

Kimball, Warren F. " '1776': Lend-Lease Gets a Number." *New England Quarterly* 42 (June 1969): 260–67.

————. "Anglo-American War Aims, 1941–1943: 'The First Review': Eden's Mission to Washington," in *The Rise and Fall of the Grand Alliance, 1941–1945.* Ann Lane and Howard Temperley, editors. London & New York: Macmillan/St. Martin's, 1995.

————. "Aus der Sicht Washingtons: Die Aussichten Deutschlands in den Jahren 1943–1945" ("German Prospects, 1943–1945: The View from Washington"), in *Die Zukunft des Reiches: Gegner, Verbündete und Neutrale (1943–1945)*/im Auftrag des Militärgeschichtlichen Forschungsamtes. Manfred Messerschmidt and Ekkehart Guth, editors. (Vorträge zur Militärgeschichte; 13) Herford & Bonn, Germany: Mittler, 1990.

————. "Churchill, Roosevelt and Postwar Europe," in *Winston Churchill: Studies in Statesmanship.* R. A. C. Parker, editor. London & Washington: Brassey's, 1995.

————. "Dieckhoff and America: A German's View of German-American Relations, 1937–1941." *The Historian* 27, no. 2 (February 1965): 230–32.

————. " 'Dr. New Deal': Franklin D. Roosevelt as Commander in Chief," in *Commanders in Chief: Presidential Leadership in Modern Wars.* Joseph G. Dawson III, editor. Lawrence: University Press of Kansas, 1993.

———— and Bruce Bartlett. "Roosevelt and Prewar Commitment to Churchill: The Tyler Kent Affair." *Diplomatic History* 5, no. 4 (Fall 1981): 291–311.

————. "Roosevelt and the Southwest Pacific: 'Merely a Facade'?" *The Journal of American-East Asian Relations* 3, no. 2 (Summer 1994): 103–26.

————. "Stalingrad: A Chance for Choices." *Journal of Military History* 60 (January 1996): 89–114.

————. "U.S. Economic Strategy in World War II: Wartime Goals, Peacetime Plans," in *America Unbound: World War II and the Making of a Superpower.* W. F. Kimball, editor. New York: St. Martin's, 1992.

Kittredge, Tracy. "A Military Danger: The Revelation of Secret Strategic Plans." *U.S. Naval Institute Proceedings,* July 1955: 731–43.

Langer, John D. "The Harriman-Beaverbrook Mission and the Debate over Unconditional Aid for the Soviet Union," in *The Second World War: Essay in Military and Political History.* Walter Laquer, editor. London & Beverly Hills: Sage, 1982.

Louis, Wm. Roger, and Ronald Robinson. "The Imperialism of Decolonization." *The Journal of Imperial and Commonwealth History* 22, no. 3 (September 1994): 462–511.

MacLean, Elizabeth Kimball. "Joseph E. Davies and Soviet-American Relations, 1941–1943." *Diplomatic History* 4, no. 1 (Winter 1980): 73–93.

Maier, Charles S. "The Politics of Productivity: Foundations of American

International Economic Foreign Policy after World War II." *International Organization* 31 (Autumn 1977): 607–33.

Miner, M. Stephen. "Stalin's 'Minimum Conditions' and the Military Balance, 1941–1942," in *Soviet-U.S. Relations, 1933–1942.* G. N. Sevost'ianov and W. F. Kimball, editors. Moscow: Progress, 1989.

Oursler, Fulton Jr., "Secret Treason." *American Heritage* 42, no. 8 (December 1991): 52–68.

Phillips, Hugh. "Mission to America: Maksim M. Litvinov in the United States, 1941–43." *Diplomatic History* 12, no. 3 (Summer 1988): 261–75.

Pollard, Robert A. "Economic Security and the Origins of the Cold War: Bretton Woods, the Marshall Plan, and American Rearmament, 1944–50." *Diplomatic History* 9, no. 3 (Summer 1985): 271–72.

Pollock, Fred E. "Roosevelt, the Ogdensburg Agreement, and the British Fleet: All Done with Mirrors." *Diplomatic History* 5, no. 3 (Summer 1981): 203–19.

Polonsky, Antony. "Stalin and the Poles 1941–7." *European History Quarterly* 17 (1987): 453–92.

Poole, DeWitt C. "Light on Nazi Foreign Policy." *Foreign Affairs* 25, no. 1 (October 1946): 130–54.

Prazmowska, Anita. "Churchill and Poland," in *Winston Churchill: Studies in Statesmanship.* R. A. C. Parker, editor. London & Washington: Brassey's, 1995.

———. "Poland Between East and West—The Politics of a Government-in-Exile," in *Soviet Foreign Policy, 1917–91: A Retrospective.* Gabriel Gorodetsky, editor. London: Frank Cass, 1994.

Resis, Albert. "Spheres of Influence in Soviet Wartime Diplomacy." *Journal of Modern History* 53 (September 1981): 422–36.

Reynolds, David. "Churchill and Allied Grand Strategy in Europe, 1944–1945," in *World War Two in Europe The Final Year.* Charles Brower, editor. New York: St. Martin's Press, in press.

———. "Churchill the Appeaser? Between Hitler, Roosevelt and Stalin in World War Two," in *Diplomacy and World Power: Studies in British Foreign Policy, 1890–1950.* Michael Dockrill and Brian McKercher, editors. Cambridge: Cambridge University Press, 1996.

———. "Lord Lothian and Anglo-American Relations, 1939–1940." *Transactions of the American Philosophical Society* 73, pt. 2 (1983).

———. "Roosevelt, Churchill, and the Wartime Anglo-American Alliance, 1939–1945" in *The 'Special Relationship.'* Wm. Roger Louis and Hedley Bull, editors. Oxford: Clarendon Press, 1986.

———. "A 'Special Relationship'? America, Britain and the International Order since the Second World War." *International Affairs* 62, no. 1 (Winter 1985–86): 1–20.

Robbins, Ron Cynewulf. "Reporting Churchill: A Journalist Remembers." *Finest Hour* 76 (1992): 8–10.

Roosevelt, Franklin D. "Our Foreign Policy: A Democratic View." *Foreign Affairs* 6 (July 1928): 573–86.

———. "Shall We Trust Japan?" *Asia* 23 (July 1923): 475–78ff.

Rossini, Daniela. "Isolationism and Internationalism in Perspective: Myths and Reality in American Foreign Policy," in *From Theodore Roosevelt to FDR: Internationalism and Isolationism in American Foreign Policy.* Daniela Rossini, editor. Staffordshire: Keele University Press/Ryburn, 1995.

Rzheshevsky, O. A. "The Soviet-German Pact of August 23, 1939: Was the War Inevitable?" The *Newsletter* of the Society for Historians of American Foreign Relations, vol. 22, no. 1 (March 1991): 13–32.

Schlesinger, Jr., Arthur. "Roosevelt's Diplomacy at Yalta," in *Yalta: Un Mito che Resiste,* Paolo Brundu Olla, editor. Rome: Edizioni dell'Ateneo, n.d. (1987).

Slavinsky, Boris. "The Soviet Occupation of the Kurile Islands and the Plans for the Capture of Northern Hokkaido." *Japan Forum* (April 1993): 95–114.

Smith, Bradley, F. "Anglo-Soviet Intelligence Co-operation and Roads to the Cold War," in *British Intelligence, Strategy and the Cold War, 1945–1951.* Richard J. Aldrich editor. London & New York: Routledge, 1992.

Smith, Gaddis. "Roosevelt, the Sea, and International Security," in *The Atlantic Charter.* Douglas Brinkley and David R. Facey-Crowther, editors. New York: St. Martin's, 1994.

Steinbeck, John. "The Short Snorter War Menace," in Steinbeck, *Once There Was a War.* New York: Viking Press, 1958.

Stoler, Mark A. "From Continentalism to Globalism: General Stanley D. Embick, the Joint Strategic Survey Committee, and the Military View of American National Policy during the Second World War." *Diplomatic History* 6 (Summer 1982): 303–21.

———. "The 'Pacific-First' Alternative in American World War II Strategy." *The International History Review* 2 (July 1980): 432–52.

———. "The Soviet Union and the Second Front in American Strategic Planning, 1941–1942," in *Soviet-U.S. Relations, 1933–1942.* G. N. Sevost'ianov & W. F. Kimball, editors. Moscow: Progress Publishers, 1989.

Sullivan, Andrew. "Winstoned! America's Churchill Addiction." *The New Republic,* December 7, 1987, reprinted, with a rejoinder, in *Finest Hour* no. 58 (Winter 1987–88): 16–18.

Vitalis, Robert. "The 'New Deal' in Egypt: The Rise of Anglo-American Commercial Competition in World War II and the Fall of Neocolonialism." *Diplomatic History* 20 (Spring 1996): 211–39.

Watt, D. C. "American Anti-Colonialist Policies and the End of the European Colonial Empires, 1941–1962," in *Contagious Conflict: The Impact of American Dissent on European Life.* A. N. J. Den Hollander, editor. Leiden: E. J. Brill, 1973.

Weathersby, Kathryn. "Soviet Aims in Korea and the Origins of the Korean War, 1945–1950: New Evidence from Russian Archives." Working paper no. 8 (November 1993), Cold War International History Project, Woodrow Wilson International Center, Washington, D.C.

White, Donald W. "The Nature of World Power in American History: An Evaluation at the End of World War II." *Diplomatic History* 11, no. 3 (Summer 1987): 181–202.

Miscellaneous

Blake, Lord. "Winston Churchill the Historian," in *Proceedings of the Churchill Societies, 1988–1989*. Richard M. Langworth, editor. Contoocook, NH: Dragonwyck, for the International Churchill Societies, 1990.

Brown, Anthony Montague. Speech, in *Finest Hour* no. 50 (Winter 1985–86): 11–15.

Glantz, David M. "Soviet Military Strategy *vis à vis* Japan: An American Perspective." Paper delivered at the fourth Soviet-American Symposium on World War II, Rutgers University, New Brunswick, NJ, October 1990.

Gramer, Regina U. "Reconstructing Germany, 1938–1949: U.S. Foreign Policy and the Cartel Question." Ph.D. diss., Rutgers University, 1996.

Hoopes, Townsend, and Douglas, Brinkley. "Franklin Roosevelt and the Creation of the United Nations: A Power-Driven Dream of Peace." Unpublished draft manuscript.

Kimball, Warren F. "The Mythical Yalta Myth." Society for Historians of American Foreign Relations *Newsletter*, June 1982.

Pechatnov, Vladimir O. "The Big Three After World War II: New Documents on Soviet thinking about Post-War Relationships with the United States and Great Britain." Paper prepared for the symposium, The Second World War: War Aims—War Results, Roosevelt Study Center, Middelburg, the Netherlands, June 12–14, 1995.

Phillips, Hugh. "Rapprochement and Estrangement: The United States in Soviet Foreign Policy in the 1930s." Paper presented at the first US–USSR Symposium on the History of World War II, Moscow, October 1986.

Stoler, Mark. "The Second Front in Allied Strategy and Diplomacy, August 1942–October 1943." Paper presented at the Second Joint Symposium on the United States and the USSR in the Second World War, Franklin D. Roosevelt Library, Hyde Park, NY, October 1987. (Published in Russian in *Novaia i Noveishaia Istoriia* 5 [1988]: 58–76.)

Wilson, Theodore A. "The Road to Bretton Woods," in *Proceedings of the Churchill Societies, 1988–1989*. Richard M. Langworth, editor. Contoocook, NH: Dragonwyck, for the International Churchill Societies, 1990.

Zubok, Vladislav M. "Cooperation or 'Go Alone': Soviet Dilemma at the Transition from the World War II to the 'Cold Peace,' 1944–1945." Paper presented at the sixth US/UK/USSR Symposium on World War II, Roosevelt Study Center, Middelburg, the Netherlands, June 12–14, 1995.

LIST OF ILLUSTRATIONS

Chapter 1

1a: Churchill holding a submachine gun, inspection trip of home defenses in the north of England, July 1940. (Imperial War Museum, London)
1b: FDR at a Jackson Day Dinner, Mayflower Hotel, January 7, 1939. (T. McAvoy/*Life* magazine; copyright 1938 by Time Inc.)

Chapter 2

FDR, Churchill, and the Anglo-American Chiefs of Staff, aboard HMS *Prince of Wales,* Placentia Bay, Newfoundland, August 10, 1941. (FDR Library)

Chapter 3

Churchill and FDR, portico of the White House, Washington, D.C., December 22, 1941. (FDR Library)

Chapter 4

Joseph Stalin and FDR, Teheran, Iran, November 29, 1943. (FDR Library)

Chapter 5

FDR and Churchill, viewing the pyramids outside Cairo, Egypt, November 23, 1943. (FDR Library)

Chapter 6

Churchill and FDR, Casablanca, Morocco, January 22, 1943. (FDR Library)

Chapter 7

FDR and Churchill, White House Rose Garden, May 24, 1943. (FDR Library)

Chapter 8

Stalin, FDR, and Churchill, Teheran, Iran, November 29, 1943. (FDR Library)

Chapter 9

Churchill, FDR, and Stalin, Yalta, USSR, February 9, 1945. (FDR Library)

Appendix

App. a: Churchill at the Soviet Embassy, Kensington Gardens, London, May 9, 1945. (Imperial War Museum, London)
App. b: FDR, Yalta, USSR, February 9, 1945. (FDR Library)

INDEX

LaVergne, TN USA
10 November 2010

204333LV00002B/5/A